FEMALE ACTION HEROES

FEMALE ACTION HEROES

A Guide to Women in Comics, Video Games, Film, and Television

Gladys L. Knight

 GREENWOOD

AN IMPRINT OF ABC-CLIO, LLC
Santa Barbara, California • Denver, Colorado • Oxford, England

Library of Congress Cataloging-in-Publication Data

Knight, Gladys L., 1974–
    Female action heroes : a guide to women in comics, video games, film, and television / Gladys L. Knight.
        p. cm.
    Includes bibliographical references and index.
    ISBN 978-0-313-37612-2 (hardcover : alk. paper) — ISBN 978-0-313-37613-9 (eBook)
    1. Women heroes in mass media. I. Title.
    P94.5.W65K56   2010
    791.4082—dc22   2010004509

ISBN: 978-0-313-37612-2
EISBN: 978-0-313-37613-9

14 13 12 11 10   1 2 3 4 5

This book is also available on the World Wide Web as an eBook.
Visit www.abc-clio.com for details.

Greenwood
An Imprint of ABC-CLIO, LLC

ABC-CLIO, LLC
130 Cremona Drive, P.O. Box 1911
Santa Barbara, California 93116-1911

This book is printed on acid-free paper ∞

Manufactured in the United States of America

Contents

Preface

At a cinema near the University of Chicago in 1999, audiences went wild when, in the spectacular opening scene of *The Matrix* (1999), Trinity (Carrie-Ann Moss) duked it out single-handedly with villains. Trinity astonished moviegoers with her meteoric martial arts moves and slow-motion leg kicks, skintight black leather attire, and short, slicked-back hairdo. When Trinity tumbled downstairs while running from pursuers and then bolted upright from a prone position with two guns pointed and poised at the ready, the crowd's ecstatic shouts flooded the theater. In a more recent film, *Untraceable* (2008), Jennifer Marsh (Diane Lane) plays a smart cop, widow, and mother of a young daughter, who tracks down Internet predators. She is captured by a serial killer (who records his murders in real time for online viewing) and taken to a hidden location, where she is bound and gagged, hung upside down and slowly lowered toward a moving rotary tiller. Her male colleagues watch powerlessly from a conference room. After several suspenseful minutes, Marsh unfastens her restraints and prevails over the young, male killer. Her colleagues cheer her on with all the exuberance of a film audience.

These examples of female toughness epitomize the current trend wherein women are depicted as tough as nails and able to stand front and center in the action, but it is important to understand that this portrayal has been materializing over a long period of time in film, television, comic books, and video games. The modern depiction is significant, because it illustrates that toughness and action are not exclusive to men and that women who punch, kick, and drive fast cars can be just as cool as men who do those things. The popularity of female action heroes in the new millennium is undeniable: soaring box office receipts, fast-selling merchandise, and increasing numbers of films starring strong women speak loudly that they are accepted and in demand.

Female Action Heroes: A Guide to Women in Comics, Video Games, Film, and Television takes a look at 25 incredible female protagonists. These women and girls have appeared as vampire slayers, captains, villainesses, sharp shooters, martial arts experts, muscle-bound wrestlers, secret agents, athletes, martyrs, plucky archeologists, superheroes, vigilantes, warriors, outlaws, and more. They represent some of the most iconic heroes to have appeared since the turn of the 20th century to the present. Many of these women have had a deep impact on society. Emma Peel of the 1960s British television series, *The Avengers*, struck a chord with many young women who idolized Peel's strength, intelligence, composure, beauty, and fighting skills. The Bionic Woman of the hit 1970s series was independent, career oriented, and equipped with superpowers that made her stronger than anyone else except for her predecessor, the Six Million Dollar Man. Foxy Brown, from the eponymous 1974 film, was considered a breakout role for African American women and the first female action hero in a full feature film. Characters like Wonder Woman, Ellen Ripley, Sarah Connor, and Thelma and Louise had fan clubs that ranged from ordinary viewers to ardent feminists. Lara Croft changed the face of video game playing. She became a role model for young girls and the star of one of the most popular video games for both males and females.

This book examines a number of facets characteristic of female action heroes. Each chapter includes sections on her origins, her power suit, weapons, and abilities, the villains she grapples with, an analysis of her story, and her impact on popular culture. Discussion of recurring themes, sidebars, a glossary, bibliography, and index are also included.

ORIGINS

The origins section summarizes how each hero came to be. It features profiles on the directors and writers who developed her and the actresses who portrayed her. For example, Wonder Woman, who first appeared in comic books in 1941, was the invention of a man named William Moulton Marston, a psychologist, who believed women would one day rule the world and wanted to influence the way young boys perceived women. Joss Whedon, a director and producer, created Buffy Summers, who appeared in the film and television versions of *Buffy the Vampire Slayer* in the 1990s, to challenge the conventional portrayal of female victims. Ellen Ripley, the protagonist of the *Alien* film series (1979, 1986, 1992, 1997), was originally written as a man and emerged as one of America's favorite action heroes.

POWER SUIT, WEAPONS, ABILITIES, AND VILLAINS

The power suit, weapons, and abilities section identifies each female action hero's strengths. *Power suit*, a term popularized in the 1980s, was associated with the attire worn by business men and women to project confidence and authority. The term is especially appropriate for action heroes, for costumes were an integral part of the classic comic book superheroes. The flapping capes, latex costumes, and emblems (Superman's "S" or Spider-Man's black spider), which they wore on expansive chests, helped to denote the power that is associated with those who transcended the ordinary.

A number of the women featured in this book wore power suits, like the one-piece, stars-and-stripes costume worn by Wonder Woman and the black leather catsuits of Catwoman and Emma Peel. Black leather is also worn by Foxy Brown and Selene. In other examples, the power suit is not so obvious, but is nonetheless significant. Jen Yu in *Crouching Tiger, Hidden Dragon* (2000) prefers ordinary, toned-down robes to the fancy, delicate, and restrictive clothing typical of her high station as a privileged governor's daughter. Other women dress like men: Joan of Arc, a 14th-century warrior, gears up like a soldier in battle; Jordan O'Neil shaves her head and dons military fatigues; Thelma and Louise go without makeup and wear jeans and T-shirts, and Xena wears classic warrior vestments. Still other women prefer a feminine look, like Helen of the early 20th-century *The Hazards of Helen,* or a combination of feminine and masculine, like Chun Li, a character in the video game *Street Fighter,* who favors ox horns (a Chinese hairstyle wherein hair is worn in double buns), pantyhose, and combat boots, and The Powerpuff Girls, who fight in pastel-colored costumes.

The abilities of the female action heroes and villains vary considerably. Captain Kathryn Janeway makes tough decisions aboard the *Voyager;* Buffy has superpowered martial arts skills that she uses against vampires, monsters, and demons. Jen Yu, a fantastical wuxia warrior, uses her powers against anyone—good or bad—who stands in her way. The Bionic Woman can run 60 miles per hour, jump to and from soaring heights, and lift cars. She contends with an assortment of everyday male and female villains as well as science fiction creations. Selene, the vampire from the *Underworld* film series (2003, 2006) can also jump and heals rapidly. She wields a large arsenal of weaponry, such as guns, pistols, bow and arrows, and goes to battle against hulking werewolves called Lycans. Maggie Fitzgerald has the true-life drive, guts, and physical strength to compete as a boxer in *Million Dollar Baby* (2004). The Powerpuff Girls can shoot lasers from their eyes, run at lightning speed, and soar in the sky in the animated cartoon series that ran from 1998 to 2005. Storm is a comic book hero who can control the weather. Ellen has shooting skills to rival any cowboy as she confronts gunfighters in the film *The Quick and the Dead* (1995).

ANALYSIS

The analysis section explores how female action heroes are depicted. Historically, women have appeared in film, television, comic books, and video games as inferior to men, as either victims or damsels in distress, and have frequently been defined by their relationships to the male heroes (as mother, love interest, daughter, or sister). Their weakness functioned as a way to enhance the strength and power of the classic male hero; their role was commonly as the "prize" to be won by the hero.

Compared to male action heroes, female action heroes may, at times, be depicted in ways that undermine their own strength and power. In *The Hazards of Helen* (1914–1917), Helen is often portrayed in perilous situations that require her to be rescued by men. (Male action heroes usually rescue themselves.) Joan of Arc is depicted in the 1928 and 1948 films as emotional, whereas the male hero rarely loses his cool and keeps his emotions in check. In some examples, female action heroes are depicted as excessively masculine, like Sarah Connor in *Terminator 2* (1991), Chyna the female wrestler, and Jordan O'Neil, also known as G.I. Jane. In other ways, female action heroes meld femininity with masculinity, thus redefining what heroism looks like. This depiction demonstrates that women can be feminine, glamorous, and tough. For example, Chun-Li, with youthful features and a petite body shape, knocks out men triple her size. The women of the *Charlie's Angels* films (2000, 2003) always look fashionable but face off with villains with fierce determination. These women do not always appropriate classic male heroisms, nor do they tend to work alone. They do not always exhibit powerful muscles, and emotions sometimes show on their faces. But all female action heroes are courageous and act in ways that challenge conventional perceptions of feminine behavior. For example, The Powerpuff Girls, with their high-pitched, little girl's voices, tangle with malevolent individuals and refuse to be passive and weak, or run from danger.

Not all the female action heroes are noble and good. Some of them make no claim to either valor or chivalry. Jen Yu, for example, is self-absorbed, steals what she wants, and scoffs at tradition and rules. Thelma and Louise start off on a road trip and end up as outlaws after Louise murders a man who attempts to rape Thelma. Catwoman is a notorious supervillainess of *The Batman* comic books. She's seductive, street smart, and independent. A number of vigilantes, Chun Li, Foxy Brown, and the Western drifter Ellen, mete out justice outside the law. The portrayal of women who are bad, antiheroes, or simply villains challenges the idea that women must be typecast as good and pure. In real life, obedience to the law is important to the social order. But in fiction, audiences historically revel in the exploits of bad guys who defy the law or do the unexpected.

IMPACT

The impact section examines the influence of female action heroes on popular culture. In addition to surpassing profit expectation and breaking box office records, these women spark controversy and debate, changing the real world as well as reflecting how gender roles have changed. Action continues to be one of the most lucrative genres across all media forms, and as such, it plays a prominent role in shaping society, providing role models for young women and girls, and addressing myriad issues relevant to society.

THEMES

Among the many themes addressed in this book is *feminism*, a controversial term, because it is laden with so many negative connotations. To some, feminism is a doctrine that advocates competition between men and women, is associated with lesbianism, or is considered a challenge to traditional religious doctrines. Feminism, however, is broadly defined and can mean many things to different people. Mainstream feminism was established on the principle that men and women should be treated equally and receive the same rights and legal protections. It is largely responsible for many of the freedoms Americans benefit from each day. Today, young girls may opt to be cheerleaders or play soccer; women pursue careers and families, graduate with advanced degrees, join the military, and become doctors and formidable contenders for the presidency. But it was not always so. It is hoped that this book will illuminate the history of that change by telling the interrelated story of the female action hero.

GLOSSARY TERMS

A number of significant terms appear in bold in this book. A Glossary is therefore provided. Words such as *transgressive* refer to an act that is unconventional, that diverges from tradition or violates a written or unwritten law. For example, Chyna, a tall and muscular woman, is transgressive, because she does not look as women are expected to look. *Ageism* is a term that refers to at attitude in which individuals are discriminated against because of their age. A number of negative terms commonly identified with women, such as *bombshell*, *femme fatale*, and *vamp*, are also included.

BIBLIOGRAPHY AND MORE

This book features two resources for further reading. A Further Resources section appears at the end of each chapter, and a Selected Bibliography is included at the end of the book. These resources are presented to encourage readers to explore other books, articles, and Internet sites related to the topic of female action heroes. The Index will help readers locate names and topics that appear in this book. Sidebars provide additional information on pertinent topics and individuals.

Finally, this book in no way attempts to condone or encourage violence or to express in any fashion the idea that any one gender is better than the other. This book is intended to illuminate the history and sociological issues of female action heroes, as well as to bring to light the female action hero herself in all her splendor and complexity as she treads in and out of boundaries, probes limitless space, and plunges into danger, adventure, and triumph.

ACKNOWLEDGMENTS

Many thanks to the extraordinary team at ABC-CLIO, notably Kristi Ward, eMarketing Manager, and George Butler, developmental editor, who made this book possible. Special thanks to Susan Owen, professor of communication studies at the University of Puget Sound, who introduced me to the fascinating world of film, television, and media criticism, and to Ellen Larson, a real-life Wonder Woman whose counsel and recommendations are worth more than gold. I am deeply grateful to Scott Braut, a picture editor of outstanding skill and work ethic, who provided the bulk of the photo research for this book. Special thanks to my family, friends, and the creators of the female action heroes who challenge us to be more than we dare possible!

Introduction

There is something utterly irresistible about toughness when it is transferred to the fictional world of film, television, comic books, and video games. Only there can toughness surpass the bounds of the mundane, the ordinary, and the laws of physics as we know them. Individuals who embody toughness can transcend anything—harrowing obstacles, impossible situations, and terrible, fiendish adversaries in particular.

Female Action Heroes: A Guide to Women in Comics, Video Games, Film, and Television is a venture into the incredible world of 25 of the most iconic and popular women and girls of action—women who run, pounce, throttle villains, and save the day—as they have been portrayed since the early years of the 20th century. This book explores the ways in which these women grew in power and independence or were undermined by longstanding gender stereotypes rooted in America's past.

Historically, men—not women—have set the standard for toughness, while women were portrayed in ways that reflected traditional gender roles. Nonetheless, beginning in the 1900s, female action heroes have evolved into the extraordinary phenomenon we see today. In the first decade of the new millennium, female action heroes have proliferated like never before, beating box office records and exceeding profit expectations as if they had been born to do so.

TRADITIONAL MALE ACTION HERO

The female action hero has roots in both traditional concepts of femininity and in the portrayal of traditional male action heroism. The male action hero was endowed with so-called masculine traits such as independence, physical strength, aggression, intelligence, competence, reticence, and cool-headedness. He showed little, if any, emotion and was often equipped with an extraordinary, superhuman skill. The male action hero was by definition associated with activity, and thus endowed with the ability to perform a se-ries of harrowing feats. He was the one who did the rescuing, while others who did not have the power to save themselves were positioned in a passive role. Symbolically, the male hero represented power, and his weapons were phallic symbols. *Phallic*, derived from the Greek word for an erect penis, is a term frequently used by psychoanalysts (scientists interested in the con-scious and unconscious processes of the human mind) to identify objects that may either resemble the male penis (and in some contexts fertility), or, more importantly, represent the physical and social power that is historically associated with men. For the action hero, fertility holds little importance, as most male heroes are childless and generally unencumbered by monoga-mous romantic relationships. The male hero operates best alone, avoiding anyone (a wife) or any ties (marriage, permanent home, social obligations, and responsibilities) that might civilize him or force him to remain station-ary. His sole purpose is to be active and free. His power is therefore most often used to dominate or defeat others, such as a villain or nemesis, who would try to bridle or constrain him, and to demonstrate physical and men-tal strength.

TOUGHNESS DEFINED FROM THE MALE PERSPECTIVE

Another attribute of the male action hero is toughness. Sherrie A. Inness explains in her book *Tough Girls: Women Warriors and Wonder Women in Popular Culture* (1999) that toughness involves the presentation of the hero in four areas: body, attitude, action, and authority. Although Inness focuses on toughness as it applies to tough women or girls, the male hero is the pro-genitor of the term.

To use action heroes in film as an illustration, a tough body translates into the barrel-chested physique of John Wayne, a legend of war and West-ern films from 1926 to 1976; the rippling muscle-bound Arnold Schwarze-negger, whose action hero career lasted from 1970 to 2003; and the disciplined musculature of Sylvester Stallone, who starred in iconic roles such as the bloodied boxing champion Rocky Balboa (1976–2006) and the sweaty and grimy one-man-army John Rambo (1982–2008).

Attitude, which surfaces as a nervy, quiet confidence conveyed by the fa-cial expression and comportment of the male action hero, is all important. The steely eyed grimace of Clint Eastwood, who played a series of man-of-few-words loners in Western and cop films from the 1960s to the 1980s, is a prime example. Another is the don't-mess-with-me swagger of Vin Diesel, playing a mercenary who goes by the name of Toorop and wears a camou-flage poncho, which shows that he is unfazed by the gritty chaos of a futur-istic Russian city in the opening scene of *Babylon A.D. (*2008). As Diesel makes his way along a concrete path, we hear the words "You ain't never seen a bigger threat" in the background song ("Deuces," by AchoZen). At the end of the song, Diesel aggressively grabs a man by the collar. The music, the intimidating walk, the camo, Diesel's sangfroid, and the rough handling of a man who has cheated Toorop in a gun purchase function as film code or indicators that this Toorop is a mighty tough guy.

In classic action hero films, the action is constantly on show; the action hero's identity is inextricably linked to his actions: running, pounding bad guys, being chased, leading chases, and, sometimes, like Superman, fighting villains in the stratosphere. Fighting is one of the most seminal actions of the hero, whether it's combat with a weapon, or with the balletic skills of martial artists like Bruce Lee, who starred in films and television shows until his death in 1973, and Jackie Chan, who rose through the ranks of low-budget Hong Kong films to star in contemporary blockbusters.

Action heroes must also be able to command authority or effectively use the authority bestowed upon them by rank or position. For example, Captain James T. Kirk of the *Star Trek* television show that ran from 1966 to 1970 was rarely, if ever, challenged by those under his command. His orders were followed without question. However, rank is not necessary for true heroes, who naturally elicit the trust, respect, and awe of others.

TRADITIONAL FEMALE TRAITS: SUGAR, SPICE, AND EVERYTHING NICE

Men epitomized physical power, emotional control, and brawn, and women were deemed to be their polar opposites. Traditional elements of femininity included docility, delicateness, virtuousness, modesty, gentleness, emotionalism, physical weakness, dependency, gullibility, ability to nurture, and a lesser intelligence than men. Women with a short stature (shorter than men), curves, and smooth (undefined) musculature indicating a high percentage of body fat (not muscle) were considered the ideal. While men swaggered or walked with long gaits to show confidence, women were expected to mince their steps. A "lady" did not run; not only was she perceived to be physically incapable of doing it but she didn't have to—her place was deemed to be in town or city, that is, in a civilized environs or in the home, where she could be protected and sheltered from danger. The local area outside the home and particularly the unknown and potentially barbarous world beyond the cities were considered acceptable only for men. At various times this concept of "outside the home" included the workplace, taverns, and positions of leadership. While men were expected to be active and adventurous, women were required to be passive and stationary.

The ideal feminine voice was deemed to be soft, high-pitched, and gentle. The feminine appearance included long, flowing hair, flawless, clean, and fair-complexioned skin. Feminine embellishments, such as earrings, makeup (but not too much), ribbons and bows, perfume, and long and frilly dresses, were essential.

EVOLUTION OF THE FEMALE ACTION HERO

The women and girls of action films, television, comic books, and video games have come a long way in the past hundred years, moving away from stereotypical feminine roles and toward those traditionally appropriated to men. Their development is tightly entwined with contemporaneous societal changes and current happenings in the real world. In the late 19th century, women were second-class citizens, a situation that was reflected in the literature of the time, from novels to dime novels and newspapers (all that was available before the advent of radio, television, and films). Women were typically portrayed as weak, unintelligent, and needing to be rescued (damsels in distress).

But even then, there were signs of what was to come. Although the woman of action was a rarity, she did occasionally appear in novels and women's popular fiction. Dime novels gave glimpses of early archetypes like Calamity Jane, a real-life woman of action who dared venture into the wild spaces of the frontier and was renowned for her scouting and fighting skills. She was a novelty amid the scores of dashing male heroes, especially the Western hero, a longstanding American symbol of masculinity, freedom, and ruggedness. Her adventures made a thrilling read for women, who, in real life, were confined to the home and to roles as wives and mothers. This was not always the case; for example, since slavery times, black women were often required to work like men in the fields and as domestics.

1900s–1920s

When silent films emerged in the 1890s as the newest medium for storytelling, it was no surprise that male heroism dominated. Women took their expected place as loving mothers or damsels in distress, appearing regularly as the fainting or hysterical woman tied to train tracks, waiting for the handsome male hero to arrive on horseback and save the day—like Andromeda tied to a rock who must be rescued by the Greek hero Perseus. But there were some socially acceptable exceptions in the new medium, just as there had been in dime novels.

Because film contained no dialogue, action was of paramount importance, and film makers were pressed to provide an endless stream of threatening scenarios and thrilling escapes. Thus were born the serial queens, a term that refers to the spunky female leads of short films that were released weekly and played before the featured film. These unmarried women dressed in trendy fashions (still the conservative long dress but without the feminizing ornamentation) or, in some episodes, disguised themselves as men. They bounded through assorted capers with surprising athletic skill and nerve. Among the popular serials were *The Perils of Pauline*, *The Exploits of Elaine*, *The Hazards of Helen*, and *The Ventures of Marguerite*. Though tame in comparison to today's female action heroes, in their day, the serial queens were considered groundbreaking. They were a stimulus to changing social perceptions, embodying the spirit of rebelliousness exhibited by women in real life, the suffragists, the reform women, and the New Woman.

Between 1890 and 1920, American society underwent significant changes in terms of industrialization and women's roles. Inventions such as the automobile, the airplane, motion pictures, radio, and television made the world smaller and thus sped up the pace of social change. These and other inventions, machines, and factories spurred economic growth in the cities. Women's roles were changing too. They stayed single longer, went to college more often, and moved to the growing cities where they took jobs as secretaries and in factories and lived on their own. Women took more public roles, organizing clubs, marching, and protesting their exclusion from the voting process. Suffragists, as they were called, had struggled long and fiercely for the right to vote. Many women also answered the call of reform work, trying to improve living conditions and better lives for impoverished and immigrant communities in the cities. The suffragists and reform women tended to be conservative and moralistic. Their progressive counterpart was the *New Woman*, a term applied to the younger generation of women who challenged the conservative norm of modest dress and polite behavior with their short hair styles, heavy makeup, knee-length dresses, and liberated views on sexuality. The New Woman also smoked cigarettes, which "proper" women did not do. By 1920, the Nineteenth Amendment to the U.S. Constitution, which gave women voting rights, had been ratified, the serial queen phenomenon was no longer in vogue.

1930s–1950s

In the 1930s, comic books became all the rage and the commercialization of television began. *Famous Funnies* was the first comic book to be published in America. Four years later, Superman, one of the most popular superheroes in American history, appeared, balancing a car over his head with his red cape undulating behind him. Comic books were most popular with young boys and played a prominent role in establishing the traits of the male action superhero.

Though they would remain the minority for decades to come, female versions of the new male action heroes quickly followed. (This was a common practice, particularly in comic books and television, wherein, Supergirl followed on the heels of Superman, The Bionic Woman followed The Six Million Dollar Man, and Janeway followed Kirk.) The *Nancy Drew* mystery series for girls followed a few years after *The Hardy Boys* detective series for boys. Nancy Drew, a 16-year-old amateur detective, was depicted as smart, independent, and conventionally pretty in books and low-budget films. She became an influential role model for young girls soon after her initial appearance in 1930. At the start of World War II in 1941, William Moulton Marston introduced Wonder Woman, the first major female action hero in her own comic book series. Her red, white, and blue one-piece costume and her heroic adventures on the frontline endeared her to many Americans. Marston intended her to be a feminist character, showing young boys the illimitable possibilities of a woman who could be considered just as strong as the famed Superman.

Marston was significantly ahead of his time, as women in real life were excluded from leading roles and combat during the war. They did, however, sign up in droves to join the Women's Army Corps, beginning in 1942, though they were restricted to supporting positions. On the home front, large numbers of women went to work for the first time in the factories that produced components needed for the war. Rosie the Riveter, with her trademark polka-dot headscarf and flexed arm, was a ubiquitous face in wartime propaganda aimed at encouraging women to work in war factories. Contemporaneous film and television, however, failed to produce a single significant portrayal of a wartime woman of action. And when the war ended, Rosie the Riveter was quietly retired. Women were encouraged to go home.

From the 1940s to the 1960s, many films and television programs targeted boys and appealed to male fantasies. Cowboys like the Lone Ranger were all the rage. The horse, cowboy hat, and gun became popular accessories and powerful symbols of masculinity for boys. A blanket tied around the neck to imitate the cape of a superhero or a cowboy hat and pistol instantly transformed young boys into masculine heroes. This effectively excluded most girls, who were not generally encouraged to participate in this form of child's play. In the films of this period, women were portrayed as glamorous beauties bathed in soft lights, femme fatales, and bombshell celebrities. Marilyn Monroe, whose persona was largely predicated on her curvaceous, pin-up body, while her intellect was downplayed, became a superstar. Irish McCalla, who played the television lead in *Sheena, Queen of the Jungle*, was also depicted as an eye-candy archetype. But she was among the very few female action heroes of the era. During this post-war period, few gains were made for women, and the traditional stereotypes became entrenched.

1960s

But starting in the mid-1960s, women again made staggering progress. This was a tumultuous time of change, led by the emergence of the long-simmering civil rights movement, in which African Americans protested segregation and other discriminatory practices. Racist violence against nonviolent activists was shown on television, shocking the nation and leading to change. *Second-wave feminists* (a term used to describe advocates of equality for women in the 1960s) took the cue. They vigorously opposed longstanding discrimination against women in the workplace and vigorously opposed domestic violence and other crimes specific to women. They condemned the objectification of women in the media, in beauty contests, and in pornography.

In 1963, Bettie Friedan wrote *The Feminine Mystique*, which explored how women were denigrated in society. The 1960s saw the deathblow to racial segregation and established voting protection for African Americans. With regard to women's issues, the birth control pill was introduced, laws to prohibit sex discrimination in the workplace were established, and women's studies programs in colleges and universities emerged. Breakout roles featuring the new progressive women tended to be spies or sleuths such as Cathy Gale and Emma Peel, who partnered with John Steed in the British television show, *The Avengers*; April Dancer, who starred in the television series *The Girl from U.N.C.L.E.*; Modesty Blaise, a comic book version of the James Bond character who was adapted to film in 1966; and an extraordinarily tough red-haired hoyden named *Pippi Longstocking* (1969).

Meanwhile, traditional female roles persisted. The television series *Gilligan's Island*, which aired from 1964 to 1967, served up two stereotypical images—the glamorous sexpot, Ginger, and the ingénue, Mary Ann—while *Leave it to Beaver*, which ran during the 1950s and 1960s, popularized the flawlessly coiffed and preternaturally mild-mannered housewife and mother, Mrs. June Cleaver.

1970s–1980s

Over the next two decades, second-wave feminism became a major influence in popular culture. Title IX of the Education Amendments Act was passed, prohibiting sex discrimination in educational institutions. Women were permitted entrance into military academies. Legislation outlawed discrimination against married and pregnant women in the workplace. Paralleling these changes, producers launched television series that showcased the progressive, independent female action hero—even if she was stereotypically beautiful and feminine and failed to exude quite the same effectual command, confidence, and prowess as classic male heroes. Among the slew of such shows in the 1970s were *Police Woman*, *Wonder Woman*, *The Bionic Woman*, and *Charlie's Angels*. African American women pioneered the female action hero in film with portrayals such as *Cleopatra Jones* (1973), *Coffy* (1973), *Foxy Brown* (1974), and *Sheba, Baby* (1975). In this same decade, Storm, the first major African American woman comic book superhero, was introduced.

In the 1980s, women secured greater power in the workforce, in music, and sports, and so did the fictional female warriors in the media. The increased power of women in the workplace was underscored by a striking change in work attire: angular power suits with large shoulder pads and minimal jewelry or other feminine identifiers. Pop singers like Madonna and Cindy Lauper sang songs advocating the pursuit of romantic relationships, girliness, and fun. Women in sports, such as gymnast Mary Lou Retton and heptathlete and long jumper Jackie Joyner-Kersee, received clamorous media attention. Women's lib was a movement that was acknowledged in television and film. In the movie *Nine to Five* (1980), women demonstrated through humor that they wanted to be taken seriously and not treated as sex objects or servants.

The most iconic film protagonist of this era was Ellen Ripley of the *Alien* film series, which began with *Alien* in 1979. She embodied the ideal woman of the times who eschewed the stereotypical markers of femininity, had a career in the space industry, and wore a uniform (in 1983, Sally Ride, wearing a similar uniform, would become the first American woman in space). She also single-handedly defeated one of the most horrifying space monsters ever to grace the screen. Ripley emanated toughness with her low, even pitch; she did not resort to hyper-emotionalism and proved stronger than her colleagues on the spaceship, all of whom died horrible deaths.

Other landmark female action heroes included Superman's female counterpart *Supergirl* (1984), *Red Sonja* (1985), who had first appeared in the comic book *Conan the Barbarian*, and She-Ra, He-Man's counterpart in an animated series. The 1980s also featured the award-winning series that cast the first-ever female detective team, *Cagney and Lacey*. This series was celebrated for depicting its leads as ordinary and unglamorous women, and for addressing hard social issues such as racism, alcoholism, and rape.

Although video games had their start in the 1960s with *Spacewar*, a computer game developed by a MIT computer programmer, they would undergo a popularity boom in the 1980s. Atari, a major player in arcade and video game console production, made its mark in the 1980s with games like *Pac-Man*, developed by Namco, and *Donkey Kong*, developed by Nintendo. The technological advances were staggering, and thus video games became the newest form of narrative storytelling—one that reinforced old female stereotypes. Video games like *Donkey Kong*, released in 1981, and *Super Mario Brothers*, developed in 1985, largely portrayed females as damsels in distress; women were never the center of action. Female versions of existing games, like *Ms. Pac-Man*, were an afterthought, attempts to repackage the product to expand sales.

1990s and Beyond

Female characters in video games underwent a drastic change in the 1990s, paralleling a surge of female action heroes in film and television and giant leaps for women in society. In the 1990s, a burgeoning new movement, third-wave feminism (a term that refers to the younger generation of women whose issues frequently clashed with second-wave feminists) embraced concepts such as femininity, ambition, and independence. Also in that decade, 35,000 women participated in the Gulf War, women athletes became icons of popular culture, and independence and toughness in women were in vogue.

Many of the female action heroes who emerged from the late 1990s onward reflected the spirit of third-wave feminism, with its advocacy of looking good and being powerful (though in films, television, comic books, and video games, this sometimes translated to excessive violence, bravado, and over-the-top combat moves.) Still, some women appeared who reflected values of second-wave feminism. Samus Aran, a bounty hunter in the *Metroid* series, was considered one of the first major tough female protagonists in a video game. Debuting at the end of the previous decade, she was followed by Princess Zelda, Lara Croft, and others. The list continues to grow. In film, Sarah Connor in *Terminator 2* (1991) helped to popularize hard-bodied female action heroes. Captain Kathryn Janeway, Xena, and the animated women of *Sailor Moon* were popular action women and girls on television who operated on a par with men. In 1997, Chyna matched the strength and musculature of the men in World Wrestling Entertainment, and Lieutenant Jordan O'Neil showed the world that a female soldier could be just as tough as a man in *G.I. Jane* (1997).

Youthfulness, girliness, and combativeness increasingly defined many of the female action heroes who appeared from the late 1990s onward. Buffy, a pretty high school girl, slew vampires on television in *Buffy the Vampire Slayer* (1997–2003), and three cute and cuddly kindergarteners fought with viciousness in the animated *The Powerpuff Girls* (1998–2005). A sexy assassin fought hard and kept her cool in the television series *La Femme Nikita* (1997–2001). Thrill-seeking archeologist Lara Croft appeared on film in 2001 and 2003, exhibiting the kind of extreme stunts that women amateurs and professionals were beginning to do in real life. No longer limited to love interests, mothers, wives, and sisters, strong women increasingly became the standard in a variety of action roles. They might be martial arts heroes, fierce vampires, heroic cheerleaders, space adventurers, or sangfroid assassins. These heroes may also be represented as second- and third-wave types or merge both types together.

The progress of female heroes notwithstanding, some issues remain. Leading female roles continue to be dominated by white women, with few positive roles permitted to women of color. The few women of color who are represented in action genres are generally reduced to sidekick status or portrayed in negative ways. The issue of body image is an example of how film, television, comic books, and video games can negatively affect society by perpetuating the all-impossible beautiful and svelte figure.

However, female action heroes are still in flux. As we have seen, she has been changing and shape-shifting from one form to another for over a hundred years. Thus we can be sure that there is something new waiting just around the corner. Whether we will see her dressed in ankle-length robes, a patriotic swim suit, cargo pants, or jeans and a T-shirt, the one thing that is clear is that for her, all things are possible.

Timeline

1778	Impersonating a man, Deborah Sampson becomes the first female soldier to join the army. She serves for a year and a half before she is given an honorable discharge.
1856	Kate Warne is the first female detective in the United States.
1890s	Seventeen percent of women are working. Common jobs include domestic and factory workers, teachers, and nurses. First-wave feminism begins and continues into the early 19th century. First-wave feminists primarily advocate for suffrage.
1898	Sharpshooter Annie Oakley is denied entry into the military.
1900s	Women's fashion trends: women wear corsets, long and heavy dresses that completely cover a woman's body, and long hair frequently worn in a variety of bun styles. It is considered indecent to expose any part of the body other than face and hands. Pale skin is a symbol of beauty and the upper class. Women use parasols and skin bleaching cream to keep skin fair. Twenty percent of women are working. Common jobs include clerical workers, phone operators, teachers, and factory workers.
1908	Lola Baldwin becomes the first female cop in the United States.
1911	Emma Jentzer becomes the first female special agent in the Bureau of Investigation (predecessor of the FBI).
1913	Harriet Tubman, famous for having escaped slavery half a century before and leading over 70 individuals to freedom in the Underground Railroad while wielding a gun, and for serving as a spy in the Civil War (1861–1865), dies.

1914–1917	Helen Holmes and Helen Gibson play the swashbuckling railroad telegrapher "Helen" in 119 episodes of *The Hazards of Helen* film series.
1920s	Women's fashion trends: women wear bolder makeup, flapper dresses (frequently knee length, fitted, and sleeveless), and short, bobbed hairstyles. French manicures, tanning, and cigarette smoking are in vogue for young women. This trend returns in the 1930s and 1970s, and from the 1990s onward.
1920	The Nineteenth Amendment to the U.S. Constitution is ratified, giving women the right to vote.
1928	Maria Falconetti portrays Joan of Arc, a real-life 15th century military leader, in the French silent film *The Passion of Joan of Arc*.
1930s	Women's fashion trends: shoulder pads are introduced.
1935	Mildred Burke begins wrestling men at carnivals. Out of 200 men, she purportedly lost to only one. Professional wrestler Mildred Burke wins the first World Women's Championship.
1940s	Women's fashion trends: women wear pants to work in the factories. This trend ends after the war. Thirty-eight percent of women are working in male-dominated industry jobs created by World War II. Many women lose their jobs when the war ends.
1940	Catwoman, a supervillainess, debuts in the comic book *Batman #1*.
1941	Wonder Woman, a superheroine originating from a tribe of Amazonian women, first appears in *All-Star Comics*.
1942	The Women's Auxiliary Army Corps (WAAC) is formed, marking the first time women are officially allowed to join the military. The internment of Japanese Americans occurs. "Rosie the Riveter" becomes the icon for women working in war factories.
1948	Ingrid Bergman stars in the film *Joan of Arc*.
1950s	Women's fashion trends: women wear chin-level hairstyles, frequently prepared with hair rollers worn at night, and matching hats, gloves, handbags, and dresses. The conical bra is frequently worn to provide what was considered the ideal body shape. Marilyn Monroe is one of the most popular shapely pin-up girls. Poodle skirts and pedal pushers are also popular. Thirty percent of women are working.

1954	*Brown v. Board of Education* prohibits segregated schools.
1955	Rosa Parks refuses to give up her seat on a segregated bus in Montgomery, Alabama, sparking the monumental Montgomery Bus Boycott led by Dr. Martin Luther King Jr.
1957	Jean Seaberg stars in the film *Saint Joan*.
1959	Mattel, Inc. releases Barbie, a fashion doll.
1960s–1980s	Second-wave feminists advocate for equality, reproductive rights, and other issues, challenging traditional perceptions of gender roles. Community is valued over individualism. Many scholars contend that second-wave feminism thrives concurrently with third-wave feminism.
1960s	Women's fashion trends: women wear miniskirts, Capri pants, heavy mascara and eye liner, pale lipstick, and bouffant hairstyles.
	Thirty-five percent of women are working.
1960	The birth control pill is approved for contraceptive use.
1963	The Equal Pay Act requires equal pay for women and men.
1964	The Civil Rights Act prohibits discrimination based on race and sex. Title VII of this act establishes the Equal Employment Opportunity Commission.
	Hasbro coins the term *action figure*. G.I. Joe is the first action figure.
1965	The Voting Rights Act of 1965 is passed, providing protection and enforcement of the right to vote for all citizens.
1965–1968	Diana Rigg plays Emma Peel, the female member of a spy team duo in the British television series *The Avengers*.
1966	Julie Newmar and Eartha Kitt play Catwoman in the *Batman* television series.
	The National Organization of Women is established to challenge sex discrimination laws.
	Montgomery buses are finally desegregated.
1967	Hasbro creates the first female G.I. Joe action hero, Action Nurse. She is a commercial failure.
1970s	Women's fashion trends: women wear pantsuits, bell-bottom pants, peasant tops, miniskirts, ethnic fashions, afros, and long hair. Leather and ethnic clothes are fashionable in African American urban communities. The Earthy look and disco fever are in vogue. Movies commonly feature scantily clad, shapely women with bronze tans.
	Forty-four percent of women are working. A larger percentage of women are becoming lawyers, doctors, stockbrokers, steelworkers, and railroad workers.

1970   African American activist Angela Davis becomes the third woman on the FBI Most Wanted List. Because the gun that was used in a shootout in an escape attempt at the Marin County Hall of Justice in California was registered in Davis's name, she is charged as an accomplice to conspiracy, kidnapping, and homicide. She evades the law for two months. During her flight, eventual capture, and imprisonment, she becomes an international icon. She will be released and acquitted of all charges in 1972.

1972   Title IX of the Education Amendments Act grants sex equity for all educational programs and activities, including sports.
                Congress passes the Equal Rights Amendment.
                Helen Reddy's #1 U.S. hit song "I Am Woman" is released and becomes known as the feminist national anthem.
                Gloria Steinem, a second-wave feminist leader, creates *Ms. Magazine*. Wonder Woman is featured on the cover of the first issue.

1973   Professional tennis player Billie Jean King beats Bobby Riggs in the "Battle of the Sexes."
                The first abortion law gives women the right to terminate a pregnancy.

1974   Pam Grier plays a tough African American vigilante in the eponymous film *Foxy Brown*.
                Congress prohibits sexual discrimination in housing and credit.
                Elaine Brown becomes the first female chair of the Black Panther Party.

1975   Storm, a Kenyan woman endowed with mutant powers that allow her to control the weather, debuts in Giant-Size X-Men #1. She is noted as the first major African American female super hero.

1975–1979   Linda Carter stars as Wonder Woman in the television series.

1976-1978   Lindsay Wagner plays Jaime Sommers, a secret agent empowered by cybernetic implants, in *The Bionic Woman* television series.

1976–1981   *Charlie's Angels* refers to the three female private investigators of the popular television series.

1977   Carrie Fisher plays feisty Princess Leia in the film *Star Wars Episode IV*.
                The Kenner toy company launches the first *Star Wars* action figures. The massive popularity of the action figures sparks a new trend in movie marketing.

1978	The Pregnancy Discrimination Act bars employers from firing a woman based on pregnancy.
1979	Sigourney Weaver portrays Ellen Ripley, a science fiction hero, in the film *Alien*.
1980s	Women's fashion trends: working women wear power suits with large shoulder pads and tennis shoes (changing into pumps at work). Big hair (teased and permed) and workout leotards with leg warmers are in fashion. Madonna triggers a fashion craze for shirts pulled down over one shoulder and lingerie and brassieres worn as outerwear.
	Fifty-two percent of women are in the workforce, entering a broader range of professions such as university and college professors, managers, entrepreneurs, accountants, computer programmers, truck drivers, and construction workers. The glass ceiling limits full access of and advancement in employment for many women.
1980	Carrie Fisher plays Princess Leia in *Star Wars Episode V: The Empire Strikes Back*, the second film in the *Star Wars* film series.
1981	bell hooks publishes *Ain't I a Woman? Black Women and Feminism*.
1982	The states fail to ratify the Equal Rights Amendment that was passed by Congress.
1983	Carrie Fisher plays Princess Leia in *Star Wars Episode VI: The Return of the Jedi*, the third film in the *Star Wars* series.
	Sally Ride is the first American woman in space.
1984	Linda Hamilton portrays Sarah Connor, the mother of John Connor, who is portended to lead the struggle against malevolent cyborgs, in the film *The Terminator*.
	Kathryn Sullivan becomes the first woman to take a space walk.
1986	Sigourney Weaver returns as Ellen Ripley in *Aliens*, the second film in the *Alien* series.
	The Supreme Court declares that sexual harassment violates Title VII of the 1964 Civil Rights Act.
1990s	Third-wave feminism, a controversial movement, is born. Comprising mostly individuals referred to as Generation X (born between the 1960s and 1970s) and Generation Y (born in the late 1970s and 1990s), third-wave feminists may not describe themselves as feminists at all and espouse individual empowerment and a blend of traditional and nontraditional definitions of feminine appearance and behavior.

Women's fashion trends: Brittany Spears influences girls and young women who wear revealing clothing, short tops that show the midriff, and tight jeans. Leather jackets, halter tops, and Goth clothing are also in. Women and teenagers regularly go to tanning booths and get professional manicures and pedicures. Celebrities like Linda Hamilton, Madonna, Jennifer Anniston, and female professional athletes inspire women to develop lean, athletic bodies. Many fashion styles recycle from the past with a modern twist.

Seventy-four percent of women are working, becoming scientists, politicians, executives, professional athletes, military soldiers and officers, law enforcement professionals, pilots, and artists. Although the glass ceiling continues to present challenges, women in greater numbers fill positions that were once largely held by males.

1991   Jodi Foster plays Clarice Starling, an FBI student, in the film *The Silence of the Lambs*.

The film *Thelma and Louise* stars Susan Sarandon (Thelma) and Geena Davis (Louise) as two fugitives running from the law.

Linda Hamilton returns in the role of Sarah Connor in the film *Terminator 2: Judgment Day*, the second film in the *Terminator* series.

1992   Sigourney Weaver plays Ellen Ripley in *Alien 3*.

Michelle Pfeiffer plays Catwoman in the film *Batman Returns*.

Kristy Swanson portrays Buffy in the film *Buffy the Vampire Slayer*.

Mae Jemison is the first African American woman to go into space.

1993   Catwoman gets her own comic book series.

USA Boxing recognizes female boxers. Previously, female boxing had been banned in many states.

1994   Halle Berry portrays Storm in the film *X-Men*.

The Violence Against Women Act establishes penalties against stalking and sexual violence.

1995   Sharon Stone plays Ellen, aka "The Lady," a vigilante gunslinger in the film *The Quick and the Dead*.

Captain Kathryn Janeway is the first female captain in a *Star Trek* series. The series, *Star Trek: Voyager*, runs for seven episodes.

1995–2001   Lucy Lawless plays Xena, a capable warrior in ancient Greece, in the television series *Xena: Warrior Princess*.

1996	Lara Croft, fearless archaeologist, debuts in the video game *Tomb Raider*.
	Resident Evil debuts on Sony Play Station.
	The boxing match between Christy Martin and Deirdre Gogarty is considered a landmark in women's boxing.
1997	Demi Moore plays Lt. Jordan O'Neil in the film *G.I. Jane*.
	Sigourney Weaver plays Ellen Ripley in *Alien Resurrection*, the fourth film in the *Alien* film series.
	Madeleine Albright becomes the first female United States Secretary of State.
	The second female G.I. Joe action figure, G.I. Jane, a helicopter pilot, is launched.
	Major General Claudia Kennedy becomes the first female three-star general.
1997–2001	Chyna (Joanie Laurer) is an audience favorite during her career with the World Wrestling Federation.
1997–2003	Sarah Michelle Gellar plays Buffy in *Buffy the Vampire Slayer*, the landmark television series.
1998	Uma Thurman plays Emma Peel in the American film *The Avengers*.
1998–2005	Three kindergarteners, Blossom, Bubbles, and Buttercup, are the rage in the TV animation *The Powerpuff Girls*.
1999	Milla Jovovich stars in *Messenger*, a film about Joan of Arc.
2000	Cameron Diaz, Drew Barrymore, and Lucy Liu appear in the film *Charlie's Angels*.
	Michelle Yeoh (Yu Shu Lien) and Zhang Ziyi (Jen Yu) dazzle with acrobatic martial arts fighting in the film *Crouching Tiger, Hidden Dragon*.
2000	Women's fashion trends: Many fashion styles from the past are recycled with a modern twist. Women at work wear sexier attire, low-cut tops, fitted and short pencil skirts. Young girls wear baggy sweat pants and hoodies. The metrosexual look among professional men is popular. Tatoos, once a marker for men in the military, male bikers, and gang members to signify toughness, are commonly worn by women in all walks of life.
	Angelina Jolie, who is famous for her myriad tattoos and "bad girl" image, plays Lara Croft in the film *Lara Croft: Tomb Raider*.
2001	Julianne Moore plays Clarice Starling, an FBI agent, in the film *Hannibal*.

2002   The film *Resident Evil* stars Milla Jovovich as Alice.
        The Powerpuff Girls Movie is released.

2003   Halle Berry portrays Storm in the film *X-2: X-Men United*.
        Cameron Diaz, Drew Barrymore, and Lucy Liu star in
        Charlie's Angels: Full Throttle. Demi Moore plays a former
        angel in this sequel to *Charlie's Angels* (2000).
        Angelina Jolie plays Lara Croft in the film sequel *Lara
        Croft Tomb Raider: The Cradle of Life*.
        Kate Beckinsale plays the plucky vampire Selene in the
        film *Underworld*.

2004   Halle Berry stars in the film *Catwoman*.
        Milla Jovovich stars as Alice in *Resident Evil: Apocalypse*,
        the second film in the *Resident Evil* series.
        Hilary Swank plays Maggie Fitzgerald, the indomitable
        spirited pugilist, in the film *Million Dollar Baby*.

2005   Condoleezza Rice becomes the first African American
        female United States Secretary of State.

2006   Kate Beckinsale plays the vampire Selene in *Underworld:
        Evolution*, the second film in the *Underworld* series.
        Halle Berry portrays Storm in the film *X-Men: The Last
        Stand*.

2007   Milla Jovovich stars as Alice in *Resident Evil: Extinction*,
        the third film in the *Resident Evil* series.
        Michelle Ryan plays Jaime Sommers in *Bionic Woman*, a
        remake of the 1970s television series.
        Senator Hillary Clinton of New York is a major party
        candidate for president of the United States of America.

2008   Lena Headey plays Sarah Connor in *Terminator: The Sarah
        Connor Chronicles*, a television series.
        General Ann Dunwoody becomes first female four-star
        general.
        Governor Sarah Palin of Alaska is the vice presidential
        nominee for the Republican Party.

2009   Barack Obama, the first African American president of the
        United States of America, selects Hilary Clinton to become
        the third female United States Secretary of State.
        Fifty percent of women are working.

Jaime Sommers prepares for a scene in the episode "Bionic Beauty" of the television series *The Bionic Woman*. (AP Photo/Jeff Robbins.)

The Bionic Woman

The Bionic Woman, also known as the fictional character Jaime Sommers, was an ordinary woman (albeit a professional tennis player) turned bionic action hero following a top-secret surgery to "rebuild her" after a devastating accident. *Bionic* refers to the artificial implants she received that gave her superhuman abilities. Her first appearance (1975) was in "The Bionic Woman," a two-part episode of *The Six Million Dollar Man* television series, which starred Lee Majors as Steve Austin—television's first bionic hero. Owing to intense audience demand, writer/producer Kenneth Johnson gave Sommers her own television series. *The Bionic Woman*, starring Lindsay Wagner, debuted on ABC as a mid-season replacement in January 1976 and was awarded a full second season that fall (1976/1977), after which it moved to NBC for a third season (1977/1978).

Although Sommers, like the biblical Eve in the book of Genesis who was formed from Adam's rib, emerged from Austin's story line, she achieved tremendous popularity in her own right. Sommers, with her billowy blonde hair, earthy beauty, and **ingénue** personality, could have been mistaken for the typical Hollywood heroine, but she was also physically powerful beyond human norms. Thanks to the bionics she received after a skydiving accident (one arm, both legs, and an ear), she could leap to and from the tops of buildings, run 60 miles an hour, and lift heavy objects. In a nod to societal norms, Austin's more expensive bionics were considered to be more powerful than Sommers's smaller bionics, and he was depicted, in subtle ways, as being the more powerful of the two. Nevertheless, Sommers was a force to be reckoned with, and the two superheroes worked well together as equals.

Wagner and Majors also exhibited no competitiveness, appearing on each other's shows occasionally, as well as starring together in three reunion TV movies: *The Return of the Six Million Dollar Man and the Bionic Woman* (1987), *Bionic Showdown: The Six Million Dollar Man and the Bionic Woman* (1989), and *Bionic Ever After?* (1994). As bionic-series scholar Herbie Pilato points out, the television crossover, a rarity in the 1970s, became a much-anticipated event in later action hero series like "*Buffy the Vampire Slayer* and *Angel* [and] *Xena* and *Hercules*" (Pilato, 46).

In 2007, The Bionic Woman returned in her own revamped television series, besting the Six Million Dollar Man in terms of getting a new millennium television remake. The reimagined show, titled *Bionic Woman*, starred Michelle Ryan as the new Jaime Sommers, a brooding, assertive, and edgy protagonist with shoulder-length brunette hair, who acquires her bionic parts (one eye, one arm, both legs, and an ear) after a car accident, with her boyfriend driving the car. *Bionic Woman* was launched with great promise, but a strike by the Writer's Guild of America (WGA) interfered with the new show's ability to finish scripts, and only eight episodes were televised. Though the WGA ended its strike in due course, *Bionic Woman* was not picked up for a second season.

Beauty Contests

The most famous beauty contest in America is the Miss America Pageant, which was established in 1921 and was held for many years in Atlantic City, New Jersey. In the 1950s, the contest became televised, becoming, particularly during the1960s, one of the most popular shows on television. In 1955, Lee Meriwether, who starred as Catwoman in the film *Batman* (1966), won the contest. A number of women in action films have backgrounds in beauty contests.

Notwithstanding the show's immense success with American audiences, the Miss America Pageant has had a troublous past. Until the 1970s, women of color were prohibited from participating in the contest. In the 1960s, during the rise of second-wave feminism, feminists openly condemned beauty contests, contending that they reinforced and perpetuated stereotypical gender roles and impossible beauty ideals, not to mention that the contests fostered competition for the male gaze among women.

Gradually, the contest transformed its program, welcoming women of diverse ethnicities, races, as well as political leanings. For example, Rebecca Ann King, who won the Miss America title in 1974, was a law student who supported feminist causes. Currently, the Miss America contest awards scholarships for winners. Winners are judged by a personal interview, talent, lifestyle, and fitness in swimsuit, evening wear, and onstage questions.

A number of television series, films, and other media have explored the themes of beauty contests. *Miss Congeniality* (2000) and *Miss Congeniality 2: Armed and Fabulous* (2005), starred Sandra Bullock as Gracie Hart, a tomboyish FBI agent who spars with men. Her idea of a great assignment is chasing down criminals and brandishing her gun, not suiting up in an evening gown, tottering on high heels, and wearing makeup. The contrast between Gracie and the other ultra-feminine beauty contestants appealed to audiences and demonstrated how far along women have come.

ORIGINS

The original Bionic Woman emerged at a moment in history when **women's liberation**, also known as **second-wave feminism** (1960s–1980s), was in the forefront of America's consciousness, influencing social life, working environments, and popular culture. Women were breaking new ground on several fronts: stepping out of a long history of second-class citizenship in which they had been relegated by society—with little choice—to inferior or supportive positions such as housewives, low-paid workers, and caregivers. Before second-wave feminism, if a woman worked outside the home, her job choices were usually limited to employment as a secretary, phone operator, or factory worker. Upon marriage or pregnancy, most women resigned from work and stayed at home. On television, women's roles were largely limited to nurturing mothers and love interests; women on TV were portrayed in the same roles as were found in real life.

The coming change was foreshadowed as early as 1955, when audiences watched the scantily clad and exotic buxom blonde Sheena in *Sheena, Queen of the Jungle* (1955–1957). The first—if not arguably the most influential—mainstream show to challenge the image of women in television was the British television show *The Avengers*. This show featured superspy sidekicks Cathy Gale (1962–1964), Emma Peel (1965–1968), and Tara King (1968–1969). Emma Peel (played by the tall and talented Diana Rigg) in particular fairly exploded to superstar status with her tongue-in-cheek portrayal of a karate-chopping, dressed-in black, crime fighter. Purdey, the fourth sidekick to debonair John Steed (played by Patrick Macnee) appeared in *The New Avengers* (1976–1977).

The Avengers influenced a number of subsequent shows on its road to iconic status. In 1965, Honey West of the eponymous series (1965–1966) became television's first female detective. She was glamorous, sexy, drove a sports car, practiced judo, and wielded guns. In 1966, Catwoman, a female villain in skintight black leather, appeared in the *Batman* television episodes. In the same year, the first female and African American military officer, Nyota Uhura (Nichelle Nichols), served on the bridge of the prestigious starship *Enterprise*, helmed by Captain James T. Kirk (William Shatner) in *Star Trek* (1966–1969).

The floodgates had been opened. In the ensuing decade, an influx of powerful leading ladies emerged, among them the protagonists of *Police Woman* (1974–1978), *Get Christie Love* (1974–1975), *Wonder Woman* (1975–1979), *The Bionic Woman* (1976–1978), and *Charlie's Angels* (1976–1981). Though not all were endowed with superpowers, these women had much in common: they were glamorous, exuded sex appeal, and reflected in large part the new woman of the 1970s, who enjoyed greater independence and was career-oriented.

These expanding television roles, reflecting as they did a new acceptance of women as possessed of both real and fantastical powers, shadow the changes taking place in society. Women in the 1970s enjoyed greater opportunities than at any previous time in history. And yet even they owed their advances to the 19th-century feminists, those no-nonsense women in heavy, long puritanical dresses who fought so hard for suffrage and equality. Suffrage was won in 1920, but equality proved a more elusive goal; indeed women as well as men continue to wage this battle in contemporary times. Nonetheless, the women of the 1970s wore what they wanted—pants (acceptable at work and at school for the first time in history) or long or short skirts—and they remained single longer than in any previous generation. More women graduated from college, took jobs, managed their own finances, lived on their own, owned cars, and were physically active. Thanks

Sexist Language

Sexist language refers to derogatory terms used to describe women, as well as words that specify gender. For many years, terms like *broad*, *chick*, or even *girl* were used casually in society. With the emergence of feminism, feminists made it known that such words were belittling and offensive. Feminists saw the terms as ways in which patriarchy controlled and disempowered women. Other words, e.g., *chairman*, were also deemed offensive as they excluded women, and feminists advocated for gender-neutral or gender-inclusive terms, such as *chairperson*. To some women, the word *women* was problematic, and a new spelling *womyn* emerged.

Since the 1990s, third-wave feminists have embraced some of the language, in certain constructions, that was once deemed sexist and offensive. Words such as *chick* are now common mainstream terms (i.e., chick flick). *Girl*, a term that was frequently used among African American women (e.g., girlfriend), is regularly used by the general public and some feminist scholars. Proponents contend that the way in which the words are used may not hold the same original meaning and that the use of formerly sexist words among women is a deliberate attempt to take control of their identities.

Protests against sexist language are not a new phenomenon. This early example of women who attempted to control language that referred to them comes from an excerpt in the *Springfield (Mass.) Sunday Republican* in 1901:

> There is a void in the English language which, with some diffidence, we undertake to fill. Every one has been put in an embarrassing position by ignorance of the status of some woman. To call a maiden Mrs. is only a shade worse than to insult a matron with the inferior title Miss. Yet it is not always easy to know the facts. . . . Now, clearly, what is needed is a more comprehensive term which does homage to the sex without expressing any views as to their domestic situation, and what could be simpler or more logical than the retention of what the two doubtful terms have in common. The abbreviation "Ms." is simple, it is easy to write, and the person concerned can translate it properly according to circumstances. For oral use it might be rendered as "Mizz," which would be a close parallel to the practice long universal in many bucolic regions, where a slurred "Mis" does duty for Miss and Mrs. alike.

Source: Ben Zimmer, "Hunting the Elusive First Ms." http://www.visualthesaurus. com/cm/wordroutes/1895 (accessed August 2009).

to the long and difficult **civil rights movement**, spearheaded by African American activists and organizations, blacks, as well as other minorities, including women, made great strides in terms of economic, social, and educational opportunities.

In fact, civil rights legislation helped to transform not only American society but society's view of gender roles as well. Title VII of the Civil Rights Act of 1964 prohibited employment **discrimination**. Title IX, established in 1972, banned discrimination in academics and athletics—a veritable sea change in the way professional women athletes were perceived. According to the Women's Sports Foundation, Title IX "has helped increase participation opportunities for girls and women in sports. Female high school athletic participation has increased by 904% and female collegiate athletic performance has increased by 456%" ("Title IX," *Women's Sports Foundation*). The victory of a 30-year-old professional tennis player, the bespectacled Billie Jean King, in the "Battle of the Sexes" tennis match in 1973, over Bobby Riggs, a former tennis star in his mid-fifties who contended that female tennis players were not as good as male tennis players, was a landmark moment for women. That nationally televised match in the Astrodome gave enormous positive exposure to female athletes, inspired young women to participate in sports, and showed that women were tough enough to excel in areas previously dominated by men.

Historically, women in sports were bombarded with negative **stereotypes**. Women who behaved aggressively and competitively or looked muscular were disparaged. For example, female jocks were called lesbians or not pretty enough to attract men. Muscles on women were considered "ugly" and unnatural. Society expected women to be passive and friendly, and soft-bodied. Although in the 21st century women are encouraged to have toned and athletic bodies, excessive musculature is frowned upon. Chyna, a former female bodybuilder wrestler, is a case in point.

The instant appeal of Jaime Sommers reflected a changing world. Women were challenging the status quo in a social context wherein many men (and women) continued to be reluctant to fully embrace what they perceived as a radical departure from tradition. Producer Kenneth Johnson, who gets credit for the creation of Jaime Sommers, wanted the character to reflect two ideals: the active, progressive woman and femininity. He thus named the character after a female water-skier. Johnson notes that Jaime was considered a boy's name (Jamie) at that time (but *The Bionic Woman* had an immediate effect on baby-naming trends), and that the name Sommers had a "Nice soft feel . . . [and a] kind of a warmth to it" (Pilato, 37). Images of Sommers jogging in an attractive athletic outfit, living alone, and driving to work (she was a school teacher) in her own car inspired young girls. So did the fact that she was college educated, a former professional tennis player (influenced by the real-life legend Billie Jean King), and beautiful. More than once, Sommers politely rejected or ignored the attentions of obviously interested handsome males. This seems unusual for the time, but Sommers's depiction as an independent woman was in line with the tradition of the lone male hero. This "aloneness" positioned Sommers as a "far more independent and central character than most women in 1970s shows," like the

Angels, who worked in a group and depended on "Charlie," or Emma Peel, who "had always been accompanied by Steed" (Inness, 47).

When audiences first meet Sommers, she is a love interest injected into the popular television story of Steve Austin (unlike Sommers, Austin's character came directly from the bestselling book *Cyborg* (1972) by Martin Caidin, upon which *The Six Million Dollar Man* was based). Johnson added Sommers's character "to give Six Million a bionic boost," reasoning that Austin should have "a female counterpart" (Pilato, 37). *The Six Million Dollar Man* had been on the air for two seasons before Sommers, who was depicted as a high school sweetheart, appeared. The two quickly fall back in love and become engaged. But a skydiving trip turns terribly wrong and Sommers falls to the ground. Austin convinces his supervisor, Oscar Goldman (Richard Anderson), who heads the Office of Scientific Intelligence (OSI), to rebuild Sommers's body. She receives a bionic arm, two bionic legs, and a bionic ear. After a grueling period of physical and emotional adjustment to her new bionic body, Sommers tragically dies as a result of complications related to her implants. It is clear that the producer of the show, well aware of the appeal of the lone hero, never intended for Austin's character to settle down.

But angry viewers protested. Youngsters who had never experienced life before second-wave feminism clamored for more. Fans of all ages, no longer directed by societal norms to frown upon strong, athletic, and independent women as role models, insisted Jaime Sommers be brought back to life.

Kenneth Johnson

Though Kenneth Johnson will go down in history as the man who created Jaime Sommers, he is also known for his contribution to the long struggle to make science fiction acceptable on mainstream American television. Born in 1942 in Pine Bluff, Arkansas, he graduated from the Carnegie Institute of Technology (he paid homage to his alma mater by having Sommers also graduate from Carnegie Tech). Johnson went on to produce *The Six Million Dollar Man*, *The Bionic Woman*, and *The Incredible Hulk*, all of which have a science fiction element, as well as *V*, a straight science fiction miniseries concerning an alien invasion.

Lindsay Wagner

Born in 1949 in Los Angeles, California, to Marilyn Louise and Bill Nowels Wagner, who divorced when Lindsay was seven years old, Wagner performed in plays at David Douglas High School in Portland, Oregon. After attending the University of Oregon, Wagner returned to Los Angeles and worked as a model. She appeared in the television series *Playboy After Dark*, *Marcus Welby, M.D.*, and *The Rockford Files*, and in the films *Two*

People (1972) and *The Paper Chase* (1973) before landing the starring role of Jaime Sommers in *The Bionic Woman*. During the height of her popularity, and thanks to successful negotiations when she was invited to do the series, Wagner was ranked as "the highest paid actress in a dramatic series," making "$500,000 a season, $200,000 more than Lee Majors received" (Inness, 46). Wagner had significant input into the depiction of Jaime Sommers, particularly desiring that the character maintain her femininity. Following the series that made her famous, Wagner starred in various made-for-TV movies and played minor roles in films. She is currently known best for her Select Comfort Sleep Number bed commercials and as an advocator for spirituality. She has been divorced four times, from music publisher Allan Rider, actor Michael Brandon, stuntman Henry Kingi, and television producer Lawrence Mortorff. Wagner has two sons, Dorian and Alex.

POWER SUIT, WEAPONS, AND ABILITIES

In addition to raising Jaime Sommers from the dead, Kenneth Johnson made several key adjustments to her life in preparation for his new series. Sommers was given her own moniker, *The Bionic Woman*, and became, like Austin, an OSI agent. Unlike Emma Peel or Catwoman, both of whom fought crime decked out in cool, black leather costumes, Sommers generally wore casual, comfortable clothes, mostly pants suits. In some episodes, she dressed in sophisticated styles. Like many female detectives, agents, and sleuths—notably the women of *Charlie's Angels*—Sommers wore a wide range of disguises. Like Austin, she did not wear a uniform or costume to identify her as a bionic action hero. Her bionic parts were covered by artificial skin. Her secret identity was concealed from the casual observer—unless she sustained an injury that exposed her mechanical parts or she used her bionic powers in the presence of others.

As mentioned, Sommers's powers were nearly equal to those of Austin. Both had bionic legs that enabled them to run at remarkable speeds. But some episodes reveal that Sommers might have been slower than Austin. When Sommers and Austin ran, the viewers saw them in slow motion and heard a trademark digital sound, signaling that their bionic power had been activated. When they jumped (with help, at times, from stunt doubles and trampolines hidden from the view of the camera) to extraordinary heights or from tall buildings, special effects were used to signal that the action required superhuman ability. Using their bionic arms, both Sommers and Austin could bend steel. Austin had a bionic eye, which allowed him to see great distances. Sommers had a bionic ear that enabled her to hear at a distance, and to hear whispers or phone conversations. Sommers's bionic ear was viewed as an obvious variation from Austin's bionic eye, not as inferior. A more significant difference was the cost of their bionic parts. Allegedly,

Austin's parts cost more (cf. the name of his show), but neither series ever revealed the exact cost of Sommers's bionics. Importantly, both characters were depicted with limited abilities. Unlike invincible superheroes in comic books, Sommers and Austin could sustain injuries, particularly if they over-extended their bionic parts.

Although many kids of the 1970s grew up imagining that they too had bionic powers, bionics were not solely associated with enviable ability and strength. Pilato contends that their bionic powers metaphorically identified Austin and Sommers as "different," linking them to the fictional archetype known as the Other. Many types of the Other have been memorialized in books and on film, and the difference in question can be racial, intellectual, emotional, and so forth. Both Austin and Sommers battled, for a time, with feeling different or alienated from the rest of the human race. Sommers once referred to herself as "the bride of Frankenstein," suggesting that she saw herself as abominable or monstrous. In time, both characters accepted their augmented bodies. In the last reunion movie, a paraplegic was introduced as a next-generation bionic character, suggesting the limitless potential uses (and current reality) for bionics in bettering the lives of real people with physical disabilities.

Although Sommers had her bionic powers at her command, she also knew how to use her wits and other human talents to achieve her aims. In episode eight, "Winning is Everything," Sommers is disguised as the navigator for a two-person international auto race in Afghanistan. Her driver is tormented by self-doubt and the memory of a previous crash. At several points during the race, Sommers must talk him through his doubt (reflecting the popularity of pop psychology in the 1970s). In the end, she motivates him to win, while also using her bionic strength to right their car (the driver has passed out, so he conveniently does not see her) after it tumbles over. She rescues a driver trapped under a racing vehicle, pushes his car out of a mound of soil, escapes from ne'er-do-wells when she stops to pick up a confidential package at a bar for the OSI (the purpose of her mission), and outruns a vehicle in close pursuit, stopping her pursuers by throwing a wrench at their vehicle— just another day at the office for superhero Jaime Sommers.

VILLAINS

Sommers confronted many antagonists over the course of three seasons. Generally, she contended with a new villain in each episode, but there were occasional second adventures with certain antagonists. In the first episode, "Welcome Home, Jaime," a corrupt magnate attempts to lure Sommers into working for him. Working undercover, Sommers shows an interest in him to gain his confidence. In the twelfth episode, "Mirror Image," convict Lisa Galloway is physically altered to look exactly like Sommers. Under the control of the malevolent Dr. James Courtney, Lisa becomes a threat to both the OSI and Sommers. In episode 33, "The Night Demon," Lyle Cannon, a rancher, concocts a fake "Indian evil spirit." Producer Johnson's hard-core science-fiction leanings are aired out on more than one occasion. The Fembots, robots made to look like women, wreak havoc in several episodes, such as episodes 18 and 19, "Kill Oscar, Parts I and II, and episodes 38 and 39, "Fembots in Las Vegas, Parts I and II."

THE BIONIC WOMAN (1976–1978) SERIES

For its time, *The Bionic Woman* was a revolutionary series. Because it contained various science fiction elements (not least the concept of bionics), it allowed viewers to imagine what life in the future could be like. In Johnson's original story, he explored the issue of what might happen when a woman was permitted to appropriate futuristic bionic power. Thus, in *The Six Million Dollar Man* episode, "The Bionic Woman," Sommers rejects her bionic parts, malfunctions, loses her sanity, and dies. In many ways, this reflected the societal norms of the period just ended—that women cannot cope with power. But that was not the end of the story, and like many storytellers before him, Johnson was pushed by his own viewers to rethink his original concept. The simple fact that *The Bionic Woman* came to be made at all reflects the new attitude toward women—oh yes, they can.

Given a second chance, Johnson infused Sommers's character with a wonderful mix of toughness, **feminism**, and traditional femininity, then set her out to experience a series of exciting physical adventures. Like Helen from the popular *The Hazards of Helen* film series (1914–1917), Sommers was frequently kidnapped and bound. She was also often drugged. But unlike Helen, Sommers rescued herself time and again. She single-handedly conquered all sorts of obstacles and difficulties, making her among the earliest women in television to do so. Even the hands-on Jennifer Hart (Stefanie Powers) had to repeatedly call out to her husband, Jonathan (Robert Wagner), and be rescued by him in *Hart to Hart* (1979–1984), a television series about a wealthy married couple and amateur detective team. Audiences enjoyed watching Sommers leap into bionic activity, solve problems, and triumph in her missions.

Johnson and Inness say that it was important to make audiences receptive to Sommers by also depicting her as vulnerable and feminine. Inness contends that "1970s culture . . . was deeply troubled by toughness in women" (Inness, 47). To compensate for Sommers' toughness, Johnson made her feminine, ladylike, and nonthreatening. Comparing *The Six Million Dollar Man* and *The Bionic Woman*, one can easily see how the gender difference is underscored. "[*The Six Million Dollar Man*] is mostly grim, pulse-racing, and all action, whereas [*The Bionic Woman*] starts out somber but is quickly replaced by images of smiling, laughing people, attentive schoolchildren and light music" (Pilato, 156).

Sommers's femininity came through in other ways. Frequently cheerful, good-natured, and quick to smile, Sommers is perpetually pleasant when she is not in mission mode. When Goldman talks to Sommers about her future, he insists that she should live her own life, but Sommers is eager to please, telling him she is grateful for what the OSI has done for her and indebted to them. She wants to be an agent and teach. Inness identified Sommers's decision as "reminiscent of when Mrs. Peel left *The Avengers* to pursue her married life. Both characters were divided between socially acceptable activities (being a wife or teacher) and less openly sanctioned activities (being a secret agent). Inness calls teaching "a stereotypical women's role" (Inness, 46). Even in combat situations, Sommers's femininity remained intact—rather than fight, she knocked down antagonists or pushed them out of the way.

While Austin was off in exotic locations coded as male and in the vortex of the action, Sommers was largely limited to female spaces and traditional female identities. In "Welcome Home, Jaime," Sommers spends a great deal of time using her bionics to clean up her new place. In "Brain Wash," much of the episode takes place at a beauty salon. In "Bionic Beauty," Sommers is disguised as a contestant in a Miss United States contest. She is disguised as a stewardess in "Fly Jaime," a nanny in "The Ghosthunter," and an escort in "The DeJon Caper."

Despite Sommers's femininity, there is no arguing that the character and the show itself actively promoted feminist issues and themes, especially in the episodes that featured overt male chauvinism. In "Winning is Everything," a rival race car driver taunts another driver by saying, "you drive like a woman. You fight like a woman." Rather than physically fight, the driver throws his drink on his antagonist. In a humorous twist, Sommers uses her bionic power to push his face into a bowl of cream. In "Kill Oscar!," a deranged scientist creates female robots designed to do his bidding. The scientist gloats that the female robots are servile and passive (traditional female attributes). In the end, the robots are immobilized, illustrating that in the 1970s, the world was moving on, and, like Sommers, women had a right to think for themselves, be assertive, and tough (if in a still-limited way).

Sommers's love life and ambitious career path also reflected the growing trend of independent women. Nothing illustrates this better than the fact that when Sommers got her own series, her relationship with Austin ended. Just as Johnson did not intend for Austin to settle down, he saw Sommers as a modern-day woman who had no time for marriage anytime soon. Because Sommers had amnesia when she was reintroduced, she did not remember that she and Austin had been engaged to be married. Sommers remained single for a long time, until she dated an OSI agent named Chris Williams, who promptly died while on a mission to Budapest.

In the first reunion TV movie (set 10 years from the last time Sommers and Austin saw each other), an accident restores Sommers's memory of her relationship with Austin. When Sommers challenges Austin's son Michael (who has also been fitted with bionics) to a race, he, not Sommers, wins. We can perhaps conclude from this that even by the mid 1980s, the idea of a woman beating a man at anything was still not considered acceptable by the mainstream viewer. In the second movie, Sommers trains a paraplegic named Kate Mason (Sandra Bullock) in the use of her bionics. By this time, Sommers has become a doctor and has opened a family counseling practice. This movie may well reflect the growing sense of social responsibility and the need to open doors for all members of society. In the final movie, Austin and Sommers finally marry, and Sommers receives new and improved bionics (owing to a virus that threatens her original bionic parts), including night vision. Thus there is a traditional happy ending for the superhero couple. It is, however, implied that Sommers remains childless, a life choice that by this time was no longer considered to be the tragedy it once was.

BIONIC WOMAN (2007) SERIES

When Sommers briefly returned to television in 2007 with the tagline "better, stronger, faster," fans flocked to their flat screen televisions. Not surprisingly, givin the changing times and the influence of shows like *Buffy: The Vampire Slayer* (1997–2003), *Dark Angel* (2000–2002), and *Alias* (2001–2006), this new Bionic Woman had little in common with the original. For one thing, she was four years younger (the original Bionic Woman was 28) and brunette. For another, she was a bartender, a college dropout, and guardian to a teenaged sister. She was, essentially, a third-wave feminist hero—a woman who exuded sex appeal (she had sex with a stranger she met at a bar), was aggressive (she engaged in direct combat with men and women), and was sullen rather than sultry. She also courted danger, walking down dark alleys in the city and taking on her first villain before she had been trained in the use of her bionics. That training, like most scenes, was set to edgy music performed on the electric guitar. When told she was the "property" of the Berkut Group (no longer the OSI), the new Sommers stated that if she joined the group, she would do so on her terms.

However, some things don't change. When a young girl in a car sees Sommers run through a wooded area, she tries to get her mother's attention, explaining that she saw someone running extremely fast. The mother, who is wearing a business suit and taking a business call while driving, does not believe her daughter. "I just thought it was cool," the daughter explains, "that a girl could do that, that's all" ("Bionic Woman Pilot"). According to this scene, though the bar has been raised, tough women are still a novelty, and it is up to Jaime Sommers, the bionic woman, or women like her, to challenge the status quo.

IMPACT

The character of Jaime Sommers made a lasting impression on popular culture. From an economic point of view, the character's marketing power was exceptional. As Inness notes, "like the Angels, Jaime Sommers . . . appeared on lunch boxes, posters, coffee mugs, and coloring books. You could even purchase books that featured The Bionic Woman's exploits, like Eileen Lottman's novel *The Bionic Woman: Extracurricular Activities* (1977). . . . [There was also the] Bionic Woman action figure, you could purchase a classroom, a sports car, a bionic beauty and repair station . . . and join the Bionic Woman Bionic Action Club and read the [short-lived] comic book series" (Inness, 45).

From a sociological point of view, The Bionic Woman had perhaps an even greater impact, changing as it did the perception of strong and independent women beyond the intention even of its creators. Because of Sommers, young girls across the country had a female action hero to emulate, one who broadened the horizons of a generation.

See also Charlie's Angels; Chyna; Helen; Wonder Woman.

FURTHER RESOURCES

"The Bionic Woman Files: A Tribute to the Classic Universal Studios Series." http://www.bionicwomanfiles.com.

Eck, David. "Bionic Woman Pilot." NBC, September 26, 2007.

Inness, Sherrie A. *Tough Girls: Women Warriors and Wonder Women in Popular Culture.* Philadelphia: University of Pennsylvania Press, 1999.

NBC. "Bionic Woman." http://www.nbc.com/Bionic_Woman.

Pilato, Herbie J. *The Bionic Book: The Six Million Dollar Man and the Bionic Woman Reconstructed.* Albany, GA: BearManor Media, 2007.

Rebensdorf, Alicia. "Feminism vs. Fembots." http://www.alternet.org/story/63566.

Sharp, Sharon. "Fembot Feminism: The Cyborg Body and Feminist Discourse in *The Bionic Woman.*" *Women's Studies* 36 (2007): 507–523.

White, Rosie. "Lipgloss Feminists: *Charlie's Angels* and *The Bionic Woman.*" *Storytelling: A Critical Journal of Popular Narrative* 5 (2006): 171–183.

Women's Sports Foundation. "Title IX." http://www.womenssportsfoundation.org/Issues-And-Research/Title-IX.aspx.

Buffy Summers poses confidently in the television series *Buffy the Vampire Slayer*. (TM and Copyright © 20th Century Fox Film Corp. All rights reserved. Courtesy: Everett Collection.)

Buffy the Vampire Slayer

Buffy is a petite blonde teenager who was chosen by an ancient mystical tradition to be endowed with superpowers so that she can fulfill her destiny to slaughter vampires. Buffy made her first appearance in the 1992 film *Buffy the Vampire Slayer*, starring Kristy Swanson. When we first meet Buffy, she is a superficial and vacuous cheerleader who is only interested in shopping, her female clique, and her hunky boyfriend. The mysterious Merrick Jamison-Smythe (Donald Sutherland), who calls himself a "Watcher," helps to transition her into her birthright just in time to exterminate a pack of bloodthirsty vampires who have recently come to town. The film, written by creator Joss Whedon and directed by Fran Rubel Kuzui, was a moderate success. The television series that followed in 1997, which starred Sarah Michelle Gellar and ran for seven seasons, made Buffy an unparalleled symbol of **girl power**. The show quickly became a favorite among academics and fans who voraciously studied and analyzed Buffy and the Buffyverse (the term used to designate the characters, plots, themes, and other information about the television series). Courses dedicated to the tough heroine, known as Buffy studies, cropped up at many colleges and universities.

To scholars, Buffy is one of the most important modern female protagonists to appear on the small screen. Not only did she mesmerize audiences for seven seasons, she was one of the first characters to trigger a shift in the way young women were portrayed in the media. Her story mirrored recent transformations in how young women defined and appropriated power for themselves. Buffy showed that women can be vampire slayers, not merely Dracula's love interests or victims.

Like many female action heroes, Buffy is a composite of both traditional and unconventional depictions of women; nevertheless, she contrasts sharply with her peers. As the Slayer, she is constantly torn between her duties and her desire for a normal high school life. She is not a loner like Wonder Woman, The Bionic Woman, Foxy Brown, Sarah Connor, or Clarice Starling. She fights the isolation created by her otherness, depending on an ever-expanding and close-knit network of friends. Unlike some action heroes (Wonder Woman, Helen), she changes as her world changes; her experiences have a cumulative effect upon her character, darkening her story over time.

The television series underscored themes relevant to society, not just to teenagers. Over the course of seven action-packed seasons, Buffy grows up before the viewers' eyes from teenager to young adult, developing into one of the most complicated, appealing, and fully developed female action heroes in history. She is raised by a single mother, balances school and vampire slaying, dies twice, is resurrected both times, loves, is jilted, befriends, makes mistakes, and saves the world several times.

ORIGINS

Joss Whedon created Buffy Summers with the intent of altering a very old paradigm. In his words, the concept "was my response to all the horror movies I had ever seen where some girl walks into a dark room and gets killed. So I decided to make a movie where a blonde girl walks into a dark room and kicks butt instead" (Early, "Staking Her Claim").

Classic horror movies and vampire flicks depend heavily on the terror-inducing pursuit and murder of young, nubile women. Alfred Hitchcock's *Psycho* (1960) is famous for its murder scene, though it occurs not in a dark room but a shower. Other horror movies favor images of women walking through dark alleys at night, the tap of their pumps or stiletto heels the only sound in the stygian darkness. A male predator appears and pursues. Her steps uselessly quicken; her scream pierces the air. The victim is cast as too weak and defenseless to stop the ensuing crime. Sometimes she is rescued, traditionally by a male hero or a cop. If she dies, justice is exacted by a tough vigilante, such as legendary martial artist Bruce Lee, who revenges his sister's death in *Enter the Dragon* (1973) or Charles Bronson, who plays one of America's favorite vigilantes in the *Death Wish* film series (1974, 1982, 1985, 1987, 1994).

In vampire movies, women are notoriously depicted as the victims or damsels in distress; men are the rescuers and slayers. In both renditions of *Dracula* (1931, 1992), one late 19th-century woman, Lucy, is turned into a vampire, and men fight to save the life of Mina. In a climactic end, Professor Van Helsing, the acclaimed vampire hunter, kills Dracula in the 1931 version; Mina's fiancé, Jonathan Harker, slays Dracula in the modern remake. In *Fright Night* (1985), a teenager rescues his girlfriend who is being seduced by a vampire. In the *Blade* film series (1998, 2002, 2004), Wesley Snipes plays the lead vampire hunter.

Another irony of Whedon's take on the girl-who-gets-killed scenario is that he names the girl-who-kicks-butt Buffy (an ultra-feminine name) and casts her as a stereotypical blonde Valley Girl. Historically, blonde women have had a bad rap, having been depicted in a variety of derogatory ways in film and television. Archetypes, such as the blonde **bombshell** and dumb blonde are among the host of negative images that undermine the power of women. One of the most famous blonde bombshells was Marilyn Monroe (who dyed her hair from its natural brunette color). Monroe's critical career spanned the 1950s and early 1960s and was largely based on her sex appeal, ethereal voice, wide, innocent eyes, and vulnerability. Other famous blondes included Suzanne Somers, who played Chrissy Snow in *Three's Company*, and Farrah Fawcett in *Charlie's Angels*. These women were contrasts to their dark-haired counterparts, who were projected as smarter and more serious.

The Valley Girl was an extension of previous **stereotypes** that originated in the 1980s in California. The Valley Girl was considered immature, self-absorbed, and privileged; her distinctive speech patterns were parodied nationwide. Her attitudes and exploits were commemorated in films such as *Valley Girl* (1983) and *Clueless* (1995). Although Will Smith's fictional cousin in the 1990s sitcom *Fresh Prince of Bel-Air* was African American, she talked and behaved in ways that coded her as a Valley Girl.

Since the 1960s, second-wave feminists have fought hard to obliterate derogatory and sexist images of women in popular culture and elsewhere. Women, particularly in work environments dominated by men, have had to contend with colleagues and superiors who do not take them seriously or patronize them simply because they believe women are weak and inferior. Whedon's solution to the problem of sexist stereotypes was to parody society. He gives us Buffy, who looks and sounds exactly like a blonde Valley Girl, and who wants more than anything to go to the prom—and who then slays the demons that are set to attack the event. Buffy is repeatedly shown with cuts and bruises, the result of her many violent fights, but as she says, "I'm still pretty."

Over the course of the series, Buffy grapples with heavy life issues such as her mother's death, the temptation to solve her problems through violence, and rough sex, as well as the downside of being the Slayer, an onus that forever separates her from the society she wants to be a part of. She is smart enough to go on to college, but inevitably gets involved in dysfunctional romantic relationships. Buffy may not be what some second-wave feminists envisioned as a role model for female power. But most feminists find Buffy remarkable and intriguing, agreeing that within the context of **third-wave feminism**, Buffy fits the mold—or rather shapes the mold—of the new girl-power action hero.

Girl Power and Third-Wave Feminism

Girl power is a term associated with third-wave feminism, which originated in the 1990s, overlapping with **second-wave feminism**. The proponents of third-wave feminism were distinguished from second-wave feminists by age (born in the 1960s onward) and differing viewpoints, notably the fact that some third-wave feminists appropriated terms that second-wave feminists considered sexist and tried to obliterate. Many third-wave proponents did not classify themselves as feminists at all, since that term was often perceived as derogatory and irrelevant to young women who had presumably benefited from women's struggles but had not experienced the conditions that sparked their forebears to action.

Girl power, not **feminism**, was the term that permeated popular culture in the 1990s, though rumblings of the phenomenon began before that. In the 1980s, pop singers Madonna and Cyndi Lauper embodied the traits of the new female icon, and their influence spread to a legion of young women and girls. In her twenties, Madonna blended sex appeal and girlie fashions that featured lace bows, lingerie outerwear, and fishnet stockings. Her youthful voice crooned about romantic love, materialism, and teenage pregnancy. "Girls Just Want to Have Fun," a song by Cyndi Lauper, who was popular for her quirky attire and childlike voice, was considered a feminist anthem, one that differed markedly from Helen Reddy's sober-toned 1970s hit "I Am Woman."

Helen Reddy

Helen Reddy, a popular 1970s singer and actress, was born on October 25, 1941, in Melbourne, Victoria, Australia, to parents who were both actors. Reddy began performing at four years old. She had her first child and was divorced by the time she won a contest on the Australian television show *Bandstand* and moved, shortly thereafter, to New York in 1966. In New York, Reddy married Jeff Wald, her manager.

Reddy's career grew steadily. In 1970, she signed with Capitol Records. Her first hit was "I Don't Know How to Love Him," a song from the musical *Jesus Christ Superstar.* Her second hit was the song "I Am Woman," which she co-wrote with another Australian, Ray Burton, in 1972. Reddy asserts that she was inspired to write this song by her own interest in the feminist movement and a desire to empower other women. At that time, there was no single song that encapsulated the movement, which was increasingly permeating society. The lyrics "I am strong, I am invincible, I am woman" and "I am woman hear me roar" were written during the burgeoning second-wave feminist movement. In the previous year, Gloria Steinem, a prominent spokesperson for second-wave feminism, and others, such as Betty Friedan and Fannie Lou Hamer, had established the National Women's Political Caucus to help support women's participation in politics. In 1972, Steinem established *Ms. Magazine,* a feminist magazine. Throughout the 1970s, women starred in an increasing number of American television series. As women challenged their roles in an ever-growing number of fronts, Reddy's song played in homes, on the radio, and on television, punctuating the changing times.

Reddy's star remained at its zenith throughout the 1970s. In addition to a successful singing career, she appeared in films such as *Pete's Dragon* (1977) and several musicals. In 2006, she published her autobiography, *The Woman I Am.* She has two children and has been married three times.

Many people contributed to girl power. Riot Grrrl, an underground punk movement, is considered one of the biggest influences. Mainstream performers such as the Spice Girls, a five-member all-girl band from the United Kingdom, had nicknames (Scary Spice, Posh Spice, Baby Spice, Sporty Spice, and Ginger Spice) that denoted the many ways in which young women and girls could define themselves—athletic, feminine, assertive, and sweet (or all of the above). The Spice Girls helped to rocket launch the term *girl power,* advertised on clothing, posters, watches, bikes, and stickers. At the start of the 1990s, Madonna launched her Blonde Ambition World Tour. Madonna, who is noted for her many makeovers, took on a bombshell persona for the tour, wore bleach blonde hair, dark red lipstick, and overtly sexual clothes.

In reality, Madonna is nothing like the archetype she portrayed, being driven, savvy, and disciplined.

By the late 1990s, the girl power archetype—youthful, powerful, often violent and posed as a sex object—had become a mainstay of television and film. Coinciding with this trend were dramatic changes in the lives of American women—women were going to college, entering male-dominated careers, and playing greater roles in the military and in conflicts around the world. They were asserting more control over their own lives, whether aggressively pursuing career advancement or leaving high-paying jobs to become stay-at-home moms. A concurrent social trend was the increase of men who decided to stay home as caretakers, while their wives or partners went to work.

Many popular female action heroes quickly cropped up in *Buffy*'s wake. On television, there were three adorable kindergarteners who flew and beat up villains in the animated *The Powerpuff Girls* (1998–2004), four attractive and modern-day sisters who were witches in *Charmed* (1998–2006), a twenty-something bionic bartender in *Bionic Woman* (2007), and a supercharged, athletic, and sexy CIA agent in *Alias* (2001–2006). At the movies, two *Charlie's Angels* films were made (2000, 2003) as well as two other films featuring video-game protagonist Lara Croft (2001, 2003).

Joss Whedon

Whedon, born Joseph Hill Whedon on June 23, 1964, in New York City, is a self-proclaimed feminist. He graduated in 1987 from Wesleyan University in Middletown, Connecticut. Both his parents had an impact on his professional life. His father, Tom Whedon, was a screenwriter who wrote for *The Electric Company* and *The Golden Girls*. His mother, Lee Stearns, a high school teacher and activist, had a large influence on Whedon's many strong women characters. Whedon's writing career started with the television show *Roseanne* (1988–1997), about a sarcastic working-class mother who challenged the traditional image of the polished, mild-mannered, middle-class June Cleaver archetype. After *Buffy the Vampire Slayer* (1992), his first film, he went on to write *Speed* (1994), *Toy Story* (1995), *Alien Resurrection* (1997), and *Serenity* (2005). He is most noted for producing *Buffy the Vampire Slayer*, as well as its spin-off, *Angel* (1999–2004). He produced other television shows, such as *Firefly* (2002) and *Dollhouse* (2009).

Kristy Swanson and Sarah Michelle Gellar

Kristy Swanson, who played Buffy Summers in the movie, was born Kristen Nöel in California on December 19, 1969. Both her parents, Robert and Rosemary, were physical education teachers. Swanson has been a fixture in television and film since the 1980s. Her first major role was the character

Real Women Action Heroes

Buffy, The Powerpuff Girls, and countless other female action heroes have used their special powers to defend and protect the powerless. In real life, women also answer the call when vulnerable individuals in society are threatened. Although they may not pound away at the bad guys, blast their way past obstacles in a blaze of dramatic special effects, or soar through the air, their achievements are no less spectacular.

History is replete with examples of real women of action. After escaping slavery in the American South, Harriet Tubman (1822–1913) wielded a gun as she made 13 precarious trips along the Underground Railroad, a term used to describe the clandestine movement to bring slaves to freedom in the Northern states or Canada. During the Civil War (1861–1865), Tubman served as a scout and spy. Later in life, she became a noted suffragist. Sarah H. Bradford published the first of several biographies chronicling Tubman's amazing life. Irena Sendler (1910–2008), served in the Polish Underground and in a resistance organization that opposed the German occupation of Poland during World War II (1939–1945). Thanks to Sendler's efforts to hide Jewish children and provide documents to facilitate their escape, many children were saved. Her work was extremely dangerous, owing to the fact that Adolf Hitler, notorious leader of the Nazi Party, had targeted Jews for horrific scientific experiments and extermination. Hordes of Jews were forced into concentration, labor, and extermination camps. Sendler herself was imprisoned and tortured in 1945 for her role in aiding the Jews. She lived to receive numerous awards and honors for her harrowing work. The play *Life in a Jar*, and a television movie, *The Courageous Heart of Irena Sendler* (2009), based on the book *Mother of the Children of the Holocaust: The Irena Sendler Story* (2005), were produced in her honor. Two other women who stepped up and took action to save the powerless were Ida B. Wells, an African American journalist and activist, who single-handedly fought against the rampant lynching of African Americans at the turn of the century, and former president of the Philippines, Corazon Aquino, who led a nonviolent "people power" revolt, resulting in the fall of a tyrannical leader, Ferdinand Marcos, in 1986.

Duckie in the cult classic film *Pretty in Pink* (1986), back when girls in high school in film or television had not yet started body slamming vampires and saving the world. She also appeared in another popular 1980s film, *Ferris Bueller's Day Off*, playing a minor role as a not-so-smart student, Ferris Bueller's (Matthew Broderick) classmate. She has continued to take on roles in films, television, and TV movies into the new millennium.

Sarah Michelle Gellar has had an eclectic career, playing good girls, bad girls, horror-movie victims, and action heroes. She studied martial arts, made cosmetics commercials, and is noted for her comedic abilities. Svelte and petite (5'3"), Gellar popularized a more feminine body type, one that was athletic but without the muscle definition sported by the likes of Madonna and action-hero actresses Linda Hamilton, Jennifer Garner, and Jessica Biel.

Born on April 14, 1977, in New York City, Gellar got an early start in acting. At four years old, she appeared in commercials and a TV movie. She attended various prestigious schools and made spectacular grades. After several successful years playing the daughter of legendary soap opera actress Susan Lucci in *All My Children*, she landed the role that made her famous as the lead character in *Buffy the Vampire Slayer*, the television series. Gellar's film career included the leads in the horror film *I Know What You Did Last Summer* (1997) and in the romantic comedy *Simply Irresistible* (1999). Gellar returned to her natural brunette look to play a conniving woman in *Cruel Intentions* (1999), a new and improved Daphne (with a black belt) in the *Scooby-Doo* film remakes (2002, 2004), and a go-getting New York City book editor in *Suburban Girl* (2007). She married actor Freddie Prinze Jr. in 2002.

POWER SUIT, WEAPONS, AND ABILITIES

Buffy Summers was depicted in ways that parodied and challenged traditional representations of the vampire hunter in print and on screen. Most notably, vampire hunters were historically male, frequently middle-aged or even older, wore dark, somber cloaks and hats, and were armed with an arsenal of crosses, holy water, garlic and stakes—all the folksy items believed to repel and kill vampires. Vampire hunters did not engage in hand-to-hand combat, since vampires (beginning with Dracula) were extraordinary strong and deadly.

Summers, a high school student for the film and the first three years of the series, was blonde and youthful and helplessly fashion conscious, donning an assortment of bright and trendy outfits—clothes that any ordinary young woman who frequents the best stores in the mall would wear. The colors signified girliness and playfulness, traits that figure prominently in girl-power heroes and that forced audiences to reexamine traditional concepts of power represented as male, serious, and grim. Buffy was notorious for slaying vampires in unlikely outfits and full makeup, once quipping when challenged on this point, "Don't worry, I've patrolled in this halter many times" ("The I in Team"). Even when, in the later years of the series she sometimes dressed in dark colors to reflect her position as something akin to a military leader, she never conformed to male modes of dress or appearance, as did Lieutenant Jordan O'Neil in *G.I. Jane* (1997). Buffy was allowed to stay feminine and still exert power.

Unlike her male counterparts, Buffy was endowed with slayer strength, and was thus a tough fighter. Though she had an arsenal that included the traditional crosses, stakes, and holy water (and once famously used a rocket launcher to destroy a particularly tough demon), every episode of the television series involved Buffy displaying her martial arts skills.

Unlike other vampire hunters, Summers was clearly coded as both feminine and powerful, two traditionally opposing concepts. There was also a lot of comedy in the show, and Buffy prided herself on her ability to pun when slaying. In one scene in the film, her Watcher tells Buffy that when vampires are in her presence, she will experience cramping, a sensation Summers identified as a symptom of the female menstrual cycle. For many centuries, menstruation was considered unclean, a curse, and a source of embarrassment (Although in some societies, menstruation has been considered a sacred time.) Because Summers's cramping served as an alert system, she was all-the-more prepared to slay vampires. The implication was that only females, not males, could function as slayers.

According to the mythology developed in the series, the Slayer had been reincarnated over many centuries: "Into every generation a Slayer is born. One girl in all the world, a Chosen One. One born with the strength and skill to fight the vampires" (Sherman, "Tracing"). But even though she had innate abilities, the slayer had the help of a Watcher.

In the classic vampire films and television shows, vampire hunters were usually depicted as experts, professionals, and authorities in all supernatural matters. But Whedon gave Buffy a Watcher, someone who functioned as a teacher, trainer, and a wellspring of knowledge and expertise. A Watcher also facilitated his Slayer's physical training. There were in fact many Watchers (and a Council of Watchers charged with keeping the Slayer line going), for the Slayers did not live long, and when one died, another took her place.

For some scholars, the Watcher undermined Summers's power. Frequently in films, strong female characters are assigned father figures or male guides who are depicted as essential to their development, underscoring an implied weakness or inability to go at it alone, like most male heroes do. Male feminist Whedon addresses such issues on screen, as Giles (Anthony Stewart Head), Buffy's Watcher, is fired and replace by the Council of Watchers because he is too protective of his Slayer. In due course, Buffy abandons the Council entirely and goes off on her own, thus establishing herself as an independent player. Later, she asks Giles to be her Watcher again, but their relationship is clearly one of equals, and compatible with Buffy's awareness that she needs help if she plans to live past age 25.

The emphasis on Summers's friends is one of the elements that was most celebrated in the series. In contrast to the lone male hero, Summers surrounded herself with a team (nicknamed "the Scooby gang"). She had the help of Willow Rosenberg (Alyson Hannigan), who became a powerful

Abusive Relationships

Abusive relationships are not exclusive to adult women. Teens and preteens, girls and boys, can be victims of abusers in relationships. Television series like *Buffy: The Vampire Slayer* help to bring these issues to the forefront, demonstrating that abuse is not normal and can affect anyone. Above all else, abuse in any form—physical, sexual, and emotional—should not be tolerated. Professionals recommend that children should know the warning signs of an abusive relationship and get help from friends, parents, relatives, or teachers.

Ten Warning Signs of an Abusive Relationship

1. History of discipline problems.
2. Blames you for his/her anger.
3. Serious drug or alcohol use.
4. History of violent behavior.
5. Threatens others regularly.
6. Insults you or calls you names.
7. Trouble controlling feelings like anger.
8. Tells you what to wear, what to do, or how to act.
9. Threatens or intimidates you in order to get their way.
10. Prevents you from spending time with friends or family.

Source: http://jenniferann.org/dating_violence_risks.htm (accessed August 2009).

witch, Xander Harris (Nicholas Brendon), an ordinary guy but good in a fight, Oz (Seth Green), a werewolf, and Anya (Emma Caulfield), a former vengeance demon. The Scooby Gang assisted Buffy in her quest to subdue the demons, evil spirits, and vampires that flocked to Sunnydale. Rather than undermine Summers's powers, her friends enhanced her abilities. Her friends frequently functioned as heroes themselves, or rescued Summers, even bringing her back from the dead (twice).

BUFFY THE VAMPIRE SLAYER, THE FILM

At the start of *Buffy the Vampire Slayer*, Summers is depicted as a pampered teenager who has it all. The high school years are frequently represented in film and elsewhere as a source of deep insecurity, awkwardness, and anxiety over body issues, social acceptance, and relationship issues. But Summers, an enviable character, was free from these problems. She was head cheerleader, had a handsome, athlete boyfriend, a group of equally "cool" girlfriends, and enough money to buy the appropriate clothes to match her status. Her focus was on social status, clothes, boys, and cheerleading—not academics. Blemish-free, blonde, and beautiful, Summers dreamed of marrying a celebrity and becoming a buyer (although she does not know exactly what that means). She never mentioned attending college.

Summers's status as a Valley Girl is disrupted by dreams from what she thinks are past lives—violent dreams, in which she is a peasant girl or a slave. She finds herself getting stronger, and is confused, until Merrick comes into her life and explains that she is the Slayer, and helps her through the struggle of accepting and learning about her new identity.

On her first patrol, she feigns weakness by playing the damsel in distress, singing softly, "I'm feeling helpless," before engaging the vampire. She exudes female toughness, later throwing a male student to the ground after he slaps her bottom, asserting loudly, "don't grab me." Her boyfriend intervenes, but she tells him that she can take care of herself. Realizing that the silly issues that preoccupied her in her former life are meaningless in comparison to saving the world, she tries to persuade her friends to get involved. Although bodies are turning up everywhere because of the vampire attacks, her clique is clueless. Becoming a slayer isolates Summers from her frivolous friends. It also causes her to dress down. No longer self-absorbed, she becomes obsessed with slaying vampires and saving humanity.

Though Merrick dies, Summers saves the day in a final showdown with vampires, killing their leader. Afterward, Spike and Summers (wearing a formal gown, from which she tore most of the skirt for mobility during the fight) slow dance. Neither wishes to lead the dance, underscoring Whedon's depiction, from a feminist perspective, of an equal partnership.

BUFFY THE VAMPIRE SLAYER, THE SERIES

The television series picks up more or less where the movie leaves off—and then goes on to surpass the modest success of its predecessor the way the sun outshines the moon. In the first episode, "Welcome to Hellmouth," the now Watcherless Buffy and her mother have moved to Sunnydale, California. Buffy is determined to make a new start and live a normal life with no vampires, though the prescient dreams of danger that are her birthright follow her. On her first day at high school, Cordelia (Charisma Carpenter), a popular fellow sophomore checks her out and decides she is cool enough to be one of her clique. Buffy also meets misfits Willow and Xander, and decides that she's on her way to a normal life. But she is soon reminded of her past by the principal, who is shocked to read in her records that she burned down the gym at her previous school; by Giles, the librarian, who announces himself as her new Watcher; and by the appearance in the girls locker room of a dead body with puncture wounds in her neck. This sets the pattern for the next seven years, for, as Giles explains to a resentful Buffy, Sunnydale is positioned on top of the "Hellmouth," the mystical convergence upon which Sunnydale had been built, which attracts all manner of demons, monsters, and of course, vampires. It's back to the office for Buffy Summers.

Buffy is considered a progressive hero because she is the poster child for female empowerment. Weekly, she behaved in ways that challenged male heroism. Unlike, say, Jaime Sommers, who was presented as slightly less powerful than the Six Million Dollar Man, the only creatures who are stronger than Buffy out of the literally thousands she defeats are two or three exceptionally strong demons (some of whom are ranked as gods in the Buffyverse). Most significantly, she regularly defeats her various boyfriends (human and vampire) in combat, real or feigned. Buffy never defers—never lets the boy win.

Unlike many action hero television shows, each of the secondary characters in *Buffy* is given a story arc that continues from season to season. It is no accident that the Slayer is also known as the Chosen One; the Slayer traditionally is always separated by her powers and fate—always alone—a reality that Buffy both mourns and resists. The support of her friends makes her unique among Slayers; without their help, she would face the early death that is the second most distinguishing characteristic of Slayers.

Buffy has two male friends in her life. Over the years, as Giles's relationship with Buffy changes from uptight and demanding teacher to compassionate father figure, his personal life shifts from stuffy librarian to outcast and unemployed drunk to magic shop owner and occult specialist. Though fans complain that Xander is never given enough to do, his character nonetheless goes from underachieving student and runner-up class clown to successful construction contractor. Moreover, he is Buffy's rock, the one character in the show without innate or magical abilities, the ordinary guy who is always there for her.

Willow's story line over seven years is second only to Buffy's in terms of character growth, and she becomes in her own right a female action hero. She starts off as the ultimate nerd, pining hopelessly after Xander, her oblivious best friend. She is a sweet and insecure girl who dresses in handmade clothes and shows only glimpses of the obsessive behavior that makes her such a good student and the Scooby Gang's computer and tech whiz. It is only at the end of season two that Willow displays any interest in magic, and fans had to wait until season four for her to progress to the point where, as she says, she could "float something bigger than a pencil" and for the word *Wicca* to be regularly used. It takes until season six for Willow's dormant insecurities and desire for power to explode in one of the darkest periods of the show, when, driven by grief and anger, she commits murder and sets out to destroy the world. It is this slow, inevitable, and unparalleled character growth and plot development that had fans and critics alike falling over themselves in praise of Whedon's storytelling prowess.

Although Buffy was powerful, well admired, assertive, and smart, her relationships with men were troublesome. When she loses her virginity to Angel (David Boreanaz), a vampire with a soul, she triggers a spell that turns Angel back into his former, extremely evil self. Though a terrifying plot twist that instantly gave the show a new gravitas, this is also a joke reference to all the bad things that are supposed to happen if teenagers indulge in sex ("once they get what they want, boys change"), one of many metaphors (such as "high school is hell" and "you teenagers always think it's the end of the world") that characterized the first three seasons of the show. Starting with season four, the metaphors were dropped, and as a freshman at college, Buffy enters into a relationship with a human, Riley Finn (Marc Blucas). But this too is doomed to fail, for very real reasons such as Buffy's growing isolation and Riley's awareness that he can never compete with the likes of Angel. Likewise, Buffy's relationship with the vampire Spike (James Marsters) during season six, which was violent and self-destructive, is a straightforward exploration of the devastating effects of depression and self-loathing.

Buffy was a complicated character, not a one-dimensional stereotype, such as a **vamp**, blond bombshell, or **ingénue**. She was a reflection of changing ideologies, wherein new generations of women strove for power and beauty, strong bodies, and love. It was in itself a sign of the times that it was a male feminist who created the show. But Whedon did more than reflect the times in which he lived by offering the term *slayer* as a metaphor for *empowered*. In the most powerful moment of the final episode of the series, "Chosen," Buffy states that all girls, everywhere, have the potential to be slayers, just like her. Buffy is no longer alone.

IMPACT

Buffy the Vampire Slayer was one of the most talked about television series of its time. Unlike previous television female action heroes, like Wonder Woman and Bionic Woman, she had no specific male predecessor. *Adventures of Superman* (1952–1958) preceded the 1970s *Wonder Woman* television series. *The Bionic Woman* television series emerged out of *The Six Million Dollar Man*. *Buffy the Vampire Slayer* lasted longer than either show and inspired spin-offs, like *Angel*, video games, comic books, companion books, magazines, and other merchandise such as bumper stickers asking "What Would Buffy Do?" This show more than any other paved the way for the subsequent surge of female leads in action TV women.

See also The Powerpuff Girls; Selene.

FURTHER RESOURCES

Buttsworth, Sarah. "'Bite Me': Buffy and the Penetration of the Gendered Warrior-Hero." *Continuum: Journal of Media and Cultural Studies* 16 (2002): 185–199.

Contner, James A. "The I in Team." *Buffy the Vampire Slayer*. WB, February 8, 2000.

Early, Frances H. "Staking Her Claim: *Buffy the Vampire Slayer* as Transgressive Woman Warrior." *Journal of Popular Culture* 35 (2001): 11–27.

Early, Frances H., and Kathleen Kennedy. *Athena's Daughters: Television's New Women Warriors*. Syracuse, NY: Syracuse University Press, 2003.

Goodale, Gloria. "Television's Superwomen." *Christian Science Monitor,* February 5, 1999.

Jowett, Jorna. *Sex and the Slayer: A Gender Studies Primer for the Buffy Fan*. Middleton, CT: Wesleyan University Press, 2005.

Karras, Irene. "The Third Wave's Final Girl: Buffy the Vampire Slayer." http://www.thirdspace.ca/articles/karras.htm.

Levine, Elana, and Lisa Parks, eds. *Undead TV: Essays on Buffy the Vampire Slayer*. Durham, NC: Duke University Press, 2007.

Magoulick, Mary. "Frustrating Female Heroism: Mixed Messages in *Xena, Nikita,* and *Buffy*." *Journal of Popular Culture* 39 (2006): 729–755.

Owen, Susan A. "Buffy the Vampire Slayer: Vampires, Postmodernity, and Postfeminism." *Journal of Popular Film and Television* 27 (1999): 24–31.

Sherman, Yael. "Tracing the Carnival Spirit in *Buffy the Vampire Slayer*: Feminist Reworkings of the Grotesque." http://www.thirdspace.ca/articles/3_2_sherman.htm#4.

Wilcox, Rhonda. *Why Buffy Matters: The Art of Buffy the Vampire Slayer*. New York: I. B. Tauris, 2005.

Catwoman, as played by Lee Meriwether in the *Batman* television series, poses with several of Batman's arch villains. (AP Photo.)

Catwoman

Catwoman is the supervillain and female antihero featured in DC Comics' famous *Batman* publications. Batman's fame notwithstanding, Catwoman is a legendary icon in her own right. Normally an independent player, except for when she conspires with other well-known *Batman* villains like the Joker, the Riddler, and the Penguin, Catwoman is a monumental figure in comic book history. She first appeared in 1940, in an era wherein males—superheroes or otherwise—dominated comic books and films, as well as books and mainstream society. In comic books, women were generally depicted as girlfriends and damsels in distress. Catwoman is unique in that she was conceived as a villain in her own right—a competitor to Batman and not a female version. Subsequent female action heroes were often derived from existing male heroes. DC Comics' Superwoman was based on the popular Superman. Such female superheroes were considered subordinate to the dominant male heroes and were generally less popular. It was a fact of life that comic books catered to males. Female superheroes occasionally sparked interest from girls, but were primarily intended to be **eye candy** for boys.

Catwoman, however, was a much more complex character. Always unpredictable, she embodied both conventional and unconventional characteristics in a persona that had a greater impact than most female action heroes in the comic books of the time. She appeared in numerous incarnations over the years, all of them glamorous and sexualized, but she was always, in defiance of social conventions, a "bad girl" who did as she pleased and did not abide by the rules. She refused to submit to **patriarchy** and convention and dared to challenge her morally upright foe, Batman, and his wholesome sidekick, Robin.

In a nod to feminine tradition, Catwoman was a fashion trendsetter. Her eponymic "catsuit" was such a hit that it inspired a trend among subsequent female action heroes. Emma Peel in the 1960s television series *The Avengers* famously wore a black leather catsuit. Variations were worn by Trinity in *The Matrix* film series (1999, 2003), Selene from the *Underworld* film series (2003, 2006), Seven-of-Nine in *Star Trek: Voyager* (1995–2001), and countless others.

Catwoman was frequently depicted as a woman with a troubled past. In some renditions, she was abused as a child or was a former prostitute. As an adult, she stole jewelry, caused trouble for Batman, and even gave birth to a daughter, whom she gave up for adoption (who would become known as the Huntress). After a brief period of reform, Catwoman returned to a life of crime, preferring an adventurous life, however dark, to settling down and acquiescing to traditional female roles. Shimmying back and forth across the line of transgression, Catwoman sometimes engaged in noble rescues and pursued commendable causes, thus putting her assorted powers, stunning acrobatics, agility, and fighting skills to good use. But to this day, she has not yet fully retired from her preferred position outside the law.

Catwoman's success can be measured by her refusal to go away. Created in 1940, she appeared in *Batman* comic books until the late 1950s. She resurfaced into the popular culture in several episodes of the *Batman* TV series (1966–1968), where she was first played by Julie Newmar and then by African American chanteuse Eartha Kitt. In the film *Batman Movie* (1966), Lee Meriwether played the role. In the same decade, Catwoman reappeared in DC Comics to stay, finally receiving her own comic book series in 1993. Michelle Pfeiffer was cast as Catwoman in the film *Batman Returns* (1992), and Halle Berry starred in the film *Catwoman* (2004). Catwoman has also appeared in animated cartoons and video games. Her success, spanning almost seven decades, underscores her lasting appeal to American audiences.

ORIGINS

Catwoman first appeared in *Batman #1* in 1940. She was created by Bill Finger and Bob Kane, who both began their careers in comics in the 1930s and are considered the creators of Batman. Finger, born on February 8, 1914, was a major player at DC Comics. He not only contributed to the story development of the *Batman* comic book series and co-created some of Batman's most notorious foes (The Joker, The Penguin, Two-Face, The Riddler, and Catwoman), but he also contributed to the storyline of Green Lantern, another comic book hero. Bob Kane, born on October 24, 1915, is also known for creating the two other female action heroes in the *Batman* comics: Batwoman, who appeared in 1956; and Batgirl, who made her debut in 1961. Neither Batwoman nor Batgirl would surpass the popularity of the more multifaceted Catwoman.

Catwoman's character was largely influenced by the early and mid-20th-century filmic traditions of portraying women as **femme fatales**. The femme fatales, also known as **vamps**, were sultry beauties who gained the upper hand over men through their sex appeal and sexual assertiveness. While the femme fatale was aggressive, her opposite, the **ingénue** and "good girl," was passive. Although many scholars argue that the Hollywood femme fatale image is one that objectifies women, it was one of the few roles permitted to women that showed them as active, rather than as passive, decorative, or powerless characters.

As with other successful and long-running comic book characters, Catwoman's origin story has been changed more than once. At first, Catwoman was depicted as an ordinary woman named Selina Kyle who "was a bored socialite who got in over her head during some jewel thefts and found she liked the taste of danger" (Colón, 17). In the 1950s, the story was that Selina, a former stewardess, had sustained a head injury during a plane crash. Her subsequent amnesia triggered her turn to a life of crime. In the

1980s, the comic books created one backstory in which Selina had been an abused wife who turned to robbery after stealing her jewelry from her husband, and another in which she was depicted as a prostitute who had been abused by her pimp and turned to robbery for a living. These last two origin stories are significant because they portray Catwoman as rising from victimhood to self-empowerment, though for malevolent purposes.

Catwoman's character was rooted in **transgressivness**. Although she was frequently portrayed as Batman's love interest (a typical role for a woman), she engaged in criminality, which contradicted the prevailing perception of the 1940s woman as someone who was supposed to be inherently good and wholesome. Criminals in film and comic books were predominately male. Although Catwoman was a thief, she was depicted as less violent than her male compeers. This depiction made Catwoman appear more acceptable, as women were customarily portrayed as gentle and nonviolent in contrast to males, who were permitted, if not expected, to act out aggressively and violently. Unlike so many action heroes and antiheroes, Catwoman was multidimensional, and was frequently shown struggling between doing right and doing wrong.

DC Comics

Founded in 1934, DC Comics was the birthplace of some of the world's most famous superheroes. The only other comparable comic book publisher in America is Marvel Comics. Although DC is most known for its host of incredible male heroes, such as Superman, Batman, the Flash, Green Lantern, and Captain Marvel, they also created notable female action characters, like Wonder Woman and Catwoman.

Wonder Woman, who debuted in 1941, captivated a generation of young boys. Her immense popularity spawned a long comic book career that included, as a member of the Justice League, a formidable relationship with two of DC Comics' top male heroes, Superman and Batman. Wonder Woman's status as a feminist icon was cemented when she became the star of her own wildly popular television series in the 1970s. Wonder Woman also inspired a long line of popular merchandise. Marketers rarely invested in female comic book heroes as extensively as male comic book heroes, but Wonder Woman proved a lucrative investment.

POWER SUIT, WEAPONS, AND ABILITIES

Catwoman without her catsuit would be like Batman without his bat mask and cape. However, Catwoman did not always don her famous attire. In fact, she sported multiple looks and costumes over the years. In her debut, Catwoman, known then as The Cat, wore a glamorous green dress. She wore her first distinctive costume in *Batman #3*. This costume included a full cat mask, a dress, a long red cape, and high heels. In *Batman #10*, Catwoman wore a black, full-body costume with a purple cape, and in the mid-1940s, she wore a partial cat mask, a violet dress, a cape, and high heels. In the early 1960s, Catwoman wore a scaly green body suit, green glasses, and cat ears, but by the end of the decade she wore a one-piece costume with tights, high heeled boots, and a tail. In the 1990s and beyond, Catwoman has appeared in such costumes as a body-hugging purple suit with thigh-high boots, a black PVC suit, and a sporty, Emma Peel-like catsuit and goggles.

Catwoman's costumes on television and film show further variations. In the 1960s television series, Catwoman appeared in two different renditions of the sexy, form-fitting black body suit—each suit customized for the different actress who portrayed her. The look was unorthodox, considering that 1960s television programs were predicated on squeaky-clean images, wherein women tended to cover their bodies. Sexual innuendo was discouraged, and modesty and censorship reigned supreme. Batman and Robin, the two stars of the show, were depicted with wholesome images, underscoring the trend of the1960s.

The films, released in 1966, 1992, and 2004, depicted an increasingly uninhibited Catwoman. She started off in the classic catsuit, then moved to a body suit that was even tighter and glossier, and ended up in an edgy, strappy, cleavage- and flesh-revealing costume.

Batman's costume projected masculinity and showed off his muscular form; it did not exude the unabashed sexiness of Catwoman's catsuit, a sexiness that was emphasized with plenty of **fetishizing** camera shots. However, Catwoman's costume also exuded athleticism, free-spiritedness, and disdain for traditional feminine modesty. Further, Catwoman's form was unequivocally feminine. In most renditions, Catwoman is depicted as a slim woman with an hourglass shape. She is not, like the female comic book characters of the He-Man series, large, bulky, or excessively endowed.

Catwoman wielded assorted weapons and tools. Her favorite weapon was her whip, or cat o'-nine-tails, as it was referred to in the comic books. The cat o'-nine-tails looked like an ordinary whip that diverged into several thongs at the business end. Catwoman's cat-compact contained powder that could render her opponents unconscious; she used perfume for a similar purpose. Her claw gloves provided extra fighting power when she was in combat mode. Catwoman also used a cat-apult to propel her over great distances, a catarang (boomerang), and a catmobile.

In later renditions of the comic books and the films (and reflecting the growing demand for superheroes with martial arts skills), Catwoman appeared as a far more efficient and forceful fighter, as well as naturally more acrobatic and agile. For example, in *Catwoman*, she appears effortlessly sailing through the air, turning flips, and appropriating even more primal catlike behaviors than before. In *Batman Returns*, Catwoman is depicted with nine lives, making her partially immortal.

Like other Gotham City villains, Catwoman might team up with notorious villains or henchmen. In this way, Catwoman's toughness was depicted as being on par with the cast of predominantly male villains. A number of men and women underlings did her bidding, whether for the purpose of plotting against Batman or executing a burglary. When working with villains like the Joker, Catwoman made contributions as an autonomous character with her own ideas and interests.

FOES

Catwoman's greatest foe is Batman. However, theirs is a complicated relationship, in the same way as Catwoman herself is a complicated character. Catwoman originated as one of many colorful villains living in the fictitious Gotham City, created to engineer conflict for the gallant caped crusader, Batman, his loyal sidekick Robin, and the innocent denizens of the city. But in various storylines featured in the comic books, television, and film, these two opposing characters, Catwoman and Batman, don't hide their romantic interest for each other. And Batman repeatedly tries to rescue Catwoman from her bad ways. (Catwoman is not completely bad; she shows evidence of goodness, and thus Batman believes she can be rehabilitated.) In similar fashion, Hercules, in the 1990s television series *Hercules: The Legendary Journeys*, falls for Xena, who, in the beginning, was cast as a villain, and played a large role in her departure from her evil ways. Although Xena's conversion was permanent, her relationship with Hercules was not lasting. For a time, Catwoman lived a life of reform, but this life changed and her relationship with Batman proved to be ephemeral.

THE TELEVISION SERIES

The 1960s *Batman* television series was a sensation. Established on a thrilling formula of comic book camp, the series was, for its era, an explosion of

The Antihero

The antihero is not the squeaky-clean protagonist that dominated early 20th-century film. Nor is the antihero a criminal or the classic brawny and swarthy hero with the one-hundred-watt smile. The archetype has two sides, the good and the bad, and has historically been dominated by males. Among freelance writer Shane Dayton's favorite antiheroes are grungy men such as Erik Draven (Brandon Lee) from *The Crow* (1994), a supernatural vigilante who massacres his victims, and Tyler Durden (Brad Pitt) from *Fight Club* (1999), a chiseled pugilist who rebels against society. Clint Eastwood appears twice on Dayton's list, once for his portrayal of the swaggering cop who metes out his own brand of justice in the *Dirty Harry* films and again for The Man With No Name in *The Dollars* trilogy of the 1960s.

Absent from Dayton's list are any women. This should come as no surprise, as women were commonly portrayed in film as do-gooders—nice women who followed the law. The bad women, by contrast, were generally cast as prostitutes or villains. Rarely did women appear in the complicated role as the antihero. Catwoman was one of the first prominent female antiheroes. Since then, a number of vigilantes have appeared on the big screen. In the 1990s, female action heroes in movies and television, even the "good" ones, are increasingly depicted as nervy, swaggering, and subtly outside the law. This trend has produced such iconic characters as the rebel Trinity, from *The Matrix* films, and Selene, the pouty vampire protagonist in *The Underworld* series.

avant-garde programming, showcasing newfangled color technology, high action, and ground-breaking television characters like Catwoman.

Color television was still considered somewhat of a novelty when the series debuted in 1966. So was excessive violence. Batman (Adam West) and Robin (Burt Ward) were portrayed as conventional heroes—honest, upright, and unblemished. But their appeal was heightened because they were depicted in vivid color, with fast-action adventure and fighting scenes. These heroes engaged in death-defying thrill sequences, using the latest innovations in special effects—innovations that were far superior to television's early years, though in 21st-century terms they come across as naive or simply amateurish. However, audiences of the times delighted in what they saw, including the sensational fight scenes punctuated with comic book exclamations like "Bam!" or "Pow" and flashy music.

The television portrayal of bad women in "skimpy" outfits was also innovative and controversial in the 1960s. American audiences at that time were still being fed wholesome images of women—women who filled traditional roles, and women who were fully dressed. Catwoman, in her immodest cat-suit, was among the most memorable reoccurring characters on television. Her appearance in the series was believed to have propelled her popularity after having "disappeared from the *Batman* comic books during the late 1950s" (Colón, 18). Significantly, this reappearance coincided with the burgeoning of **second-wave feminism** and the slow but sure growth of female action heroes. More and more women were emerging as characters in spy and cop shows like *The Avengers*, *The Girl from U.N.C.L.E.*, and *The Mod Squad*.

In the first and second seasons of *Batman*, Julie Newmar played Catwoman, appearing as the villain in six episodes. At six-feet tall, Newmar was already a transgressive figure, since tall women in television were still considered a rarity. Newmar gallivanted across the screen in a Lurex catsuit, bringing to mind the sultry female criminals that were more the norm in Hollywood—and something else. For Catwoman had power; she was permitted to be bad. Not only that, she was smart, in charge, and formidable enough to be ranked alongside nefarious characters like The Joker and The Riddler.

In Batman's world, power was not limited to traditional masculine markers—even male villains were small bodied or overweight. Their power resided largely in their cunning and the audacity of their challenges to Batman; they wielded just enough combat ability to put up a brief defense when confronting the heroes and largely relied on ubiquitous henchmen. Catwoman's power was enmeshed with her feminine beauty, posture, charm, and mischievousness. She did engage in the occasional tussle, but these confrontations did not stray too far from traditional female fighting conventions. Catwoman's brushes with violence were not depicted with the same excesses as the fights with male villains.

Batman further pushed the envelope when Eartha Kitt, an African American woman, was chosen to play the part of Catwoman after Meriwether could not return to the series because of an injury. Kitt appeared in only three episodes, but her role was a milestone in television history and granted her iconic status in the *Batman* universe.

Kitt's characterization of Catwoman was considered tailor-made because of her well-known "catlike" deportment (Colón, 22). Her casting was considered landmark because the part had always been portrayed by a white woman, and in the late 1960s, African Americans were rarely represented in the media. Race relations were still considered volatile in the South, where segregation had ended just three years prior, and problematic in the North, the center of the film and television industry. An African American female would not star in mainstream comic books until 1975, with the unveiling of Storm, a member of the *X-Men* team.

THE FILMS

Not only was Catwoman considered important enough to add to the *Batman* television series, she was brought back to join forces with three other infamous *Batman* villains, The Penguin (Burgess Meredith), The Joker (Cesar Romero), and The Riddler (Frank Gorshin), in *Batman Movie* (1966).

This time around, Catwoman and her **alter ego**, a Russian journalist going by the name "Miss Kitka," was portrayed by Lee Meriwether. In a plot to destroy Batman and Robin for good, Catwoman plays a paradoxical role. Her mere presence in the film underscores her importance to the franchise, and her collaboration with the other villains reveals her as a woman who is confident, smart, authoritative, and transgressive. Only Catwoman would be tough enough to brazenly walk into a tavern, where the villains have set up their headquarters, and face a pack of truculent and brawling men. Historically, both taverns and the villain's lair have been **coded as** masculine spaces.

Over the course of the film, Catwoman proves to be the villains' greatest weapon against Batman. As Miss Kitka, the beautiful Russian journalist, she destabilizes Batman, in his Bruce Wayne persona, with extraordinary ease. Bruce Wayne is helplessly captivated by her charm and beauty, especially when she becomes a damsel in distress to lure him into her net. Catwoman splendidly plays on traditional stereotypes, and Bruce Wayne is positively undone when they go on a date, complete with romantic dinner, dancing, and a carriage ride. During the inevitable visit to her home, Bruce is abducted. During the romancing of Bruce Wayne, Catwoman never loses her heart to him, maintaining a steely distance and convincing act throughout, defying the stereotype of a love-obsessed woman. In the end, it is Batman whose heart is compromised.

For all Catwoman's toughness, she is nevertheless diminished in several ways. For one, she is only permitted a limited role at the planning stage of the caper. In most of the scenes where the male villains plot and plan, she remains quiet. Only the male villains actively confront Batman, as when an attack is launched from a submarine and when Bruce Wayne is abducted from Miss Kitka's home. During one fight scene, Catwoman stands back out of the action and yells "get him," referring to Batman. Later, she pushes Batman and Robin into the ocean. That act is passive compared to the aggressive punching and fighting involving the heroes and the other villains and their henchmen. But with oddly triumphant poise, she paces alone atop a submarine, while all the males are "washed up." But this scene is short, and Batman and Robin soon climb out of the water and pursue her inside the submarine. She is ultimately apprehended after tripping and falling (an action that usually precedes a capture in films).

The Huntress

Helena Wayne is the daughter of Bruce Wayne (Batman) and Selina Kyle (Catwoman). She debuted in the November-December 1977 issue of *DC-Super Stars* #17. As the original story goes, Helena was born in 1957 and grew up in affluence. Under her parents' guidance, Helena grew to be strong and athletic. Helena took up crime fighting to avenge her mother's death. Unlike her mother, Helena fights on the right side of the law and is indeed distraught over her mother's criminal past. With long black hair, Helena paired a sexy purple costume with thigh-high boots and a crossbow and went by the name of the Huntress. The Huntress appeared in several thrilling adventures before, in the original rendition, she was killed. She reappeared in alternate storylines in subsequent comic books, as well as in the television series *Bird of Prey*, which ran on American television for the 2002–2003 season.

Not surprisingly, given the decades in which they appeared, the two subsequent films, *Batman Returns* (1992) and *Catwoman* (2004), depict a tougher and more modernized version of Catwoman. This was achieved by contrasting Catwoman with her alter ego, positioning Catwoman in a number of fierce fighting scenes, and updating the character to fit the changing concepts of female power.

In *Batman Returns*, directed by Tim Burton, Catwoman, played by Michelle Pfeiffer, gets her fair share of the action in multiple plotlines featuring Batman (Michael Keaton) and The Penguin (Danny DeVito). This film covers the imaginative origins of Catwoman, who starts out as a hapless secretary working for a tyrannical boss, Max Shreck (Christopher Walken). At work, Selina is awkward and timid; she is shown in a traditional subordinate role, refilling coffee for the men at a meeting in Shreck's office. Her boss treats her with disdain. Selina's pitiable life is underscored when she goes home to an empty apartment, save for her cat. Her home teems with feminine markers: pink walls, doll houses, stuffed animals, and other trinkets. When her love interest calls to cancel a romantic getaway, she is devastated. This is noteworthy, since although other female action heroes, like Bionic Woman and Charlie's Angels, have relished in their professional careers and contentedly eschewed marriage and romantic relationships, Selina is unhappy with all aspects of her life. She longs for a relationship and is dissatisfied with her limiting career, where the **glass ceiling** continues to keep her at the bottom of the ladder. Underscoring her sense of inferiority, Selina stutters when she speaks and talks in a circuitous fashion—speech patterns that have been used to symbolize weakness and traditional feminine ways of talking, in contrast to the so-called authoritative and direct speech of men.

Selina's transformation from weak victim of society and circumstances to empowered action antihero is heralded by her physical death. When her boss throws her from a window after she uncovers his plot to build an illicit super power station, Selina is rescued by cats. She comes back to life as a changed woman. She destroys the symbols of girlishness and traditional femininity such as her doll houses and stuffed animals. She puts her feminine skill (sewing) to a new purpose by piecing together a form-fitting catsuit. In one of her first demonstrations of physical power, she pulverizes a male predator who is about to rape a woman (also considered a feminist act). She then berates the would-be victim: "You make it so easy, don't you? Always waiting for some Batman to save you. I am Catwoman hear me roar." Her dramatic departure from the scene is marked by several whip-action backward flips. In this scene, Catwoman disparages male crime against women as well as the traditional damsel in distress. Her line "hear me roar" refers to the 1970s second-wave feminist anthem "I am Woman" by Helen Reddy.

As a symbol of second-wave feminism, Catwoman idealizes independence and female empowerment, but she also takes pleasure in her own objectification. There's no arguing that Catwoman is a sexualized figure, complete with tight black catsuit, sadistic whip, and bright-red lipstick. She moves and talks with a sultry voice and comments after her transformation that she "feel[s] so much yummier." She knows she is eye candy, but, at the same time, she refuses to settle into a relationship, even though the love connection between her and Batman is strong.

According to Jacinda Read, Catwoman represents "a complex amalgam of contradictory identities," such as "the working girl," "the victim of male violence," "the feminist avenger," "the good girl," and the "object of male desire" (Read, 197). Read believes the composite image of Catwoman represents a transitional period between second-wave feminism and **third-wave feminism**. Indeed, third-wave feminism, with its controversial embrace of femininity and the construction of girl-power philosophy, had its start in the decade in which *Batman Returns* was released. However, by the time *Catwoman* appeared in theaters in 2004, third-wave feminism was firmly rooted in popular culture, coexisting (not without some debate) with second-wave feminist ideology.

When, in 2004, Jean-Christophe Comar, who goes by the name Pitof, directed the first film in which Catwoman took the leading role, he chose to present a sexier and tougher supervillain. This Catwoman is played by the African American actress Halle Berry, a former model and beauty queen who has appeared in a number of action films, such as the *X-Men* films (2000, 2003, 2006), *Swordfish* (2001), and *Die Another Day* (2002). This film makes several references to feminist issues. Patience Phillips, Catwoman's alter ego, works at a company that produces a woman's beauty cream called beau-line. But the product is seriously defective: over time, it produces unpleasant physical symptoms and irreparable damage to skin, as well as addiction.

From the start, Patience is depicted as a passive woman. She is also wholesome, diffident, and modest, refusing to wear a sexy black-leather outfit a coworker has given her. Neither her closest friend, romantic interest, nor coworkers could have predicted what Patience would be capable of after she is murdered for uncovering the secret of beau-line. An Egyptian Mau, messenger of the Egyptian goddess Bast, chooses Patience to become the next cat-woman warrior incarnation, thus bringing her back from the dead and transforming her, in the process, into Catwoman.

As Catwoman, Patience's appearance, personality, and abilities are completely transformed. In an uncharacteristic move, Patience talks back to her self-absorbed and ruthless boss. She cuts her hair and fashions the leather outfit that was gifted to her into a provocative, body-fetishizing outfit. Her powers include super martial arts fighting abilities, acrobatic prowess, and agility. She is a fusion of physical strength, aggressiveness, as well as mischievousness (she steals jewelry), and large doses of sex appeal. The later is underscored by numerous camera close-ups of her voluptuous form and her sensual walks atop towering buildings under the moonlight.

Her new powers are validated by the woman who takes care of the cat that created Catwoman; she tells Patience/Catwoman that she is not the first Catwoman and explains that "Catwomen are not contained by the rules of society . . . you will experience a freedom other women will never know . . . you've spent a lifetime caged. By accepting who you are, all of who you are . . . you can be free, and freedom is power." This Catwoman truly enjoys a freedom outside the constraints of ordinary women. Her personality, her petite frame, and her overt sexuality are wrapped up in a package that second-wave feminists would condemn as derogatory to women, but it is also one that reinforces and perpetuates the images of which third-wave feminists wholeheartedly approve.

IMPACT

Catwoman has come a long way since her days as a comic book villain in the 1940s. She was among the first of her kind: a female villain in a patriarchal comic book world. Her popularity swelled thanks to her appearance in the *Batman* television series in the late 1960s, making her a household name. When she appeared in *Batman Returns* in 1992, audiences were responsive. The film grossed $266.83 million, suggesting that American audiences were ripe for a Catwoman revival. In 1993, Catwoman was finally granted her own comic book series.

Catwoman's popularity earned her a place among the numerous comic book films released in the new millennium. The list of such heroes includes

Spider-Man, the Hulk, the Fantastic Four, and the X-Men. Catwoman was one of only a few female comic book characters adapted to the silver screen. Although much hype surrounded the film's release, which coincided with the debut of a video game, and promos capitalized on Halle Berry's persona and her sexy catsuit, the film grossed only $82 million. Though female action heroes in other films have done remarkably well, this amount was considerably less than comic book films featuring male or mostly male leads.

Nevertheless, Catwoman is still considered an icon, and is one of the most enduring characters in comic book history. This is particularly noteworthy because she emerged at a time when women were relegated to the periphery. They were not expected to appeal to mainstream American audiences, especially when depicted in transgressive action roles, defying society's conceptions of how women should look and behave.

See also Ellen aka "The Lady"; Emma Peel; Jen Yu; Storm; Thelma and Louise.

FURTHER RESOURCES

Batman: The Tribute Pages. "Catwoman." http://adamwest.tripod.com/cat.htm.

Brown, Jeffrey A. "Gender, Sexuality, and Toughness: The Bad Girls of Action Film and Comic Books." In *Action Chicks: New Images of Tough Women in Popular Culture*, ed. Sherrie A. Inness. New York: Palgrave Macmillan, 2004.

Colón, Suzan. *Catwoman: The Life and Times of a Feline Fatale*. San Francisco: Chronicle Books, 2003.

Mainon, Dominique, and James Ursini. *The Modern Amazons: Warrior Women On-Screen*. Pompton Plains, NJ: Limelight Editions, 2006.

Read, Jacinda. *The New Avengers: Feminism, Femininity, and the Rape-Revenge Cycle*. New York: Manchester University Press, 2000.

Sims, Yvonne D. *Women of Blaxploitation: How the Black Action Film Heroine Changed American Popular Culture*. Jefferson, NC: McFarland and Company, 2006.

Kelly Garrett, Sabrina Duncan, and Jill Munroe in The *Charlie's Angels* television series. (Courtesy: Everett Collection.)

Charlie's Angels

Charlie's Angels were three alluring women detectives who worked for Charlie Townsend's private investigation agency. Over the five seasons of the show (1976–1981), there were actually a total of six angels: Sabrina Duncan, Jill Munroe, Kelly Garrett, Kris Munroe, Tiffany Welles, and Julie Rogers.

The characters who launched the series, one of the most popular shows of the 1970s, and who are most often identified with it, were Sabrina, Jill, and Kelly. Kris Munroe (Cheryl Ladd) appeared in seasons two through five, replacing Jill. Kris played Jill's little sister. Tiffany Welles (Shelley Hack) replaced Sabrina in the fourth season. When Shelley Hack left the show, Julie Rogers (Tanya Roberts) became an Angel for the final season. Dubbed "jiggle TV" because of the show's emphasis on sex appeal, the producers made sure that at least one or more of the angels appeared in a bikini, bathing suit, or towel in each episode. However, the angels were also smart, athletic, and skilled in self-defense—"skilled" in terms of the 1970s context wherein women were not normally cast as action heroes in film or television. Sherrie A. Inness defined this as "semi-tough" (Inness, 31).

Each Angel had distinguishing characteristics: Sabrina, played by Kate Jackson, a brunette with short hair, was considered the smart one; Jill, played by Farrah Fawcett, was the athletic blonde; and Kelly, played by Jaclyn Smith, had luxurious, dark brown hair and was the most skilled in combat and gun use. Fawcett, with her big, feathered hair, accrued an enormous fan base. Young women copied her hairstyle (called "The Farrah"); young girls emulated her more than the other Angels when at play, and young men affixed posters of her on their bedroom walls. The most famous of all was Fawcett in a red one-piece flashing her trademark smile.

The series debuted in late September 1976. Within a short period of time, *Charlie's Angel's* was a hit. By November of that year, "59 percent of American households were watching Farrah and her pals" (Inness, 38). And despite the bikinis, more women than men were watching. The reasons for the series' popularity were obvious. Women took pleasure in the demonstration of independent, seemingly liberated women, working together in an exciting career and living active lifestyles. Young girls liked the fact that the women were smart, beautiful, and fashionable. Men enjoyed the spectacle of glamorous women, women who were traditionally feminine and not too aggressive.

Other shows with not-too-threatening female leads were also doing quite well on television: *Police Woman* (1974–1978), *Wonder Woman* (1975–1979), and *The Bionic Woman* (1976–1978). The success of a made-for-TV film, *Get Christie Love* (1974), featuring an African American undercover cop, inspired a spin-off television series. In theatres, low-budget films like *Foxy Brown* (1974), starring African American women who solved crimes, were in vogue. *Charlie's Angels* may have been the most popular of those few women's shows, but the depiction of the Angels themselves was problematic in more ways than one.

ORIGINS

The concept of *Charlie's Angels* emerged from a brainstorming session between two major players in the television industry: Aaron Spelling and Leonard Goldberg.

Spelling was born in Dallas, Texas, on April 22, 1923. After serving in the U.S. Air Force, he attended Southern Methodist University, graduating in 1949. His second marriage produced two children, Randy and Tori. Tori Spelling's acting career started in the 1980s. She is most known for her appearance in *Beverly Hills 90120* (1990–2000), a series her father produced. Aaron Spelling started out writing scripts and acting. He later helped to produce television shows such as *The Lloyd Bridges Show* and *The Mod Squad*, making his mark in the industry. His career as a producer spanned a period from the mid-1950s to 2006. He established his own production company, Aaron Spelling Productions (later Spelling Television), in 1972.

In the 1970s, Spelling dominated primetime TV with television series such as *The Rookies* (1972–1976), *Starsky and Hutch* (1975–1979), and *Fantasy Island* (1978–1984). He also wrote scripts for popular films such as *Shaft* (1971) and *High Plains Drifter* (1973). Spelling died in 2006.

Goldberg was born in New York on January 24, 1934. He was also a prominent producer of television series, producing the made-for-TV films *Charlie's Angels* (2000) and *Charlie's Angels: Full Throttle* (2003). In 1972, he collaborated with Spelling to form Spelling/Goldberg Productions (which meant that Spelling became the head of two production companies in the same year).

At the meeting between Spelling and Goldberg, the two producers discussed an idea for a new program. They wanted a series that combined Goldberg's idea for "three Emma-Peel-like women in leather jackets who worked as freelance crimefighters" and "glamorous escapism" (Condon and Hofstede, 5).

But the trend in 1970s action TV—the trend Spelling and Goldberg had been instrumental in creating—was toward "gritty realism" (Condon and Hofstede, 5). For example, *Starsky and Hutch* was a raw series chock-full of fast-paced car chases, gunfights, and violence. The stars of *Starsky and Hutch*, Paul Michael Glaser and David Soul, were sex symbols and the epitome of masculinity, but their sexiness was associated with their brawn and good looks. The women of *Charlie's Angels* were **coded as** sex symbols because of their femininity—the exhibition of their hair, their made-up faces, and the clothes they wore. Even when they engaged in violence, which occurred with less frequency than on shows featuring male action heroes, the fight scenes were brief and less forceful.

Not all women were portrayed as sexy and gorgeous on television in the 1970s. Since the mid-1960s, **second-wave feminism** had been influencing American culture, including television, by advocating for gender equality and by questioning conventional gender roles. Male producers (very few women

The Chad

In an article entitled "Violent Femmes," Stephanie Mencimer describes a character phenomenon she calls "The Chad." The Chad, a new archetype arising in parallel and as a result of the explosive increase in the numbers of tough women and girls in film and television, is any male character who is subordinate to a strong female lead.

Chad was a character in *Charlie's Angels* (2000), the first film in the series. Chad, played by Tom Green, is weak, incompetent, and servile. While he is homely and feckless, his girlfriend, Dylan (Drew Barrymore), is beautiful, fashionable, and powerful. He makes her breakfast and obsequiously does her bidding.

Although subordinate male characters or sidekicks have appeared throughout history alongside strapping male heroes, The Chad is significant for many reasons. For one, men (not women) were normally depicted as the stronger character when both appeared together. Women (not men) were depicted as the weaker character, largely to establish or strengthen the power of the male hero. With help from The Chad, modern women are established as tough and indomitable heroes.

The Chad pops up in a number of television series and films. Two Chads, the butler and the assistant, appear in the Lara Croft *Tomb Raider* films. The cowardly Joxer plays a Chad in the *Xena: Warrior Princess* television series.

had yet cracked the glass ceiling in the film industry), picking up on the growing social influence of **feminism**, embedded feminist issues and ideas into their scripts and the characters they created. Emma Peel, one of the first such beneficiaries of the movement, was depicted as a single (her husband was presumed dead) and highly intelligent woman. Exuding both beauty and physical confidence, Peel became the most famous character on the British television show *The Avengers*. Mary Tyler Moore, of the popular 1970s sitcom *The Mary Tyler Moore Show*, was the most famous single, independent, working woman on television at the time. Although she was an ordinary woman, not an action hero, she epitomized the female empowerment that is at the core of all female action heroes and popularized the notion that single women can be happy, thrive, and successful outside of a relationship and marriage. *The Bionic Woman* glamorized the independent single woman who was satisfied with her life and committed to teaching and working as a secret agent. She frequently appeared driving in her own car, living in her own space, and saving the day single-handedly—all of which seem mundane now, but were still novelties in terms of what was seen on television at the time.

The women of *Charlie's Angels* were portrayed in a similar fashion. All three women owned their own homes. Sabrina was a divorcee, and both

Kelly and Jill were women who chose, at that time in their lives, career over dating, marriage, and children. When Fawcett left the show after the first season, it was explained that she left the agency to pursue a career as a professional race car driver. This was a **transgressive** move: she wasn't leaving to be a housewife or mother, simply making the leap from one male-dominated profession to another.

Although the idea of showcasing single career women on television was considered progressive, the series sometimes reinforced the idea that married women did not enjoy the same freedoms and opportunities as single women. When Kate Jackson, who played Sabrina, left the show after the third season, it was explained in the last episode that Sabrina was leaving the agency because she had married and was expecting a child. This behavior had its roots in the early 20th century; young women were finally able to break into the workforce, but they were nonetheless expected to return to domestic space upon marriage or first pregnancy. Sabrina was not the only female character to reflect socially constructed traditions still lingering from America's past. Emma Peel quit her exciting life of danger and espionage when her husband unexpectedly returned from the grave. It appeared that the only place for a married woman was in the home, or, as exemplified by the series *Hart to Hart*, in a career that linked her as a partner crime fighter to her husband.

Kate Jackson

Jackson, whose role as Sabrina ignited her career, was born Lucy Kate Jackson in Birmingham, Alabama, on October 29, 1949. After two years at the University of Mississippi in Oxford, Jackson dropped out to study at the American Academy of Dramatic Arts in New York. She made her television debut in the late 1960s as a ghost in the soap opera *Dark Shadows*. She played a nurse and wife in the television series *The Rookies* (1972–1976), produced by Spelling and Goldberg. After leaving *Charlie's Angels* in 1979 at the end of season three, Jackson went on to star with Bruce Boxleitner as a husband-and-wife spy team in *Scarecrow and Mrs. King* (1983–1987), and appeared in several made-for-TV films. She has survived breast cancer twice and has been married three times.

Farrah Fawcett

Born Farrah Leni Fawcett on February 2, 1947, in Corpus Christi, Texas, Fawcett was discovered from a photo after she was voted one of the top ten most beautiful students on campus at the University of Texas in Austin, where she majored in microbiology. Fawcett left the university during her sophomore year and launched her acting career with small roles in television series such as *I Dream of Jeannie* and *The Partridge Family*, also appearing in several commercials. In 1973, she married Lee Majors, famous for his role as Steve Austin in *The Six Million Dollar Man.*

Fawcett became an enormously popular cultural icon as Jill in *Charlie's Angel's*, but her career following her departure from the series at the end of the first season was lackluster. In 1982, she and Lee divorced. Reappearances on *Charlie's Angels* were not received with excitement, but her appearance in *The Burning Bed* (1984), wherein she played a domestic abuse victim, yielded her three Emmy Award nominations. She and actor Ryan O'Neal had a son, Redmond, in 1985. In the 1990s, Fawcett made appearances in several television series and posed for *Playboy Magazine* in 1995 and 1997. She died from cancer in 2009.

Jaclyn Smith

Jaclyn Ellen Smith was born on October 26, 1947, in Houston, Texas. Acting provided an outlet for expression for Smith, who was extremely shy growing up. She first performed in high school and then in the Houston Community Playhouse. She majored in psychology and studied drama at Trinity University in San Antonio. After completing one year at the university, she joined the Balanchine School of American Ballet in New York, appeared in musicals and assorted commercials, and modeled. In 1968, Smith married actor Roger Davis. They divorced in 1976.

That same year, Smith was offered the part of Kelly in *Charlie's Angels*. She was the only one of the original angels to stay with the show until its cancellation in 1981, after which she appeared in several major roles in TV movies. Since 1985, Smith has designed a collection of women's apparel exclusively for Kmart. Smith has three children, the first of whom was murdered in 1991. She married her fourth husband in 1997. She is also a breast cancer survivor.

POWER SUITS, WEAPONS, AND ABILITIES

Clothing played a large role in *Charlie's Angels*, and the Angels' wardrobe has been at the center of more than one controversy. As feminists and modern-day critics see it, the paradox of the three Angels is that they were positioned as former members of the Los Angeles Police Department and private investigators, but their appearance was that of fashion models. They exude femininity and glamour, which traditionally denote softness and weakness. In addition to bikinis, short shorts, and tight jeans, the women wore designer blouses, slacks, and an assortment of gowns. The real-life cost of keeping the women looking beautiful was exorbitant, illustrating just how important the glamour look was to the producers. There were "at least eight

Janet Guthrie

Women are often considered radicals when they break long-existing boundaries and adopt roles considered to be for men. Janet Guthrie was hard pressed to keep her wits about her when she raced as the first woman ever to compete in the Indianapolis 500 and the Daytona 500.

Born March 7, 1938, in Iowa City, Iowa, Guthrie attended the University of Michigan at a time when women in the media were depicted in passive roles. Athleticism in women was not encouraged, and race car driving was a field intended for the fiercest, bravest, and most ambitious of young men. The first Indianapolis 500 car race took place in 1911; the first Daytona 500 race occurred in 1959. Both to this day are dominated by male race car drivers.

Guthrie, an aerospace engineer, started racing in 1963, during the early days of the second-wave feminist movement. At that time, the most transgressive women in the media were the karate-fighting costars of the British television series *The Avengers*. Despite intense resistance to her presence in the racing world, Guthrie went on to compete at the foremost racing venues, the Indy 500 and Daytona 500, in the 1970s. In 2008, Danica Patrick became the first woman race car driver ever to win an Indy car race. Patrick's role as a race car driver and her achievement are still considered an anomaly, despite the numerous gains women have made in recent history.

costume changes throughout each episode," and "each Angel was given her own high-fashion 'look' at a cost of $20,000 per episode" (Gough-Yates, 91).

In numerous promotional photos, whether dressed in casual wear, evening gowns, or their many undercover costumes, the Angels struck alluring poses, sometimes with guns, blurring the lines of glamorous femininity and toughness, or intentionally minimizing their toughness. A number of people have argued that this preoccupation with the women's bodies was exploitive. While the Angels dolled it up, their male counterparts in action series wore trench coats, leather jackets, and uniforms that coded them as men of authority and power, men who were taken seriously.

However, within the context of 1970s television in general, and *Charlie's Angels* in particular, one can counter argue that glamour and sex appeal were how the Angel's power was frequently defined. This power was demonstrated in the fact that they consistently exerted control over men when working undercover. They also drew high ratings, which caused men to take notice of them and women to want to be like them. According to Dawn Heinecken, "objectification sometimes brings . . . feminine success" (Heinecken, 198). When Kelly wore a white bikini in "The Mexican Connection," she easily reeled in her target, the owner of a Mexican airline who was also a drug dealer. Men and young boys tuned in to the series for glimpses of sexy women. Women shopped for the latest fashions and sported "The Farrah" to emulate a sex symbol. The underlying belief was that audiences wouldn't find appeal in women dressed in garb that was considered masculine, frumpy, or too conservative. But this belief is considered problematic to critics who contend that women's power should not be confined to glamorous clothes and sex appeal and that shows, such as *Charlie's Angels*, reinforce impossible goals for young girls in terms of appearance and body image.

Another major difference between male TV detectives and the Angels was the weapons they wielded. In most episodes, the Angels did not carry guns, even though they received gun training and had the necessary licenses and permits. Compared to their male counterparts, the Angels engaged in hand-to-hand combat and gun fights much less often. In fact, the series was markedly less violent than those gritty shows of the 1970s featuring male leads, and the Angels very rarely killed villains.

Indeed, the lack of violence was a conscious decision on the part of the producers of all the shows with female leads in that era. Kenneth Johnson, who created Jaime Sommers, the female bionic hero in *The Bionic Woman*, believed that audiences would reject a woman that was characterized as too violent or too masculine. Others considered the trend a progressive step toward making violence less glamorous. In *The Bionic Woman* and *Wonder Woman*, the emphasis was placed on utilizing other methods to solve problems and apprehend victims. Second-wave feminists liked this trend, as they had long advocated against violence (because glamorizing any violence inevitably includes glamorizing violence against women). Others who favored less violence (or none at all) were concerned that shows like *Starsky and Hutch*, which were excessively violent, had a bad influence on children.

VILLAINS

The villains in *Charlie's Angels* changed with each episode. Adversaries, male and female, were portrayed in a variety of roles. In "Hellride," a boyfriend and girlfriend team were responsible for the death of a female race stock car driver, and it's up to the Angels to stop them. When Jill goes undercover as a centerfold for *Feline Magazine* in "Lady Killer," she is shocked to discover that a woman is responsible for the deaths of two centerfolds. In the last episode of the first season, "The Blue Angels," the Angels must contend with corrupt cops at a police academy. In "Angels on the Air," the Angels must find a male stalker. In "The Sandcastle Murders," the Angels track down a male serial killer, and, in season three, a male nightclub owner hires three women to pose as the Angels and wreak havoc in "Counterfeit Angels." Subsequent seasons feature more thieves, murderers, and pimps.

CHARLIE'S ANGELS, THE SERIES

The concept of women who fight crime was, at the time *Charlie's Angels* was aired, still very revolutionary. Other revolutionary concepts were implanted into the series, reflecting second-wave feminist principles such as the idea that women could break through barriers if given the opportunity and that defying tradition was in itself an American tradition. These concepts coexisted side by side with the many gender **stereotypes** on the show. For example, in the opening sequence of each episode, the women are seen engaging in tough activities while at the police academy: on the practice range, slamming a man to the floor, and undergoing rigorous training. But they are also called "little girls," a term that many people felt was condescending. At the time in America, it was not unusual for women to be referred to as girls, but it was considered dismissive for men to be referred to as boys.

The writers of the show blurred the lines of stereotypical and transgressive traits in other ways. For example, Bosley (David Doyle), who functioned as Charlie's assistant, was depicted as a benign character. He stayed mostly in the office, not in the vortex of action like the Angels. The real "muscle" and brains of the agency were the Angels, who went out in the field and solved cases themselves.

The Angels were consistently identified in ways that challenged stereotypical perceptions of women, but were nonetheless frequently depicted in traditional terms. As the smart one, Sabrina defied the stereotypical view of women and girls as less smart than men and boys. In sitcom after sitcom, female characters were shown playing dumb to appeal to male characters. Smart girls were depicted as marginal players and unattractive. Indeed, in some ways, Sabrina was characterized as the least attractive of the three Angels. Depicted with short hair, while the two other women wore long, glamorizing styles, Sabrina was not shown in bikinis or bathing suits. Only twice did she appear in a towel. And when undercover, Sabrina was rarely portrayed on the front lines as a prostitute or seductress.

While Sabrina used her intelligence, in some episodes she undermined her own abilities. In "The Mexican Connection," she asked a male how she performed after an encounter with a bad guy and deferred to him on how to handle a situation. In "Hellride," she downplayed her race car driving skills.

The other Angels were portrayed in similarly contradictory ways. Kelly, the best shot of the three, was frequently characterized as emotional. Jill was the athletic one, a former swimming champion and sports buff, showing that women can be pretty and feminine as well as physically active. Historically, women were either depicted as physically weak, or, if athletic, as masculine, unfeminine, and unattractive. Jill challenged one stereotype and reinforced another in how she was often "written as Charlie's most airheaded Angel" (Condon and Hofstede, 162).

Nancy Drew

Nancy Drew was created in 1930, a decade that otherwise did little to add to the number of tough female action heroes. Drew, an adolescent, was marketed to young girls. Contrasting with the social perception that girls were neither smart nor adventurous, Drew was not only intelligent, courageous, and active, she was attractive, good-natured, and sensible. This was a radical archetype nestled within the guise of acceptable norms of female behavior.

Nancy Drew appeared in numerous books, as well as on television and in film. She was one of the earliest progressive role models for young girls, inspiring future leaders such as Sandra Day O'Connor, former Supreme Court Justice, and Secretary of State Hillary Rodham Clinton. In *Girl Sleuth: Nancy Drew and the Women who Created Her* (2005), Melanie Rehak expounds on the social significance of this early female action hero.

For all the paradoxes and mixed messages, for all the stereotypical disguises as nurses, prostitutes, models, and beauty contestants, *Charlie's Angels* addressed issues that were important to women. At the opening of each episode, the story of how the three women became Angels is told. Because of **sexism** within the police academy, women were relegated to inferior positions, working behind a desk or as a crossing guard or parking ticket attendant. Although they were depicted in multiple shots as just as capable as the male cops, the women were expected to stay out of the action. Charles Townsend provided an outlet for the women to work without constraints. The series also painted the women in a positive role when they were shown working cooperatively and effectively together, rescuing one another, and assuming mentor-like roles to other women who were frequently portrayed as victims or unsure of themselves.

Numerous other scenes showed the Angels behaving transgressively, doing things that women did not normally do and were not expected to do at that time. In "Hellride," Sabrina drives a race car. In "Bullseye," Jill and Kelly go undercover at an army base. Sabrina plays a nurse, while Jill and Kelly wear army fatigues. In "Consenting Adults," Jill engages in one of the more iconic episodes, wherein she flees from a group of bad guys on a skateboard. Among the episodes that depict Kelly riding a motorcycle are the pilot and "Circus of Terror." In "Angels in the Backfield," all three Angels (Sabrina, Kelly, and Kris) go undercover on a women's football team.

After *Charlie's Angels* was canceled in 1981, the show went into successful syndication. Numerous nostalgic reunion shows were planned but never filmed. The innate conventionality of *Charlie's Angels* notwithstanding, more transgressive spinoffs of the show were at least considered. In the episode "Toni's Boys," legendary actress Barbara Stanwyck played the owner of a detective agency in charge of three handsome men. In the late 1980s, a new Angels series was planned and a pilot produced, featuring four women, one of them African American. Despite the changing times (blatant sex appeal was no longer considered acceptable in an action hero), or perhaps because of them (**girl power** had not yet fully kicked in), the show was not picked up and the pilot never aired.

CHARLIE'S ANGELS, THE FILM SERIES

In the new millennium, two decades after the original run, the series was adapted into two films, *Charlie's Angels* (2000) and *Charlie's Angels: Full Throttle* (2003), which melded action and comedy. This reimagining of the three detectives emerged in a period when women leads and powerful sidekicks in action film and television appeared with greater regularity than ever before. *Crouching Tiger, Hidden Dragon* (2000) and *Lara Croft: Tomb Raider* (2001) were films whose success paralleled that of action films starring male leads. Television shows such as *Xena: Warrior Princess* (1995–2001), *Buffy the Vampire Slayer* (1997–2003), and *Charmed* (1998–2006) were among the most widely watched series on TV.

Charlie's Angels and *Charlie's Angels: Full Throttle*, which were enormous box office successes, reinvented the three detectives as bubbly incarnations of girl power. The movies cast three perky women as Angels: Natalie Cook (Cameron Diaz), Dylan Sanders (Drew Barrymore), and Alex Munday (Lucy Liu). The first film grossed over $260 million dollars; its sequel grossed slightly less at $250 million dollars, demonstrating that the new versions of the characters appealed to men and women.

Girl power is a term that was coined during the emergence of **third-wave feminism** in the 1990s, a form of feminism that was, in many ways, perplexing to the proponents of second-wave feminism. Second-wave feminists celebrated the stoic, mature, intelligent, and makeup-free female heroes like Ellen Ripley of the *Alien* film series and Kathryn Janeway, the first female captain of a *Star Trek* series, who helmed her own ship and television series, *Star Trek Voyager*. These kinds of women were not depicted as sex objects. Nor did they giggle like school children or engage in conflict just for the thrill or fun of it. Girl power heroes, however, were made from different material.

The Angels as represented in the two films embodied the new female action hero. They were smart and playful, fierce and girly, independent and boy crazy, and had loads of sex appeal. Alex could defuse bombs; Dylan dodged bullets. Unlike the original Angels, all three women were expert martial artists and had no qualms, as evident in the sequel, about taking on a den of pugnacious men in Mongolia. When the Angels fought, they engaged in long, brutal fights that drew blood. This is exemplified in a culminating scene when they confront former Angel Madison Lee (Demi Moore), who plays the villain in *Charlie's Angels: Full Throttle*.

Other differences show the shift from the stereotypical portrayal of femininity typical of the original Angels and the girl power version of the new Angels. These Angels ogle good-looking men like teenagers, have boyfriends, and are evidently sexually active. Extremely playful and flirtatious, Natalie, in a scene in the first movie, is dancing to pop music before her bedroom mirror after waking up when a delivery man rings her doorbell; she opens the door in her underwear. The Angels use their sex appeal in a scene in the sequel where they perform a sexy dance routine on stage before men. During the routine, Dylan performs a pole dance, and Alex dances provocatively for a man in the audience.

In the context of the new girl power films, sexiness—as well as aggression, equal power, and convention—are frequently turned upside down. A common trait in these kinds of films is to depict men in roles that were traditionally relegated to women. These men served as love interests and dudes in distress and appeared physically weaker and more emotive than the female heroes. They get none of the intense action that their girlfriends thrive on. For example, Alex dated an actor who played an action hero, but Alex was the one with real power. Dylan dated the man known as "The Chad." He is described as "a scrawny boat owner who gets up early and cheerfully makes [Dylan's] pancakes for breakfast, only to have her dash away to meet up with the other angels for some daring mission" (Mencimer, "Violent Femmes"). While Dylan pursues danger, Chad must stay behind.

IMPACT

The success of the *Charlie's Angels* films demonstrated not only how director McG was able to turn an outdated series into a relevant and appealing production, but that American audiences could still be fascinated by the Angels.

Despite the multiple arguments against the glamorization of women in television, the glamour of the original Angels helped to make the underlying transgressive messages of the series more palatable to male and female viewers and more marketable to consumers. And as with Foxy Brown, the negative stereotypes have since become fewer in number in real life, while the transgressive messages have bloomed. Showing pretty women working as detectives, confronting danger, riding motorcycles, and running marathons softened the blow of unconventional behavior and was a way to normalize the association of activities that were once deemed improper for women. The implication was that society did not have to feel threatened by women who engaged in male activities—that male activities such as detective work and sports did not make women unattractive, unfeminine, or masculine.

The mass production of *Charlie's Angels* dolls (not quite action figures) and paraphernalia was made possible in large part because the Angels' beauty was so marketable, and, as a result, a generation of young girls was introduced to new forms of play. The original Angels inspired an assortment of toys and games bearing the Angels' famous smiles, symbolizing, beneath the gleam of attractiveness, women who challenged **patriarchy**, even if in small ways. Whereas Barbie, the fashion doll that was created in 1959, was limited to glamorous fashions, *Charlie's Angels* dolls offered costumes that ranged from gowns to athletic outfits complete with accessories like a skateboard. Girls could also play with the *Charlie's Angels* target set, which came with two guns and six darts with which to practice. The *Charlie's Angels* paraphernalia allowed girls to operate symbols of power under the guise of traditional femininity that made such things as target practice more acceptable. These symbols of power helped to empower young girls to think outside the norm and to explore all the possibilities that life holds.

See also The Bionic Woman; Emma Peel; Foxy Brown; Lara Croft; The Powerpuff Girls; Wonder Woman.

FURTHER RESOURCES

Chadwick, Roberts. "The Politics of Farrah's Body: The Female Icon as Cultural Embodiment." *Journal of Popular Culture* 37 (2003): 83.

Condon, Jack, and David Hofstede. *Charlie's Angels: Casebook*. Beverly Hills, CA: Pomegranate Press, 2000.

Gough-Yates, Anna. "Angels in Chains? Feminism, Femininity, and Consumer Culture in *Charlie's Angels*." In *Action TV: Tough Guys, Smooth Operators, and Foxy Chicks*, ed. Bill Osgerby and Anna Gough-Yates. New York: Routledge, 2001.

Heinecken, Dawn. "No Cage Can Hold Her Rage? Gender, Transgression, and the World Wrestling Federation's Chyna." In *Action Chicks: New Images of Tough Women in Popular Culture*, ed. Sherrie A. Inness. New York: Palgrave Macmillan, 2004.

Hopkins, Susan. *Girl Heroes: The New Force in Popular Culture*. Annandale, Australia: Pluto Press, 2002.

Inness, Sherrie A. *Tough Girls: Women Warriors and Wonder Women in Popular Culture*. Philadelphia: University of Pennsylvania Press, 1999.

Krulik, Nancy. *Angels: The Inside Scoop on the Stars of Charlie's Angels*. New York: Aladdin, 2000.

Mencimer, Stephanie. "Violent Femmes." http//www.washingtonmonthly.com/features/2001/0109.mencimer.html.

Mitzejewski, Linda. *Hardboiled and High Heeled: The Woman Detective in Popular Culture*. New York: Routledge, 2004.

O'Day, Marc. "Beauty in Motion: Gender, Spectacle, and Action Babe Cinema." In *Action and Adventure Cinema*, ed. Yvonne Tasker. New York: Routledge, 2004.

White, Rosie. "Lipgloss Feminists: *Charlie's Angels* and *The Bionic Woman*." *Storytelling: A Critical Journal of Popular Narrative* 5 (2006): 171–183.

Chun Li is considered to be the first female character in a fighting video game. (© Courtesy of Capcom. Reprinted with Permission.)

Chun Li

Chun Li is considered the first female playable character in a fighting video game. She debuted in *Street Fighter II: The World Warrior* in 1991, along with seven other playable characters, all of them men. Her entrance into the massively lucrative video game industry stirred excitement among avid game players. Indeed, Chun Li became one of the favorite characters in this ground-breaking series. The appearance of blood in the game, as well as the bold, vivid cartoonish graphics, sound effects, and spectacular fighting moves, made *Street Fighter II* one of the most controversial and popular games around at that time. Although Chun Li debuted before the renowned Lara Croft from the *Tomb Raider* video game series, she was not the first female (i.e., nonfighting) protagonist in video game history. That honor goes to Ms. Pac-Man, the sequel to Pac-Man, launched in 1981, who was followed by Samus Aran in 1986.

Chun Li, of Chinese heritage, has stunning fighting capabilities and combines brutal power, girliness, and sex appeal. She is best known for her kicking power (which she demonstrates using various martial arts techniques) and she has powerful, protruding thighs and calves to show for it. Although her legs are her most prominent feature, she has large breasts and a small waist, the trademark dimensions of female comic book heroes and video game characters, geared to appeal to male fantasies.

Though her birth date is given as March 1, 1968, making her 33 years old when she premiered in *Street Fighter II*, she looks much younger. Underscoring her youthfulness, Chun Li wears ox horns, a popular hairstyle for young girls in China, uses a high-pitched screaming voice when she gets pummeled, and giggles like a school girl after defeating an opponent. After finishing off her final opponent, M. Bison (who long ago murdered her father), in *Street Fighter II*, she visits her father's grave and announces, through subtitles, that she has vindicated his murder. She also proclaims, while posing gleefully, that now she "can get back to being a young single girl." Thus Chun Li is depicted as an independent, powerful, and unconventional girl fighter.

Chun Li reappeared in subsequent video games in the series as well as in other fighting games and manga, which refers to Japanese comics and cartoons. She also appeared in three feature films: an animated film, *Street Fighter II: The Animated Movie* (1994), and the live action films *Street Fighter* (1994) and *Street Fighter: The Legend of Chun-Li* (2009). Nearly two decades after her debut, Chun Li is recognized as an icon in video game history.

ORIGINS

Chun Li and other similarly large-muscled playable characters were the product of the design team at Capcom. Capcom, a major developer and publisher in the video game industry, is located in Japan, a country that has

Samus Aran

Samus Aran is a character from the *Metroid* video game series. She was created by Makoto Kanou and designed by Hiroii Kiyotake and debuted wearing a futuristic power suit in 1986. In a clever twist, game players did not know Samus Aran was a woman until they successfully completed the game and watched as she discarded her power suit, revealing long hair and feminine form in a hot pink bikini and boots. The final reveal surprised game players who were not accustomed to tough female characters.

As the origin story goes, Samus Aran was born to human parents on Earth colony K-2L. Space pirates attacked the colony when she was just three years old. All the inhabitants, save for Samus, were killed. An alien species known as the Chozo found Samus and raised her on their home planet. There, they infused Samus with Chozo DNA and gifted her a power suit imbued with powerful technology. (Later, she would also receive Metroid DNA.) After working as a bounty hunter, she worked for the Galactic Federation, where her primary objective was to destroy malignant alien species known as Metroids and the Mother Brain, a central computer system. Samus Aran and the *Metroid* series is considered one of the most popular games in video game history.

long been in the vanguard of computer and video game technology. Capcom's *Street Fighter* games were largely propelled by Akira Yasuda, otherwise known as Akiman, who played an integral role in designing all the *Street Fighter* characters. Other designers included Akira Nishitani, Shoei, Nishimura Kinu, and Ikeno.

Street Fighter II was neither the first (as the number suggests) nor the last installment of the video game. Preceded in 1987 by *Street Fighter*, an arcade game, it was followed by *Street Fighter II—Champion Edition* (1992), *Street Fighter II—Hyper Fighting* (1992), *Street Fighter II—The New Challengers* (1993), *Super Street Fighter II Turbo* (1994), and *Hyper Street Fighter II* (2003). The franchise also includes several related series, such as the *Street Fighter Alpha* series (1995–1998), the *Street Fighter EX* series (1996–2001), the *Street Fighter III* series (1997–1999), the *Vs.* series (1996, 2002, 2008), the *Street Fighter IV* series (2008), and *Street Fighter Online: Mouse Generation* (2009). Each series features a host of changes, new characters, new fighting options and graphics, and augmented storylines. The *Vs.* series pits *Street Fighter* characters against comic book characters in *X-Men vs. Street Fighter* and *Marvel Super Heroes vs. Street Fighter*.

The *Street Fighter* franchise is known for the high-octane power of its playable characters, action heroes who perform a variety of spectacular moves, throwing fireballs, thrashing with incredible fist action, kicking, and leaping. Each character has a specialty move; some characters are known to be either slower or more agile than others.

The original cast included Ryu, Ken, E. Honda, Blanka, Zangief, Guile, and Dhalsim. Japanese-born Ryu, who was depicted as the leader, had brown hair and wore a karate gi (or uniform) with the sleeves ripped off and a headband. Ryu's specialties included his powerful fist action and side kick. Ken was a blonde American who wore a sleeveless martial arts training uniform and performed moves similar to Ryu. E. Honda was a muscled sumo wrestler. Among his signature moves were the "Hundred Hand Slap" and a torpedo-head butt move. Raised in Brazil, Blanka was green with bright orange hair. His trademark move caused electricity to run through his body, inflicting some serious damage on his opponents. Zangief, a Russian fighter and former wrestler, wore a Mohawk and was one of the more hefty characters to appear in the games. Guile, a blonde American with a tall angular hair style, wore a tank top, military cargo pants, combat boots, and an American flag tattoo on his arm. He wielded a powerful punch called the "Sonic Boom." Dhalsim, a lanky yoga practitioner from India, wore indigenous dress and a skull necklace. His strengths lay in his exceptional flexibility. For example, he could stretch his arms and legs to extraordinary lengths while executing moves. Dhalsim could also teleport. Other characters were introduced in subsequent games, such as T. Hawk, a Native American; Dee Jay, a Jamaican; and several women, like Cammy, a 19-year-old British MI6 agent; Elena, an adolescent African girl; and C. Viper, an American spy.

When *Street Fighter II* arrived in America in 1991, the effect was extraordinary—largely because dramatic fighting games with fantastical characters with exaggerated features were new, bold, and exciting. And Chun Li epitomized the new bold character of the 1990s, first because she was a woman, and second because she **transgressed** the pattern of the typical 1980s action woman, personified by Ellen Ripley of the *Alien* series.

Ripley combined the traits of an ideal second-wave feminist female action hero. She was a woman who worked in a male-dominated field, exuded confidence, authority, and can-do, and who was, importantly, not depicted as a sex object. In *Alien* (1979), she wore an ordinary, unfeminine uniform. In the second film, *Aliens* (1986), she wore an unglamorous T-shirt and pants and sported a short hair cut.

By comparison, Chun Li was a hybrid female action hero, reflecting the growing ascendancy of **third-wave feminism**. Though she burst through several **glass ceilings** at once—the video game industry, a fighting game, and the taboo against strong, masculine-like musculature—she was, in the tradition of two extremely popular Japanese genres, anime (animation) and manga (comic books), girly and sexy as well as powerful. Chun Li was a woman who could punch and kick aggressively and then exert girlish zeal. She wore youthful and feminine styles of clothing that would have horrified

Ellen Ripley. Her name, which means "Spring Beauty" in Mandarin Chinese, her pastel-colored outfits, and her combat boots punctuate this point. This meshing of femininity and masculine toughness would become the norm in the final decade of the century.

The 1990s witnessed an onslaught of super-confident, sexy, and hard-fighting female action heroes, many of whom exhibited traits that came to be known as **girl power**. In the film *La Femme Nikita* (1990) and the subsequent television series, Nikita is a smart, sexy assassin in high heels and form-fitting dresses. Buffy Summers, the high-school cheerleader turned vampire slayer made her debut in *Buffy the Vampire Slayer* (1992) and became a hit in the television series that ran from 1997 to 2003. Young girls in short skirts with super powers were all the rage in the animated *Sailormoon* (1992–1997), while in *Tank Girl* (1995), a film adapted from the British comic book, the lead female action hero was aggressive and depicted with a punk look. In video games, Chun Li was followed by Lara Croft and a host of others, like the women of the *Resident Evil* video game series. Alongside the increasing numbers of tough female action heroes in video games, there was an ever-expanding population of women and young girl video game players, some of whom called themselves feminist game players.

Chun Li's Backstory

Chun Li's story shares its starting point with any number of other action heroes: she longed to avenge her father's death. Vengeance has long been a common motivational theme for male heroes, and has proved just as effective among female action heroes. In *For a Few Dollars More* (1967), a gunslinger is spurred to action after a vile outlaw causes the death of his sister. Famed martial artist Bruce Lee starred in a number of revenge movies, like *Fist of Fury* (1972), where he fights those responsible for his master's death. In *Commando* (1985), Arnold Schwarzenegger plays John Matrix, who launches a violent attack on the men who kidnapped his daughter. The popular comic book character Spider-Man was also incited to action after his Uncle Ben is murdered.

Since the Greek Tragedies were written over two thousand years ago, and since Hamlet pondered the pros and cons of action, males have been the progenitors and instigators of violent revenge. This is one of the ways they are perceived to fulfill their roles as protectors of society and overseers of the honor and safety of loved ones and important figures. It is therefore a transgressive twist for women to fill the role as vengeance seekers in modern film. Ellen, also known as The Lady in *The Quick and the Dead* (1995), transformed herself into a gunfighter so that she could kill the man who had murdered her father. Other female agents of revenge include Jodie Foster, who played Erica Bain, a woman who became a vigilante after the murder of her fiancé in *The Brave One* (2007). The female protagonist in *Foxy Brown* (1974) took revenge on the leaders of the illicit organization that murdered

Damsels and Princesses: Traditional Video Game Archetypes

Damsels in distress and princesses are centuries-old storytelling archetypes that were easily adapted into film, television, and comic books. When narrative video games became all the rage in American popular culture, these archetypes also made that transition. In the 1980s, Pauline was the damsel in distress in the video game *Donkey Kong*. While Mario, the mustached hero, was at the forefront of the action, Pauline was the captive of the ferocious ape known as Donkey Kong, and her role was limited to anxiously awaiting rescue. Like the shrieking and fainting woman of the wildly popular Japanese-inspired King Kong films of the early 20th century, Pauline was reduced to a stereotypical victim role.

The beautiful princess Zelda first appeared in 1986 in *The Legend of Zelda*, a role-playing game that is still massively popular today. Zelda is perhaps one of the most well-known princesses in video game history. Although her name receives top billing in the prodigious video game series and she does demonstrate a smattering of magical power, she is primarily just another damsel in distress. Link is the real protagonist of the series. He endures danger, solves puzzles, fights villains and foes, and saves the day when he rescues Princess Zelda.

In 2009, a new princess emerged on the video game scene, sparking an uproar among game players. In the midst of the growing number of tough female protagonists who challenged traditional female archetypes, the game *Fat Princess* confounded critics. In this game, teams are established to keep their princesses from being rescued by their opponents. This is done by feeding the princess so that she becomes too heavy to be easily carried away. This game exacerbates the traditional passive and victim role by mixing in issues concerning overeating and obesity.

her boyfriend and her brother, and *Thelma and Louise* (1991) wreaked havoc on **sexist**, rude, and violent men. Other characters in the *Street Fighter* series also harbored desires for vengeance against M. Bison, including Guile and T. Hawk. Bison reputedly killed Guile's best friend and T. Hawk's father.

Just as The Lady entered a gun fighting contest to gain the chance to pay back her father's murderer, Chun Li entered the violent industry of male-dominated fight tournaments looking for an opportunity to revenge her father. Chun Li obtained her martial arts and other fighting skills from her father and, in adulthood, from an assassin named Gen. Chun Li's final opponent in the *Street Fighter II* video game is M. Bison, the man who killed her father. After M. Bison's defeat, Chun Li presumably returns to her normal life.

As with Lara Croft, Chun Li's story is expanded in other installments of the game. In *Super Street Fighter II*, game players may choose a normal life or a career as a police officer for Chun Li. In *Street Fighter Alpha: Warriors' Dreams*, Chun Li is an agent working to bring M. Bison and his criminal organization to justice, and in a game from *Street Fighter III*, Chun Li is back in action after one of her students (she has become a martial arts teacher) has been kidnapped, and she must set out to rescue the young girl.

POWER SUIT, WEAPONS, AND ABILITIES

Traditionally, soft colors and women's apparel and hair styles signify weakness and femininity, but Chun Li has fun with those symbols by melding them with equally well-established symbols of power. Visually, she is depicted as both girly and physically strong. Behavior-wise, she is, again, girly, but is also ultra aggressive. Chun Li wears a variety of fighting costumes, but her trademark outfit is a blue *qipao*, a traditional Chinese dress worn by early 20th-century girls. Her hairstyle is known as ox horns, which is similar to Princess Leia's iconic cinnamon-bun look. Two buns are worn on either side of the crown in both styles, but Chun Li's hair buns are smaller and worn above the ears. With the exception of the *Alpha* video games, Chun Li adorns her ox horns with brocades and ribbons. These adornments allegedly signify the fact that she is mourning over her father, but they also make her appear more feminine. Other wardrobe accessories include brown tights and combat boots. In *Street Fighter Alpha*, Chun Li wears an "embroidered vest, leotard and athletic shoes, as well as studded wristbands" ("Chun-Li: The First Lady of Video Games").

Game players viewing Chun Li in a fight get an eyeful: a vivid spectacle of a woman who fights extraordinarily well but is also feminized and objectified. Her specialties include several kicking techniques and energy attacks. She generally calls out the names of her techniques as she executes them. Among her numerous famous kicks, many of them executed while she is in midair, are the Spinning Bird Kick, the Supreme Heaven Ascent Kick, the Supreme Mountain Kick, the Phoenix Fanning Wings, the Hundred Tearing Kicks, and the Thousand Tearing Kicks. One avid game player described how her abilities change over the course of the franchise, alternately becoming weaker and then more powerful. In *Street Fighter Alpha 2*, it was alleged "that Chun-Li was the strongest character in the game. . . . A particularly powerful Custom Combo of hers was to start with a crouching strong kick, rise from it and follow through with a strong Hyakuretsu Kyaku [Japanese for Hundred Tearing Kicks]. When it succeeded, 70–80% of an opponents' health was taken off" ("Chun-Li: The First Lady of Video Games").

Chun Li's fighting abilities were such that she gained a formidable reputation within the video game itself. One opponent, Urien, confronts Chun Li; "he wants to fight her, because her legendary legs are said to have destroyed [Shadowloo]" ("Chun-Li: The First Lady of Video Games"). (Shadowloo is a crime syndicate.) The comment about Chun Li's legs reflects her fearsome physical prowess as well as her feminine allure and the common practice of objectifying the female body in the media.

Chun Li's depiction is studded with feminizing and sexualizing markers in addition to her hair style, hair accessories, and exaggerated female form. Chun Li's voice is high pitched. When she performs a certain move, her underpants show. When she wins a fight, she jumps up and down and giggles. Her prettiness, coupled with a move that "showed Chun-Li sticking her butt out and firing both hands forward to launch the attack," are believed to have augmented Chun Li's popularity in *Street Fighter II: The New Challenge* ("Chun-Li: The First Lady of Video Games").

Exacerbating her sex-object status, Chun Li is frequently depicted in promotional images posing provocatively and at times in skimpy outfits. To second-wave feminists, these images are troubling because they appear to reinforce the **stereotypical** roles women have historically played in the media, wherein they were dolled up, adorned, and represented in ways designed specifically for the **male gaze**. Third-wave feminists, however, tend to equate sexual power with physical power and believe that women who are beautiful and draw the male gaze can be **coded as** powerful. Thus, what was once deemed derogatory and sexist was labeled empowering during this period.

Although Chun Li was smaller in stature than other *Street Fighter* characters, her unusually large musculature unequivocally established her equality in terms of power. The muscled female body was not new. In the 1980s, She-Ra, from the animated cartoon series, also had a large frame, though she was still considerably smaller than her male counterpart, He-Man. In contrast to real-life society, where women were traditionally expected to maintain small, feminine frames, bulky builds were the norm for women in the He-Man comic book and film franchise.

Chun Li's body size served as a symbol of power, but it bothered many game players. In the several renditions of Chun Li in the series, she is always depicted with powerful legs and sinewy arms. A popular online fan complaint was that "Chun-Li's thighs are too big. Her arms are too muscular. She looks like a man now!!!" (Nelson, "Retro Gamer"). Nelson, however, defends Capcom, stating that "From Chun-Li's muscular build to the petite Cammy to the tomboyish Sakura—this is one fighting series that has an incredible variety in their character designs" (Nelson, "Retro Gamer").

VILLAINS

Chun Li faces off with myriad opponents. For example, in *Street Fighter II*, she must fight the seven other players before challenging four bosses (a video game term used to refer to villains). The seven players include the other male characters—Ryu, Ken, E. Honda, Blanka, Zangrief, Guile, and

Portal

In 2007, Valve Corporation released the video game *Portal*. This game is considered one of the most progressive video games in recent history. In the starring role is a woman named Chell. Unlike her predecessors, Chun Li and Lara Croft, Chell's body is not depicted as exaggeratedly muscular or buxom. Chell has a slender and feminine form. Importantly, her physical appearance is not overly sexual or glamorous. Chell's primary strength is her intelligence, which is exhibited through the game player's skill at negotiating through assorted puzzles, obstacles, and hazards in each level. There is little violence in this game, save for the destruction of Chell's primary nemesis, an artificial intelligence named GLaDOS.

Dhalsim. The four bosses, which are controlled by the CPU, include Balrog, Vega, Sagat, and M. Bison.

Balrog, who bears a resemblance to Mike Tyson, a former American boxing champion, is portrayed as an African American boxer with an enormous and frightful frame. He is six feet, five inches tall and favors solid, debilitating punches over kicks. Vega, who hails from Spain, wears a mask and has large muscles and long metal claws on one of his hands. He is the only character in *Street Fighter II* to possess a weapon, giving him an unfair advantage over his opponents. His fighting style is a combination of Spanish bullfighting and Japanese ninjutsu. Sagat, who is from Thailand, towers over the other characters at seven feet, four inches and has a muscular build. He is bald and has a scar on his chest and a patch over his right eye. Both injuries (his lost eye and the chest wound) signify his toughness and fierceness. M. Bison, the final boss, is not only physically strong and supremely skilled, but he has abilities such as "Psycho Power" that allows him to levitate objects. He is the malevolent leader of the crime organization Shadaloo.

One extraordinary element of the series is that although Chun Li is considerably smaller than her foes, and a woman (the first one in the series), she was created with the potential to beat all her opponents.

STREET FIGHTER MOVIES

In addition to the *Street Fighter* video games, the character of Chun Li appears in different types of media developed by the *Street Fighter* franchise: manga, Japanese anime, American comics, and an animated television series. She also appears in three films: first, as an animated character in *Street Fighter II: The Animated Movie* (1994), and then as a live-action character in *Street Fighter* (1994) and *Street Fighter: The Legend of Chun-Li* (2009).

The Animated Movie is a step backward for Chun Li, and the producers' ready dismissal of third-wave, let alone second-wave feminism is obvious. For one thing, Chun Li sees only limited action. Worse, she is greatly objectified, particularly when her nude body is exposed (the nudity is censored in some countries) in a shower scene, a scene that also shows her being attacked by Vega. She fights him off, but lapses into a coma after the battle and stays in the hospital, missing out on all the action, particularly the critical part when Ryu and Ken subdue Bison.

In *Street Fighter*, Chun Li continues to be portrayed in a supporting role. This 1994 movie casts action hero icon Jean-Claude Van Damme as Guile, who takes the lead role, while Chun Li, played by Ming-Na Wen, is effectively marginalized. At the end of the film, Guile takes on Bison during a spectacular, heavy-action fight scene and prevails.

She finally gets her day in *Street Fighter: The Legend of Chun-Li*, which concentrates on the origins and rise of the Chun Li character. Unlike the previous two attempts, this 2009 film's depiction of Chun Li returns to the standard of how other female action heroes had been portrayed since the 1990s: forceful and violent as well as feminine and alluring. This blended personality type is what audiences have come to expect in modern-day female action heroes.

Kristin Kreuk (known for playing Clark Kent's love interest Lana Lane in the popular TV series *Smallville*, a role which, at least in later years, allowed her to flex her muscles in various fight scenes) plays Chun Li in this rendition. Kreuk, only 26 years old when she appeared in the film, has a soft, youthful face, but is also sporty and svelte. She has a background in gymnastics from her high school days. Kreuk, who is of Dutch and Chinese ancestry, is considered to be extremely pretty.

According to the film, Chun Li's father raised her to be both refined and physically powerful. In a voice-over flashback at the start of the film, she explains that her father (who proudly watches a young Chun Li in ox horns at the piano) wanted her to be a concert pianist. Traditionally, classical music and most things associated with cultural achievements and elite society were symbolized as soft and feminine. In subsequent scenes, her father is shown teaching Chun Li martial arts and giving her a spinning bird necklace (alluding to one of Chun Li's signature moves). Clearly, Chun Li is largely influenced by her father and not at all by her mother, who is depicted as a peripheral character. Her mother is never a part of the action; she is traditional, passive, fearful (in a later scene she worries about Chun Li's safety), and, later, sickly in a hospital. She is the antithesis of the strong mother type as depicted by Sarah Connor, who toughens up to protect her son, John, predestined to lead the resistance against the machines in the *Terminator* films (1984, 1991). At the conclusion of the flashback, we learn that Chun Li's father was abducted before her eyes by the villain Bison and his ruffians.

Chun Li grows up to become a concert pianist, but she is haunted by memories of her father. Following a performance, Chun Li receives a scroll that instructs her to go to Bangkok and seek out a man named Gen. After the death of her mother, Chun Li obeys, though it means leaving her lavish home and pampered lifestyle.

The trip to Bangkok is a pivotal juncture in Chun Li's life, one that is traditionally reserved for men. The male rite of passage is common in many cultures. The walkabout, practiced by Australian aborigines, and the vision quest, undertaken by Native Americans, are examples of rites that are intended to usher boys into manhood. Likewise, in the hero quest, males must undergo a series of tests, endurances, or challenges before advancing toward their goal—transcending one state and reaching the next (much as is the case in many video games). When female heroes set out upon a quest, the journey is the same.

In *The Quick and the Dead* (1995), Ellen travels to an unknown town, where she must face her fears and challenge her opponent to death. Lieutenant Jordan O'Neil leaves the comfort of her home for the rigors of an army barracks, where she must overcome personal weaknesses, physical challenges, and negative perceptions to complete the rigorous elite training program in *G.I. Jane* (1997). Chun Li must do the same when she leaves the security of home and goes to live alone amongst the homeless and dangerous denizens of the streets of Bangkok.

In an early encounter, she challenges thugs who attempt to rob a man. After she takes them down, she passes out, taking on a traditional role as Gen, who she had been unsuccessfully pursuing, rescues her. Gen, who offers to help her find her father, acts as a mentor to Chen Li. The mentor is a common character in the hero quest, one of several "helpers" along the journey. Gen is an older man, and highly skilled; he gives Chun Li purpose and hope and also helps to further develop her fighting skills. He teaches her how to create balls of energy. He plays a large role in Chun Li's transition to a stronger, more powerful warrior. But he is also depicted as a nurturer. This is an atypical role for a male warrior, as the nurturing helper is traditionally a mother figure or croon. But with the advent of female heroes, the male nurturer has been on the increase. Lo, for example, in *Crouching Tiger, Hidden Dragon* (2000), nurtures the rebellious Jen Yu back to health when she collapses in a desert, and a monk heals Lara Croft's wound in *Lara Croft: Tomb Raider* (2001).

Throughout the film, Chun Li is generally depicted as strong and capable, up to the challenges she must face. She is tough enough to investigate her father's whereabouts on her own, though she is captured by Bison, who kills her father (who had been assisting Bison's criminal activities with his crimes in exchange for glimpses of Chun Li) in front of her. Like a true hero, Chun Li does not come unglued after the murder of her father. She instead rescues herself from her entrapment, something her father seemed powerless to do.

But viewers are constantly reminded that Chun Li is also feminine. Her size, petite and slim, and her soft voice and features are markers of femininity.

In two scenes, Chun Li dresses glamorously, once for a piano concert and once when she seduces a female villain, first dancing with her and then beating her up in the women's restroom of the dance club. Chun Li is also coded as feminine when she is positioned as a damsel in distress whom Gen must rescue, and when, unlike the traditional male hero, she relies on the assistance of others to help fight her enemies. However, she beats Bison without assistance in the final showdown.

Chun Li is not the only tough female action hero in this film. Detective Maya Sunee, played by Moon Bloodgood, is also portrayed in contrasting but still paradoxical terms. Chun Li is something of a tomboy—a youthful girl who is not afraid to sweat, get dirty, and fight forcefully. Maya, on the other hand, is characterized as an overtly sexy woman, though, unconventionally, she doesn't flinch at the sight of a grotesque murder scene. Where Chun Li favors a boyish look and sporty outfits, Maya is mature, sophisticated, and stylish. She rides a motorcycle and has a take-charge attitude, but wears long, glamorous, salon-fresh hair and designer clothes. Both women, each in her own way, incorporate character traits that were previously held to be contradictory. They thus define the modern image of female toughness: feminine and aggressive, sexy but not identified by a romantic relationship.

IMPACT

Critical praise for *Street Fighter: The Legend of Chun-Li* was muted. Some even said the film was worse than the previous *Street Fighter* film, which was generally panned by the critics. Audiences were for once aligned with the critics. Nevertheless, it is significant that the film sets Chun Li front and center of the action, not on the periphery or disabled in a hospital room as she was in the animated movie and the first *Street Fighter* film.

Movies aside, Chun Li is credited with having broken new ground in the realm of fighting video games, as well as showing the world that a female character can be just as popular as the standard male hero in a video game. She helped transform the landscape of the once all-male world of video gaming, illustrating that social change can shift even the oldest paradigms. This helped make possible the female characters who would follow: Lara Croft, the women of *Resident Evil*, and others.

Chun Li takes her place as one of several "girl power" action heroes who arose during the 1990s, creating the framework for a new kind of female hero, one who was celebrated for being both girly and aggressive, two traits that had traditionally been at odds. Though second-wave feminists continue to be troubled by some implications of treating sex as power, and of placing an emphasis on physical appearance, there is no denying that Chun Li helped expand the playing field for women across all the modern media formats.

See also Chyna; Ellen Ripley; Lara Croft; Maggie Fitzgerald; Princess Leia.

FURTHER RESOURCES

Cassell, J., and H. Jenkins, eds. *From Barbie to Mortal Kombat: Gender and Computer Games.* Cambridge, MA: MIT Press, 1999.

"Chun-Li: The First Lady of Video Games." http://www.retrojunk.com/details_articles_569.

DeMaria, Rusel. *Reset: Changing the Way We Look at Video Games.* San Francisco: Berrett-Koehler, 2007.

Hopkins, Susan. *Girl Heroes: The New Force in Popular Culture.* Annandale, Australia: Pluto Press, 2002.

Kent, Steven L. *The Ultimate History of Video Games, from Pong to Pokémon: The Story Behind the Craze That Touched Our Lives and Changed the World.* Three Rivers, MI: Three Rivers Press, 2001.

Nelson, Carl. "Retro Gamer: A Look Back at Street Fighter Character Designs." http://www.hardcoreware.net/retro-gamer-a-look-back-at-street-fighter-character-designs.

"Street Fighter." http://www.streetfighter.com/flash/#/home/en.

Watts, Steve. "Women Who Changed Gaming: Part 3—Chun-Li." http://steven-cwatts.newsvine.com/_news/2007/03/09/583957-women-who-changed-gaming-part-3-chun-li.

Chyna in ringside with Jesse Ventura, guest referee, and Triple H. (AP Photo/David Sherman.)

Chyna

Chyna (pronounced "China"), also known as "The Ninth Wonder of the World," is the name that wrestling personality Joanie Laurer assumed when she wrestled in the World Wrestling Federation (WWF) between 1997 and 2001. Chyna, with her long black hair, searing black eyeliner, and racy black-leather outfits, instantly conjures up images of a **dominatrix** or a tough, bad-girl biker chick. But her sizable muscles and ripped abs are evidence of a woman whose persona extends beyond simple sex object archetypes.

Chyna was a pioneering wrestling personality who broke new ground in the wrestling industry and became a mainstream phenomenon. Before Chyna, women wrestlers in the WWF, a television phenomenon in itself, were not pitted against men wrestlers. When women did fight, they fought other women. The women were characteristically smaller than Chyna, with large breasts, slender waists, and dressed in suggestive, barely there clothing. Indeed, women were generally depicted as the male wrestlers' "managers" but served also as love interests and "damsels in distress," providing drama for the already sensationalized wrestling program (Heinecken, 185).

Chyna built an empire on her spectacular musculature and extraordinary strength. Although she did serve time as a love interest, she was always a tough, muscle-bound woman. The way she stood (arms akimbo and legs apart) and grimaced (a rock-hard expression) had long been a posture appropriated by men of power, but Chyna, who stood five feet, ten inches, came to own the pose. Chyna could lift a sizeable grown man over her head and hurl him to the floor (a body slam); she could bench-press over 300 pounds. When she became the first woman to triumph over a man in a title fight (winning the industry's Intercontinental Championship in 1999), Chyna sealed her claim as one of the toughest women in wrestling history.

Though Chyna exhibited power, her prowess was restricted within the boundaries of the often tortuous scripts. Laurer contends she once heard Vince McMahon, the man who built the WWF empire (which became the World Wrestling Entertainment [WWE] in 2002), claim that the organization was "a variety show, more soap opera than action adventure, sometimes it's more Comedy Central" (Laurer, 29). There was a time in the 1980s when die-hard fans refused to believe that their favorite wrestling personalities—Hulk Hogan, Andre the Giant, "Rowdy" Roddy Piper, and so forth—engaged in staged competitions conceived by writers who determined the wins and losses and the melodramatic storylines.

In recent years, the WWE has made no attempt to hide the fact that the histrionics that unfurl within each television episode are staged. Episodes feature long-winded dialogues and soliloquies as well as infectious one-liners that fans recite on cue. The seemingly impromptu skirmishes between wrestlers sometimes involve the audience (actors disguised as fans) and feature outrageous posturing, gimmicky costumes, and flashy names. There are entrance themes for each wrestler, as well as theatrical devices and crude

Body Image

Body image is an issue that affects individuals of all ages, though in the media, the campaign to address this issue is largely directed at females. Body image concerns the way individuals perceive their outward appearance—the skin, teeth, face, hair, or any other part of the body, as well as body size and shape. The attempt to mold one's body to all-too-often impossible societal standards can result in extreme stress, low self-esteem, or emotional disorders, which sometimes manifest as symptoms.

Since ancient history, women have endured societal pressure to conform to certain beauty standards, such as flawless skin, immaculate body shape, and gleaming teeth. The pursuit of beauty has sometimes proved fatal. During the Renaissance, cosmetics such as a product containing lead to perfect the complexion, caused hair loss or death if used for a prolonged period of time. Some mascaras caused blindness. Corsets worn as early as the 16th century presented health risks to the wearers. Foot binding in China crippled women and often resulted in fatal infections.

In modern times, cosmetics are safer than ever before, but other problems remain. Many American women receive breast implants and undergo cosmetic surgeries knowing the serious risks involved. Others attempt to drastically control their weight through unhealthy methods. Bulimia nervosa involves binge eating followed by any variety of ways to remove the calories from the body through excessive exercise, fasting, the use of diuretics, enemas, and laxatives, or self-induced vomiting. Individuals suffering anorexia are excessively underweight, but still perceive themselves to be fat. Eating disorders, if not remedied, lead to serious health issues and complications.

weapons such as chairs and sledgehammers. The complex storylines always feature wrestlers who play "bad guys" (also known as heels) and "good guys," though the names and identities are in constant flux. The action often spills out of the "squared circle" and into the aisles or backstage. Die-hard WWE fans tune in frequently and fill the auditoriums.

Indeed the WWE has permeated popular culture. In addition to Saturday morning cartoon adaptations, video games, and multiple paraphernalia, the WWE show airs multiple times a week on television, with "at least three primetime spectacles fans can tune into: *Raw*, *Heat*, and *Smackdown*" (Heinecken, 184). Many wrestlers have attained name recognition outside the wrestling world, thus helping to further the exposure of WWE. "Rowdy" Roddy Piper appeared in several films and television shows from the late 1970s to the present. Andre the Giant, known as the "Eighth Wonder of the World," stood at seven feet, four inches and weighed 500 pounds. He played Sasquatch in an episode of *The Bionic Woman*, a giant in *Conan The Destroyer* (1984), and a Turkish wrestler in *The Princess Bride* (1987). Hulk Hogan appeared in *Rocky III* (1982), *No Holds Barred* (1989), and *Mr. Nanny* (1993), and starred in his reality television show *Hulk Knows Best* (2005–2007). Triple H played a vampire in *Blade: Trinity* (2004) and Tyler Mane was cast as the villain Sabretooth in *X-Men* (2000). The film *The Wrestler* (2008), which received positive attention from critics and audiences, as well as several Oscar nominations, provided a serious, dramatic glimpse into the world of wrestling through the life of Randy "The Ram" Robinson (Mickey Rourke), a hapless professional wrestler who tries to redeem himself and his career.

Over the decades, it was always male wrestlers who put wrestling into the spotlight and kept it there. Despite this formidable barrier, Chyna managed to penetrate the male-dominated world of wrestling and build a spectacular career, becoming in the process a household name and a highly unconventional symbol of empowerment.

ORIGINS

History of Wrestling

As far back as the historical record goes, there has been wrestling. In some cultures, both men and women engaged in this sport, but it has always been a predominantly male sport. Wrestling matches were important events in many countries, such as France, England, Egypt, and Japan. Wrestling was also practiced by Native Americans. In 708 BCE., wrestling was added to the Olympic Games in Olympia, Greece. Wrestling played an important role in Greek mythology, legends, and literature, and was a massively popular competitive event.

Depending on the period and the culture, the form and rules of wrestling changed, but in most cases, hitting and kicking were not allowed. Weapons were also generally barred. Winners forged their reputations by their ability to subdue an opposing wrestler using strength and agility. In Iceland, where wrestling is called *glima*, wrestlers try to cause each other to fall to the ground, using a plethora of highly stylized moves.

In America, wrestling has always been a marginalized sport. In the 18th and 19th centuries, matches were largely conducted in dilapidated buildings in dangerous neighborhoods or at traveling carnivals and country fairs. Eventually, competitive (Greco-Roman) wrestling found a more acceptable form in schools and universities. In the mid-1920s, attempts were made to legitimize wrestling as a professional sport. But if professional wrestling was considered a minor sport, women's wrestling was all but nonexistent.

In the early decades of the 20th century, career limitations kept most women at home, in secretarial positions, or in factories. But there is always a leading edge pushing into new territory, and women were making breakthroughs in competitive sports, including wrestling. In 1935, Mildred Burke was recognized as the first winner of the Women's World Championship. Burke would later establish the World Women's Wrestling Association.

History of the WWE

Jess McMahon, a former boxing promoter, Joseph Raymond Mondt, a former professional wrestler, and others collaborated to form the Capitol Wrestling Corporation. This organization later joined the NWA. In 1953, Vincent J. McMahon replaced his father, Jess, continuing along the path to success. In 1963, McMahon and his associates established the World Wide Wrestling Federation (WWWF) and shortly thereafter left the NWA. In 1979, the WWWF became the World Wrestling Federation (WWF). A law suit forced the WWF to change its name to World Wrestling Entertainment (WWE) in 2002.

Vincent K. McMahon, Vincent J.'s son, took professional wrestling to another level. Beginning in the 1980s, McMahon renovated the entire sport, transforming it into a pop culture sensation—albeit one enjoyed mostly by a niche audience, mostly male, mostly preteens to young adults. By featuring colorful wrestlers on television, cable, and pay-per-view shows, McMahon made television history. By fusing 1980s pop culture icons like Mr. T, a muscle-bound African American man who talked tough and sported a Mohawk in the action adventure television series *The A-Team* (1983–1986), and Cindy Lauper, a singer known for upbeat songs like "Girls Just Want to Have Fun" and a quirky fashion sense, the WWE further increased its appeal. During this period, it quickly swallowed up competing wrestling organizations.

A public steroid controversy that implicated many wrestlers and threatened to mar the reputation of the organization nearly ended McMahon's dynasty. In an attempt to rescue the WWE, new wrestling personalities were created. One of the traits that set the new wrestlers apart from the former wresters was muscle definition. The new wrestlers were more athletic, less flabby, and the storylines became increasingly elaborate. To further draw fans, cliffhangers were employed, drawing back viewers from week to week.

In the second half of the 1990s, the WWE was experiencing a resurgence in public interest. McMahon was again laying plans for expansion, but he did not dream that it would include an iconic female superstar. Then, on February 16, 1997, an unknown woman with expansive arms and exotic looks took a seat amongst the audience, waiting for the cue that would signal her first appearance as a character in the WWE.

ORIGINS OF CHYNA

Childhood

Chyna's story is inextricably linked to the life of Joanie Laurer, and the line between them—between the action hero and the woman who not only

Mildred Burke

Mildred Burke (1915–1989) was born Mildred Bliss. She started out life as a waitress and a stenographer, two conventional jobs for women in the first half of the 20th century. After seeing a wrestling match for the first time, Mildred discovered her passion. In the 1930s, the only arena where women could wrestle was at carnivals, where the fantastic and unusual attracted spectators from far and wide. Mildred received her early training from her future (second) husband, Billy Wolfe. Burke excelled at wrestling, besting hundreds of men. She held the World Woman's Championship title (now known as NWA World Women's Championship) from 1935 to 1945.

Burke nurtured an entrepreneurial spirit, and helped to establish other women in wrestling. She founded the World Women's Wrestling Association in Los Angeles, California. She helped found International Women's Wrestlers, Inc. and managed a school for women wrestlers in Encino, California.

"played" her but for all intents and purposes "was" her—is often blurred. Born on December 27, 1970, in Rochester, New York, Laurer was the youngest of three children. Her parents, Janet and Joe Laurer, divorced when she was four years old. The marriage is said to have ended shortly after Janet threw a plate of spaghetti at her husband, and he reacted by stabbing his wife in the thigh with a butter knife.

For Laurer, family life was difficult. While she contends that her biological father had been an alcoholic, she says her mother's issues with two subsequent husbands made for a stressful home life. In her best-selling autobiography, *Chyna* (2001), Laurer describes a mother who was withdrawn and at times severe with her children, like the time she destroyed her son's model toys after he confessed (to protect Laurer) that he broke a record player.

Laurer experienced many challenges in her childhood. She was self-conscious about her size; she was always bigger and taller than her classmates. In high school, she attempted to manipulate her weight by purging. She described herself as a bulimic, eating whatever she wanted and then forcing herself to throw up. After Laurer's mother accused her of abusing drugs, Laurer moved in with her biological father to evade being forced into a drug rehabilitation center. Laurer was 16 years old.

That was a critical year in other ways for Laurer. She started dating, had a benign tumor removed from her ovaries, and began taking steps to change her physique. Although aerobics were popular in the 1980s with both men and women, bodybuilding and weightlifting were still considered a male domain. The first female bodybuilding contest had occurred only recently, in 1978. Laurer forged ahead, sculpting her body—not yet to the size she would eventually develop as an adult—through weightlifting.

After graduating from high school in 1988 (studying her senior year in Spain, where she learned to speak fluent Spanish), Laurer set out to live her father's dream: joining the Secret Service, another endeavor historically dominated by men. Thanks in large part to her father's insistence, she found herself embarking on a life that was considered unconventional for a woman. Although women then enjoyed more opportunities than in previous generations—receiving advanced degrees, becoming working mothers, climbing the ladder of corporate leadership, and entering male-dominated fields like construction—many traditionally male fields remained just that.

University of Florida

Laurer applied to the University of Florida without any reservations and was accepted. The University of Tampa in Florida presented both opportunities and challenges for Laurer. She continued to lift weights, steadily improving her level of fitness. She participated in the Reserve Officers' Training Corps (ROTC), and relates how "being phobic about losers, I went into it whole hog. I shot M-16s. I rappelled off giant towers. We dug foxholes. We crawled on our bellies through slop and mud. We went on recons in the middle of the night with a map. We followed clues to where something like a box of ammo or whatever was buried" (Laurer, 124). Laurer was a serious and involved student, becoming a residential assistant and making good grades.

Post-Graduate Years

After graduating in 1992 with a degree in Spanish literature, Laurer joined the Peace Corps, a two-year volunteer program that gives people the opportunity to work in foreign countries. Like the Secret Service, the corps was her father's idea. He believed the experience would better Laurer's chances of getting into the Secret Service. Laurer felt out of place in the Peace Corps program and decided it was not for her. After spending two unhappy months in Guatemala, Laurer returned home.

Back in America, Laurer started and ended a problematic relationship and worked a string of jobs. The relationship was with an ex-convict, who had served several years in federal prison for smuggling drugs; following several incidents when he physically abused her, Laurer finally stood up to him. She had several interviews with the FBI for a Secret Service position while she worked as a cocktail waitress and a 900-line operator. For a while she sold beepers and considered becoming a flight attendant. She also entered several fitness and bodybuilding competitions with little success, as she was normally passed up for smaller women who exhibited more conventional notions of femininity and sex appeal.

Television proved to be the turning point in Laurer's career. While watching wrestling on television, she had an epiphany: she wanted to be a professional wrestler. To Laurer, the wrestlers looked like they were having "fun. And [she] wanted in. It was kooky, it was wrong-headed, it was MY CHOICE" is how she recalls the moment (Laurer, 144). From that point on, Laurer decided to follow her own dreams rather than her father's aspirations for her.

Wrestling School and Independent League

In the mid-1990s, Laurer enrolled in Walter Kowalski's wrestling school. Like the obstinate coach Frankie Dunn (Clint Eastwood) in *Million Dollar Baby* (2004), Kowalski was neither accustomed nor thrilled about training a woman. But Laurer more than proved her ability and eagerness. She stunned the other men when she lifted a man over her head and body slammed him, and when she bench-pressed over two hundred pounds. She could easily lift more, but did not want to show off. She was proud of her first black eye, an accident that occurred during practice, and considered it a defining moment in her life. Wrestling was the career path for her.

While practicing in Kowalski's warehouse in Malden, Massachusetts, Laurer picked up skills rapidly. In 1995, after she was laid off from her job selling beepers, Kowalski planned to assign Laurer to wrestling matches in the Independent League. Kowalski thought that "[Laurer] was too big, too strong" to wrestle other women, so he lined her up with a match against a man disguised as a woman (Laurer, 156). Laurer's experience in the Independent circuit was a step forward, but it paid little and did not compare to wrestling for the WWF.

Becoming Chyna

A tip from a friend in 1996 led Laurer to a WWE match that was being held in Springfield, Massachusetts. There she met with an agent whom she hoped would provide her access to wrestling for more money, but it did not go well. However, a chance meeting with wrestlers Triple H (Paul Michael Levesque) and Sean Michaels that same night brought her the opportunity she had been waiting for. Later that night, Laurer showed Triple H (also known as Hunter Hearst Helmsley, a man whom she dated after her career picked up) and Sean Michaels her portfolio, along with a video of her wrestling. They liked what they saw and worked in the ensuing weeks to convince Vince McMahon to employ her. This was no easy task. McMahon did not think audiences would respond positively to a heavily muscled female wrestler who wrestled men. But America had undergone numerous changes since women had started wrestling in the 1930s.

Girl Wrestlers

In 2009, the Internet lit up with news about 15-year-old Alyssa Lampe, who made history in Wisconsin when she became the first female ever to qualify for a state wrestling tournament. Lampe is as tough as the boys, sustaining injuries and bruises all for the love of a sport. Lampe, who attends Tomahawk High School in Wisconsin, started wrestling in kindergarten and is extremely disciplined. She wrestles in an environment that is generally supportive. Indeed, the overall environment for girls in sports has changed drastically over the years.

According to statistics, there were 404 girl wrestlers in 1992/1993, 1,907 girl wrestlers in 1997/1998, and 3,769 girl wrestlers in 2002/2003. The notion of girls in sports is increasingly accepted. No longer are girls expected to play traditional roles, wherein they were believed to be afraid of danger, inactive, and passive. Lampe's involvement in wrestling was made possible by Title IX, an amendment passed in 1972 that prohibited the discrimination of women and girls in educational programs and activities, like school athletics. Today girls sweat, play hard, and make history, excelling at such sports as tennis, basketball, boxing, snowboarding, and surfing.

The 1990s in particular was a watershed decade on multiple levels: in the workplace, in how young women and girls began to perceive and express themselves, and, importantly, how television and films had responded to America's changing outlook on women's roles. More women were working and more were entering the historically male-dominated positions than in the previous decade; women soldiers were allowed to play greater roles in the military during the conflict in the Middle East. In short, America was becoming increasingly more acclimated to the changing roles of women.

Film and television producers took ever-greater risks, casting strong female leads in traditionally male action hero roles, such as *G.I. Jane* (1991), *Xena Warrior Princess*, and *Buffy the Vampire Slayer*. In 1992, Linda Hamilton popularized the lean, toned, and low–body fat look for women when, for *Terminator 2*, she transformed her previously soft feminine body. In so doing, she sparked a trend in women's fitness, increasing the acceptance—if not the expectation—of women with hard bodies or at least toned arms, flat stomachs, and calf muscles that visibly flexed. Female athletes, including powerhouse tennis professionals Venus and Serena Williams, with their unconventionally strong bodies, made headlines thanks to their remarkable performances and multimillion-dollar marketing deals. Amateur female athletes began to participate in greater numbers in outdoor sports and competitions such as snowboarding, triathlons, and marathons.

Television shows like *The Powerpuff Girls* and all-girl bands like the *Spice Girls* advocated **girl power**. Young women and girls began to assert their personal power, take pride not only in their good looks, but in academic prowess (especially in math and science) and athletic toughness. Being ambitious was no longer necessarily seen as a negative.

But women moving into the last bastion of maleness known as professional wrestling was still largely perceived as radical idea, and McMahon took a lot of convincing. Hunter pointed out that Laurer would create a media sensation. He told McMahon about the female bodybuilder, Corey Everson, who convincingly "beats everybody up" in the film *Double Impact* (1991), starring action hero star Jean-Claude Van Damme (Laurer, 216). McMahon finally agreed to open the WWE doors to Laurer.

A Difficult Entry into the WWF

Laurer's wrestling career with the WWF started humbly enough in 1997 with a minor role as a crazed fan, followed by a series of appearances supporting male wrestlers. She gradually graduated to playing major roles as a villain or good guy, wrestling solo and as part of a team, over time (several months) amassing more and more popularity.

McMahon gave Laurer the name Chyna, a play on words considering that she was neither soft, nor delicate, nor domestic. The first year in the WWF were emotionally harrowing. Many male wrestlers opposed Laurer's presence and did not want to fight her. Some called her names. Laurer also found it difficult having to maintain her look. She contended that men had it easier; they did not have to deal with the challenges of body image and hair and makeup maintenance. The media depicted her as a "monster" and a "freak" (Heinecken, 186, 197). Laurer's extraordinary size and the fact that she fought men disrupted societal notions of femininity. It also went against the norm for other women in the WWF, most of whom were depicted as "extremely feminine," "petite," and "large-breasted," and functioned in noncombative roles (unless they fought other women) as "managers," "wives," and "damsels in distress" (Heinecken, 185).

Becoming Successful

In time, Chyna was accepted by most of her peers, as well as by the audiences. Indeed, she eventually became a raging success. Chyna contends that her acceptance was largely predicated on trends in television, such as talk shows like *The Jerry Springer Show* and reality television shows, where scandalous affairs, heated arguments, and fist fights were regularly aired. These shows pushed the envelope in terms of "how shocking we could all get," thus "mak[ing] it a little easier for [Chyna] to wrestle men in the WWF" (Laurer, 184).

Heinecken points out that Chyna's success came about after she underwent a radical makeover, receiving breast implants in 2000 and "facial reconstruction" (Heinecken, 199). She started to "walk . . . in the familiar feminine manner, with arms swaying side to side across her body" and appeared in *Playboy Magazine* more than once (Heineken, 199). However, as Heinecken points out, "female sexuality and objectification" can be **read** as "signs of female success" (Heinecken, 198). At one time, **to-be-looked-at-ness**, a common term used in film criticism, was considered negative. With the advent of the girl-power movement, being an object of desire became a way young women and girls felt empowered. To some, Laurer's new look may have compromised her depiction. To others, it compounded her appeal. When she retired from wrestling in 2001, she wrestled independently until 2004 and pursued an acting career.

POWER SUIT, WEAPONS, AND ABILITIES

Chyna's carefully crafted look was a part of her depiction of power and sex appeal. Her black leather attire and high-heeled shoes were crowd pleasers. Her clothes were usually tight short-shorts and bondage-style bustier. Black also traditionally indicates badness and mystery, which, in 21st-century terms, can be a virtue. This is a radical shift from the 1950s, when the good girl or the **ingénue** was the ideal archetype.

Chyna's power is coded in other ways. Her sheer size, high-exposure fights, and ability to perform well for audiences helped her gain status. Among her most famous fights was the series of "Battle of the Sexes" fights, culminating with the "Good Housekeeping Match." In these fights, Chyna was pitted against Jeff Jarrett, who was cast as a male chauvinist. In the final big fight in 1999, the writers gave Chyna the victory. This fight was reminiscent of the famous 1973 "Battle of the Sexes" tennis match between Billie Jean King and Bobby Riggs, which King won. Although wrestlers are often criticized, particularly by non fans, for acting in over-the-top ways to the point of campiness, fans expect wrestlers to be overly dramatic. Chyna stated that action films and video games helped teach her how to better perform during matches.

In the ring, Chyna fought as hard as her male peers, using a variety of trademark moves. Her specialty moves included the Flippy, also referred to by other names such as the Chyna Spring Roll or ninja somersault. Other moves included the Pedigree, Powerbomb, Gorilla press slam, DDT, Handspring back elbow, Jawbreaker, Low blow, and Powerslam.

IMPACT

Chyna opened the door for women in modern professional wrestling. Though she was a real person, with real combat skills, who sustained injuries and did her own stunts, Chyna can be counted as one of a growing number of female action heroes to emerge in the 1990s—women who shattered traditional images of females as weak, small bodied, inactive, and subordinate to a male hero. She was a woman who dared to fight other men when it was not popular to do so; she became one of the most popular wrestling personalities in history, a position normally reserved for men.

Following her departure from the WWF in 2001, the line between Laurer and Chyna that had always been blurred became more clearly defined. Laurer has yet to find a place in mainstream television and films that parallels her wrestling career. She has had several awkward run-ins with mainstream Hollywood. For example, when she attended the Emmys one year, she felt conspicuous in the presence of the many actresses who maintain thin frames. At the same event, she was passed up for an interview from a co-host on the red carpet who did not recognize her. When she tried out for the part of the cyborg in *Terminator 3: Rise of the Machines* (2003), a woman with traditional feminine beauty and body got the part instead. This is a noticeable contrast to the experiences of male bodybuilders like Lou Ferrigno, who played the Hulk in the 1970s television series, and Arnold Schwarzenegger, one of the top action heroes in film history. With the exception of several reality television shows, some appearances in film and television, a contingent of mainstream society has yet to embrace Laurer and her glaring defiance of societal norms.

See also G.I. Jane; Maggie Fitzgerald; Xena: Warrior Princess.

FURTHER RESOURCES

Assael, Shaun, and Mike Mooneyham. *Sex, Lies, and Headlocks: The Real Story of Vince McMahon and World Wrestling Entertainment.* New York: Three Rivers Press, 2004.

Heinecken, Dawn. "No Cage Can Hold Her Rage? Gender, Transgression, and the World Wrestling Federation's Chyna." In *Action Chicks: New Images of Tough Women in Popular Culture,* ed. Sherrie A. Inness. New York: Palgrave Macmillan, 2004.

Heinecken, Dawn. *The Warrior Women of Television: A Feminist Cultural Analysis of the New Female Body in Popular Media.* New York: Peter Lang, 2003.

Laurer, Joanie, with Michael Angeli. *Chyna.* New York: HarperTorch, 2001.

"Official Site of World Wrestling Entertainment." http://www.wwe.com.

Tasker, Yvonne. *Spectacular Bodies: Gender, Genre, and the Action Cinema.* New York: Routledge, 1993.

Ellen aka "The Lady" rides her horse looking stalwart in the film *The Quick and the Dead*. (© TriStar/Courtesy: Everett Collection)

Ellen aka "The Lady"

The Lady is the lone female gunfighter in the Western film *The Quick and the Dead* (1995). In the movie, she participates in a deadly gun-fighting contest in the town of Redemption for the opportunity to take vengeance on John Herod (Gene Hackman). Herod was responsible for the death of her father (a marshal), stringing him up with a noose and forcing Ellen, who was only a child and knew nothing of guns, to try to shoot the rope and set her father free. Instead, Ellen missed and killed her father. During the contest, a grown-up Ellen is simply referred to as "The Lady," and no one, including Herod, knows who she really is. *The Quick and the Dead* was not a financial success, grossing only $18,636,537 in the United States.

Though women are not generally associated with frontier masculinity, nor do they often play the lead in the Western genre, The Lady, played by Sharon Stone, is an exceptional protagonist. She combines feminine beauty and the rugged characteristics of the classic Western hero. Her long, blonde hair is unkempt and her pretty features show the signs of wear and tear from the long days on the road and exposure to hot sun and beating rain. This hero does not bother with makeup on the trail. Like her male compatriots, she wields symbols of power: her cowboy hat, her horse, and her gun. When she first appears in the film, the camera follows her movements from afar, her horse slowly plodding along. Her gender is indistinguishable to the audience, as well as to an outlaw, Dog Kelly (Tobin Bell), who shoots at her, not wanting to be seen as he searches for his buried gold in the sere ranges of the frontier. She falls to the ground. Dog Kelly inspects the body, not suspecting that his victim is playing possum. The Lady suddenly throws him to the ground and handcuffs him to a wagon wheel. She then stands triumphant, with the sun directly behind her. Removing her hat, her golden hair spills loose, and her identity is revealed: a woman whose cunning and skills have outdone Dog Kelly and will be the undoing of her intended target, the villainous Herod.

The West, with its sweeping cast of tall and noble cowboys, reckless outlaws, vast spaces, and unforeseen dangers, figures prominently in American heroism, legends, fables, folklore, and literature, as well as in the modern storytelling media of film and television. What is depicted in film and on television about the West is a mix of both fact and fiction. But one thing is undeniable: almost all real cowboys were male. Indeed, it largely is from our perceptions of the West that our American concept of masculinity takes its form and shape.

Masculinity is epitomized by the restless loner who is only free when crossing the vastness of the wild frontier. His skills are honed by years of hardship; he is most alive when in the dangerous environs of outlaws, ne'er-do-wells, and scavengers. His might is expressed through his prowess with a gun. He's steady, emotionless, and speaks little. His reputation is often amplified by the stories that are told about him, the machismo of his name, or the number of his kills. The books, films, and television series that were

Annie Oakley

On the American frontier, women who used rifles were not completely uncommon. Women, like men, were often required to know how to use guns for hunting and protecting the family—their family's survival depended on it. There were also independent women, like frontierswoman Calamity Jane, who lived bold, combative, daring lives out of sheer passion. Annie Oakley (1860–1926), the sixth of eight children, hunted with a rifle as early as nine years old. She was so skilled that she helped provide for the family after her father's death. The income she brought in paid for the family farm. At 21 years old, Oakley, who had attained considerable notoriety for her sharpshooting skills, entered a shooting match with Frances E. Butler, whom she married in 1882. Shortly after their marriage, they toured as a traveling show. They later joined the popular Buffalo Bill's Wild West Show, where her fame soared. Oakley traveled throughout the nation and in Europe. Despite her skills, then-President William McKinley turned her offer down when she wrote him, requesting that she and several other women sharpshooters join the nation's armed forces in combat.

After suffering a serious injury in a railway accident in 1901, Oakley left Buffalo Bill's Wild West Show, but her subsequent life was no less thrilling. She appeared in a stage play, *The Western Girl*. She continued to dazzle audiences with her shooting skills into her sixties. After her death, Oakley inspired a number of films, such as *Annie Oakley* (1935), *Buffalo Girls* (1996), the musical *Annie Get Your Gun* (1946), and the eponymous television series that ran from 1954 to 1956.

based on Western traditions featuring strong male cowboys were long ranked as America's most popular.

But there were also more than a few women—Latino, Native American, black, and white—in the West. Women living in the frontier were expected to be tougher than the women who lived in town. The "pioneer women in the American West were a different breed. They worked on ranches, famously performed in Wild West show[s] and competed in rodeos, often in addition to customary gender duties such as taking care of home and family" (Mainon and Ursini, 325).

In the Western movie genre, women tend to live in town or on the homestead. They are mostly positioned as mothers, wives, daughters, sisters, or prostitutes. The woman in a Western is the antithesis of the masculine Western hero. Where he is strong, free, and masculine, she is weak, bound to restrictive gender roles, and feminine. His place is roaming the vast and open spaces of the frontier; her place is restricted to the boundaries of civilization. She is separate from the free-spirited loner who goes wherever he dares to go and stays alive by using his wits and his gun.

A significant number of books explore the lives of both real and fictional women and girls who were also sharpshooters and who could handle a horse with the same skill as a man. Film and television have shed more light on such topics. The Lady is among a handful of women to be depicted in a genre that has traditionally been dominated by action heroes like John Wayne and antiheroes like Clint Eastwood.

ORIGINS

History of Women as Western Heroes

Despite the preponderance of male cowboys in the movies, there has been a smattering of women Western heroes as far back as the silent era. *The Bad Man* (1907), *The Girl Sheriff* (1912), *The Bandits of Death Valley* (1915), *Arizona Cat Claw* (1919), and *As the Sun Went Down* (1919) featured women who shared in the action with the male leads, rescued men, and wielded gun power. These films were among the 60 films of assorted genres that starred young women, known as **serial** queens, in ongoing adventures. For the times, the characters played by the serial queens were considered active and powerful, though they were not unfettered by **stereotypical** constraints. For example, they wore long dresses and did not engage in hand-to-hand combat.

The female Western hero returned in subsequent decades. Actress Barbara Stanwyck portrayed several strong women in this genre. She starred as *Annie Oakley* (1935) and played Jessica Drummond in *Forty Guns* (1957). In *Johnny Guitar* (1954), a film that is considered a feminist Western, Joan Crawford was cast as Vienna, a woman who takes down a tough female villain in a showdown. *Gunslinger* (1956) also pitted two strong female roles against each other: the hero played by Beverly Garland and the villain by Erica Paige. In this film, men were positioned in subordinate and weak roles. The character known as "The Woman," played by Millie Perkins in *The Shooting* (1966), is a feisty, self-absorbed character who unflinchingly shoots to the death her horse and a bird while on a hazardous quest for revenge. Although her appearance in *The Shooting* is **transgressive**, the film was never released in theaters. In 1971, Raquel Welch was cast as Hannie in *Hannie Caulder*, a film about a woman who takes up a gun to mete out revenge against a band of thieves who raped her and murdered her husband. Such films challenged general industry trends that cast women as **femme fatales** or glamorous love interests. Notable exceptions from other genres included the kind of smart and independent roles for which Katharine Hepburn was so well known.

The Quick and the Dead was released in the 1990s, a period in which films increasingly challenged how women were portrayed in action films in myriad genres such as science fiction, thriller, and horror. Clarice Starling penetrated the male-dominated field of the FBI in *The Silence of the Lambs* (1991). Thelma and Louise co-opted the male space of the open road and were positioned as outlaws in the eponymous film, released in 1991. A female vampire slayer was introduced in *Buffy the Vampire Slayer* in 1992. Four female outlaws appeared in *Bad Girls* (1994), and Jordan O'Neil succeeded in an all-male environment in an elite branch of the military in *G.I. Jane* (1997). The Lady, a female Western hero, was thus a part of a burgeoning trend for action women in film.

Simon Moore, who wrote the script for *The Quick and the Dead*, was inspired by Sergio Leone's spaghetti Westerns—only he wanted a woman in the starring role. Spaghetti Westerns, a subgenre of the Westerns, were so called because they were filmed in Italian. These low-budget films were actually filmed in Spain by various Italian and Spanish companies in partnership, and featured a mixture of Italian and Spanish actors. In America, the most well-known spaghetti Westerns were films such as *A Fistful of Dollars* (1964), *For a Few Dollars More* (1965), and *The Good, the Bad and the Ugly* (1966), all directed by Sergio Leone. These films helped to catapult Clint Eastwood into stardom as one of the most important male action heroes of the 1960s and onward.

One of the key elements to Eastwood's character in these spaghetti Westerns was that his identity was frequently withheld from both the audience and the other characters in the film. He was commonly known as the "Man With No Name." Depicted as a lone drifter, his power was heightened by the fact that no one knew his name, his background, or his agenda, for familiarity would have made him less threatening. In the Western, strangers represent uncertainty, as well as the threat of potential danger. Moreover, Eastwood spoke little and his movements were minimal and deliberate. His power could be glimpsed in his clear blue eyes, which saw everything without betraying his knowledge. Those eyes narrowed as he sized up a dangerous situation or determined in an instant who he should shoot first. His motions were rapid and sure as he pulled his weapon's trigger again and again. And there would always be more than one villain skulking atop the buildings, peeking out a window, or lurking in other unexpected locales. These villains were usually ferocious men who killed quickly and without remorse.

In *The Quick and the Dead*, Sharon Stone (who coproduced the movie) and director Sam Raimi agreed to cast an up-and-coming Australian actor, Russell Crowe, as the lead male, Cort. Cort's role was unconventional for a Western. Depicted as a former member of Herod's gang, Cort turned to religion because of his remorse after Herod forced him to kill a priest. Herod forces Cort to enter the gun-fighting contest, which turns out to be his way

Lozen

Warrior women existed in many indigenous cultures and ancient societies, despite the enormous pressures to conform. Rather than learn the traditional women's work of her Apache society, Lozen (1848–1890) chose to run fast, ride horses, and use weapons (activities associated with Apache males). She also dressed like a man and refrained from marrying, as was the custom of women in any society of that time. Like the male warriors, Lozen went on a solo quest to the Sacred Mountain, situated in New Mexico, for several days. In her lifetime, she became a well-respected member of Apache warrior society, well known for her extraordinary skills—healing, locating enemies, and riding horses. Her work as a medicine woman, however, was not so unusual for a woman. In indigenous cultures in America or Africa, medicine women were typical.

of taking out his competition before they can rise up to challenge him. Cort is reluctant, having given up his wild ways, killing, and his gun. Peace and religion are Cort's way of finding redemption—an unusual method, considering that masculinity in the West was so clearly defined by guns and bravado, not by settling down and eschewing danger and violence. This was also an atypical role for Crowe, whose successful American career would be largely based on his ultra-masculine and tough guy roles such as those he played in *Gladiator* (2000) and *Cinderella Man* (2005).

While Cort settles down and is **coded** in a traditional nonmasculine role, The Lady chooses revenge. She wields a gun (a **phallic** symbol representing power) and plunges headlong into the masculine world of gun fighting and vengeance.

Sam Raimi

Samuel Marshall Raimi was born on October 23, 1959, in Royal Oak, Michigan. Raimi's films depict women in varied ways, from heroes to damsels in distress, somtimes in the same film. For example, in *The Quick and the Dead*, The Lady oscillates between power and weakness; although she refuses to allow others to stereotype her or to cower when in male-dominated spheres (like the frontier or a town run by the ruthless Herod), she demonstrates weakness on several occasions. In the *Spider-Man* films (2002, 2004, 2007), which Raimi directed, women are often portrayed as screaming damsels, needing to be rescued by the costumed comic-book character Spider-Man. In *Drag Me to Hell* (2009), an ordinary woman toughens up when demons harass her after an elderly woman curses her. In the end, however, the demons capture the female protagonist and drag her to a horrific fate.

Raimi also produced one of the most iconic television shows of the 1990s, *Xena: Warrior Princess*, the series that made Lucy Lawless, cast in the lead role, famous. Xena, an ancient warrior with long brown hair, tall and solidly built, was an icon for women and young girls, who delighted in her unabashed strength and power.

Sharon Stone

Sharon Stone is known for her strong and controversial film roles. Born on March 10, 1958, in Meadville, Pennsylvania, Stone studied briefly at Edinboro University of Pennsylvania before starting a modeling career. Switching to acting, she made her film debut in *Stardust Memories* in 1980. Her appearance was brief but landed her important roles in a string of films in the 1980s such as *Irreconcilable Differences* (1984), *Action Jackson* (1988), *King Solomon's Mines* (1985), and *Above the Law* (1988). In several of those films, such as *Action Jackson*, starring Carl Weathers as the African American male lead, and *Above the Law*, starring action icon Steven Seagal, Stone played stereotypical roles, while men took the lead.

Total Recall (1990), a science fiction film starring Arnold Schwarzenegger as Doug Quaid, was Stone's breakout role as a female action character. Stone plays Quaid's wife, Laurie, who was in reality an enemy agent ordered to keep watch on Quaid. The two eventually confront each other in a violent sequence. Stone, a slender, albeit athletic Hollywood beauty, is pitted against an action-film legend and former Mr. Universe. She fights convincingly and takes punches with a stoicism not ordinarily depicted by women in film. She ultimately looses the battle but puts on a good show in the process. In the same year, Stone appeared nude in *Playboy* magazine, and two years later, in 1992, she played a serial killer in *Basic Instinct*.

Stone has continued to act, appearing in films such as *Casino* (1995) and *Catwoman* (2004; opposite Halle Berry, who played the notorious villain in catsuit) as well as becoming involved in assorted philanthropies. Stone has divorced three times and has three adopted children.

POWER SUIT, WEAPONS, AND ABILITIES

In *The Quick and the Dead*, The Lady dons the masculine attire of the rugged cowboy and gunslinger. She takes on the look so well that Dog Kelly thinks that she is a man when he sees her from a distance. When she takes off her hat, her long, golden hair codes her as a woman. But her clothes—the leggings, the boots, and the cowboy hat—associate her with symbols of masculinity and power.

Women warriors often adopt men's clothing. In the 14th century, Joan of Arc wore men's clothing and, during battle, was fitted with battle armor that weighed some 60 pounds. During the American Civil War, some women disguised themselves as male soldiers to have the opportunity to fight. Officially, women in America are still forbidden to engage in combat.

There are myriad reasons why women of action don men's clothing. Some scholars contend that Joan of Arc may have discarded her traditional peasant dresses because they were too cumbersome and constricting, were not functional for travel or battle, and were not an effective symbol of authority (dresses were associated with femininity and vulnerability, while nothing emanated power like gleaming armor). Some scholars argue that dressing like the male soldiers she traveled with might have facilitated their acceptance and tolerance of Joan's presence or enabled her to maintain her modesty. Women who customarily traveled with soldiers were either prostitutes or wives.

The Lady's gunslinger wardrobe aligned her with her new identity. When she was a child, weak and incapable of freeing her father who hung from a rope, she wore a traditional dress. As an adult, bent on vengeance and having perfected her gun and combat skills, her masculine Western attire was more than fitting, accentuating not only her skill but her masculine behavior. Ellen's power resided not only in her clothing but in the gun she carried. Men, not women, traditionally wielded guns throughout history.

Ellen has other skills. In at least three scenes, she shows off her hand-to-hand combat skills. In the opening scene, she sends Dog Kelly to the ground in a flash. After entering Redemption, she sends a saloon owner to the floor after he insinuates that she is a prostitute, and in another scene, she punches a rapist and then shoots him in his penis.

VILLAINS

Many of the gunslingers who come to Redemption to enter the gun-fighting contest are criminals and outlaws—common enough characters in Westerns. But the primary villain is Herod.

Herod is a stone-cold killer who heads a gang that does his bidding without question. Herod's greatest strength appears to be not his shooting skill, which he flaunts by deriding the skills of his cocky, illegitimate son, The Kid (Leonardo DiCaprio), but his ability to feel no remorse or guilt for what he does, even after he shoots his son to the death. Herod is a bully in every sense of the term. He oppresses Redemption, the town he rules without legal sanction or mercy, and extorts money from its poor citizens. The residents are so downtrodden that they spend what little they have to hire a gunslinger, a talented and confident African American man named Sergeant Clay Cantrell (Keith David) to enter the contest in the hope that he will kill Herod.

Hackman, who plays Herod, is notable for his villainous roles, including Lex Luther, Superman's arch enemy. Traditional Western villains generally

The Women of *Kill Bill*

Quentin Tarantino directed the *Kill Bill* film series (2003, 2004), which featured several incredibly violent and fierce female assassins. The movie fuses the Western and martial arts genres to tell the gory and graphic tale of a former assassin, Beatrix Kiddo (Uma Thurman), also known as The Bride or Black Mamba. Kiddo was a blonde beauty whose trademark outfit, a yellow suit, was originally worn by Bruce Lee in *Game of Death* (1978). She seeks revenge for her husband-to-be, who was murdered on their wedding day. She targets Bill (David Carradine), her former boss, and his lethally trained female killers. These include Vernita Green, played by African American actress Vivica A. Fox; O-Ren Ishii (Lucy Liu), who heads a malevolent organization of her own; Gogo Yubari (Chiaki Kuriyama), a feisty teen who dons a school uniform; and an eye-patch-wearing Elle Driver (Daryl Hannah).

The *Kill Bill* movies were a huge success when they hit American theaters. Audiences enjoyed the newfangled way in which Tarantino melded fast-paced action, a twisted plot, and violent women. The films were particularly groundbreaking because they featured a diverse cast of all-female combatants. The protagonist, The Bride, was aggressive and didn't flinch at the sight of blood, but unlike traditional male heroes, she was also thin and pretty. Gogo Yubari, a defiant teen, reflected the increasing number of girls with power who have appeared with regularity since the 1990s.

appear physically threatening, either excessively large or with some physical defect, like the character Le Chiffre whose eyes tear blood in *Casino Royale* (2006). Hackman's threat is not based on his appearance or size but on his ability to emanate emotional coldness and cruelty. With Herod, Hackman crafts a character who appears unstoppable and whose evil knows no bounds. But Ellen finds a way—by challenging gender roles.

THE QUICK AND THE DEAD, THE FILM

When The Lady first appears in the film, she is riding a horse, traveling alone. Her presence challenges conventional gender roles. Even tough frontierswomen rarely traveled alone in real life, nor were they allowed in many saloons. The rough and wild spaces of the frontier, and the guns and clothing that were necessary to survive there, were intended for men, not women. When she manacles Dog Kelly to a wagon wheel, Ellen sets the tone of the film—no ordinary Western here.

After coming into the town of Redemption, Ellen must deal with people who try to force her into stereotypical roles or exclude her from areas where women were not customarily allowed. Asking for a room, a saloon owner insists that the prostitutes stay next door. Ellen kicks a stool from under him; he hits the floor hard while she pours herself a drink. The saloon owner immediately has his daughter ready a room. Ace Hanlon (Lance Henriksen), arriving in town to participate in the contest, enters the saloon shortly thereafter. He brandishes his machismo, she quips back at him smartly, then walks out, ignoring him. Outside, Scars (Mark Boone Junior), a man recently released from prison, appears. This man is so monstrous that when a man who had been in the saloon see him, he runs for his life. Scars shoots him from a distance, nonetheless, then, using a knife, he tallies the kill on his forearm. But when he confronts The Lady, she does not cower. "You're pretty," he tells her, his sinister smile portending a potential sexual assault. "You're not," she quips back. "I need a woman," he says, and she replies, "you need a bath." The Lady is full of repartee like this—comments that identify her as fearless and bold. But in a later scene, men balk at the idea of allowing her to join the gun-fighting contest. Women "just can't shoot" one man calls out. Shortly thereafter, Ellen sees Cort standing on a stool with a rope around his neck—just like her father. Herod shoots at the legs of the stool, giving Cort only two options: join the gun-fighting contest or die. Ellen proves her marksmanship when she shoots the rope with which Cort is about to be lynched.

The saloon owner's adolescent daughter provides a stark contrast to The Lady. Katie (Olivia Burnette) performs traditional female duties, such as cleaning and drawing bathwater for customers, and wears the traditional dress that all women of that period and place wore. She is talkative, wide-eyed, and gullible. Ellen, who, like classic male heroes, doesn't talk much, is annoyed by Katie's incessant chatter and ignores her rapid-fire questions as well as her youthful exuberance over The Lady's shooting skills. Ellen makes it clear to Katie that what she does in the gun-fighting contest is not for fun, that there is nothing glamorous about shooting and killing. Ellen is not interested in the money that is promised to the victor. She has her steady gaze on Herod, waiting for an opportunity to kill.

Not only does The Lady contrast with Katie's traditional girlishness, she also appears in many ways more masculine than Cort. First, she rescues him from being hanged. Later, five young boys beat on Cort, who lies chained and defenseless on the ground. The Lady strides up to him and the boys flee in fear. Ellen does not understand why Cort chooses religion and peace, stating that "some people deserve to die." Thus, in an unusual twist, a man is associated with religious values and pacifism, while a woman pursues vengeance and violence. In another example of role reversal, Cort denigrates The Lady for cavorting with The Kid, but she shows no qualms when she wakes up one morning with The Kid, implying that they had sex.

Madeleine Albright's Pins

Guns and fancy fighting skills are not the only way to get a tough message across. Madeleine Albright (1937), the first woman to serve as secretary of state in America, wielded a different kind of weapon: pins. In her book *Read My Pins: Stories from a Diplomat's Jewel Box* (2009), Albright discusses how she used her pins not only as decorative accessories but to convey deliberate messages during international encounters. During light and uplifting moments, Albright was known to wear flower or butterfly pins. But when she wanted to demonstrate toughness, she paired a serious demeanor with a serious pin, such as a wasp. When she wore an arrow-shaped pin, a Russian foreign minister thought it was an interceptor missile; Albright did not discourage the impression.

Albright was born in Prague, Czechoslovakia. She moved to America in 1948. Albright attended high school in Denver, Colorado. Inspired by her diplomat father, she studied political science in college, graduating from Wellesley College in 1959. In 1957, she became a U.S. citizen. Shortly thereafter, she married Joseph Albright (they divorced in 1982), with whom she had three daughters. She received a PhD at Columbia University in 1976. In 1993, President William Clinton appointed her U.S. ambassador to the United Nations. She served as secretary of state between 1997 and 2001.

Traditionally, sexuality was acceptable for the male hero and was in many cases employed to heighten his aura of masculinity. In women, sex was coded as bad.

But The Lady's behavior is not always depicted in masculine terms. She is often depicted as weak (at least according to some scholars) or portrayed in distinctly feminine ways. When it is The Lady's turn to fight, she is visibly nervous. Her success is dependent on Cort, who gives her a tip (once the gunfight starts, Cort rises to the challenge). It is obvious that Ellen is not a hardened killer. Emotion frequently shows on her face as she watches the contest. At dinner, she dresses in a traditionally feminine, off-the-shoulder dress. When Herod invites her to his home, her courage wilts and she becomes emotional, leaving without completing her mission. But Ellen's underlying humanity, emotions, and heart provide a vivid contrast to the heartless Herod.

Ellen beats up and shoots to death Eugene Dred (Kevin Conway), who seduces and rapes Katie (but only after he is about to shoot Ellen). This retaliation is coded as a triumph for women, because the act vindicates a young female victim who received no protection from traditional masculinity. The girl's father was too powerless to do anything about his daughter's victimization, and none of the other characters would get involved. After The Lady kills Dred, she cries and later rides out of town. Unlike male heroes, she expresses her emotions to Doc Wallace (Roberts Blossom), her father's friend, who comes to talk with her. She divulges that she could not kill Herod because she is scared of dying. Emboldened by her conversation with Doc Wallace, The Lady returns to Redemption.

Back in town, The Lady gets another chance at Herod, with the help of Cort. Before a showdown between Cort and Herod, The Lady sets off an explosion. She emerges from the smoke, sweltering flames rising behind her, looking tough and determined. Cort takes down Herod's hoodlums, while Ellen faces off with Herod. Herod, who had previously admired her for her beauty, her admirable shooting skills, and her mystery, finally learns that The Lady is the daughter of the man he tricked her into killing. "You're not fast enough for me," Herod says confidently and truthfully; as good as The Lady is, her skills are not on par with Herod or Cort. Undaunted, she replies, "Today, I am." Her voice is authoritative and low. Tears stream down her face. She shoots, and Herod falls back from the force and dies. She tosses her father's badge to Cort and then rides out of town on her horse in true hero fashion.

IMPACT

Historically, Westerns have been the path to stardom for many male actors, and the genre's immense popularity has underscored how deeply American culture values masculinity and heroism. Although this film did not advance Stone's career in any profound way and did not spark a frenzy at the box office, many critics and scholars responded positively to the film. Importantly, *The Quick and the Dead* challenged the traditional Western hero role. The Lady was depicted as a Western hero who was tough but had feelings, pretty but not afraid to get dirty, skilled but not showy. Scholars could easily argue, as many have done in regard to female action heroes in other films, that her power was undermined by her emotionalism and by her reliance on men (Doc and Cort) as she navigated the rough town of Redemption. But, in the end, it was Ellen's softness that made her human, in contrast to the monstrous Herod, and it was Ellen, not Doc or Cort, who left town when the job was done. In the Western, the mythic hero rides off into the sunset, while the ordinary townsfolk stay behind.

See also Chun Li; Chyna; G.I. Jane; Joan of Arc.

FURTHER RESOURCES

Carlson, Howard Paul. *The Cowboy Way: An Exploration of History and Culture.* Lubbock: Texas Tech University Press, 2006.

Flood, Elizabeth Clair, and William Manns. *Cowgirls: Women of the Wild West.* Santa Fe, NM: Zon International, 2000.

Inness, Sherrie A. *Tough Girls: Women Warriors and Wonder Women in Popular Culture.* Philadelphia: University of Pennsylvania Press, 1999.

Kitses, Jim, and Greg Rickman, eds. *The Western Reader.* New York: Limelight Editions, 1998.

Knobloch, Susan. "Sharon Stone's (An)Aesthetic." In *Reel Knockouts: Violent Women in the Movies*, ed. Martha McCaughey and Neal King. Austin: University of Texas Press, 2001.

Mainon, Dominique, and James Ursini. *The Modern Amazons: Warrior Women On-Screen.* Pompton Plains, NJ: Limelight Editions, 2006.

McGee, Patrick. *From Shane to Kill Bill: Rethinking the Western.* Carlton, Australia: Blackwell, 2007.

Mellencamp, Patricia. *A Fine Romance: Five Ages of Film Feminism.* Philadelphia: Temple University Press, 1995.

"A Woman's Place: Tied to the Railroad Tracks?" http://xroads.virginia.edu/~HYPER/HNS/Westfilm/heroine.htm.

Ellen Ripley is geared for action in the film *Aliens*. (AP Photo/File.)

Ellen Ripley

Lieutenant Ellen Ripley is the protagonist of the *Alien* science fiction film series (1979, 1986, 1992, 1997). The standard glamorous Hollywood archetype is usually blond and buxom and the hero's love interest, sidekick, or victim. Ripley is five feet, eleven inches tall, lean, brunette, and brown-eyed. She is grim-toned, her face is unembellished by makeup, and she visibly sweats and grimaces as she chases Aliens through darkened tunnels dressed in the functional attire of a space industry (cargo pants and heavy boots). Ripley is no sidekick, and she is certainly no one's victim.

Sigourney Weaver played Ripley in all four movies. She was not the first to depict a female action hero in film or television, but following her appearance in *Alien* (1979), she became a revolutionary film icon. Among the reasons for her iconic status is that she was one of the first **final girl** archetypes to defeat a villain without any help or rescue from a man.

The Ripley character was a hit with men and women. Second-wave feminists liked that Ripley emitted power, intelligence, and confidence, striding across the screen in manner and appearance that was far from typical for that era. Ripley's tough character appealed to men too, and she did not have to emanate sex appeal to do it. In *Aliens* (1986), the second film in the series, Ripley returned in an even grittier role, one which some believe positioned her as the first female Reagan-era hero.

Heroism in the 1980s was big business. Actors like Arnold Schwarzenegger, Sylvester Stallone, Mel Gibson, Bruce Willis, and Jean-Claude Van Damme set the standard for muscle-bound heroism. They dominated the film industry with movies infused with new, never-before-seen, high-powered action and special effects, producing over-the-top explosions, gun fights, car chases, and fight sequences.

Ripley set the standard for a new kind of cinematic female action hero, one that was tough as nails and dynamic enough to stand front and center in a major blockbuster, not to mention an entire film series. The films themselves met the standards of the time, with innovative special lighting and effects, subdued color tones, orchestral background music, and startlingly realistic Aliens. It is believed that Ridley Scott, who directed *Alien*, was inspired by another landmark science fiction film, *Star Wars* (1977). But the realism of the *Alien* movies is a marked departure from the campiness of *Star Wars*-style science fiction. The scene in the first film (*Alien*, 1979), in which an Alien erupts from the chest of a crew member, is considered a milestone in cinematic horror.

The *Alien* series was enormously popular with film critics. They picked and prodded the films to interpret the societal values and prejudices they presented, as well as the changing perceptions of gender roles in America. The films also established Ripley, faults and all, as foremother of a steadily growing succession of female action heroes.

ORIGINS

There would be no Ellen Ripley without Sigourney Weaver, and the two are inextricably linked in terms of action hero lore. However, Ellen Ripley's role

Final Girl

The term *final girl* was coined by Carol J. Clover in the book *Men, Women and Chain Saws: Gender in the Modern Horror Film* (1992). Among other things, the final girl is depicted as typically nonsexual (she doesn't usually get amorous with the boys) and frequently tomboyish, quick-witted, and capable. She stands out from the rest, guys and girls included, because she's the one left standing at the end of the day, smudged with grime and bruises, the consequences of her harrowing trial. Her survival is all the more poignant if she rescues herself without any external help.

The term *final girl* was originally associated with horror and slasher films, but it is now associated with any female lone survivor in a film. Final girls are often considered progressive and subversive, because they challenge the longstanding tradition of depicting women as hysterical victims immobilized by fear or, worse, victimized by monsters and other villains. Traditionally, girls died (or were raped) in movies and television to provide a motive of revenge for men.

Final girls appeared in increasing numbers in the movies of the 1970s and 1980s. Laurie Strode (Jamie Lee Curtis) was a progenitor of the final girl archetype. She appeared in 6 of the 10 *Halloween* films. The first movie, released in 1978, showed Strode's first triumphant encounter with the serial killer Michael Myers. Although it was a psychiatrist who finished off Myers in the film, Strode demonstrated remarkable sense and will as she eluded the killer's grasp (early films represented women as feeble and easy prey). Other final girls quickly followed in the wake of the positive reception of Laurie Strode: Alice Hardy in *Friday the 13th* (1980), Nancy Thompson in *A Nightmare on Elm Street* (1984), and Sidney Prescott in *Scream* (1996).

was originally meant for a man. The switch was made by Alan Ladd, former president of 20th Century Fox, who believed "that audiences would become more engaged in the story if a woman were in peril" (Gallardo-C and Smith, 16). Allegedly, the writers merely inserted "she" wherever the storyline referred to the character. Their approach worked well, and Ripley would become one of the most iconic figures in action hero history.

When, in 1979, the first of the *Alien* films was released, Ellen Ripley's presence was a big deal. Strong female protagonists in action films that were void of sexual and sexist overtones were not the norm. This is not surprising, as women in male-dominated fields such as construction, politics, law enforcement, and politics, and in management and executive positions were scarce, and women were generally relegated to subordinate status as mothers and wives. However, women such as Gloria Steinem, spokeswoman for **second-wave feminism**, were in the news, voicing their frustrations with traditional women's roles and the suppression of women's rights, issues, and equality. Steinem helped found *Ms. Magazine* in 1972. Wonder Woman was on the cover of the magazine's first issue.

Wonder Woman, as well as The Bionic Woman and Charlie's Angels, were among a handful of female action heroes in the television shows of the 1970s. These women were largely glamorized, with long, billowy, feminine hairstyles, and made-up faces. They engaged in campy fight sequences, showing nowhere near the same toughness and seriousness as later characters like Ripley. In theaters, there was *Foxy Brown* (1974), but she used her glamour and sex appeal to get things done. Final girls, like Sally Hardesty in *The Texas Chainsaw Massacre* (1974), required help to get away from a cannibalistic antagonist. Even Princess Leia's power was restricted in *Star Wars* (1977) because she was not the primary protagonist. In *Alien*, Ripley not only destroys the adult Alien on her own but executes her own escape.

Ridley Scott

Each film in the *Alien* series was directed by a different director. *Alien* (1979) was director Ridley Scott's first major American success. Following a substantive start in his native England with several adventure series, Scott moved to America in the late 1960s. His first film, *The Duellists* (1977), did not appeal to audiences, but the groundbreaking *Alien* did. *Blade Runner* (1982), achieved cult status. Like *Alien*, his films *Thelma and Louise* (1991) and *G.I. Jane* (1997) changed the status quo. Subsequent films like *Gladiator* (2000), *Black Hawk Down* (2001), and *Hannibal* (2001) were met with widespread success.

James Cameron

Canadian-born James Cameron, who directed *Aliens*, entered the world of filmmaking after seeing *Star Wars*. Perhaps Princess Leia made a marked impression on him, for he went on to create or direct a series of empowered women heroes. His claim to fame includes two of the four *Terminator* films, which feature another iconic female hero, Sarah Connor (Linda Hamilton). Cameron's *The Abyss* (1989) casts Dr. Lindsey Brigman (Mary Elizabeth Mastrantonio) as a smart and feisty character, much like Ripley. In 2000, Cameron created the popular *Dark Angel* television series, starring Jessica Alba playing a super soldier called Max Guevara, one of very few Latina action heroes in television. The *Spy Kids* trilogy (2001, 2002, 2003) and films starring Jennifer Lopez, like *Anaconda* (1997) and *Enough* (2002), have also featured Latina heroes.

David Leo Fincher

Though *Alien 3*, director David Leo Fincher's debut film, was not considered a favorite among audiences, he did go on to direct several successes.

Seven (1975) featured two male detectives, played by Brad Pitt and Morgan Freeman, who solve a serial murder case. *Fight Club* (1999), a film about male underground fighting, is considered a cult classic.

Jean-Pierre Jeunet

French director Jean-Pierre Jeunet directed *Alien: Resurrection*, the last film in the series. This was Jeunet's first American film. Although Jeunet began his career directing action films, his films following *Alien: Resurrection* mostly dealt with romantic love.

Sigourney Weaver

When Sigourney Weaver was chosen to play Ellen Ripley, she was an unknown—a risky maneuver in a major film production. Born Susan Alexandra Weaver on October 8, 1949, in New York City to Sylvester L. Weaver, an NBC television executive, and Elizabeth Inglis, a former actress, Weaver had a privileged upbringing. As an aspiring actress, she was keenly aware that she did not fit society's image of curvaceous female beauty, as she was boyishly thin and tall, with a square face with small features.

Weaver received a BA in English from Stanford in 1972 and an MFA from Yale in 1974. In an interview, Weaver divulged that she had aspirations to be a Shakespearean thespian, not a Hollywood actor. Weaver married Jim Simpson in 1984, giving birth to daughter Charlotte in 1990. She managed a production company and appeared in well-known films such as *Ghostbusters* and its sequel (1984 and 1989), *Gorillas in the Mist: The Story of Dian Fossey* (1988), *Working Girl* (1988), *Dave* (1993), *Copycat* (1995), *Galaxy Quest* (1999), and *Holes* (2003). In *Galaxy Quest*, a film that lampoons science fiction action movies, Weaver's character laments the fact that her "job" is to translate the computer (which speaks English).

POWER SUIT, WEAPONS, AND ABILITIES

Ripley's strength, power, and authority are enhanced by the clothing she wears and the weapons she uses. Ripley's power look is most evident in the first, second, and fourth movies. In *Alien*, Ripley wears a unisex one-piece uniform. The army-green color traditionally denotes seriousness and masculinity (in contrast to alleged feminine colors like yellow and pink). The uniform is an outward symbol that one has successfully passed a variety of trials, tests, and requirements and indicates official membership in an elite organization. Significantly, Ripley has an athletic body and wears a loose-fitting uniform. In the 1960s and 1970s, revealing costumes and shapely bodies were the norm for women in science fiction films. In her battle

The Descent

The Descent, a British film that was released in 2005, gave a unique spin to the final girl genre, with its all-female cast of sporty adventurers. The film featured five transgressive women—athletic thrill-seeking friends. Three of the women start off the film white-water rafting, then join two other friends to go caving or spelunking, a sport that involves exceptional skill, confidence, and upper-body strength. In the caves, the horrific tale unfolds.

A rock slide blocks the way out, forcing the women to work together and testing their endurance, skill, and strength while attempting to rescue themselves. Making matters worse are the monstrous predators stalking the women, killing them one by one. Sarah (Shauna Macdonald) emerges as a valiant warrior, who kills the predators and alone escapes the cave.

against an adult Alien, she uses a flamethrower. The battle culminates with Ripley, in a spacesuit, harpooning the Alien out an airlock into space.

At the start of the action in the second film, *Aliens*, Ripley has short hair and wears drab, bulky masculine clothes. Having had her fill of death, she is temporarily weaponless, while the forceful-looking Colonial Marines are loaded with gleaming nukes, pulse rifles, explosives, and smart guns. Midway through the film, Ellen morphs into super Alien slayer; she discards her jacket, revealing a grimy T-shirt, and packs a heavy weapon. This is the typical garb and accessory of a 1980s male hero, personified by Rambo (though many times the male hero goes without a shirt altogether, revealing a defined physique, usually glistening with sweat and smudged with grime—symbols of toughness). *Aliens* includes iconic fighting scenes wherein Ripley, in one scene, blasts Aliens with a flamethrower and grenades, and in another scene steps into a power loader and faces off with the Alien Queen.

In *Alien Resurrection*, Ripley as we knew her is no more (She threw herself into a fiery furnace as an Alien Queen embryo erupted from her chest in the third movie.) But scientists clone her, creating a Ripley human/Alien hybrid. Her stony, emotionless expressions, hinting at the Alien aspect within, as well as her leggings, fitted top baring muscled arms, and long hair are reminiscent of the Conan the Barbarian figure of comic book fame.

Of the four films, Ripley's appearance is the most weak and vulnerable in *Alien 3*. Stranded on Fiorina "Fury" 161, a penal colony, Ripley must shed all physical trappings of power; she wears androgynous clothes and has a shaved head like the other (male) prisoners. Exacerbating matters is that there are no weapons on the colony; the prisoners (including Ripley) have only their wits, one another, and fire to combat and destroy an adult Alien.

VILLAINS

Extraterrestrials

Ash, the science officer android in *Alien*, called the Alien entity a "perfect organism," "a survivor," stating that "its structural perfection is matched only by its hostility." The physiology of the Alien species makes it a seemingly indestructible foe—tough exterior, acid for blood (acid can also be spewed from the Alien's mouth), razor-sharp teeth set in a retractable mouth, super strength, and quick speed—not to mention that the adult Aliens can scale walls and ceilings and walk upright.

The primary villains in the *Alien* films are the Alien monsters, or xenomorphs, as they are sometimes called. The Aliens appear in several stages—the egg, the Facehugger, the Chestburster, and the adult Alien, the last of which is represented most impressively by the Alien Queen. The development of this species is complex. The Alien Queen, like many real animals or insects, lays eggs containing Facehuggers. Upon approach of a potential host, a Facehugger will spring from its egg and attach itself to the face of its host and deposit a Chestburster inside the host's body. After several hours or days, the Chestburster will erupt from the host's body and then further develop into an adult Alien or Alien Queen.

Institution

The Aliens are not the only antagonists depicted in the *Alien* series. The Weyland-Yutani Corporation (in the first three films) and United Systems Military (in the last film) are fictional institutions whose principal aims are to seize the creatures for use as biological weapons by any means necessary.

THE *ALIEN* FILM SERIES

Alien begins when the crew of the *Nostromo* is prematurely awakened by the ship's computer (MU/TH/UR 6000, or simply "Mother") to investigate a distress signal. The crew includes three white males, two white women, one white male artificial life form, and one black male: Captain Dallas (Tom Skerritt), Executive Officer Kane (John Hurt), Warrant Officer Ripley (Sigourney Weaver), Science Officer Ash (Ian Holm), Navigator Lambert (Veronica Cartwright), and Engineers Brett (Harry Dean Stanton) and Parker (Yaphet Kotto). After the crew lands on the planet in response to the signal, Dallas, Kane, and Lambert leave the ship to investigate. Unbeknownst to the others, Kane happens upon an Alien nursery, where a Facehugger promptly attaches itself to his face. Ripley gives the first glimpse of what she's made of by refusing to allow the team back onto the ship because

Kane has been compromised. But she is overruled, and all three return to face the horror of watching an Alien embryo erupt from Kane's chest. As the Alien develops into an adult warrior, it kills all but Ripley and the ship's resident cat, Jonesy.

The film includes several gender transgressions. Ripley, one of only two women on the ship, is third in command, making her the highest-ranking officer left on the ship when her two superior officers join the landing party. Kane's stumble while in the Alien nursery is a trademark slasher film cue that he will, more than likely, be the film's first victim. Clumsiness and weakness are always punished in the horror/slasher genre, and Kane is horrifically violated in what scholars consider a metaphorical rape and then dies during the violent birth of a Chestbuster. A subsequent killing invokes the classic Alfred Hitchcock scene in *Psycho* (1960), in which Marion Crane (Janet Leigh) is murdered while taking a shower. In *Alien*, Brett, in his search for the adult Alien, stops and refreshes himself under a shower of condensation in the engine room and is shortly thereafter attacked. Though Dallas is a seemingly gallant and experienced captain, he consistently makes bad decisions, such as going into the shaft to try to kill the intruding Alien with a flamethrower, upon which he is promptly killed. This puts Ripley in command.

Ripley is a capable commander, though she is repeatedly challenged by her crewmates. There would have been no Alien invasion if the crew had listened to Ripley (and followed protocol) and desisted from bringing Kane back into the ship. But the crew of the *Nostromo* appears to have learned little. When Ripley facilitates a debriefing with the two remaining crew members, Parker and the hysterical Lambert, they are argumentative and resistant to her leadership.

Ripley's worth as a leader stands out sharply. Parker and Lambert suggest flawed plans and are both depicted as overly emotional. Parker is too eager to fight an Alien that he continues to underestimate; Lambert, tottering in hysteria, only wants to run. Ripley coolly thinks through the crisis and comes up with a better plan: get away by shuttle and blow up the ship with the Alien on it.

Though Ripley is a credible hero, she is not bereft of all codes of femininity. Her hair is shoulder length, though in a suspenseful scene she pins it up as she prepares the ship for autodestruct, signaling that her long hair (feminine code) is an obstacle. On several occasions, she holds and pets the cat, speaking to it using a soft feminine voice. When she is attacked by Ash, the android who is in league with "The Company" to capture the Alien, it is in a symbolically sexual fashion: he rolls up a porn magazine and thrusts it in her mouth with the intent to suffocate her. Gallardo-C and Smith posit that "his assault mimics the Facehugger's invasive aggression" and "is thus coded as a rape, with the added significance of the implied violence against women commonly associated with pornographic material." While Ripley is in her

Dian Fossey

Born in San Francisco, California, Dian Fossey (1932–1985) grew up to be a prominent zoologist, famous for her work to save gorillas in the Rwandan rainforests. In 1954, when Fossey received a bachelor's degree in occupational therapy from San Jose State College (now San Jose State University), women who went to college to study the sciences were not the norm. Moreover, she largely worked her way through college, taking on a series of jobs, some traditional, such as a job in a department store, others not so typical, such as when she took a job as a machinist.

   Fossey first went to Africa in 1963; in 1967, she established a camp in Rwanda. She rocketed to national fame in 1970 when she appeared on the cover of *National Geographic Magazine*. In 1976, she earned a PhD in zoology from Darwin College at Cambridge University, England. Fossey continued to scour the Rwandan rainforests to document the life and behavior of great apes, animals that were becoming seriously endangered because of illegal poaching. She became a controversial figure and made enemies who viewed her pro-gorilla stance as detrimental to tourism and economic development. In 1985, she was murdered at her camp, a crime that is still unsolved.

weakest position in the film, she must be rescued by Parker and Lambert (Gallardo-C and Smith, 48).

Aliens picks up where the first film leaves off, with Ripley in cryo-sleep. The film starts off with shots within Ripley's shuttle—it is a shambles and in darkness—before Ripley is rescued by a salvage crew. Later, she wakens in a hospital with severe post-traumatic stress disorder to find that her shuttle went off course and decades have passed. She is told that she had a daughter who died of old age. Shattered and fearful, she takes a low-paying warehouse job on the space station. Eventually, she is coaxed by the Weyland-Yutani Corporation into joining a unit of Colonial Marines on a search-and-rescue mission of a terraforming colony on the same planet where Ripley and crew in the first film encountered the Aliens. Ripley sees this mission as an opportunity to overcome her fears and to try to save others from going through what she went through.

On the planet LV-426, Ripley and the marines face many terrors, as it slowly becomes clear that military brawn is no match for the Aliens. Ripley, emerging as even more heroic than in the first film, rescues young Newt (the only survivor of the terraformers) and the admiring Hicks, last survivor of the Colonial Marines, and eventually escapes (with the help of the android Bishop) before the colony is blown up.

This film is rife with **transgressive** images and scenes. First, when Ripley and the others are awakened from cryo-sleep, they begin dressing in a coed room. And though all the classic masculine war themes are on parade—tough-talking cursing soldiers (men and women), a cigar-smoking Sergeant (Al Matthews), muscled biceps, and gun power—the soldiers themselves poke fun at these male demonstrations and symbols of power. In one scene, a soldier tells the Sergeant that cigars (traditionally a **phallic** symbol) can cause cancer (and potentially his death). In another, when told to get rid of their weapons because they are too close to the colony's nuclear reactor, a soldier sarcastically asks if they are supposed to attack the Aliens with "harsh language."

Over the course of the film, Ripley slowly emerges as a hardened warrior. She shows the tough soldiers, men and women, that she knows how to use a weapon and that her brand of toughness is more effective than symbols. While preparing for the trip, Ripley asks to be part of the action, rather than sit around and do nothing. The Sergeant lets her put her warehouse experience to use by manning a power loader to help load weapons onto the ship. Both Hicks and the Sergeant are visibly impressed with her skill. In another scene, Hicks tells Ripley that he has noticed that "she can handle herself." When Hicks teaches her how to use the marine weaponry, she learns rapidly and easily. By relying on the smarts of Newt to navigate through the complex and not just on gun power, Ripley demonstrates that toughness requires strategy, not just brawn.

Ripley shows herself to be transformative in other ways. When the unit is overwhelmed by the first Alien attack, it is Ripley who responds proactively, while Lt. Gorman (William Hope) freezes in fear. She takes the helm of the vehicle despite her fear, charging right through the walls of the colony complex to rescue the remaining soldiers. In several scenes, Ripley shows she is smarter than everyone else. For example, it is she who first deduces the existence of an Alien Queen. And when a potential romance is introduced between Ripley and Hicks, it is Hicks, the man, who takes on the subordinate role as love interest.

Ripley is not the only transformative tough female action hero. Vasquez's musculature, tough talk, and demeanor mark her as an obvious example of female toughness. But she is nevertheless revealed to be subordinate to Ripley and even to Newt, whose small and doll-like appearance belies the cool toughness and survival smarts she exhibits.

Film, television, and animation are replete with images of young female action heroes, and Newt is an often overlooked addition to the canon. Newt was nine years old when the terraformers, including her own family, were decimated by the Alien attack. She is found traumatized (like Ripley after her rescue in the opening scenes) and feral by Ripley and the marines. Newt's very existence is astounding, considering that all the other families were either killed or transformed into hosts for Alien parasites. Newt survives, not by might, strength, or gun prowess, but by intellect, courage, and the fact that she is small enough to easily scramble through the airshafts. Even she knows that brawn alone is not enough. Even she scoffs at the idea that the marines are going to be her knights in shining armor.

In a significant parallel to the Alien Queen, who attacks to protect her eggs, Ripley becomes a surrogate mother to Newt, equally bent on protecting her child at all costs. By taking on the mother role, Ripley is strengthened. Her mother's instinct—something no male hero ever had—functions as a source of power for Ripley, enabling her to overcome her fears and giving her the will to conquer. These two Titans slug it out in masculine fashion with a sort of "don't you forget it" brilliance.

In the subsequent film, Ripley's escape pod crashes on a penal colony planet peopled by male convicts who have served out their time but choose to live isolated from the rest of society, especially women. They blame women for their crimes (rape, assault, murder) and embrace a radical religion built around that theme. The men object to Ripley's presence; she is a woman and thus threatens the status quo and their "tranquility." Ultimately, they rely upon her strength and wit to save them.

The twist comes when Ripley discovers that she has been impregnated with a xenomorph. In Ripley's final act, she kills herself (and the Alien Queen that is just beginning to erupt from inside her). Her death not only shocks audiences but divides scholars. Some **read** her death as an empowering act; others interpret Ripley's death as a punishment for the transgressive role she played from the start. From any angle, Ripley demonstrated fortitude to end her own life in order to end the life of an Alien. This was her final act of power and strength.

In the final film, Ripley is brought back to life as a clone—part Alien, part human. As a clone, Ripley is a "superhuman: she has superior strength and speed, lightning reflexes, and heightened senses. Her acid blood burns through metal. [But] she is a freak" (Gallardo-C and Smith, 163). In essence, Ripley has become the ultimate action-hero fighting machine. She is tougher than the mercenaries (several men, one adult woman, one disabled male, and a young female android) she is thrown in with, who unwittingly supply live humans to be used in a malevolent plot to harvest Aliens for weapons research. She is undaunted by the military, who prefer the Alien clones over Ripley and keep her caged (like a slave or pet) and do not permit her to roam the outer space military science vessel. In the end, Ripley helps the surviving mercenaries escape, enabling their (and her) liberation from the science vessel by destroying her unredeemable Alien kin, and looks forward to a new life on Earth.

IMPACT

The *Alien* franchise was a huge success, spawning action figures, paraphernalia, games, comics, and movie spin-offs, as well as influencing the emergence of a string of new strong female roles in film, television, and video games. From the 1990s and onward, female action heroes (even those who appear girlier and sexier than Ripley) were so well represented that female toughness has increasingly become a conventional construct for new generations of boys and girls.

The *Alien* series also inspired several spin-offs. The director of *Alien vs. Predator* (2004) cast an African American woman, Sanaa Lathan, as the film's hero. *Alien vs. Predator: Requiem* (2007) features a mostly male cast of survivors. Overall, these films received poor reviews, and the protagonists would not eclipse the iconic status of Lieutenant Ellen Ripley.

See also Foxy Brown; Princess Leia; Sarah Connor.

FURTHER RESOURCES

Berg, Charles Ramirez. *Latino Images in Film: Stereotypes, Subversion, Resistance.* Austin: University of Texas Press, 2002.

Clover, Carol J. *Men, Women, and Chainsaws: Gender in the Modern Horror Film.* Princeton, NJ: Princeton University Press, 1992.

Gallardo-C, Ximena, and Jason C. Smith. *Alien Woman: The Making of Lt. Ellen Ripley.* New York: Continuum, 2004.

Grant, Barry Keith. *The Dread of Difference: Gender and the Horror Film.* Austin: University of Texas Press, 1996.

Jeffords, Susan. *Hard Bodies: Hollywood Masculinity in the Reagan Era.* Piscataway, NJ: Rutgers University Press, 1993.

The Greenwood Encyclopedia of Science Fiction and Fantasy: Themes, Works, and Wonders. Westport, CT: Greenwood Press, 2005.

Emma Peel is a spy in the British television series *The Avengers*. (AP Photo/ho.)

Emma Peel

Emma Peel was a secret agent, the second of three sidekicks who partnered John Steed on numerous high-action escapades in *The Avengers*, a British television show that ran for six sensational seasons between 1962 and 1969. However, there were gaps between the seasons, referred to as series in the United Kingdom, which were not all of the same length.

"Mrs. Peel," as she was famously called by Steed, was played by Diana Rigg, an attractive, tall, and svelte brunette. Rigg's character is considered one of the "toughest women in 1960s television" (Inness, 33). Peel (whose tenure lasted from 1965 to 1968) was one of a handful of precursors to the female action heroes who would appear in modest numbers in the mid-1970s and rise to critical and financial prominence in the 1990s and 2000s. Moreover, she was one of an even smaller number of women who fought with intensity and frequency. Skilled in judo and karate, Peel also fused her own style into her combat technique. But fighting was not the only talent for which she was celebrated. She was also known for her intelligence, imperturbable confidence, and the trend-setting black leather catsuit she wore. An intrinsically mysterious character, she matched wits and exchanged quips on a par with the sophisticated Steed.

Diana Rigg shot to stardom thanks to her portrayal of Peel in *The Avengers*. She was twice nominated for the prestigious American Emmy Award for Outstanding Continued Performance by an Actress in a leading role in a dramatic series. She was bested both times by Barbara Bain for her role as Cinnamon Carter, a secret government agent, in *Mission Impossible*, a popular American television series. Unlike Peel, who was a scientist and could hold her own in combat, Carter was depicted in more conventional ways as a **femme fatale** who had worked as a model before becoming a secret government agent. In 1969, Rigg played Countess Tracy di Vicenzo, James Bond's love interest in the film *On Her Majesty's Secret Service*. Succeeding ventures in film, the London stage, and series television in America attest to Rigg's staying power and skill, but nothing ever matched the attention Rigg received during her period with *The Avengers*.

The Avengers was a television show that was before its time, defying many of the conventions that restricted women's roles in television, film, as well as in society. Although Peel could be classified as Steed's female sidekick (she was referred to as a "talented amateur" in contrast to his "top professional") and was repeatedly rescued by him, she transcended her second billing every time she appeared on screen. Exchanging witticisms with conniving villains, she was never a vulnerable and powerless damsel in distress. Beautiful and sexy, she was never the femme fatale who relies more on sex appeal than on wits and physical prowess. Doughty and cool, Peel was the harbinger of every female action hero to come.

ORIGINS

Dr. David Keel (1961)

The Avengers emerged in the wake of a widely watched British series, *Police Surgeon*, starring Ian Hendry. Looking for a new series for the actor when *Police Surgeon* ended, Sydney Newman, a Canadian, was instrumental in coming up with the idea for *The Avengers*. The show, filmed in black and white, made its debut in the winter of 1961, with Hendry cast as Dr. David Keel, and was characterized as "combin[ing] toughness with compassion, and serv[ing] as the conscience of the team" (Rogers, 14).

In early episodes, John Steed (Patrick Macnee) was a hard-nosed character in a trench coat, an agent with a mysterious background. He was depicted as "a wolf with the women" and someone who "revels in trouble" (Rogers, 14). The two first met when Steed assisted Hendry in finding his fiancée's murderers. The other regular in the series was Carol Wilson (Ingrid Hafner), Keel's nurse and secretary. Although she assisted with some of the missions, her role was severely limited. She did not take part in the action, other than to play the damsel in distress. After Hendry left the show to pursue a movie career, Steed became the main character. All the producers needed was a sidekick.

Catherine Gale (1962–1964)

To fill Keel's spot on the show (although demoted to supporting-role status), producer Leonard White came up with a female character named Catherine Gale in an effort to create a "version of [an] emancipated young woman" (Rogers, 32). Gale can be said to be a product of the burgeoning **women's liberation movement** (now referred to as **second-wave feminism**). Women in developed countries aspired to break free of traditions that deprived them of protection from sexual harassment and gender **discrimination**; they wanted control over their bodies and career choices and unrestricted roles in society. In the early 1960s, such desires were considered revolutionary, if not radical. Women's liberation coincided and interacted with the **civil rights movement** in America, wherein African Americans demanded the end of racial discrimination and other racist practices.

Gale, played by Honor Blackman, was, in large part, the epitome of the spirit of resistance. Her existence belied the erroneous myth that femininity must equal vulnerability and weakness. Her depiction challenged the rampant typecasting of women in real life and on television as subordinate and inferior. In Blackman's own words, Gale was "the first feminist to come into

Bond Girls

Bond girls, who appear in the spy-thriller *James Bond* films, are notoriously voluptuous, glamorous, and frequent deadly. The most famous are known primarily for their appearance; usually scantily clad, these women are prey to the male gaze. Although multiple Bond girls can appear in a single film, some are more popular than others. For example, Ursula Andress, who played Honey Ryder in *Dr. No* (1962), appears in an iconic scene in a bikini on a beach (a number of Bond girls end up in similar scenarios).

Since the first Bond film in 1962, the Bond girls have played a number of roles. Some are portrayed as villains or MI6 spies; others serve no other purpose than to appear in scenes and look alluring. Some wind up in a relationship with Bond, the swarthy protagonist who has been played by Sean Connery, Roger Moore, and others. Most recently, Daniel Craig portrayed Bond in two films, *Casino Royale* (2006) and *Quantum of Solace* (2008). Although most of his romances are depicted as temporary, Bond was once given a wife, Tracy Di Vicenzo, played by Diana Rigg, in *On Her Majesty's Secret Service* (1969). He had a more serious love interest, Vesper Lynd (Eva Green) in *Casino Royale*, for whom he temporarily left the agency. Both women tragically died.

Although the Bond girls are almost always overshadowed by the suave protagonist-hero James Bond, the girls figure prominently in the series, and it is generally considered a coup for an actress to play one. What concerns some critics is that the Bond girls are largely objectified; they serve no other role than to make the male protagonist appear more cool and enviable to a predominately male audience. Moreover, the women are frequently positioned as victims, though this excludes some villains and agents who flaunt some spectacular combat moves.

a television serial; the first woman to fight back"; she was portrayed as a widowed "anthropologist, an academic, all brain and what she doesn't have in the way of brawn, she makes up for in motorbikes, black boots, leather combat suits and judo" (Rogers, 32). Margaret Mead, the acclaimed anthropologist, and Margaret Bourney-Smith, a celebrated photographer, served as inspiration for Gale's character and were real-life examples of women who dared to live adventurously and outside the barriers of conventionality.

The character of Gale did not have an easy birth. Blackman vocalized her dissatisfaction as scripts were reworked to reflect the switch from Keel to Gale. "My problem," she explained, "was that they continued to write it as they'd *always* written women's parts until then; she waited for the man to make the decision; she had no mind of her own and was incapable of any logical thought process" (Rogers, 32). Upon her husband's suggestion,

Blackman insisted that they keep the original scripts. The writers agreed, only making changes after Gale's character had been established. Ellen Ripley, the protagonist in *Alien* (1979), was another role that was originally written for a man. Director Ridley Scott kept the original script, and Ripley, like Gale, became a renowned female action hero. Gale, however, was depicted with more glamour than Ripley. With her glossy hair and sexy, fashionable outfits, Gale was a confluence of beauty, intelligence, and toughness.

Gale's presence was the most radical change in *The Avengers* at the start of the second season, but there were others. Steed was supplied with a new look—his trademark bowler hat, formal suits, and cane—and given an assortment of secret weapons and trick gadgets. He became impeccably well mannered, though he was ever ready with his sharp wit and double entendres. In the second season, Steed had three alternating assistants as the producers tried out various costars—Martin King (Jon Rollason), 3 episodes; Venus Smith (Julie Stevens), 6 episodes; and Cathy Gale, 17 episodes. Venus (as the name implies) was all glamour and no combat, with undertones of romantic interest in Steed. It is a fact that the show only began to hit its stride with Cathy Gale. Another change in the format of the show was the inclusion of "a lot of sexual fetishes, leather, bondage . . . but in a very very light way" (Rogers, 38). Macnee explained that the purpose of the fetishes was to tantalize audiences, and that "Cecil B. DeMille had been doing that in the 20s and the 30s, under much heavier censorship" (Rogers, 38). Others, such as Wonder Woman's creator, William Moulton Marston, did the same. Marston, a prominent psychologist, believed that audiences responded favorably to scenes wherein women were bound and gagged. The manacling of women in distress was a trademark of many early film series and **serials** and in early Wonder Woman comic book storylines. The practice served to escalate drama and was symbolically associated with sexual innuendo and sadomasochism. In the 1960s, fetishes, innuendo, and sex scenes were still largely taboo subjects. For that reason, *The Avengers* pushed the limits of tradition but did not traverse too far (e.g., real sex scenes were out of the question).

Gale enthralled British audiences. It is in no small part because of her success that female partners became the norm in the series. She not only sparked a fashion trend (the catsuit so identified with Peel was a Gale trademark first) but she showed the world, through her demeanor, combat skills, and gun use, that a woman could be just as tough as her partner.

After two seasons, Blackman, like Hendry, left the series to pursue a career in film. The 52 episodes she made of *The Avengers* were not shown in the United States until 1991. She starred in *Goldfinger* (1964), one of the most popular James Bond films, featuring Sean Connery as the debonair British agent Bond. She enjoyed a successful acting career that continues to this day.

Girl Heroes

Susan Hopkins, who wrote *Girl Heroes: The New Force in Popular Culture* (2002), had this to say about why the term *hero* is more relevant than *heroine* when referring to female heroes:

> The current generation of girls and young women won't accept submissive, weak and dependent role models. Their heroes are active and aggressive in pursuit of their own goals. I use the term "hero" deliberately, to distinguish this new breed of female character from the delicate, servile heroines of the past. To some extent the new girl hero is in fact anti-heroine—she is everything the traditional heroine was not supposed to be. Where the traditional heroine is dutiful, gentle and invariably "good," the new girl hero thrives on sexual and moral ambiguity . . . she has staked her own claim to the privileges of both femininity *and* masculinity. She is not the overly emotional victimized heroine—she does her own hunting, fighting and monster-slaying.

Source: Susan Hopkins, *Girl Heroes: The New Force in Popular Culture* (Annandale, Australia: Pluto Press, 2002), p. 3.

The Avengers comes to America: Emma Peel (1965–1967) and Tara King (1968–1969)

Emma Peel replaced Cathy Gale at the start of the show's third season. The following year, *The Avengers* was televised for the first time to American audiences, starting with the Emma Peel episodes. The increasingly popular show made the move to color in its fourth season.

In the 1960s, *The Avengers* stood out strikingly from all the other major dramas. For example, there was a recurring male official in the agency referred to as "Mother," and a female agent was once given the code name of "Father." This type of gender-blurring playfulness would have been frowned on in American television, where the majority of the shows reinforced conventional gender roles. In *The Andy Griffith Show* (1960–1968), males took the lead as sheriff, cops, and leaders in the conventional town of Mayberry, North Carolina; women functioned as love interests and nurturing characters like the matronly Aunt Bee. In *Hogan's Heroes* (1965–1971) men served in the army, while women, Helga and Hilda, worked as secretaries. In *I Dream of Jeannie* (1965–1970), a submissive and beautiful female genie complies with the wishes of a man she's in love with. *The Beverly Hillbillies* (1962–1971) featured stereotypical country folk who struck oil and became rich but did not eschew their humble origins. Out of all the characters, "Granny" was the most **transgressive**, speaking her mind freely and in one episode fighting men in a wrestling match.

Batman (1966–1968) and *Mission Impossible* (1966–1973) were among the few unconventional sitcoms of the time. *Batman* featured the villainous Catwoman, who was no less conniving and powerful than her male compeers. The producers, hoping that a female superhero would draw female audiences, introduced the character of Batgirl to the show. Before plans could be implemented to make Batgirl another of Batman's sidekicks, the series was canceled. *Mission Impossible* introduced a handful of female agents, but their power was portrayed in largely conventional ways. Cinnamon Carter and Lisa Casey were femme fatales, and Dana Lambert could not fight well.

Peel, on the other hand, was a masterful fighter, an expert with a variety of weapons, courageous, and forceful when she needed to be. Rigg quickly made the role her own, appearing as Steed's equal from the start. Indeed, the rapport between the two characters, and their obvious concern for each other's safety, had audiences speculating that they were romantically involved (a speculation only strengthened by the unfailingly polite use of "Mrs. Peel" by the dapper Steed). Emma Peel became, in short order, a household name in the United Kingdom and then in the United States. But after two seasons and 51 episodes, Diana Rigg, like her predecessors, decided to move on. Mr. Peel abruptly returned; Steed and Peel exchanged the last in a series of meaningful glances, this time imbued with shock and loss; and Emma Peel disappeared for good.

Steed was given yet another new partner, Tara King (Linda Thorson). King's depiction diverged markedly from her two catsuited predecessors. For starters, she was the only female partner to be single (Gale's husband had died; Peel's husband had been missing). She was also the most traditionally feminine of the bunch, relying from the first, "on feminine guile [rather] than muscular skill" (Rogers, 160). She was considered "soft, feminine and vulnerable, yet adventurous, resourceful and assertive when she had to be" (Rogers, 162). King appeared in only one season (33 episodes). *The Avengers* was cancelled following declining popularity due to the departure of Rigg and the fact that it could not compete on American television with the comedy show *Laugh-In*.

Sydney Newman

Sydney Newman was most noted for his instrumental role in creating two popular British television series, *The Avengers* and *Dr. Who*, a science fiction drama. Born in Toronto, Ontario, on April 1, 1917, Newman attended Central Technical School. He had wanted to make a career out of drawing film posters, but working directly in the film industry proved more profitable. He made the shift from film to television, and given his drive and innate creativity, Newman's career blossomed. After working for a time in New York, Newman was offered a job as a managing director of the Associated British Corporation (ABC) in the United Kingdom. He eventually became one of the big names in the television industry in that country, far from home, in the 1950s and 1960s.

Newman, who believed in stirring things up, wanted to change traditionally elitist British programming. He had a hand in the *Armchair Theater* anthology series, producing episodes that highlighted social issues. During the 1960s, an important decade for action TV, he launched several popular series, including *Police Surgeon*, *The Avengers*, and, after his move to the British Broadcasting Corporation (BBC), *Doctor Who*.

In the aftermath of his impactful television career, he worked in British film with less success. He returned to Canada in the 1970s and served in an assortment of positions, as chairman of the National Film Board of Canada, director of the Canadian Broadcasting Corporation (CBC), and special advisor on film to the Secretary of State. He died in 1997.

Diana Rigg

Rigg was born Enid Diana Elizabeth Rigg on July 20, 1938, in Doncaster, a large town in northern England. She was only two months old when her father, a railroad executive, moved the family to India, where they lived for eight years. She attended a boarding school in Fulneck, a village situated in an urban county, West Yorkshire, in England. Rigg began acting in her adolescence. She was 17 when she appeared in *The Caucasian Chalk Circle* (1955), a play that takes place after the end of World War II in the Soviet Union. In 1959, she joined the Royal Shakespeare Company, and in 1965, she tried out for the part of Emma Peel, allegedly, just for the fun of it. She got the part.

Following her departure from *The Avengers* in 1968, Rigg maintained a busy acting schedule in film, television, and the theater. She appeared in television series such as *Diana* (1973–1974), starring in the lead role as a divorced woman who moves from London to New York City and in several films, including *On Her Majesty's Secret Service* (1969), *The Assassination Bureau* (1969), *The Hospital* (1971), *Theater of Blood* (1973), *In This House of Brede* (1975), *A Little Night Music* (1977), *The Great Muppet Caper* (1981), and *Snow White* (1987). In the 1990s, she performed in plays, such as *Medea*, *Mother Courage*, and *Who's Afraid of Virginia Woolf?* Into the new millennium, she has appeared in musicals such as *A Little Night Music* and *Morecambe and Wise*.

Rigg has been married twice. Her first marriage was to Menachem Gueffen. Her second marriage, to Archibald Stirling, produced a daughter, who was born in 1977.

POWER SUIT, WEAPONS, AND ABILITIES

Peel was famous for her black leather catsuit and tall leather boots (also known as kinky boots). As noted, the iconic leather suit actually originated

Margaret Mead

Margaret Mead (1901–1978) was one of the best-known anthropologists in the world. She obtained her bachelor's degree (1923), master's degree (1924), and PhD (1929) during the era of the New Woman, when women in large numbers and immense zest tested the waters of independence, free-spiritedness, and the working life. Mead plunged bravely into a world dominated by men—academia (within the discipline of the social sciences)—and ventured off to foreign lands to do field study. She produced a number of seminal works, including *Coming of Age in Samoa* (1928), writing unabashedly about unconventional sexuality and behavior. Her work not only changed the face of anthropology but inspired young women, including her daughter, Mary Catherine Bateson, to follow in her footsteps.

with Cathy Gale, who required clothing that would give her mobility and had to be made out of material that would withstand numerous action sequences. In 1964, Honor Blackman and Patrick Macnee recorded the song "Kinky Books," promoting the trend of leather boots for women and young girls of any background. Boots, they crooned, that were once for men and symbolized masculinity could now be embraced by females too.

The fitted leather suits conveyed individuality, fashion, and toughness, as well as sexiness. The suit distinguished Peel from everyone else on the screen, for she was usually the only one in such attire. The suit also contrasted with and set her apart from Steed, who, in his flawless and tasteful suits, came across as conventional and proper.

Peel's catsuits set the mold (literally) for the outfit worn by the 1960s Catwoman, whose black leather made her disruptive, seductive, and powerful. Peel was not a villain, but she was not at all the typical ingénue, either, being far from wide-eyed and gullible. Despite the fact that her power clothing suits were **coded as** fetishes, she was not depicted as an overtly sexy woman, though the attraction between her and Steed was frequently plain to see. For a time, Peel's outfits were marketed to the mainstream, sparking a fashion craze.

Another symbol that signaled Peel's power was the Lotus Elan she drove. The Lotus is an extremely fast sports car. Historically, high speeds and sports cars are associated with masculinity, while women have a history of being depicted as incompetent drivers. The Lotus gave Peel social status, as well.

Peel was not only one of the most fashionable secret agents, she was also well balanced in terms of fighting skills and weapons expertise. Rigg performed much of her own stunt work (a fact that gave her moves excitement for viewers) and is given credit by many for being the first person to perform a karate kick on television. Peel expertly wielded a gun, sword, or any other object she could get her hands on. From the perspective of 21st-century audiences, the fighting sequences were very tame (this was true for men and women), but in the 1960s, a woman in active combat, especially against the opposite sex, in film or on television, was a groundbreaking, not to say earth-shattering event. Film and television would undergo several developments over the years before fight sequences would come to be as brutal and realistic as they currently are.

Indeed, Peel's martial arts skills surpassed many of her successors in action TV. Despite her super strength, The Bionic Woman never got into fisticuffs, preferring to push and shove her opponents. In "Winning is Everything," she shrank in her chair at the thought that she would have to enter a race car contest for an undercover mission (she was relegated to the passenger seat instead). Samantha in *Charlie's Angels* also cringed when she had to enter a race car contest. Intimidated at the thought that she had to win the race, she was told that all she had to do was to look the part. Whereas the other women of hit 1970s American shows were somewhat girly and giggly, Peel was mature, reserved, and somewhat stern.

VILLAINS

The villains of *The Avengers* generally changed from episode to episode but were always extremely dangerous and malicious, frequently two-dimensional, and occasionally campy. There was a science fiction comic book element to the show, illustrated by the fact that villains created fantastical machines or utilized malevolent means, like "a giant man-eating plant; torrential rainstorms; agents being brainwashed in a Manchurian concentration camp," as well as cybernauts and robots to disrupt society or foil Steed and Peel (Rogers, 91). Most of the villains were male.

In "Murdersville," an entire village engages in murderous activities. In "How to Succeed . . . at Murder," "a group of modern-day suffragettes intent on the elimination of all men" are the foes (Rogers, 118). As with the female adversaries in "How to Succeed . . . at Murder," feminism is frequently depicted in conflicting ways, echoing the discordant social perceptions of feminism in the real world. Feminists are sometimes represented as strong, progressive, but moderate women (like Peel) and sometimes as spiteful and extreme men haters who want to rule the world. Jade Fox, in the film *Crouching Tiger, Hidden Dragon* (2000), is an example of the extreme feminist, who murders a Wudan master who will not allow women into his school, steals a secret manual, and is depicted as a vengeful, witch-like villain.

THE AVENGERS

With a host of rogues at her heels, danger at every corner, and mysteries to solve, Peel was in her element. According to the Web site Avengers Forever,

Peel was born to wealthy parents and was destined to be a secret agent. At 21 years old, she became chairman of her father's corporation. Though endowed with book smarts (especially in the sciences), artistic talent, and heaps of analytical and combat skills, Peel did not take full advantage of her talents until after her husband, Peter Peel, a test pilot, was declared missing when his plane crashed, and then she was invited to partner with John Steed. Although Peel kept her married name and continued to use her married title, she was, according to Maria Alvarez, "a 'bachelor girl' with a bachelor pad and a bachelor lifestyle," though not in terms of sexual relations but rather in terms of having the freedom to do and to go whenever she pleased" (Alvarez, 16). Alvarez went as far as to regard Peel and John Steed as equals.

The banter between Steed and Peel was one of the highlights of every show, and one of the ways they were presented as equals. Peel was often sent out on solo missions as the "front man" for the team. Working in an undercover job in a lingerie department in "Death at Bargain Prices," Peel played the dominant role to unravel the mystery behind the murdered body found at the department store. When fighting, Peel was depicted as aggressive as, if not more so than, Steed, an impression that was reinforced by the fact that Patrick Macnee was clearly no athlete. Indeed, Peel handled her own fights even when Steed was present; he rarely lent a hand, knowing that she was more than capable.

For all of Peel's power and bravado, she was not completely bereft of the old **stereotypes**. For one thing, she dressed sexily. For another, she struck glamorous, provocative poses, as well as the stoic, don't-mess-with-me postures, in promotional photographs. Her name suggests her positioning as a sex object. Marie Donaldson, a press officer, used the industry phrase "Man Appeal" to denote part of Peel's character. From these two words came "M appeal," which was turned into Emma Peel (Rogers, 87). In several episodes, men acknowledged her beauty and sex appeal in a variety of ways, with a glance, or unabashed frankness. Steed himself flirted with Peel, and she flirted back from an electricity-charged distance. In response to other men's attentions, she was cool and nonchalant.

Peel was represented in other problematic ways. Sherrie A. Inness points to the episode "A Touch of Brimstone," wherein Peel is confronted by a man who threatens to whip her, while she is "dressed as the 'Queen of Sin,' complete with a corset, high leather boots, and an iron collar with three-inch spikes—transforming her into an object of male sado-masochistic sexual fantasy" (Inness, 36). In many episodes, Peel played the damsel in distress. In some episodes, such as in "The House that Jack Built," Peel rescues herself or rescues Steed. But in a score of other episodes, Peel is rescued by Steed, as in "The Gravediggers," wherein Peel is tethered to a railroad track and must be saved in the nick of time.

In the final episode featuring Peel and Steed together, Peel leaves secret agent work after her husband surfaces. This implies that married women

Tough Women and Girls Who Are Weapons

Female action heroes don't only have to know how to use a gun, a sword, or a flamethrower, some women *are* the weapons. In *The Fifth Element* (1997), Milla Jovovich plays the titular character, who is an essential piece of the weapon that will destroy the Great Evil that plans to destroy the world. Milla is a weapon in a slight, feminine body, swaddled scantily in white strips of fabric, with flaming-orange hair and a girlish babbling voice. In appearance, Milla's character looks childlike and thin, but her fighting skills and the fact that she is a deadly weapon make her the most formidable character in the film.

In *Serenity* (2007), River Tam (Summer Glau) is an adolescent girl with doe-like eyes, an oval face, and long hair who appears to be mute and benign—except when someone blurts out the magic words that set her off fighting. She turns out to be the psychic fighting machine the nemesis of the film desires to claim. When her powers are unleashed, she becomes a flurry of martial arts kicks and hand moves, single-handedly hurling men triple her size across the room.

Other women or female entities whose powers and extraordinary abilities were coveted by corrupt and evil agents were Jean Gray/Phoenix in *X-Men: The Last Stand* (2006) and the Alien Queens who appeared in the *Alien* film series.

must return to respectable roles in the domestic sphere—that work, especially careers fraught with peril, is tolerable for single women but not for women with husbands or families.

IMPACT

The Avengers had a pronounced effect on the world. Even before Emma Peel reached American shores, at least forty countries were already hooked on the series. America received *The Avengers* with a certain degree of trepidation. The dry British humor and sexual innuendo were not what conservative audiences were used to or wanted. Indeed, the show never did as well in mainstream America as expected. But that did not lessen its influence one iota.

The character of karate-fighting Emma Peel had an immediate influence on other female action heroes. For a time, Wonder Woman underwent a dramatic change in the comic books, morphing into an Emma Peel-like character who was into fashion and an expert martial artist. Although *The Avengers* had been canceled in 1969, the series returned as *The New Avengers* in 1976. Steed, still played by Patrick Macnee, was given two new sidekicks, Mike Gambit (Gareth Hunt) and Purdey (Joanna Lumley). In 1998, *The Avengers* film was released to theaters. John Steed was played by Ralph Fiennes and Emma Peel was played by Uma Thurman, who was a hit in the *Kill Bill* film series.

Peel's influence on female action heroes was like a dominant gene that reappeared in every subsequent generation: the catsuit, the karate, the wry quips, and the combo of looks and intelligence. Starting the year after *The Avengers* ended, women regularly appeared on television as cops, detectives, and undercover agents. Some were only sidekicks, but as time went on, more and more stood alone as tough heroines who could do it all.

See also The Bionic Woman; Catwoman; Charlie's Angels.

FURTHER RESOURCES

Alvarez, Maria. "Feminist Icon in a Catsuit." *New Statesman* 11 (1998): 16.

Inness, Sherrie A. *Tough Girls: Women Warriors and Wonder Women in Popular Culture*. Philadelphia: University of Pennsylvania Press, 1999.

Mainon, Dominique, and James Ursini. *The Modern Amazons: Warrior Women On-Screen*. Pompton Plains, NJ: Limelight Editions, 2006.

Mitzejewski, Linda. *Hardboiled and High Heeled: The Woman Detective in Popular Culture*. New York: Routledge, 2004.

O'Day, Marc. "Of Leather Suits and Kinky Boots: *The Avengers*, Style, and Popular Culture." In *Action TV: Tough Guys, Smooth Operators, and Foxy Chicks*, ed. Bill Osgerby and Anna Gough-Yates. New York: Routledge, 2001.

Rogers, Dave. *The Complete Avengers: The Full Story of Britain's Smash Crime-Fighting Team!* New York: St. Martin's Press, 1989.

The Avengers Forever. http://theavengers.tv/forever/guide.htm.

Tracy, Kathleen. *Diana Rigg: The Biography.* Dallas: BenBella, 2003.

White, Rosie. *Violent Femmes: Women as Spies in Popular Culture*. New York: Routledge, 2007.

the film *Foxy Brown*. (Courtesy:

Foxy Brown was the African American vigilante of the titular film released in 1974. Pam Grier, who played Foxy Brown, is known as the "Queen of Blaxploitation" for her multiple roles as an afro-sporting, tough-talking, gun-wielding action heroine in a string of B-flicks in the 1970s. Foxy Brown combined sex appeal with traditional female traits, black consciousness, independence, and aggression to create an archetypal *superwoman*, a term denoting a positive and empowered archetype. This was an unprecedented depiction, considering that film producers did not, as a norm, give strong, leading roles to either African American men or women. Generally, blacks received negative and **stereotypical** roles. Indeed, Brown's starring role in *Coffy* (1973), the precursor to *Foxy Brown* (1974), placed her in two remarkable categories as the first female action hero in a full-length American film and the first female African American action hero created deliberately for urban black audiences.

The so-called **blaxploitation** films, first starring male protagonists and shortly thereafter female heroes, were a mainstay in theaters between 1970 and 1975. To some blacks—particularly the middle and upper classes—the term has negative connotations. The National Association for the Advancement of Colored People (NAACP), the leading civil rights organization, frequently publicly denounced films of this genre. Nonetheless, blaxploitation, a film genre that was characterized by violence, sex, nudity, posturing, and black slang and was replete with emblems of urban life—drugs, prostitution, pimps, corrupt villains, and **racism**—was, at the beginning, geared toward and received with enthusiasm by black audiences and eventually spread to mainstream audiences. The films were raw (if not campy) and frequently flawed. Although blaxploitation films were made on low budgets and were thus less glossy and realistic than mainstream films, profits were high.

The films were all the rage largely because the characters, the subject matter, and the plots resonated with African Americans living in poverty in drug- and crime-infested cities where racism was rampant, and where the influence of militancy and black power and nationalism of the mid-1960s still lingered. The films were also popular because black heroes, male or female, were a novelty and filled a gaping need. Blaxploitation films introduced the first ever strong, assertive African American role models, heroes whom black youth could look up to. Historically, African Americans had been stripped of power—economic, social, and political—beginning in slavery days, and denied culturally relevant figures in the media. African American women in particular suffered numerous negative depictions and challenges. Black women did not fit the beauty ideal, nor were they permitted to exert much power, either in the media or in society. Brown, as well as subsequent African American female action stars such as Tamara Dobson, Jeannie Bell, and Teresa Graves, with their tour-de-force performances, changed that.

ORIGINS

Images of Black Women in Film

Foxy Brown and her compeers drastically challenged the historical images of black women in film. In the early years of film, the roles blacks played reflected their inferior status in mainstream society. **Racism, discrimination, segregation**, and exclusion were a way of life for most African Americans. One of the earliest troublesome images for blacks was the black face, wherein white men painted their faces black and parodied stereotypical black behavior, speech patterns, music, and appearance. This form of entertainment was offensive to many. Among the many negative images of black women were the mammy, the tragic mulatta, and the matriarch.

The mammy was a ubiquitous image in early films, particularly during the 1930s and 1940s. In real life, many African American women worked in the capacity of a domestic in white households, cleaning, washing, caring for babies and children, and frequently providing emotional support. The mammy figure was frequently characterized as portly, cheerful, puritanical, religious, and dark complected. This stereotype was fueled by the real-life subjugation of black women in domestic roles and erroneous perceptions of ideal racial relations. Actress Hattie McDaniel is arguably the most famous mammy figure; she won an Oscar for her supporting role in *Gone with the Wind* (1939). Lena Horne in the 1930s and Dorothy Dandridge in the 1950s were frequently **typecast** as the tragic mulatta, a biracial woman who is reduced to an exotic "sex object," "entertainer," "seductress," and "mistress," often meeting a tragic or fatal end (Sims, 37, 38, 39).

In sharp contrast to the obsequious mammy and the powerless, immoral "tragic mulatta" images, the matriarch image emerged in the 1960s, largely in response to the Moynihan Report of 1965. This report, prepared during a period of intense rioting in black communities, was an attempt to address the tumultuous history of blacks in America and the inequities and assorted issues that continued to embroil many blacks in poverty, crime, and general crisis. The report reasoned that, among other things, racism and single-mother-led homes (the matriarch figure) were largely at fault. The matriarch was depicted as an aggressive, dominant, and controlling black female figure, frequently an impoverished single mother on welfare.

These images plagued the portrayal of black women in film for many decades. Although black directors employed black actors and actresses in films referred to as "race films," which were popular between 1927 and 1948, women were generally cast in passive roles. The era of the **civil rights movement** yielded films like *Porgy and Bess* (1959), directed by a Jewish American, which featured an African American heroine (tragic mulatta) addicted to drugs and involved in an abusive relationship, and *A Raisin in the Sun* (1961), a film that incorporates the matriarch image. Although these

Vigilante Women

There is no shortage of women in film who take the law into their own hands, meting out justice vigilante style. Vigilante women pop up in myriad film genres. The film *The Shooting* (1966) featured Millie Perkins as "The Woman" who hired a gunslinger and two guides and relentlessly scoured the oppressively hot Western frontier to avenge the death of an undisclosed person. Although she was small framed, with a dainty woman's voice, and couldn't even carry her own travel bags, she talked tough, demanded her own way, and shot with surety and without remorse. In the end, her unfulfilled quest led to her own demise. Other vigilante women in the Western genre include Ellen, also known as "The Lady," who lived a solitary and hard life in search of her father's killer in *The Quick and the Dead* (1995). The Lady entered a gun-shooting contest and, with the help of a thug-turned preacher, was able to fulfill her long quest of vengeance. In *Enough* (2002), Slim (Jennifer Lopez), a victim of spouse abuse, learns self-defense, overcomes her fears, and emerges triumphant. In *Kill Bill* (2003), "The Bride" (Uma Thurman) is no stereotypical victim of tragedy when everyone at her wedding is killed. She mounts a relentless attack on those she holds responsible. Erica Bain (Jodie Foster) declares war on the gang that murdered her fiancé in *The Brave One* (2007).

films were considered important contributions to African American film history, they reinforced negative stereotypical perceptions of black women.

The emergence of the black hero, as the film industry finally opened up to African Americans in the 1970s, was a radical shift, brought about largely because of several social changes taking place. Civil rights activism and the gains it produced, such as the Civil Rights Act of 1964 that eliminated segregation, the Voting Rights Act of 1965 that empowered black voters, and many poverty programs, helped start the process of leveling the economic, political, and social playing fields and brought the plight of blacks to mainstream consciousness. The mid-1960s saw the emergence of a formidable black power movement. Black power proponents advocated black pride, assertiveness, and a militant response to white domination, racism, and oppression, challenging the racist view that black race was inferior. When, in the same period, blacks rioted in their communities in cities in the North, they demonstrated an aggression that had long been suppressed, particularly in the South, where backlash from law enforcement and racist white organizations like the Ku Klux Klan was immediate, brutal, and often fatal.

Second-wave feminism also appeared in the 1960s (women also benefited from the civil rights gains) but its influence among black women was limited.

Many black women did not feel welcome in the movement, which comprised mostly middle- and upper-class white women. Black women felt that their experiences and issues were different, as historically, black women contended with a complex set of issues concerning race and gender. For example, black women were always expected to work, while middle-class white women fought for the right to work. During slavery, black women were depicted as beasts of burden, whereas white women were regarded as delicate and weak. As a result of these differences, black women eventually formed their own brand of feminism, known as black feminism.

The rapid social changes of the 1960s, a flourishing black consciousness, and the fact that militant personas appeared regularly in the news (Malcolm X, Huey P. Newton, Elaine Brown, and Angela Davis) helped to inspire new African American roles in film and television. African American males were the first to benefit. Black men appeared in films as cowboys, detectives, and super bad (tough) urban action heroes. Blaxploitation films such as *Shaft* (1971), *Superfly* (1972), and a stream of others, were among the most popular. These films depicted African American men who swaggered, dressed to the rhythms of black fashion trends, used black slang—all set to the sounds of popular black music forms, funk and soul. These films frequently glorified street culture and all that it entailed—pimps, prostitution, and criminality. Above all else, black males were permitted to appropriate power, wield weapons, and assert dominance in their environment. Urban black audiences, who had been so long without a black hero in film, television, or comic books, were ecstatic.

American International Pictures launched Pam Grier, the first major female African American blaxploitation star, in 1973. Many had issue with the depiction of black women in these films, as the women frequently appeared with little or no clothing and relied heavily on sex appeal to achieve their goals. It was as if these characters were created for little else than to be subjected to the **male gaze** and to be framed as an object of male fantasy. Black scholars called her a "superwoman." According to Ida Banks, "the superwoman image presented black women as the action heroines of their communities, willing to protect family and community by any means necessary. The superwoman image portrayed black women as strong and invincible. The message was sent that black women could endure and overcome all odds"; moreover, she was "empowering and intimidating" (Banks, 78, 80).

American International Pictures

Established in 1954 by Jim Nicholson and Samuel Arkoff, American International Pictures (AIP) specialized in producing low-budget films. Independent from the mainstream film industry, AIP wielded more control over the films they wanted to make. Whereas mainstream studios showed no interest in films with radical inner-city black heroes and maintained mainstream and

Fannie Lou Hamer: A Tough Woman of the Civil Rights Movement

Men were not the only ones at the forefront of the action during the civil rights movement. Women like Fannie Lou Hamer (1917–1977) labored to help better the racial climate in America and obtain basic rights for and address the needs and issues of all marginalized citizens. In the 1960s, economic, political, and social oppression was prevalent in most African American communities.

Fannie Lou Hamer, a descendant of slaves and a former sharecropper born in Montgomery County, Mississippi, was a major player on the national level. As vice chair of the Mississippi Freedom Democratic Party, she bravely retold the story of her traumatic incarceration after registering to vote and spoke of the perils of living in a racist society at the 1964 Democratic National Convention in Atlantic City, New Jersey. Armed with her faith in God and her arsenal of spirituals, Hamer waged a campaign to increase black voting and political power in her home state of Mississippi. She provided food and opportunities for poor blacks and lent a hand to other civil rights projects. She also protested against the discriminatory and heinous practices of sterilizing poor women of color.

middle-class objectives and values, AIP built their success on a subversive formula, "appealing to a different audience," casting "unknown" actors, following "current popular trends" and producing "cheap movies that, while perhaps lacking in artistic quality, were profitable as double features at drive-ins, which appealed to much of the youth market." The studio "earned its reputation by shamelessly copying and mass-marketing trends or whatever social problem received great publicity in American culture" (Sims, 62). Many of AIP's early films dealt with rebellious youth.

In the mid- to late 1960s, the eruption of riots in black neighborhoods put black urban communities in focus. In 1971, African American director Melvin Van Peeble's *Sweet Sweetback's Baadasssss Song* was released and was a box office success. Black culture, complete with afros, music, and hip ways of talking came into vogue, and AIP planned its campaign. Its first film, *Coffy*, directed by Jack Hill and starring Pamela Grier, about a vigilante black nurse who rescues her community, was a phenomenal success. Rather than create a sequel to that film, Jack Hill directed *Foxy Brown*, a film intended to stand on its own.

Jack Hill

Jack Hill was a prominent writer and director of blaxploitation films. He is also white. A number of white males directed so-called black action films, profiting off a genre that was made for African Americans. Hill's prolific career is examined in a biography written by British writer Calum Waddell in *Jack Hill: The Exploitation and Blaxploitation Master, Film by Film* (2009). Born on January 28, 1933, in Los Angeles, California, Hill is responsible for having helped create the black female action hero persona. He wrote the screenplay for and directed *Coffy* (1973) as well as *Foxy Brown* (1974). The themes and depictions of blacks were considered stereotypical and problematic for some, and the fact that Hill was white anguished many blacks because, among many reasons, they saw his role as a continuation of historical racial exploitation. Hill contends that though he took his job seriously, "AIP had nothing but contempt for the audience they were making movies for. Not just the Black audience but the whole audience that they made movies for. They didn't understand Black pictures. . . . I had to really fight to keep elements in the picture that I felt the audience would respond to" (Sims, 128).

Pam Grier

Pam Grier, whose appearance in films of the 1970s gave her cult status as a symbol of male fantasy on the one hand and a superwoman on the other, has devoted her life to acting. During the height of her fame, Grier challenged writers, producers, and directors to give more depth to the characters she portrayed, and she has long defended her roles against critics who deemed her characters **sexist** and offensive.

Pamela Suzette Grier was born on May 26, 1949, in Winston-Salem, North Carolina. Her father, Clarence Ransom Grier, was a mechanic and technical sergeant in the United States Air Force. Her mother, Gwendolyn Sylvia, was a nurse. Brown has two siblings, a brother and a sister. She was popular in high school (East High School in Denver, Colorado). She performed in plays and participated in beauty contests.

Although Grier planned to attend Metropolitan State College in Denver, she instead moved to Los Angeles, California, landing a job as a receptionist at AIP. Jack Hill, a white film director at AIP, cast Grier in prison films such as *The Big Doll House* (1971) and *The Big Bird Cage* (1972). In *The Big Doll House*, Brown plays a supporting character, a bisexual prostitute who, along with several other women, is being tormented by a female warden and guard. In *The Big Bird Cage*, Grier plays Blossom, the tough, gun-wielding girlfriend of a revolutionary. She and another woman execute a breakout from a women's prison.

The film *Coffy* (1973) pushed Grier to the forefront of an entirely new genre of film, blaxploitation. After *Foxy Brown*, Grier went on to starring roles in *Friday Foster* (1975) and *Sheba, Baby* (1975). In the wake of her brief but shimmering action hero career, Grier took on traditional female roles. She was a prostitute in *Fort Apache the Bronx* (1981), a witch in

Something Wicket this Way Comes (1983), and a detective sidekick in *Above the Law* (1988). Finally, in 1997, director Quentin Tarantino cast Brown as the title character, a flight attendant turned tough hero (she helps take down a big-time smuggler), in *Jackie Brown*. In 2004, she played Kit Porter in the HBO television series *The L Word* and a minor role as a recurring character in the television series *Law and Order: Special Victims Unit*. Grier has never married.

POWER SUIT, WEAPONS, AND ABILITIES

Foxy Brown is notorious for her curvaceous body and aggressiveness, which translate into her wardrobe, her arsenal of weapons, and her ability to be tough. She exhibits multiple looks in the film. For the first, she wears classy, conservative pantsuits, indicating her status as an ordinary, independent career woman (her occupation is never identified). Brown's wardrobe is surprisingly conservative, considering the hype that surrounds her figure and the emphasis on her shapely body in the film's opening credits. In those credits, audiences get glimpses of Brown in a sultry, Bond-girl-imitation silhouette, dancing provocatively. This is her second look, which is also seen as the cameras get close-up and full-body shots of Brown in a bikini. For the third look, she has a black leather outfit, in which she mixes dance moves with karate kicks.

In the early scenes (before her boyfriend dies), Brown is confident, independent, has a home of her own, and has a boyfriend—an image that reflects the progressive woman of the 1970s who is a product of the changes brought on by second-wave feminism. Brown is a multifaceted woman, one that is conventional, oozes sexuality, and becomes an agent of action. The image also implies that Brown would have maintained her normalcy if only the villains had left her brother and boyfriend alone. In the theme song, a sonorous voice—a vintage 1970s sound—sings, "don't make her angry, or you'll find out she's super bad." For Brown, anger is a catalyst for action.

In other scenes, Brown is transfigured as a symbol of power and sex appeal. Brown wears various disguises, working undercover to solve crime vigilante style (Brown is not a member of law enforcement). Brown exposes her body in lingerie and sexy outfits in many scenes. In one scene, in which she goes undercover as a prostitute, she wears the wardrobe of the profession (body-clinging dresses) and strips down to lingerie. Although from one perspective these outfits position Brown in a stereotypical female role and as a sex object (male action heroes don't use their bodies to get what they're after), some scholars claim that Brown uses her sensuality as a weapon, and that in the scenes where she exudes sensuality, she has the upper hand over the men, whom she easily foils with her feminine power.

Brown also wears wigs, covering up her afro. The wigs (straight hair styles) allow her to achieve an instant Hollywood glamour look, one that

Elaine Brown and the Black Panthers

At the heels of the civil rights movement of the 1960s, which promoted nonviolence and integration, a new movement emerged among blacks in the urban North. The Black Power Movement did not espouse one single ideology but rather comprised an array of alternative perspectives. Generally, the movement inspired Afrocentric regalia, like African shirts, called dashikis, natural hair styles such as afros (unstraightened black hair that is combed into a round shape), and advocated a militant reaction to racist attacks on the black community, which faced serious disparities and social problems. Some black power leaders advocated separatism, rejected assimilation into American culture, and even encouraged rioting to protest adverse conditions in black ghettos.

In this context, Huey P. Newton and Bobby Seale founded the Black Panther Party for Self-Defense in 1966 in Oakland, California. Originally, this organization was established to monitor encounters between law enforcement and locals. Police officers were notorious for harassing and abusing African Americans and unfairly singling out black men for crimes they did not commit. The Black Panthers wore uniforms (black berets, leather jackets, blue shirts, and black pants) and wielded guns during patrols.

In 1974, Elaine Brown (b. 1943) became the first woman to chair the Black Panther Party. Born and raised in the rough neighborhoods of Philadelphia, Pennsylvania, Brown had no problem challenging the chauvinistic tendencies of some of the male members. Backed up by armed guards, Brown led with a no-nonsense style and spoke in a quick and aggressive speaking style that writers have referred to as rapid-fire. Under her leadership, the organization thrived, although the Black Panthers increasingly became associated with controversial criminal activities. Brown's leadership ended in 1977. She has written an autobiography, *A Taste of Power* (1992), and continues to lecture nationwide, advocating for the poor and protesting the racial inequities that remain in the judicial system and in law enforcement.

historically has been codified as acceptable and ideal, demonstrating that Brown knows how to manipulate her look in order to achieve a certain effect. Not all critics approve of disguises on women, but the ploy has been used by many female action heroes over the years (Emma Peel, Charlie's Angels, The Bionic Woman, and the **protagonist** in Alias). Scholar Sherrie A. Inness contends that tough action heroines are often "undermined in a variety of ways, such as through [their] repeated use of masquerade and disguise" (Inness, 35). Indeed, male heroes are rarely seen in disguise. When they want something, they simply break down or gun down a door to get it.

Brown's third look is coded as her most powerful, as evidenced in the culminating scene when Brown confronts Miss Katherine, the leader of an illicit organization. In this scene, Brown sheds her disguises, reveals her afro, and stands in a cool poise in a black leather outfit. Afros, worn since the mid 1960s by college students, were considered outward symbols of resistance to mainstream culture and were a way for students to reclaim their roots, challenging the centuries-old construct that unstraightened hair was inferior to silky, Caucasian hair. In the black power movement, the Afro was a symbol of militancy, black pride, and the new assertiveness that was sweeping over a generation of young African Americans. For Brown, the Afro made her relevant to 1970s black audiences, coded her as being connected with her African American heritage, and gave her power.

The black leather outfit or long leather trench jacket were staples of many blaxploitation films. This fashionable outfit confers coolness and status upon the hero, a status that was much more relevant to black communities then the spandex and patriotic costumes that characters like Superman and Wonder Woman wore. This look has been imitated in television and film. For example, in "Fool for Love," an episode that flashes back to the 1960s, in the television series *Buffy the Vampire Slayer* (1997–2003), a character named Spike kills an African American vampire slayer. The slayer is African American, tall, strong, and she wears an afro and an ankle-length black-leather coat. Spike takes the coat, wearing it throughout the series.

Tough Talk, Gun, Bar Stool, Fists, and Airplane

Brown makes use of a number of weapons to vanquish her foes. Traditionally, women in society were expected to keep quiet, to speak softly (and politely), and to refrain from violence or weapons associated with violence. Images of women fumbling with guns, shooting clumsily and off mark, and wielding small "ineffective" firearms are replete throughout the history of film. Brown challenges the stereotypical images of women and symbols of toughness. In this, Brown is imaginative, resourceful, and commanding.

In an early scene, Brown speeds in her car, cursing at the villain who topples onto her car and clings on. She swerves the car until he falls off, then picks up her brother, whom she has come to rescue, and speeds away. In other scenes, Brown uses rapid-fire talk to intimidate others, including her brother, when she demands that he give her the name of the person (Katherine Wall) who ordered her boyfriend's murder. When her tough talk does not work, she grazes her brother's ear with a bullet from the handgun her deceased boyfriend recently gave her so that she could learn how to use it. Brown is a quick study.

In another scene, Brown takes on women in a Lesbian bar who attack her when she comes to the rescue of a woman she met while undercover. She uses a bar stool and instinctive, raw fighting techniques, overcoming even a woman who boasts that she is a martial arts expert. (Most female action heroes will come to use some form of martial arts fighting techniques; Emma Peel of the 1960s British television show *The Avengers*, was among the forbears of the practice.) And in one of the final action scenes, Brown gets in the cockpit of a plane and drives it through the midst of the big fight between the gang she has enlisted to help her and the villains.

VILLAINS

Mob members are the villains in *Foxy Brown*. In most blaxploitation films, corrupt and racist whites are usually portrayed as antagonists, reflecting 1970s attitudes toward the dominant white culture and incorporating the themes, experiences, and issues that were relevant to black communities from slavery onward. At the top of the hierarchy of the white mob is a woman named Miss Katherine (Kathryn Loder) and her boyfriend, Steve Alias (Peter Brown). In scenes taking place at mob headquarters, Brown is called a "broad," a sexist term, and Brown's boyfriend is referred to as a "nigger," a racist epithet. This mob is the same organization that loaned $20,000 to Foxy Brown's brother, Link Brown (Antonio Fargas), and then hunted him down to force him to pay back what he owed. They also enslave women to prostitution. In one scene a villain says, "give me a sawed-off shot gun. We're gonna kill us some nigger." This invokes imagery from the harrowing years following slavery, when African Americans were routinely hunted down by racist whites in many parts of the South.

FOXY BROWN, THE FILM

Slavery is a prominent theme in *Foxy Brown*, and Brown takes a hard-hitting approach to the subject. In the film, drugs are referred to as the "new slavery." To be sure, poor African American neighborhoods in the inner city during the 1970s were ravaged by drugs and crime. But Brown has nothing to do with drugs. She harangues her brother for his bad choices (resorting to selling drugs and getting involved with criminals); he feels he has no other options.

Brown refuses to be a victim to society or to anyone; moreover she helps others by deed and example. When she meets Claudia, a prostitute who is hooked on drugs and bound to an illicit organization fronting as a model agency led by Katherine, Brown, who is working undercover as a prostitute, encourages her to go back home to her husband and son. In one scene, she rescues Claudia from a female predator in a bar, and in another she wrestles with the bad guys, thus enabling Claudia to escape. After Katherine discovers Brown's true identity, she has Brown tortured and then sent to an intermediate location called "the ranch" to be processed before being sent out to Haiti for a life of sexual enslavement (Haiti was one of the regions African slaves were sent during slavery times). Brown's processing is horrific. She is bound to a bed while a miscreant forces heroin into her veins and rapes her. Heroically, Brown, using a razor on a nearby dresser, loosens her constraints, stabs a man with a hanger, and blows up the drug house.

Brown's toughness extends beyond her refusal to be a victim. When her boyfriend and brother are murdered, she does not linger in pain or feelings of powerlessness, but instantly moves into action, choosing the way of the vigilante over the law. This is a common choice for action heroes, like the sharp shooter Ellen, in *The Quick and the Dead* (1995), whose presence and skill disrupt the traditional Western film, though she succeeds in shooting and killing the man who murdered her father. As a vigilante, Brown works outside the law, on the fringes of normal society. In this way, she is free to do as she pleases.

Brown is tough, but she is not entirely the "one chick hit squad" the theme song proposes. Although many male action heroes have been portrayed as one-man armies, female action heroes are often dependent on others for support. In the first *Alien* movie, Ellen Ripley finishes off the alien and escapes, assuming the status of last person standing; but in subsequent films, she works with others. Depending on the scholar, this dependence can either be a good thing or a bad thing. Dependence undermines traditional male heroism, but it also challenges the concept of individualism. Brown enlists the aid of a local grassroots gang of all-male vigilantes to attack Katherine's hoodlums in the climactic scene near the film's end. While the men shoot with guns, Brown drives a plane, creating havoc for the adversaries.

In a raw and surprising scene, men from the grassroots gang that she got together to fight the mob castrate Katherine's boyfriend (castration was a method employed by racists when terrorizing or lynching black males in the early 20th century). Brown delivers the item personally to Katherine. "I want you to live," Brown tells her, ". . . I want you to suffer." In the end, Brown gets her revenge.

IMPACT

Foxy Brown and the other women of blaxploitation cinema are credited with being among the progenitors of the female action hero in American film. AIP and other studios were able to create these heroines because they did so independently of the major studios that relied on the traditional male hero archetype. Even so, as Yvonne D. Sims points out, the female action hero was not new; she had "appeared for quite some time in martial arts movies made in Hong Kong and Taiwan" (Sims, 17). Sims asserts that the women of the blaxploitation films not only "paved the way for other action heroines, but also redefined the ways in which women in general were represented in film by portraying a new character who held her own among men *and* women" (Sims, 17). Succeeding female action heroes, however, would rely less on baring their bodies and seducing men.

See also The Bionic Woman; Storm.

FURTHER RESOURCES

Banks, Ingrid. "Women in Film." In *African Americans and Popular Culture: Theatre, Film, and Television*, ed. Todd Boyd. Westport, CT: Praeger, 2008.

Collins, Patricia Hill. *Black Feminist Thought: Knowledge, Consciousness, and the Politics of Empowerment*. New York: Routledge, 2000.

Guerrero, Ed. *Framing Blackness: The African American Image in Film*. Philadelphia: Temple University Press, 1993.

Inness, Sherrie A. *Tough Girls: Women Warriors and Wonder Women in Popular Culture*. Philadelphia: University of Pennsylvania Press, 1999.

Long Island University. "African-Americans in Motion Pictures: The Past and the Present." http://www.liu.edu/cwis/cwp/library/african/movies.htm.

Pennicott, Elaine. "'Who's the Cat That Won't Cop Out?' Black Masculinity in American Action Series of the Sixties and Seventies." In *Action TV: Tough Guys, Smooth Operators and Foxy Chicks*, ed. Bill Osgerby and Anna Gough-Yates. New York: Routledge, 2001.

Sims, Yvonne D. *Women of Blaxploitation: How the Black Action Film Heroine Changed American Popular Culture*. Jefferson, NC: McFarland and Company, 2006.

Taylor, Quintard. BlackPast.org. http://www.blackpast.org.

Waddell, Calum. *Jack Hill: The Exploitation and Blaxploitation Master, Film by Film*. Jefferson, NC: McFarland and Company, 2009.

Lieutenant Jordan O'Neil in the film *G.I. Jane*. (Courtesy: Everett Collection.)

G.I. Jane

"G.I. Jane" functions doubly as the title of the movie that stars Demi Moore as fictional military hero Jordan O'Neil and as the moniker conferred upon O'Neil during the film. *G.I. Jane* (1997) is considered one of Moore's most transformative roles. She shaved her head and bulked up during the course of filming to power through one-handed push-ups and the myriad physical obstacles that were part of the ultra-strenuous training regime for the fictional Navy Special Reconnaissance program. O'Neil's participation in the training program was a test case to presumably integrate the special male-only units (combat, special operations, etc.) of the military. Director Ridley Scott, whose father and oldest brother served in the military, based his movie on the real-life United States Navy Sea, Air and Land Forces, otherwise known as Navy SEALS, which continues to prohibit women. Scott addressed head-on the issues and colossal challenges and struggles a woman in such circumstances might experience. In the end, he showed that O'Neil could not only survive, but triumph in a world constructed for masculinity.

According to Linda Ruth Williams in "Ready for Action: *G.I. Jane, Demi Moore's Body and the Female Combat Movie*," O'Neil's character emerged during a major shift in the portrayal of male action heroes. Actors who played iconic male heroes were suddenly being cast in "sensitive roles"; for example, Arnold Schwarzenegger, of *Conan* and *Terminator* fame, starred in *Kindergarten Cop* (1990) and *Junior* (1994); Harrison Ford, famous for his appearances as Han Solo in the *Star Wars* films and as Indiana Jones in the eponymous films, starred in the heart-warming *Regarding Henry* (1991); and Mel Gibson, the uninhibited and reckless police cop of the *Lethal Weapon* films, appeared in *Hamlet* (1990; Williams, 169). On the other end of the spectrum, Meg Ryan, popular for her roles as the appealing love interest in films such as *When Harry Met Sally* (1989), played a pilot in *Courage Under Fire* (1996), and Meryl Streep toned up for the action-packed *The River Wild* (1994). When *G.I. Jane* appeared in theaters, American audiences, primed to receive the popular Moore's portrayal, welcomed the film with considerable open-mindedness.

ORIGINS

G.I. Jane addresses one of the most controversial topics involving women's historic struggle for equality and opportunity in the military. Women have wanted to join the war effort since America's beginnings, back when gender expectations were more restrictive and the consequences of disrupting societal norms posed potentially greater risks. To get around this issue, some women impersonated men or simply dressed like them. Joan of Arc, the 15th-century female crusader, dressed in male armor to lead the troops. In the late 18th century, disguised as a man, Deborah Sampson served in the Continental Army during the American Revolution. During the Civil War,

Harriet Tubman, a former slave, served as a spy. Before America went to war with Spain in the late 19th century, Annie Oakley, as well as her offer of 50 female sharpshooters to help in time of combat, was turned down. When, during the first two world wars, the armed forces opened their doors to women, women were subjected to restrictions. Women worked largely in auxiliary positions and as nurses. Among the reasons women had historically been denied entrance in the military and then severely restricted even after barriers were partly broken down was that society perceived that women were nurturers, not fighters; soft, not hard; passive, not aggressive; and that certain physical differences predisposed them to be a risk, a threat, or a liability.

Compounded by other societal changes, the Gulf War, which took place between 1990 and 1991, brought forth revolutionary change in terms of women's involvement in the military. In the 1990s, working women had become the norm. The highly public fight for equality and women's rights, starting in the late 19th century and reemerging in the 1960s, had, by the 1990s, cooled considerably. Although the struggle continued beneath the surface, many women were simply reaping previous gains; social attitudes were changing, and, in academic settings, topics that had once been taboo, such as **feminism** and multiculturalism, experienced a wave of interest. Underscoring these changes was the fact that society no longer disparaged a woman for working outside of the home or looked askance at a young girl in shorts playing on a soccer team.

Women's involvement in the Middle East conflict was a landmark moment in history. According to one Web site, "mobilization for the Gulf war included an unprecedented proportion of women from the active forces (7%) as well as the Reserve and National Guard (17%). It was the largest female deployment in U.S. history. Over 40,000 U.S. military women served in key combat-support positions throughout the Persian Gulf Region. Women in Desert Storm did everything the male troops did except engage in ground combat—they could essentially get fired upon—they just weren't, by existing regulations, theoretically allowed to shoot back!" ("Women in Desert Storm"). Some women contended that, in some circumstances, they did fire back.

The expression "G.I. Joe," a generic term referring to a male soldier, emerged during World War II. *G.I.* stands for "government issue," while *Joe* is considered to be a nondescript, generic name for a man. Though the army formally renounced the use of the term in the 1990s, it is still sometimes used by the media and society in general; we refer, for example, to the well-known G.I. Bill, which concerned educational funding for those with military service.

Due to the shortage of male soldiers in World War II, increasing numbers of women were called upon to enlist in the war effort or to fill traditional male occupations on the home front while the men were away. Thus the term *G.I. Jane* first appeared only shortly after the term *G.I. Joe* was coined, reflecting a time of great change for women in the military. In 1942,

Women in Combat in History

In American history, women often had to disguise themselves as men to fight in combat. In other parts of the world, women warriors fought openly and honorably. Several queens, such as the Celtic warrior queen Boudicca, a towering woman with long red hair and a notoriously intimidating disposition, led her tribe, the Iceni, in a battle against the oppressive Romans. During battle, Boudicca was said to rely upon the guidance of Andraste, a goddess of war. In the Celtic tradition, both men and women were trained to be warriors.

Other cultures also permitted women to fight. The Dahomey Amazons served as guards and later functioned as a militia under the king who governed the West African region now known as Benin. In Japan, women were generally allowed to become samurai and ninja. In 1568, a group of some three hundred women fought in Haarlam, Holland, in the Spanish invasion. The Woman's Death Battalion was established in 1917 in Russia.

the Women's Army Corps (WAC) was formed, and a year later, the Women's Army Auxiliary Corps (WAAC). During World War II, some 150,000 women participated in both groups. However, women in the military were still viewed as subordinate or a minor counterpart to the male soldier.

Before there was *G.I. Jane* (1997), there was *The Story of G.I. Joe* (1945), a film directed by William Wellman and inspired by the heroism of soldiers that Ernie Pyle, a war correspondent, witnessed during World War II. In the 1950s, the first appearance of a blonde and shapely G.I. Jane was marked by a short-lived and otherwise unmemorable comic book. In the ensuing decade, however, Jane's male counterpart would become a major character in popular culture.

In 1963, Hasbro, a major toy company, coined the term *action figure* and marketed the first ever "doll" for boys. The idea for a toy doll specifically for boys was inspired by the overwhelming success of the Barbie doll. Unlike Barbie—a confection of pastel colors, long blonde hair, and fashion clothes with preternatural physical dimensions—the first action figure, named Rocky, was a marine. In subsequent years, a black G.I. Joe and an assortment of international soldiers were added. A female version of G.I. Joe—a nurse—was not marketed until 1967. It was a commercial failure.

Ridley Scott

Ridley Scott, who directed *G.I. Jane*, began his career in the 1960s. Scott was born in Tyne and Wear, in northeast England, on November 30, 1937. He has directed a sizable collection of films that deal with both traditional and transgressive themes. Films that portray traditional male heroes include *The Duellists* (1977), a film that highlights military power and fencing brothers; *Legend* (1985), the dreamy classic tale of a male hero who must vanquish evil; *White Squall* (1996), a narrative that pits young men on a sailing trip against nature; and *Gladiator* (2000), a historical epic about herculean men forced to fight one another to the death.

A number of Ridley Scott films have been praised for departing from the norm. Heading the list is *Alien* (1979), the horror/science fiction film that gave the world Ellen Ripley, a celebrated female lead who singlehandedly outwitted the alien enemy and out survived a cast of mostly men. In 1991, Scott directed *Thelma and Louise*, a film that is deemed one of the most important feminist films in history. And, in 1991, he directed *Hannibal*, featuring popular female protagonist Clarice Starling. Released in 1997, *G.I. Jane* pushed the boundaries further still.

Demi Moore

Demi Moore, the woman chosen to play the lead in *G.I. Jane*, was at the time (the 1990s) one of the highest-paid actresses in Hollywood, having been a budding star in her teens and cutting her teeth in the soaps. In 1996, she was rated in *People* magazine as one of the 50 most beautiful people in the world. Born Demetria Gene Guynes on November 11, 1962, Moore was allegedly named after a shampoo, though Demetria also happens to be the name of a female deity in Greek mythology, the goddess of agriculture or fertility.

Moore's successful career is intertwined with controversy. Her childhood was troubled; she dropped out of high school at 16 and for a short time worked as a pin-up girl. She appeared nude, while pregnant, on the cover of *Vanity Fair* in 1991. She portrayed a married woman who agreed to have sex with a wealthy man for money in *Indecent Exposure* (1993), a provocateur in a sexual harassment case in *Disclosure* (1994), and a mom who danced topless for a living in *Striptease* (1996). In 2003, she played a villain in *Charlie's Angels: Full Throttle*. She was in her early forties when the film was released, appearing fit and toned and in a bikini, sparking a media sensation. In 2005, she was the subject of media headlines when she married actor Ashton Kutcher, who is 15 years her junior. Moore is still among the biggest headliners in Hollywood.

POWER SUIT, WEAPONS, AND ABILITIES

In *G.I. Jane*, power is associated with the military uniform, elaborate artillery, helicopters, tanks, and the sparse environment in which the men sleep and eat. The power of the soldiers is demonstrated by their ability to maintain weapons and the meteoric speed in which these weapons are fired, and by their ability to strategize and function in spite of injury, duress, hunger, and adverse environmental factors. Power is also associated with rank (the soldier who gives orders and is in command), credibility (the veteran who has seen combat), and heroism (the soldier with medals and honors). During the course of the film, Jordan O'Neil exhibits all these forms of military power. She endures the weight of the military uniform, multiple accessories, and the sterile, all-male environs of the barracks and cafeteria. She excels in weapon use, survives the harrowing training process despite multiple injuries and health issues, and emerges heroically from a combat situation. All in all, O'Neil is equipped with the symbols of militant power, compounded by an unstoppable determination.

In *G.I. Jane*, Scott blatantly violates the conventions of gender through the role of Jordan O'Neil who not only learns, but masters, the forms and mannerisms of masculinity, wins the acceptance of the other male soldiers, and goes to war (combat).

VILLAINS

G.I. Jane features several archetypal villains. One is the ominous man in charge of training, master chief John James Urgayle (Viggo Mortensen). His last name suspiciously resembles the word *gargoyle*, a demonic creature made from stone or metal originally perceived, in medieval and ancient cultures, to function as a guardian against evil spirits. Symbolically, Master Chief Urgayle is positioned in a similar manner to the gargoyle, only he functions as a guardian of the sacred male space of the elite unit, protecting against anything or anyone (i.e., females) that might pollute the organization or compromise the efficiency of its soldiers. Urgayle's chiseled face and sinister facial expressions lend themselves to the gargoyle metaphor, and on several occasions he demonstrates his hostility to O'Neil's presence. Urgayle is the epitome of toughness and hardness, and yet Scott transgresses this character in scenes in which he recites and reads poetry and gets his hair trimmed while listening to classical music. By the end of the film, Urgayle has been repositioned as O'Neil's supporter.

Other villains in the film are Senator Lillian DeHaven (Anne Bancroft) and the other soldiers in training with O'Neil. During most of the training, O'Neil's peers are antagonistic to her. They ridicule her and ostracize her until she proves her worth and wins their admiration. Senator DeHaven is originally adamant about integrating all military units and has handpicked O'Neil to serve as the first woman to challenge the system of elite training. She states that if O'Neil is triumphant, she will attempt to eliminate the exclusionary practices of women, who are prohibited from joining combat units. But DeHaven is repositioned as a nemesis when, given the choice of supporting O'Neil or going along with Congress's wish to end the gender experiment (or else face base shutdowns), she chooses to foil O'Neil's progress.

Deborah Sampson

Deborah Sampson (1760–1827) is the first known woman to serve in combat in an American military unit. She was born in Plympton, Massachusetts. In her childhood, she did traditional women's work, such as sewing and spinning, as well as men's work, such as carpentry and plowing fields. Instead of marrying right away, Sampson chose to become a teacher. In 1778, she did the unthinkable and enlisted in the army during the American Revolutionary War. Binding her breasts and donning men's clothes, Sampson served in the army under the name Robert Shurtliff. She fought valiantly and was injured during one battle. After a year and a half in the military, Sampson was honorably discharged.

Sampson married in 1785 and had three children, but she did not settle entirely into a traditional life after her military career. Indeed, when her secret became known to the public, it caused her trouble. Sampson waged a long campaign to receive back pay for her military service (she had repeatedly been denied pay owed to her because she was a woman). Her success in this endeavor, as well as the lectures she gave about her experiences in the war, made her one of the most well known of the women who impersonated men during American wars.

O'Neil's literal enemy is represented by Middle Eastern nationalists who confront the soldiers-in-training when help is abruptly needed to rescue the rangers in the Libyan desert. The fictionalized real-life mission ends with success and with her colleagues considering O'Neil to be a hero.

G.I. JANE, THE FILM

The opening scene of the film involves Senator DeHaven, a female chairman of the Armed Services Committee, who chides a candidate for Secretary of the Navy for the discriminatory report on a female aviator whose craft crashed. She is vocal about her disappointment that there are areas in the military that are still "off limits to women." Shortly thereafter, a deal is made: Senator DeHaven can have her wish granted (full integration of women in the military or "gender-blind Navy") if a woman can pass several tests, the first of which is the rigorous U.S. Navy Combined Reconnaissance Team training, where the dropout rate is 60 percent.

In a subsequent scene, a satellite systems analyst struggles to come up with a plan to rescue a pilot stranded in Asia. Lieutenant O'Neil comes up with a plan, which presumably works out well. In this scene, O'Neil is portrayed in a feminine manner, with her long hair tied in a bun, makeup, and earrings.

Another scene shows Senator DeHaven assessing a pool of female candidates for the first test case. She rejects women, including a marathon runner and a woman body builder, who are too masculine-looking, reflecting that society's acceptance of transgressive women is conditional: tough women must still retain some femininity and beauty. She chooses O'Neil, who has a commendable background, is athletic, but is also feminine-looking. O'Neil accepts the challenge, but later that night, tells her boyfriend, Royce (Jason Beghe), while they are in a bath together, that she does not "want to be turned into some poster girl for women's rights." She insists that she just wants an opportunity to advance in the military, since, without combat training, her career is at a standstill. She credits her readiness to the fact that she "survived Basic Training and three brothers." However, she gets no encouragement from Royce. He is skeptical, asserting that a special operations unit is no place for a lady. He also comes across as insulted that she expects him to wait for her if her career causes her to travel to dangerous locations for any length of time. The conflict this decision has created between O'Neil and Royce continues until the end of the film.

Prior to the training, O'Neil tells the commander officer, Salem (Scott Wilson), that she does not want special treatment, but he informs her that she will receive special accommodations nonetheless: she will have separate barracks and will have separate physical standards. He wants her to alert him if anyone harasses her in any way, in line with the military's policies of no sexual harassment and no gender and racial **discrimination**.

Salem is frank about his less-than-enthusiastic response to her presence on his base. Her femininity is a nuisance to him, if not the military system. But he's tolerant enough, stating that her long hair is no problem as long as it stays "off [her] collar and out of [her] eyes." Nonetheless, O'Neil's hair does pose a problem for her, and she later resolves it in a way that is as shocking to the viewer as it was in real-life gossip magazines, which marveled over the courageousness of a woman who would shave her head for a part in a movie. The commanding officer asserts that he does not want to "change her sex," though, as some critics state, this is what happens as the film progresses.

In the training program, O'Neil is faced with hostile attitudes, strenuous physical challenges, and her reactions to her own physical weaknesses. Scott shows the tension felt by the men in response to O'Neil's presence during a scene in the mess hall. A group of raucous men at one table complain bitterly about O'Neil's presence; one man implies that a woman has too much body fat to make a good soldier. However, an African American soldier, McCool (Morris Chestnut), interjects that he doesn't mind a woman's participation if she can hold her own. Later, McCool puts O'Neil's status as the first woman in combat training into historical perspective when he tells the group (in O'Neil's presence) that his grandfather had been prohibited from fighting in World War II because of his race. The metaphor of race is also seen in the notion of a "test case," as civil rights activists repeatedly staged tests (like blacks and whites riding on interstate buses in the 1960s during the Freedom Rides) to challenge racially discriminatory practices, and in the fact that O'Neil does not like that she has to be separated or segregated from the male soldiers. Racial segregation was a term used to describe the legally upheld practice of racially separating public spaces and amenities in the South following the emancipation of black slaves. As evidenced by the few minorities among the male soldiers, such as McCool and Cortez (David Vadim), the elite group has yet to yield progress in terms of racial diversity.

To remedy one of the issues she faces, O'Neil goes to the commanding officer to request equal treatment: she wants the double standard, which has left her feeling like an "outsider," eliminated. During this encounter, the officer tells O'Neil that he begrudges the idea of women in the military and of concepts such as sensitivity training, and challenges O'Neil by asking her if the "**phallic** nature" of his cigar "offend[s] . . . [her] fragile sensibilities." What he is really asking her is if male power intimidates her. At the end of the meeting, he agrees to do away with the double standards, and O'Neil moves into the barracks, replying with tough comebacks to the men who protest.

Other obstacles with which O'Neil must contend are the grueling training courses, called "evolutions" in the film, and her personal weaknesses. Though the male soldiers must also overcome physical challenges, the implication is that the challenge is harder for women. It is established that anyone at any time can opt out of the training program simply by ringing a bell located on the premises. To match the strength of her peers, O'Neil must constantly work out in her private time. She suffers the consequences of her hard work in the form of tendonitis, wounds on her back, and jungle rot on her foot. In the process of acclimating to her role, her body stops menstruating. The nurse explains that this occurs when a woman's body fat decreases beneath a certain percentage, a common occurrence with athletes.

O'Neil relentlessly powers through her various challenges, the grueling exercises in water, weapons training, the combat assimilation course, and jumping out of planes. Unbeknownst to her, her progress is monitored and reported back to authorities who do not want to see her succeed because they do not want the integration of special military groups. Behind the scenes, the mostly male leadership call her names like Super Girl and Joan of Arc, labels that should be empowering, but out of their mouths, in their incredulous tones, are meant to be derogatory.

The physical challenges culminate when O'Neil, a team leader of a simulated mission, is captured and interrogated, a training scenario that is horrifically realistic. O'Neil is viciously singled out by Urgayle. His attack visibly confounds the other soldiers, and even one of the interrogators verbally disagrees with the rough handling of O'Neil. But Urgayle dismisses this concern. O'Neil's face becomes bloodied and bruised. Urgayle bends

Lieutenant General Ann Dunwoody

Lieutenant General Ann Dunwoody received her fourth star in 2008, becoming the first woman in America to do so. The following is a quote by Dunwoody after the Senate confirmed her on July 23, 2008: "I have never considered myself anything but a Soldier. I recognize that with this selection, some will view me as a trailblazer, but it's important that we remember the generations of women, whose dedication, commitment and quality of service helped open the doors of opportunity for us today."
   Women are still barred from combat.

Source: http://www.army.mil/-quotes/2008/08/25/11883-lt-gen-ann-e-dunwoody (accessed June 2009).

her over across a table and threatens to rape her, while simultaneously instructing the other men that the threat of rape is one of the reasons a woman can bring harm upon herself in a combat situation. O'Neil snaps back that the same thing can happen to a man. Before Urgayle goes further with his rape threat, she tackles him and kicks him as the watching soldiers shout their approval. Urgayle rises to his feet and recovers his dominance over her, punching her full in the face. He explains to the group that he's "saving her life and yours" by pointing out her weaknesses. She gets back up. He tells her to "seek life," in other words, give up what he considers a fruitless battle, and she quips back "suck my dick." Her defiant command settles the matter. Urgayle, bloodied by her attack, nods at her and desists. In the aftermath, her fellow soldiers reward her by inviting her into their male clique in a trip to a bar. Essentially, they have accepted her as one of their own. At the bar, O'Neil talks tough along with the men and devours hard liquor.

   After this heroic moment, O'Neil must still face two more challenges. In one, she faces off with Senator DeHaven, who attempts to ruin her reputation with falsified accusations that she is a lesbian. She does this to save her job and the Texas naval bases that are under threat of elimination because of the unpopularity of O'Neil, who has created a media frenzy. The tension causes O'Neil to ring the bell at training headquarters.

   O'Neil's departure is only temporary. O'Neil threatens to tell the truth to the public and forces the senator to reinstate her. After she returns to the training program, the group is sent off on an operational readiness exercise. En route to the assignment, the trainees are called to participate in a real-life extraction of rangers who have retrieved a satellite fueled with weapons-grade plutonium in the Libyan desert. At the start of the rescue mission, a skirmish ensues between Middle Easterners and O'Neil's team. The master chief is shot (though not fatally), and O'Neil drags him to safety. This harkens back to an earlier scene in which he berated her for not doing the same thing in a simulation, accusing her of not having the upper body strength to do so.

At the conclusion of the film, all the trainees in O'Neil's team are honored with awards and inducted into the Combined Reconnaissance Team. Urgayle leaves a book of poetry in O'Neil's locker, an intimate and quiet gesture of his pride in her accomplishment.

IMPACT

Despite the groundbreaking subject matter and the spectacular show of a woman toughing out the most challenging training course in the military and overcoming a landslide of obstacles, *G.I. Jane* was not universally admired. The film's gross domestic box office was $48,169,156, which is better than several of Scott's films but does not come close to the $100,000,000 plus enjoyed by successes such as *Gladiator* (2000), *Black Hawk Down* (2001), and *American Gangster* (2007). Among O'Neil's fans were Roger Ebert, of Siskel and Ebert fame—two critics who reviewed movies on a popular television show between 1986 and 1999—and a number of feminist critics, who heralded O'Neil as a strong and powerful icon for women.

Other critics were bewildered by the images and messages emanating from the film. Phyllis Schlafly, a longtime opponent of feminism, decried the film because it justified violence against women and portrayed women as physically equal to men. A number of critics concede that the masculinization of O'Neil is problematic. One critic argued that O'Neil "can only achieve success as a Navy SEAL by putting her femininity behind her" (Brown, 55). Another scholar explained that "critics saw the film as a story of G.I. Jane becoming G.I. Joe" (Williams, 181). Hilary Neroni is concerned that only when O'Neil becomes more masculine (through the systematic shedding of feminine symbols such as her hair, the absence of her menstruation, her soft physique, and a polite manner of communicating versus the rough talk she engages in with her peers) does she become accepted by her male peers. By removing her femininity, O'Neil removed the threat to the military. Although Owen, Stein, and Vande Berg underscore triumphant points in the narrative, they contend that it portrays "the female body [as a] primary problem that needs 'solving,'" or indeed, fixing. This O'Neil does masterfully and is, as a result, rewarded with induction into the special operations force and social acceptance by the male soldiers, including the master chief (Owen, Stein, Vande Berg, 212).

The issues some scholars have with O'Neil's gradual "masculinization" contrast with other perspectives. One of the original arguments of **second-wave feminists** (1960s–1980s) was that women should demonstrate equality with men, as well as be treated equally. Many second-wave feminists were critical of portrayals of women who were not taken seriously, who had traditional long and fancy hairstyles, who dressed femininely, talked softly, and whose mannerisms and modes of communication projected timidity and weakness. Action heroes like Ellen Ripley from the *Alien* series were considered the second-wave ideal. Her heroism, not her looks, is what she is most remembered for.

The lasting effect of *G.I. Jane* is evident in the palpable silence that followed in its wake. *G.I. Jane* did not go on to produce massively popular video games, clothing, toys, comic book characters, and other paraphernalia; the film has yet to inspire a sequel. Nevertheless, O'Neil remains an enduring symbol of power and radical transformation.

See also Ellen aka "The Lady"; Joan of Arc.

FURTHER RESOURCES

Brown, Jeffrey A. "Gender, Sexuality, and Toughness: The Bad Girls of Action Film and Comic Books." In *Action Chicks: New Images of Tough Women in Popular Culture*, ed. Sherrie A. Inness. New York: Palgrave Macmillan, 2004.

Browne, Kingsley. *Co-ed Combat: The New Evidence That Women Shouldn't Fight the Nation's Wars.* New York: Sentinel HC, 2007.

Inness, Sherrie A. "It's a Girl Thing: Tough Female Action Figures in the Toy Store." In *Action Chicks: New Images of Tough Women in Popular Culture*, ed. Sherrie A. Inness. New York: Palgrave Macmillan, 2004.

Lioness. Directed by Meg McLagan and Daria Sommers. New York: Room 11 Productions, 2008.

Meyer, Leisa D. *Creating G.I. Jane: Sexuality and Power in the Women's Army Corps during World War II.* New York: Columbia University Press, 1996.

Military Women Veterans. "Women in Desert Storm." http://userpages.aug.com/captbarb/femvetsds.html.

Neroni, Hilary. *The Violent Woman: Femininity, Narrative, and Violence in Contemporary American Cinema.* Albany: State University of New York Press, 2005.

Owen, Susan A., Sarah R. Stein, and Leah R. Vande Berg. *Bad Girls: Cultural Politics and Media Representations of Transgressive Women.* New York: Peter Lang, 2007.

Schlafly, Phyllis. "G.I. Jane Is a Role-Model for Evil." http://www.eagleforum.org/column/1997/sept97/97-09-10.html.

Williams, Linda Ruth. "Ready for Action: *G.I. Jane*, Demi Moore's Body, and the Female Combat Movie." In *Action and Adventure Cinema*, ed. Yvonne Tasker. New York: Routledge, 2004.

Wise, James E., and Scott Baron. *Women at War: Iraq, Afghanistan, and Other Conflicts.* Annapolis, MD: Naval Institute Press, 2006.

Helen Gibson in the episode "Race for Your Life" in *The Hazards of Helen*. (Image courtesy Joyce Godsey.)

Helen

Helen was the star of the wildly popular *The Hazards of Helen* film series, one of more than 60 **serials** released between 1912 and 1920. Helen, a generally proactive protagonist who went through physical and dangerous adventures in every episode, can be considered one of the earliest female action heroes in film history. These films were not feature films; rather each episode of *Helen* was about 12 minutes long. Kalem Company, an American film studio, produced 119 episodes of *The Hazards of Helen* between November 7, 1914, and February 24, 1917. This makes it one of the longest running serials in silent film history. *The Hazards of Helen* serials were produced by Kalem.

Helen in no way resembled the frail, diminutive archetype that had been idealized in previous centuries. She was a sturdy, athletic, and independent young woman with a career as a railroad telegrapher. Though she was outfitted in modest loose-fitting shirts and cumbersome, long skirts, she was at least liberated from the tight corsets and frilly embellishments women had commonly worn. Her dark hair, frequently worn in a braid or pony tail draped over her shoulder, was reminiscent of modern-day tough adventurer Lara Croft. Helen had a free and easy, long stride. She performed daring stunts in car chases, on horseback, and on a runaway train, and had frequent skirmishes with villains. This female hero lived to leap, climb, run, and fend off ne'er-do-wells, and she was the one who saved the day at the conclusion of most episodes. Though at times she was depicted as the damsel in distress, most of the time she was the one solving the problems, and she rescued her fair share of men.

Four women were cast in the title role. Helen Holmes (who lent her name to the character, a common convention in the silent film era) portrayed Helen for the first 26 episodes. Anna Q. Nilsson stood in for Holmes at least once while Holmes recovered from an illness. When Holmes left the series with her then-husband, director J. P. McGowan, to establish their own film production company, Elsie McLeod temporarily took over the role, performing in 22 episodes. Rose Wenger Gibson, who was renamed Helen by the film company, filled the role in episodes 50 to 119. Holmes and Gibson became celebrated stars during their time in *The Hazards of Helen*, particularly since they performed most of their own stunts.

ORIGINS

Helen was a product of numerous influences, including literary tradition, the changing social perceptions and realities of women's roles, and industry marketing practices. In the 1800s, dime novels and serial fiction in newspapers were mass produced at affordable prices, greatly contributing to the massive popularity of the print medium. These stories commonly featured male heroes and disempowered women. Over time, male authors, as well as female authors, began to create strong female characters, serving as either subordinate characters or protagonists. Illustrious dime novelist Edward L. Wheeler wrote numerous Westerns, such as the "Deadwood Dick" series and other tales featuring tough women like Hurricane Nell, Wild Edna, and Calamity Jane. Dime novels were popular with men, as well as with a growing number of women who were beginning to enjoy more leisure time and greater freedom than ever before.

From the birth of America in 1776, society imposed many restrictions upon women. During the colonial period, men received more education than women. Married women were not permitted to make decisions on their own, own property, or file a suit in a court of law. They were expected to submit to their husbands' authority. In many regions, wives were considered property. No woman was given the legal right to vote.

Although single or widowed women enjoyed opportunities that were denied married women, the unmarried woman was frequently dependent upon her family for protection and shelter and had to suffer ridicule for having not married or borne children. Single women who owned and managed stores and farms or occupied traditional occupations, such as blacksmiths, gunsmiths, butchers, and publishers, were the exception, not the rule.

During the westward expansion of the 19th century, more men than women made the precarious journey to stake out opportunities for wealth, new beginnings, and adventure. The West, ultimately, would become a symbol of masculinity—of limitless space, freedom, independence, adventure, and danger—while women would function as civilizing agents, tending to home, children, husbands, and others (as needed). Nonetheless, some women, for a number of reasons, did brave the West alone. Armed with rifles and resourcefulness, they defended their homes from the threat of outlaws, wild animals, and warring Native Americans, grew their own food, made the family's clothes, and served as doctors and midwives. Other women who subverted the **stereotype** of the "weak woman" were Native American women, who frequently served leadership positions in their communities, and black female slaves, who were forced to toil on slave plantations alongside male slaves and received equal punishment for transgressions, real or imagined.

In the 19th century, the ideology of the cult of true womanhood, or cult of domesticity, was extremely popular. During this period, many women and men succumbed to the idea that women should be confined to domestic roles, and be pious, pure, and submissive. Importantly, these rules were meant for white middle- and upper-class women.

During this time, gender differences were underscored and encouraged, as well as amplified through numerous etiquette books and newspaper articles that endorsed the image of the ideal woman, who was lily white (not tanned, which was associated with the lower class or masculinity), delicate, and feminine. In keeping with this ideal, a lady never cursed, spoke or laughed loudly, loitered in male spaces like saloons or the out-of-doors, or

Pants Timeline

1839–1901	During the Victorian era, progressive women advocate for dress reform. Desiring more comfortable and functional clothing, some first-wave feminists protest wearing long and cumbersome dresses, which all women were expected to wear.
1851	Elizabeth Smith Miller wears pants under a skirt, similar to the Turkish style. Amelia Bloomer popularizes Miller's fashion and the term *bloomers* is born. Bloomers are not popular with mainstream women and are heavily discouraged by the general press.
1860s	The invention of the bicycle is one precursor of the coming revolution in women's fashion.
1890s	Sportswear is introduced for active women. Skirts are shortened to the tops of the ankles and more streamlined for walking and playing tennis. Bloomers and knickerbockers are also worn for bicycle riding and other sports. The Wigan pit brow girls spark controversy when they wear bloomers to work in the coal mines.
1914–1918	Women who go to work in the factories during World War I wear pants, but the practice stops at the end of the war.
1930	Marlene Dietrich appears in trousers in the film *Morocco*.
1930s	Famous actresses Marlene Dietrich and Katherine Hepburn customarily wear trousers, but the fashion is still considered transgressive.
1939	*Vogue* magazine features women in trousers.
1960s	Fashion trendsetter Audrey Hepburn wears Capri pants in *Breakfast at Tiffany's* (1961). Other celebrities help to popularize the fashion trend.
1970s	Women regularly appear in film and television wearing pants. Pants are commonly worn by American women. The fashion symbolizes women's burgeoning liberation and equality with men.

behaved like a man. She always needed protection and chaperoning. She took short "dainty" steps, never ran, or allowed herself to lose her temper. Many women did not work, except as homemakers. Their job was to support their men as wives and manage their homes as mothers. Poor—often immigrant—women, however, were required to work and often served as domestics for the middle- and upper-class women. In contrast to prostitutes, who resided in rural communities as well as urban cities, the true woman never wore too much makeup or exposed her body.

Though many women may have followed some of the guidelines of true womanhood, a number found ways to challenge the status quo. Women abolitionists, club members, and eventually **suffragists** (women who fought for women's right to vote) forged outlets to protest societal wrongs and disparities. They became agents of social change and community leaders, giving speeches, organizing, and generally disrupting accepted gender roles.

Among the conventions that women challenged were marriage and motherhood, career, and education. Although many women reformers were mothers and wives, an increasing number of leaders did not marry. Many women pursued careers and motherhood simultaneously; some delayed marriage and children until later in life or not at all. An increasing number of women pursued higher education and advanced degrees, though it was rumored by some misguided traditionalists that higher education was harmful to a woman's health.

The emergence of the assertive woman, also known as the "**New Woman**," coincided with a time of many exciting new inventions and the urbanization of America at the turn of the century. The "New Woman" was not necessarily a feminist. With the invention of new technologies, women were relieved of many traditional chores such as house cleaning, laundry washing, and food preparation. Inventions in transportation, the establishment of theaters and other places of entertainment, urban growth, and the fact that single women were taking jobs in the cities helped to mold the image of the New Woman— an independent and single woman who frequently lived in a boarding house and went to plays and social functions, many times without a chaperone. In appearance, the New Woman was brazen, donning shorter dresses, wearing more makeup than was customary, and sporting a short hairstyle. The New Woman was considered cheeky, and she frequently appropriated traditional male attributes in her zeal for fun and sexual expression. Another attribute of the New Woman was her relative economic independence.

According to statistics, "10 percent of women worked in paid labor in 1880; by 1910, over 40 percent of young, single women worked for several years before marriage, and the figure was probably over 60 percent in urban areas" (Singer, 177). Notwithstanding these staggering percentages, women were paid significantly less than men and worked in environments **segregated** by gender. While men worked in the railroad and construction industry, joined the military, and held positions of power in all fields, women worked in clothing factories, for example, and as secretaries and phone operators.

Although the New Woman is considered a **transgressive** archetype, she permeated pop culture. Book and newspaper publishers parodied her. When silent film emerged as the new medium in the first decade of the 20th century, film makers were quick to leap on the bandwagon. In an attempt to target a female audience and reflecting the New Woman trend, Edison Studios created the first serial queen, a term that refers to the female stars of silent film serials. Her name was Mary, and she was the protagonist of *What Happened to Mary?* (1917). This was followed by countless serials and series in rapid succession. These serials were one of the precursors to the action genre and came in many forms, such as the Western, detective story, Gothic, and working girl.

Changing social conditions were not the only influence on the emergence of serial queens who engaged in action. Silent films needed and had a preference for action, because they had no dialogue and wanted to be visually interesting. This opened a door that might otherwise have remained closed much longer (and indeed was re-closed when the talkies arrived). Technology and its limitations helped to break down barriers. And it helped that the serial queens were pretty and in constant peril, a combination that appealed to audiences.

History of Film Serials and Series

The era of the film serials spanned the 1900s to the mid 1950s. During the silent era, which began in the 1890s, films were produced in black and white, because the technology to reproduce colors on film did not yet exist. Nor did the technicians understand—or think much about—how to add audio to film. Production was basic and frequently crude. To compensate for the lack of sound, as well as to help create emotion, a piano player often accompanied the showing of the films. For important productions, an orchestra might be employed.

Generally, serials and series episodes (which were short one- or two-reelers), were shown before a feature film. Each episode of a serial lasted about 12 or about 24 minutes and usually ended with a cliffhanger, a moment of climactic suspense wherein the resolution of the story is not disclosed until the next episode. In a series, the narrative played out from beginning to end during each episode. Still, there were plenty of shorts that were neither serial nor series that were shown along with a feature film. Those shorts could be anything: comedy, serial, series, documentary, or news.

One popular motif that is often identified with the film serials and series of the silent era was the damsel in distress—the woman fettered to train tracks by a villain and who must be rescued by the gallant male hero. It is uncertain who had the honor of first putting this on film; some point to *The Perils of Pauline*, one of the most popular serials ever filmed, and some to *The Hazards of Helen*.

The many serial queens of the silent era were considered in their time to be tough, active, and independent, frequently rescuing themselves as well as the men. They went by many names: Dolly of *The Active Life of Dolly of the Dailies* (1914), Kathlyn of *The Adventures of Kathlyn* (1913), Pauline of *The Perils of Pauline* (1914), as well as Elaine, Lucille, Peg, Ruth, Helen, and others. In *A Lass of the Lumberlands* (1916), the protagonist, named Helen, rescues a man who has been tied to the train tracks, reversing the

Elizabeth Smith Miller

Elizabeth Smith Miller (1822–1909) explains why she decided to wear pants: "In the spring of 1851, while spending many hours at work in the garden, I became so thoroughly disgusted with the long skirt, that the dissatisfaction— the growth of years—suddenly ripened into the decision that this shackle should no longer be endured. The resolution was at once put into practice. Turkish trousers to the ankle with a skirt reaching some four inches below the knee, were substituted for the heavy, untidy and exasperating old garment."

Source: http://www.nyhistory.com/gerritsmith/esm.htm (accessed July 2009).

roles in the customary scene. These women are considered precursors of female action heroes who engaged in intense chases and rescues.

In the sound (or talkie) era, the film serials and series underwent a dramatic change. Beginning in the 1930s, the female action hero became nearly obsolete, as studios depicted women in more glamorous, less active roles. They returned to a policy of giving preference to male heroes in such film series and serials as *The Three Musketeers* (1933), *Tarzan the Fearless* (1933), *Dick Tracy* (1937), *The Lone Ranger* (1938), *Buck Rogers* (1938), *Flash Gordon Conquers the Universe* (1940), and *Batman* (1943). By 1950, film serials and series dropped out of popularity and were brought to an end. They would reappear years later, though never again with the frequency and public appeal that had distinguished them in the early days of silent film.

Kalem Company

Though Helen was a heroic figure, she was immersed in a world of men who functioned as villains and railroad personnel. She was also created by men. Originally conceived as the protagonist of a book written by John Russell Corvell and later adapted to a play by Denman Thompson, Helen's successful existence as a serial queen was overseen by two directors at the Kalem Company, J. P. McGowan and James Davis. Kalem Company, which was established in New York in 1907, was dominated by men, as women at that time had not penetrated the upper echelons of the so-called "male professions" such as the film industry. Kalem produced a substantial number of serials, such as *The Ventures of Marguerite*. In 1917, Vitagraph studios purchased Kalem, ending its decade-long existence.

J. P. McGowan and James Davis

Both directors enjoyed much acclaim thanks to the *Helen* series, and rightfully so, considering how much they brought to the project. The first director to work on the series, J. P. McGowan, was born in Australia in 1880. His early life mirrored two hero archetypes—the cowboy and the soldier. Australia, in the 18th century, was similar to the oft-romanticized period of the American West, with plenty of open space and a rich horse culture. He would later serve in the Second Boer War. In America, McGowan put his riding skills to good use, performing as an actor as well as a stunt man. While directing *The Hazards of Helen*, he married Helen Holmes, the original star of the series. They left the series together after 26 episodes to form their own production company, which they managed together until they divorced in 1925.

J. Gunnis Davis, born in England in 1873, directed the series after McGowan's departure. He appeared in more than 30 films prior to his role as director and ushered *Helen* into several more years of thrilling adventures.

Helen Holmes and Helen Gibson

The two real-life Helens gave the cinema Helen shape, form, and credibility. It is a fact that at one time, women were not allowed to act. For example, during William Shakespeare's lifetime, men dressed in lavish women's clothing, wigs, and makeup to portray female characters on the stage. Though athletic women in the early 20th century were still very much a rarity, real women played the parts of the active female heroes, frequently performing the stunts themselves. Thus they exemplified the courageous and independent spirit of their characters. This was the case with Helen Holmes and Helen Gibson.

Holmes (born in Indiana in 1893) ended plans to become a model because she allegedly did not have the look that was in vogue at the time. But she found her niche as the resourceful "Helen." After marrying McGowan, they established Signal Film Productions, a joint venture that was particularly exemplary considering that women were still expected to perform auxiliary roles within marriage and had not yet, in great numbers, shattered the barriers dominated by men. Holmes adopted a baby girl, whom, she boasted, would upon growing up wear overalls and "play with a monkey wrench" (Stamp, 222). After the dissolution of her marriage in 1925, Holmes married a second time and started an animal-training business with her new husband. Later, she managed a home-based business selling antiques.

Born in Ohio in 1892 and one of four sisters, Rose Wenger Gibson, the second "Helen," was a real hoyden in her childhood, no doubt with the approval of her father, who had wanted a son. Though others discouraged her, she engaged in dangerous activities designated for boys such as riding horses and audaciously performing tricks on horseback. She went on to become, among other things, a trick rider, a rodeo performer, and the first American professional stunt woman. After Holmes left *The Hazards of Helen*, Gibson stepped in, acting in 69 episodes. In 1920, in an attempt to recreate her career after the demise of the *Helen* series, she founded her own, albeit short-lived, production company, Helen Gibson Productions. She also performed in other films, and tried, unsuccessfully, to sell real estate. Throughout the course of her career, Gibson was resilient, despite many trips to the hospital because of accidents she suffered while doing stunt work. She married twice.

POWER SUIT, WEAPONS, AND ABILITIES

Helen, the hero of *The Hazards of Helen*, always wore long skirts (women wearing pants did not become commonplace until the 1950s). The long skirts code her as wholesome, traditional, and virginal, contrasting the image of the liberated New Woman, who daringly wore shorter dresses, bared her naked arms, and consorted with men.

Although Helen is positioned as traditionally feminine by her dress, her clothes were, nevertheless, not ornamental but rather, within the context of the era, functional. Her tops and skirts were plain. Glaringly absent were ruffles, bows, and corsets—symbols of femininity. Her look, essentially, was intended to denote an early 20th-century adventure woman who did not stray too far outside the bounds of social expectation, but whose clothing permitted her more freedom and range of motion than traditional women's clothing. The wardrobe of the serial queen was intended to inspire real-life fashion trends.

Helen's toughness was depicted in other ways that were largely defined by the times in which she first appeared to audiences. For one, she was no waifish, delicate person. She was hardy and hale, embodying early 20th-century ideals of what a healthy and athletic person should look like. Helen was also brave, if not brazen, in the face of danger; she maintained her calm and displayed athleticism and resourcefulness. Unlike some heroes, whose heroism is attached to a pistol, a sword, or a shield, Helen's courage, intelligence, and physical prowess were her primary weapons, though she could use a gun or other object to achieve her aims. Helen worked either alone or with the assistance of a man or several men.

VILLAINS

The "hazards" Helen faced included accidents, technical malfunctions, and thugs. Helen's antagonists were always male. They ranged from maleficent cowboys, as in episode six, "The Black Diamond Express," to robbers, who appeared in several episodes, and malcontented employees in the railroad industry. Trains and railroads were popular in the films. There were abundant opportunities to create thrilling action and danger. Characters could jump on and off trains, race across the tops of trains, and get run over or tied to the railroad tracks. These tricks were repeated from episode to episode.

THE HAZARDS OF HELEN, SERIALS

The life of a Hollywood actor in the 1910s was far from the norm, but nothing could come close to the sort of fantastical life that Helen led in her

Tough Women Who Wore Dresses

Although many women reformers challenged traditional women's wear, a number of women in history demonstrated that one could be tough and follow social customs and traditions at the same time. Ancient times are full of tales of women who managed pregnancy, birth, children, and a life of high action all at the same time. Phung Thi Chinh went to battle while pregnant, gave birth, and continued fighting with her baby tied to her body. Other women, such as Empress Jingo-Kogo, Salaym Bint Malham, and numerous women who secretly served in the American Civil War, went to battle while pregnant. Susan B. Anthony, a prominent leader in the women's rights movement, wore traditional hairstyles and long dresses. Other women engaged in rebellious activities, such as marching and picketing, in full dresses, many pushing baby strollers. Ida B. Wells Barnett, a turn-of-the-century activist, disappointed some of her peers when she went the way of custom and married and had children. But Barnett also took one of her newborn babies with her on her lecture tours and managed to pursue her career throughout her lifetime as well as raise a family.

In modern American society, women have greater fashion freedom. Women in construction and other blue-collar positions wear jeans to work. Women in the military wear the same uniforms as men. In politics and other high-power positions, women alternate between pants suits and skirts.

serials. Daring female action heroes were unprecedented in the early 20th century. Audiences were aware of changing roles, attitudes, and behaviors of progressive women. But compared to the New Woman, Helen was extreme, for women in dresses did not, in real life, leap onto trains, run down villains, or conduct car chases—many times outperforming burly men. Even women athletes were considered marginal and the exceptions to the rules that dictated women's roles in the early 20th century. The emergence of serial queens, like Helen, came out of the blue, spurred on by the fact that because of the state of the medium, they needed action. It wasn't the kind of action that is seen today, and it was filled with coded images that would be problematic to feminists. Moreover, the serials were repetitive and badly plotted, but for its time it was amazing.

However, it was Helen's novelty that yielded success. Jennifer M. Bean contends that serial-queen films were "designed to flaunt difference, to defamiliarize the familiar, to unsettle (rather than restore the viewer's equilibrium)" (Bean, 28). The woman-in-action serial queen shocked and enthralled audiences, resulting in substantial profits for film studios like Kalem.

Helen broke many rules, thus epitomizing the role of a transgressive and progressive woman. Other films depicted women as screaming hysterical women, who either froze or ran when confronted by terror or danger. Helen never shirked from danger; she ran toward it, rather than seeking shelter or waiting to be rescued. For example, when, in "The Broken Circuit," episode 10, thieves rob the paymaster's office, she single-handedly confronts them. When, in "The Girl at the Throttle" episode three, Helen finds out about a runaway train, she charges toward the danger to warn the engineer and save the day. From start to finish, Helen is quick to act, steely and determined under pressure, and rarely ruffled, even when she is outnumbered by bandits.

Helen is also considered progressive because she was the star of the show, lived in a male-dominated environment, and was depicted as an independent working girl. Unlike Batman and Robin, Helen had no major sidekick, though from time to time she received assistance or was rescued by men. When men did appear in an episode, they were rarely addressed by name, and they did not appear on screen with the same regularity as Helen, though it was evident that males dominated the train industry.

The spirited Helen ignored the social conventions that would have put her in a factory, behind a desk, or at home. So-called genteel or proper ladies did not consort with men by themselves or enter male spaces, but Helen did. She worked in a male-dominated railroad industry, never appearing in traditional domestic spaces or with female friends, and no one appeared to mind. An **ingénu**e archetype, Helen was friendly with employees and moved confidently in the work space. Although men repeatedly asked for her hand in marriage, Helen always declined.

Obviously, Helen's single status was what made her lifestyle and the series possible. In the early 20th century, middle- and upper-class married women tended not to work. Some women who delayed marriage did so with the idea that fun, adventure, and career could only be had when single. After marriage, women were expected to "settle down" to the full-time responsibilities of housewife and mother. Thus, by depicting Helen as a single woman, producers did not challenge the perceptions of traditional wives and mothers; only single women could appropriate traditional male heroism.

Although Helen is a striking character, especially given the time in which she was popular, she was frequently undermined. In one episode, a man holds Helen's hand as they run across the top of a train, though Helen has proved in many episodes that she is more than capable of managing a stunt like that. "In Danger's Path," Helen strikes a classic damsel-in-distress pose, with her arm pulled dramatically across her face when criminals lock her into a train car. She paces the floor, visibly fretting, until she conceives a plan to start a fire, which signals help.

One problematic depiction of Helen is that she is repeatedly assaulted, a common feature in silent movie series and serials featuring female leads. Helen is often bound and gagged, locked in a closet or a box car, or tethered to a railroad. While driving, a man in the passenger seat suddenly leaps upon Helen. Helen fights back, struggling at first and then throwing him out of the car, leaving him stranded. Scholars are uneasy with these repeated assaults, believing that these scenes depict women as victims. Silent film scholar Ben Singer surmises that serial queens were victimized because, metaphorically, they trespassed alone in the wild and uncertain spaces dominated by men; they dared to venture outside social conventions. This phenomenon, however, was a sign of the times and was considered acceptable as a way to develop dramatic tension at the time (and now, for that matter). The touring plays of the era (no TV, little radio) had their own aesthetic and conventions, and treating women like victims was one of them—like *Birth of a Nation* (1915), all the rage at the time, but soon condemned as **racist** of the sort that can't be ignored.

IMPACT

Helen and the other serial queens were a hit with audiences nationwide. Singer contends that Helen and her ilk intrigued men and women differently, with men finding enjoyment in the action sequences "and its sporadic imagery of female victimization" and women finding appeal in the "fantasies of [female] emancipation and power" (Singer, 170, 172).

For the times, Helen embodied independence and female power. She did everything her time and the conventions of filming allowed her to do. She also was a role model for and anticipated the women of the Roaring Twenties, who were just about to emerge. Helen, however, looks quite different from the women of action in today's films, television series, and video games.

See also The Bionic Woman; Buffy the Vampire Slayer; Jen Yu; Lara Croft.

FURTHER RESOURCES

Acker, Ally. *Reel Women: Pioneers of the Cinema: 1896 to the Present*. New York: Continuum International, 1997.

American Women's Dime Novel Project. http://chnm.gmu.edu/dimenovels/intro.html.

Bean, Jennifer M. "'Trauma Thrills': Notes on Early Action Cinema." In *Action and Adventure Cinema*, ed. Yvonne Tasker. New York: Routledge, 2004.

Estad, Nan. *Ladies of Labor, Girls of Adventure*. Irvington, NY: Columbia University Press, 1999.

Kava, Beth, and Jeanne Bodin. *We, the American Women: A Documentary History*. Lincoln, NE: iUniverse, 2001.

Singer, Ben. "Female Power in the Serial-Queen Melodrama: The Etiology of an Anomaly." In *Silent Film*, ed. Richard Abel. New York: Routledge, 1996.

Stamp, Shelley. "An Awful Struggle between Love and Ambition: Serial Heroines, Serial Stars, and Their Female Fans." In *The Silent Cinema Reader*, ed. Lee Grieveson and Peter Krämer. New York: Routledge, 2004.

Jen Yu and Yu Shu Lien fight spectacularly in the film *Crouching Tiger, Hidden Dragon*. (© Sony Pictures Classics/Courtesy: Everett Collection.)

Jen Yu

Jen Yu (Zhang Ziyi) is a 19-year-old aristocrat in the film *Crouching Tiger, Hidden Dragon* (2000), a film produced in Mandarin Chinese and directed by Ang Lee. The film was based on a five-part wuxia novel, *Crouching Tiger, Hidden Dragon* (1945), written by Wang Du-lu. American audiences do not normally flock to see foreign films with English subtitles, especially artsy ones, but this film was action packed and shown, in some regions, in mainstream theaters for months after its release. Among the several prestigious awards the film received were Oscars for best art direction–set decoration, best cinematography, best foreign language film, and best music. It grossed $128 million in the United States.

The film was widely praised as a stunning, lavish display of natural landscapes and graceful fight sequences, accompanied by traditional Chinese music featuring melancholy strains and drums that propelled the action scenes forward. Peter Pau did the choreography; Tan Dun composed the score. Famous cellist Yo-Yo Ma was featured on the soundtrack. The fight scenes were not the ordinary, run-of-the-mill variety; women glided up the sides of buildings, soared gently over rooftops, shot up in the sky like comic book heroes, and flew toward the horizon. In one sequence, Jen Yu and Li Mu Bai (Chow Yun Fat) battled it out on the tops of tall bright green trees. Yuen Woo Ping, who choreographed the martial arts sequences, is also known for the meteoric fighting scenes in *The Matrix* (1999).

Women play a prominent role in this complex tale set in 19th-century China. The main plot concerns Jen, a privileged 19-year-old, daughter of a governor, who is unhappily the subject of an arranged marriage that will advance her father's career. Jen has romantic views of warrior life and longs to be a warrior herself, free and unencumbered from social obligations. Jade Fox (Pei-pei Cheng), Jen's mentor, has been secretly training her. At one point, a 400-year-old legendary sword, the Green Destiny, an ancient **phallic** symbol that belongs to Mu Bai, a master swordsman who desires to give up the warrior life, is delivered by Shu Lien, a swordswoman (Michelle Yeoh), to Sir Te in Peking. Jen disguises herself as a thief and steals the sword, making Jen an antihero, like Thelma and Louise. Shu Lien and Mu Bai struggle to retrieve the Green Destiny; Mu Bai tries to persuade Jen to be his protégée and pursues Jade Fox, the woman who murdered his master. Shu Lien pines for Mu Bai, privately longing to settle down in marriage.

Lee's *Crouching Tiger, Hidden Dragon* depicts powerful women as a normal part of society, though they must nevertheless contend with social expectations and obligations. The two strong female characters, Jen and Shu Lien, are presented as opposites. Jen is young, coddled and spoiled, irreverent and reckless; Shu Lien is an older woman, mature, disciplined, wise, and loyal. Shu Lien is also a business woman; she manages her deceased father's security business. Both women exhibit masterful skills in martial arts and sword fighting. When the women fight against each other in an electrifying battle, Jen gets the upper hand. Still, Shu Lien's abilities, weapons expertise, and steely determination are extraordinary. In the end, Mu Bai dies at the hands of Jade Fox, who, forgoing kung fu or sword fighting because her skills are inferior to Mu Bai's, resorts to a less-than-admirable weapon—poison— but not before Mu Bai manages to kill Jade Fox with a swift, effortless flourish. Shu Lien lives, but Jen, who undergoes a redemptive moment, propels her body from a precipice near the Wudan school.

ORIGINS

Lee directed *Crouching Tiger, Hidden Dragon* using many of the standard devices of the traditional Chinese genre called wuxia. Wuxia, which stands for fighting skills (wu) and chivalry or gallantry (xia), incorporates kung fu and weapons training, ancient legends, magic, and the supernatural. It has long been a popular genre in China, focusing on tales of noble martial artists—men, as well as women. The genre now permeates much of Chinese popular culture.

In ancient times, martial arts school proliferated in towns, mountainous regions, and the country. The Shaolin Temple, a famous spiritual center, also served as a martial arts training ground for monks. Many martial arts schools, like Shaolin, did not open their doors to women. However, women did emerge as legendary swordswomen and were revered equally to male warriors.

In spite of China's legacy of strong women warriors, women in everyday life were long subjected to male control and dominance. Similar to the experience of women in America's history, Chinese women were expected to behave in ways that were associated with femininity, serving men, and maintaining social and gender roles in society. Traditionally, women did not advance in education or enter into work or careers delineated for men. Women were also not allowed to sing in Chinese opera or enter temples. Foot binding, a practice that originated in the 10th century and ended in the early 20th century, was practiced by women from all economic classes who desired small feet, believing that the ideal of a beautiful foot was three inches long. The practice involved intentionally breaking bones and crippled the woman for life, was often imposed by men, and at the very least by the sort of societal pressures that lead to modern-day self-destruction like anorexia and bulimia—not to mention that one of the main points of foot binding was that it kept the women at home. Starting in 1949, the Chinese government advocated for gender equality, though many long-held traditions have not been easily eliminated.

Women and the History of Kung Fu Films

China, Hong Kong, and Taiwan are the leading producers of kung fu and wuxia films. These films have been produced in two major periods: the

Mulan

Mulan is the subject of a singing ballad or poem originating in ancient Chinese history. The ballad tells the story of a young girl who first appears doing traditional women's work, weaving. After seeing a list of men who were ordered to go to war, wherein her father is listed because he has no son to go in his stead, Mulan decides that she should become a soldier. She acquires a horse, a saddle, and other equipment and goes alone on a long journey to join the war. She goes to battle for 12 years and, at the end, is recognized for her valiant fighting. After returning home, she is welcomed by her parents and siblings and appropriates a traditional appearance, putting on makeup and styling her hair. When the other soldiers see her, they are taken aback—they had thought Mulan was a boy.

Mulan's tale is one of several such stories found in ancient Chinese literature that position women as leading heroes in action. This story is among the more popular, influencing a number of adaptations in China and Hong Kong, such as the films *Hua Mulan Joins the Army* (1927), *Mulan Joins the Army* (1928, 1939), and *Lady General Hua Mulan* (1964). Disney popularized Mulan for American audiences with the animated adaptations *Mulan* (1998) and *Mulan II* (2004).

Source: "Ode to Mulan," http://www.yellowbridge.com/onlinelit/mulan.php (accessed July 2009).

golden ages, which took place in the 1920s and between the 1960s and 1980s; and the modern era, comprised of films made from the 1990s onward. Male actors and male writers have dominated the film industry, but several popular films and film **serials**, such as *Lady Sword Fighter of Jian-Nan* (1925), *Red Heroine* (1929), and *Swordswoman of Huangjiang* (1930), featured strong roles for women and catapulted actresses like Chin Tsi-Ang, Fan Xuepeng, Xu Qinfang, and Wu Lizhu to stardom. This feat alone was extraordinary, considering that unconventional women, including ancient female warriors, were not the norm in China. But the women who portrayed them did so by bending the rules.

Chin Tsi-Ang, for example, grew up with privileges and freedoms few Chinese girls enjoyed. She was permitted to live the life of a boy, sometimes even dressing like one, because a fortune-teller allegedly warned her parents that their daughter might otherwise die. She started martial arts training at eight years old, and when she grew up, acted in wuxia films and performed her own stunts. After marrying, she and her husband formed a production company. Another star, Fan, who was born in poverty in 1908, was raised by an extraordinary woman, who single-handedly educated and provided for the child after her husband died. As an adult, Fan married twice and "worked hard at mastering the skills [that film studios] demanded, such as riding, boxing, archery and, of course, swordsmanship," rising to become one of the popular female action heroes in China between 1927 and 1931 ("Fan Xuepeng"). After 1931, the thrilling warrior films subsided for numerous reasons: lack of interest, government censorship, and Japan's attack on China. Fan's action hero career also ended. As an aging actress, she was **typecast** as a mother, appearing in many "conventional roles in melodrama" ("Fan Xuepeng").

Chinese women were not the only ones to be depicted as powerful heroes in film. Early American films had their own assortment of unconventional women, generally appearing in action-adventure serials. Helen, the adventurous hero of *The Hazards of Helen* (1914–1917), was famous for the daring she showed, constantly risking life and limb as she faced weekly peril. The striking difference between characters such as Helen and the female Chinese warriors is that Helen and her ilk rarely wielded weapons or engaged in violent confrontations. After the advent of the talkies, women of action virtually disappeared and did not turn up again in Western nations until the 1960s, when such television shows as *The Avengers* appeared. Substantial numbers of American female action heroes would not emerge in TV or film until a decade after **second-wave feminism** got underway.

Wuxia films returned to Asian theaters in the 1960s and have remained there to this today. But there were dramatic changes, reflecting advancements in technology and a changing society. Women continued to figure prominently. Among the films that featured tough women warriors are *A Touch of Zen* (1971), *Hapkido* (1972), and *Come Drink with Me* and *The Fate of Lee Khan* (1972). In 1987, a woman, Teresa Woo, directed *Angel*, "a low-budget action thriller that is basically a rip-off of the American television series *Charlie's Angels*" that depicts the three female protagonists as relatively passive until the end of the film, when two women engage in a spectacular fight (West, 172–173).

Michelle Yeoh Choo Khen, born in Ipoh, Malaysia, on August 6, 1962, started her career in Hong Kong in the 1980s and was among the handful of stars to make the leap to America. Because of a spinal injury, Yeoh was unable to pursue her original goal, a professional career in ballet. But she credits her ballet training for helping her transition into becoming a kung fu star. Yeoh obtained a bachelor's degree in creative arts. After winning the Miss Malaysia beauty pageant in 1983, she appeared in Hong Kong commercials and debuted in her first film, *The Owl and Dumbo* (1984), shortly thereafter. After a brief marriage, Yeoh returned to acting in 1992, combining beauty and toughness in a busy action film career. She starred in an action comedy, *Police Story 3: Supercop* (1992), alongside Jackie Chan. The film was released to American audiences as *Supercop* in 1996. Her American film debut was as a lead Bond girl in *Tomorrow Never Dies* (1997). But it was

Crouching Tiger, Hidden Dragon (2000) that made Yeoh an international star. Yeoh has gone on to star in multiple Chinese and American films. Among her notable American films are *Memoirs of a Geisha* (2005), *The Mummy: Tomb of the Dragon Emperor* (2008), and *Babylon A.D* (2008). Yeoh, in her late forties as of this writing, has every intention of continuing to wield a sword and demonstrate her extraordinary fighting skills in future movies. She thus emerges as one of the few women action heroes who has defied the longstanding Hollywood tendency of **ageism**.

Kung Fu Films Come to America

Not long after kung fu action films experienced a resurgence in Asian countries, the excitement spilled over to America. In the 1970s, America experienced a kung fu craze that continues to influence its television and film industry to this day. Bruce Lee is considered the first and most influential kung fu star in America. His success is of particular import because America film and television rarely represented ethnic groups as heroes. Small, but powerfully quick and sinewy, Lee sparked mainstream interest in kung fu and challenged the American concept of a hero as either a tall, lanky, blue-eyed drifter or a tall, muscle-bound, American soldier. Born in San Francisco, California, on November 27, 1940, Lee began acting in kung fu films in Hong Kong at an early age. His reputation was such that he landed a plum role on American television, played Kato, the masked sidekick in *The Green Hornet* (1966/1967). In Hong Kong he went on to make the films that made him famous: *The Big Boss* (1971), *Fist of Fury* (1972), *Way of the Dragon* (1972), and the big-budget *Enter the Dragon* (1973).

The kung fu effect was far-reaching. The British television show *The Avengers* for a time featured Emma Peel, a spy and martial arts expert (although what actually appeared on-screen in the way of kung fu was very tame). In the late 1960s, Wonder Woman appeared in comic books as a kung-fu-fighting super hero. In the 1960s and 1970s, the number of martial artist action heroes in film and television increased, though they were primarily white males or Chinese nationalists. Chuck Norris, a karate champion, starred as Lee's adversary in *Way of the Dragon* (1972), the role that launched him to stardom. David Carradine, who was not Chinese, starred as Kwai Chang Caine, a biracial orphan who was trained by Shaolin monks in the 1970s series *Kung Fu*. Later, Jackie Chan, a star in Hong Kong, and Jet Li, a famous actor in Hong Kong and mainland China, became household names in America. Kung fu fighting became a staple in many action films and television series.

Despite the influx of Asian men introduced to American audiences between the 1970s and 1990s, Asian women were rarely depicted as action heroes. This fact is particularly confusing as the American girls and women appearing more and more regularly in action TV and film (*The Powerpuff*

Samurai Women and Ninja Girls

In Japan, between the 12th and 19th centuries, women warriors were not unusual. Some martial arts schools welcomed women, and others proactively instructed young girls and women in the ways of the samurai and kunoichi or ninja. Samurai women received education, traditional training in skills such as housekeeping, and learned how to fight with and without weapons such as a knives, daggers, and bows and arrows. Some Samurai women fought in battles, while others stayed at home and managed the family affairs, always vigilant in case of trouble (samurai wives often had to defend their homes in time of conflict).

Ninja women were frequently required to serve as assassins and spies. These women fought as fiercely as did male ninjas. Female ninjas often resorted to wearing disguises to accomplish their missions. At other times, they wore the all-black garb most often associated with the ninja.

Girls, *Buffy the Vampire Slayer*, *The Matrix*, *Kill Bill*), particularly in the 1990s and beyond, employed kung fu methods with increasing regularity. Instead, Asian women were either characterized as docile or malevolent and violently aggressive. The negative images associated with Asian women in America include "geisha, housewives, exotic Cathay Girls, China Dolls, Suzie Wongs, Madame Butterflies, powerful Dragon Ladies, martial arts mistresses, and the like" (Prasso, xiii). Ang Lee helped to bring female Asian kung fu stars to the forefront, subverting **stereotypical** images of Asian women in American film and television.

Ang Lee

Ang Lee was born in Taiwan on October 23, 1954. He received a bachelor's degree in theater at the University of Illinois at Urbana-Champaign and a master of fine arts degree from the Tisch School of the Arts of New York University. Controversial filmmaker Spike Lee, who directed several films that address **racism** and African American culture, attended the Tisch School of the Arts at the same time as Lee.

Ang Lee first came to international attention as the director of *Sense and Sensibility* (1995), a British film set in the 19th century, based on the novel of the same name written by Jane Austen about traditional romantic love and marriage. This film featured conventional gender roles and happy endings—although the author is considered notoriously independent and intelligent and was far ahead of her time, but his later films moved swiftly toward action and controversy. *Crouching Tiger, Hidden Dragon* depicts women who defy tradition and challenge socially constructed barriers. In 2003, he directed the first movie version of the *Hulk*. This film was among the first of a wave of revival films based on mostly male comic book action heroes. In 2005, he directed the controversial *Brokeback Mountain*, a movie about forbidden homosexual love. In 2007, he directed *Lust, Caution*, a film that portrayed a Chinese college-student-turned assassin whose love for her target caused her to disclose the assassination plans. In this film, the female lead is punished because of her inability to stay detached and follow through with her mission. Her forebears, Nikita from *La Femme Nikita*, Samantha Caine from *The Long Kiss Goodnight* (1996), and Fox from *Wanted* (2008) were too cool, professional, and unwavering to foil an assignment over love or any other emotion.

Zhang Ziyi

Zhang Ziyi was born in Beijing, China, on February 9, 1979. After graduating from the Central Academy of Drama in China, Zhang appeared in *The Road Home* (1999). This love story did not portend the high-action films like *Crouching Tiger, Hidden Dragon*, *Hero* (2002), and *House of Flying Daggers* (2004), for which she is most known. She also played a fierce villain in *Rush Hour* 2 (2001), starring Jackie Chan as Chief Inspector Lee and Chris Tucker as Detective James Carter. This film was Zhang's American film debut. She appeared in several other roles, such as a geisha in *Memoirs of a Geisha* (2005) and an empress in *The Banquet* (2006).

POWER SUITS, WEAPONS, AND ABILITIES

In *Crouching Tiger, Hidden Dragon*, men and women wear flowing robes, thus leveling out the historic playing field in terms of dress. Men and women appear majestic in long robes, especially as the robes flow with their movements during fight scenes or when, for example, Mu Bai is alone executing moves with the Green Destiny under the soft light of the moon. Jen, however, is restricted in her formal attire. Her robes restrict her mobility. Jen prefers the black garb of a thief and the attire worn by individuals of lower status. In this way, she can move freely and fight.

Women in *Crouching Tiger, Hidden Dragon* wield both supernatural and martial arts powers. They can dart up buildings, flutter and glide with the nimbleness of a ballerina, and perform martial arts with believable and authoritative finesse. Jen's favorite weapon is the Green Destiny, a sword coveted by many warriors. In one scene, two men sit and admire the sword, discuss its ancientness, measurements, beauty, and power: "It comes alive only through skillful manipulation." Shu Lien is skilled in all the accoutrements of martial arts—swords, spears, and other weapons—but tells Jen she prefers the machete.

Jen is good at fighting, and she knows this. Jen, however, is rebellious. Her rebelliousness is what pushes her to excel and transform as a combatant. Unlike Jade Fox, Jen fights purely in masculine ways. Jade Fox, however, compensates for her lesser combat abilities by using poison. Traditionally, poison is coded as a feminine weapon, one that is passive and does not depend on physical combat or skill. In kung fu, skill and technique are paramount.

Mu Bai, as well as everyone else, recognizes Jen's amazing skills. But he and Shu Lien desire to teach her restraint. Mu Bai wants to train her further, for, in truth, he is still more powerful than she is.

VILLAIN

Although Jen is depicted as a bad girl (she steals things that do not belong to her, flirts with the dark side, masquerades as a villain, and fights the good guys), Jen is in reality a misguided young woman who eventually has a change of heart. The real villain is Jade Fox.

Jade Fox has an unfortunate storyline; indeed, she is one of the more complex villains in film history. Like Jen, she dreamed in her youth of becoming a great warrior. She went to Wudan Mountain, where men were trained in the secrets of Wudan martial arts. She alleged that Mu Bai's master would only sleep with her, not teach her martial arts, because women were not allowed. Exclusion is a feminist theme—one that in the 21st century is less common than it was say a century ago, when women in America and China were excluded from many activities and careers. In anger, Jade Fox murdered Mu Bai's master and stole the Wudan manual, which contained secret techniques. To underscore her evilness, she is depicted as a witch, a stereotypical image that is associated with craggy, old sorceresses of fairy tales and is reflected in the tragedies of women in the 17th century who were, falsely or not, accused of witchery and executed. Indeed, Jade Fox is a mature woman who dresses in black, contorts her face wickedly, and uses magic and poison.

Jade Fox is bitter and powerful; her evil exploits are notorious throughout the region. After Jen, in disguise, secretly steals the Green Destiny, people mistake the thief as Jade Fox. Word goes out that Jade Fox is in town, and everyone trembles. One man thinks Jade Fox is a man, automatically assuming that a woman cannot be a villain or strong and powerful. Traditionally, criminality and power were associated with masculinity, a line few women crossed. An inspector informs the man that Jade Fox is indeed a woman and goes on to explain how she killed his wife, who was a martial arts expert. In this film, most women know martial arts, including the inspector's daughter.

Jade Fox's abilities notwithstanding, she is not the most powerful character in this film. She has limited reading skills and cannot decipher all the symbols

Tomoe Gozen

Born circa 1100 in Japan, Tomoe Gozen was a well-known female samurai. She fought in many battles, attaining legendary status. According to one legend, she fought in a battle with her husband, a general named Kiso Yoshinaka. She killed many—including one of the leaders on the enemy side—utilizing her favorite weapon, the *naginata*, a long pole usually made of bamboo. Many revered her for her extraordinary fighting skills, as well as her beauty.

Tomoe Gozen appears in *The Tale of the Heike*, a book that was transcribed from oral stories told by monks in the 1300s, considered an important classic of medieval Japanese literature. She is also the only female warrior protagonist to appear in Noh theater, a form of theater originating in 14th-century Japan.

in the secret manual. Jen, with her privileged education, can and does. Behind Jade Fox's back, Jen teaches herself all the secret methods of fighting, surpassing her master and everyone else save for Mu Bai. Mu Bai is also more powerful than Jade, who in the end must depend on poison to kill him.

CROUCHING TIGER, HIDDEN DRAGON, THE FILM

In action films—including those that, as with foreign films, are perceived to be radically different from what mainstream Americans are used to seeing—skill as well as sangfroid, toughness, and independence are essential ingredients. Jen exhibits these qualities, but in unconventional ways. For example, when Jen is at home, she plays the role of aristocrat with a cool steadiness. She is coy, demure, feminine, and charming. This **alter ego**, akin to Wonder Woman's Diana Prince, or the many disguises used in undercover work by Charlie's Angels, The Bionic Woman, Catwoman, or Supergirl, functions as a way to divert attention from her true intentions. Unlike other action heroes, Jen's ploy is sinister. No one but a shrewd woman like Shu Lien could guess that Jen, a young woman and aristocrat, was capable of stealing the Green Destiny.

Jen's earliest demonstrations of toughness occur when she steals Mu Bai's sword "for fun," much like how Lara Croft, the video game protagonist, is depicted as getting a playful, childlike thrill out of reckless extreme behavior and adventuring. In a flashback, Jen relentlessly pursues a wild desert bandit who stole her comb. Feeling contained by her sheltered, aristocratic life, impending marriage, and other social expectations, and longing for an unbridled warrior lifestyle, Jen breaks up with the bandit (Lo) after a love affair, rejects his rescue attempt on her marriage day, and makes a run for it on her own. Stopping for a meal, Jen is challenged by two rough warriors with fearsome names, Iron Eagle Sung and Flying Cougar Mu Bai Yun. She dauntlessly crushes them, as she does all the men she encounters in an ensu-ing scene at a restaurant populated by exclusively male warriors. Before she fights them, she insults them, making fun of their warrior names. During the fight, someone asks who she is. Announcing herself, she sings out a paean commencing with "I am the Invincible Sword Goddess, armed with the Green Destiny that knows no equal."

Jen demonstrates toughness and independence in other ways. By spurning romantic relationships (like other female action heroes such as Helen of *The Hazards of Helen* and Lara Croft), Jen maintains her autonomy, a classic trait of male heroes. She rejects enticing offers from Mu Bai, who wants to be her master and rescue her from her mischievous ways, telling her that there is "no growth without assistance," and Jade Fox, who wants to com-bine forces with her. Jen, who is largely self-taught and formidable, thus demonstrates individualism and rebelliousness (she has no regard for tradi-tion or protocol). She breaks rules to get power; she forges her own path.

Jen's brand of toughness includes fierce ambition and unabashed confi-dence in herself. Traditionally, ambition is a masculine trait. Confidence is too. But Jen goes one better by plotting behind Jade Fox's back, hiding the fact that she has trained herself in the most secret techniques of the Wudan manual. When the truth of her powers is revealed during a fight with Mu Bai, Jen is quite brutal when she tells Jade Fox that she realized a long time ago that she was the more powerful.

Jen's nature further comes to light when she is contrasted with the other characters in the film. Jen's rebelliousness has its opposite in Shu Lien's reserve, dutifulness, and sense of responsibility. Shu Lien recognizes that her power is limited and less than Mu Bai's. She knows that only men are per-mitted to train in the prestigious martial arts school. Unlike Jen, Shu Lien wants to be in a romantic relationship and feels no passion about her posi-tion as a swordswoman. During Jen's brief relationship with Lo, Lo is char-acterized with feminine traits; he is nurturing, caring, and anxious to spend the rest of his days with Jen. However, when it comes to Mu Bai, Jen's powers fall short. He can easily subdue her; she must resort to game play to try to outdo him, telling him when he has cornered her, "if you can take [the Green Destiny] in three moves, I'll give it to you." He effortlessly pro-pels the sword out of her hand. Racing after it, Jen grabs it. She is then res-cued by Jade Fox, who takes flight and eludes Mu Bai.

In the end, after Mu Bai has been poisoned by one of Jade Fox's darts, Jen has a change of heart. But her shocking leap over a cliff, in the presence of Lo after a night of lovemaking, demonstrates that Jen—with all her unconven-tional passion, ambition, and independence—could not find a place in that world. Other female action heroes meet a similar fate. Thelma and Louise, outlaws on the run, drove over a cliff rather than face imprisonment or the ennui and constraints of their traditional lives. Joan of Arc, in real life and on film, was executed because she rebelled against authority and tradition.

IMPACT

Crouching Tiger, Hidden Dragon was a watershed event. The film helped to launch the careers of Zhang Ziyi, Michelle Yeoh, and Chow Yun Fat in America and paved the way for the subsequent release of foreign films such as *Hero* (2002) and *House of Flying Daggers* (2004) in America. In terms of female action heroism, Ang Lee gave audiences two powerful women. One reflected the influence of **third-wave feminism** that was becoming the norm: a swaggering girl hero who mixed danger and pleasure and did things her way, whether with sex appeal, childlike fervor, or excessive violence. The other was both traditional and unconventional: an experienced woman who executed power with responsibility and demonstrated virtue, loyalty, and obedience to the law.

See also Catwoman; Emma Peel; Thelma and Louise.

FURTHER RESOURCES

Aarons, Wendy. "If Her Stunning Beauty Doesn't Bring You to Your Knees, Her Deadly Drop Kick Will: Violent Women in the Hong Kong Kung Fu Film." In *Reel Knockouts: Violent Women in the Movies*, ed. Martha McCaughey and Neal King. Austin: University of Texas Press, 2001.

The Chinese Mirror. "Fan Xuepeng (1908–1974): Swordswoman 'Thirteenth Sister.'" http://www.chinesemirror.com/index/2009/07/fan-xuepeng-1908-1974-swords woman-13th-sister.html.

Inness, Sherrie A. *Tough Girls: Women Warriors and Wonder Women in Popular Culture*. Philadelphia: University of Pennsylvania Press, 1999.

Jiwani, Yasmin. "From Dragon Lady to Action Hero: Race and Gender in Popular Television (Part 1)." http://lists.econ.utah.edu/pipermail/margins-to-centre/2006-July/000884.html.

Jiwani, Yasmin. "From Dragon Lady to Action Hero: Race and Gender in Popular Television (Part 2)." http://lists.econ.utah.edu/pipermail/margins-to-centre/2006-July/000885.html.

Mainon, Dominique, and James Ursini. *The Modern Amazons: Warrior Women On-Screen*. Pompton Plains, NJ: Limelight Editions, 2006.

Prasso, Sheridan. *The Asian Mystique: Dragon Ladies, Geisha Girls, and Our Fantasies of the Exotic Orient*. New York: Public Affairs, 2005.

Reynaud, Berenice. "Glamour and Suffering: Gong Li and the History of Chinese Stars." In *Women and Film: A Sight and Sound Reader*, ed. Pam Cook and Philip Dodd. Philadelphia: Temple University Press, 1993.

Slampyak, Diana E. "Chivalric Virtues in Female Form: *Crouching Tiger, Hidden Dragon*'s Wudan Warrior Princess as Medieval Hero." In *The Medieval Hero on Screen*, ed. Martha W. Driver and Sid Ray. Jefferson, NC: McFarland and Company, 2004.

West, David. *Chasing Dragons: An Introduction to the Martial Arts Film*. New York: I. B. Tauris, 2006.

Joan of Arc leading battle in the film *The Messenger: The Story of Joan of Arc*. (AP Photo/Gaumont.)

Joan of Arc

Joan of Arc is a historic figure whose brief and dramatic life has been adapted into numerous adaptations, films, and television series. Joan of Arc was born in the winter of 1412 in the sylvan village of Domremy, France. In Joan's time, France was wracked with social instability, government corruption, and a centuries-old brutal conflict between France and England and England's supporters, like the Burgundians. Bit by bit, England seized land belonging to the French. Raiders pillaged villages, burned homes to the ground, and terrorized the inhabitants.

At the age of 13, Joan began hearing voices. She told no one what she heard and saw until near the end of her life, when she was being interrogated during her grueling trial before her martyrdom. During her trial, she claimed that she had visions of Christian saints, which were not perceptible to others. Their voices gave her commands (which Joan sometimes referred to as "counsel"), telling her to do extraordinary things such as to crown Charles VII and to lead the French to victory over the English. Catholicism was the national religion of France, but the people were still largely influenced by beliefs and fears of the supernatural, demons, fairies, and witches.

Despite being a woman of humble origins, Joan of Arc rose to prominence by following the commands of her voices. In a period of less than two years, she brought about the crowning of Charles VII and saw the French through many heroic battles, dressed in her trademark men's clothes and with her hair cut short like a man. Ultimately, she was captured, as the voices had said she would be. After enduring a lengthy trial, Joan of Arc was burned at the stake in 1431. Her ecclesiastical judges claimed she was a heretic because she heard voices that they alleged came from demons and failed to show remorse for her contempt of religion and custom by dressing in men's clothing. Nearly five hundred years later, in 1920, Joan of Arc was canonized by the pope. She is today one of the three patron saints of France.

In 1928, the first film adaptation of Joan of Arc's life was made. This seminal work, a highly acclaimed silent film entitled *La Passion de Jeanne d'Arc* or *The Passion of Joan of Arc*, was directed by Carl Theodor Dreyer. *Passion* starred Maria Falconetti and covered Joan's trials and martyrdom in 110 minutes. A second major film, *Joan of Arc*, was released in 1948. It was directed by Victor Fleming and cast Ingrid Bergman in the leading role. This film ran 145 minutes. There was also *Saint Joan* (1957) directed by Otto Preminger. Jean Seaberg was cast as Joan of Arc. *Procès de Jeanne d'Arc* or *The Trial of Joan of Arc* (1962) starred Florence Delay and received the Special Jury Prize at the 1962 Cannes Film Festival. In 1999, upcoming actress Milla Jovovich (a mainstay in 1990s action films) played Joan in *The Messenger: The Story of Joan of Arc*, a film that ran 160 minutes. In that same year, CBS in the United States and CBC in Canada released a two-part television miniseries, *Joan of Arc*, starring LeeLee Sobieski, which detailed Joan's short life from birth to death. In the new millennium,

Amber Tamblyn played an adolescent Joan of Arc in the television series *Joan of Arcadia* (2003–2005).

Most renditions of her story include quotes from Joan herself, which were recorded by scribes during her trial. Joan has been depicted in a number of different ways—as lachrymose, restless, or eager for action—all of which show, with varying degrees of creative embellishment, how Joan rose to power, endured courageously her harrowing trial, and died with faith intact. Her strength and toughness was underscored by the conservative times she lived in, when only men could be soldiers, and women, especially youth, did not challenge societal roles, let alone their government and their religion.

ORIGINS

The stories of real-life legends, male and female, have always fascinated society and prompted a steady stream of retellings down through the centuries via first the oral traditions, then nonfiction books, novels, and plays, and in the last century, film and television adaptations. Queen Elizabeth, the redoubtable red-haired leader of England who reigned between 1558 and 1603, has inspired numerous plays, films, and a television miniseries. The lives of extraordinary people are deemed to transcend the ordinariness of normal life, and thus they become the very stuff of legend, archetypes of heroism or infamy. Famous people, those legends-in-the-making, act, speak, and behave in ways that **transgress** custom and demonstrate heroism, especially those who protect the lives of ordinary people. Their stories, reshaped over time, long outlive them.

Because women were not historically associated with heroism, a woman hero transcends the ordinary. When the hero is a child, like David, who battled the giant Goliath with a mere slingshot, as the biblical narrative goes, audiences are all the more amazed.

The Life of Joan of Arc

Like Queen Elizabeth and David, Joan of Arc is considered exceptional in part because of her youth. Like David, her upbringing did not portend greatness. In medieval times, men of valor and honor became knights (fighting soldiers). They wore armor and fought in service to the king. Women wore dresses and lived exclusively in the home, as dictated by gender roles. During Joan's childhood, she was no different. She lived in a small village and was not taught to read or write, let alone train in combat or strategy.

Young Joan was accustomed to women's work, such as sewing and spinning. Described as extraordinarily pious and compassionate, Joan, at 13, was considered quiet and withdrawn. She prayed often and kept the secret

Medieval Women in Film

Historically, the medieval woman was depicted in films as a prize to be won by charming princes, knights, and other gallant men or as a damsel in distress, awaiting rescue from a ravenous dragon or evil wizard. A score of films in recent times have challenged this stereotype, featuring women who are commanding, forceful, and powerful. In the *Shrek* films (2001, 2004, 2007), Princess Fiona and other princesses flaunt spectacular martial arts moves. Guinevere (Keira Knightly) in *King Arthur* (2004) is radically different from her predecessors. Wearing a strappy warrior outfit, with tribal-looking markings on her face, this Guinevere pelts out a battle cry and fights with bow and arrow and sword. In the climactic battle of *The Return of the King* (2003), the third installation in *The Lord of the Rings* film trilogy, Eowyn (Miranda Otto) enters battle disguised as a man and kills the terrifying Nazgul.

of her voices to herself. Scholars like to debate the source of the voices: whether they were a sign of mental illness, hallucinations, her subconscious or intuition, or, perhaps, truly from God. Joan herself believed that the voices belonged to St. Michael, St. Margaret, St. Catherine, and others.

Joan Goes to See the Governor at Vaucouleurs

In the spring of 1428, the same year her village was attacked, Joan acted upon the voices' commands. She was told to "go to Vaucouleurs, get help from the Governor, Robert de Baudricourt, and prepare to go to the rescue of the exiled Dauphin and his besieged town of Orléans" (Brooks, 27).

With the English threatening to take over the whole country, Joan believed God wanted her to help save France and crown the son of the deceased French king. However, Joan first had to escape from her parents. She knew that they would not allow her to pursue such a dangerous and unconventional mission. Her father had allegedly dreamed that Joan would go off with the soldiers and had vowed that that would not happen.

Joan managed to get away with the help of her uncle, who transported her to Vaucouleurs, where she went before the governor. He was skeptical, but Joan was persistent. Eventually, she was able to convince him to help her gain an audience with Charles VII. In the process, she won the loyalty of the people of Vaucouleurs, who believed in her God-inspired mission. Divine crusades were considered a normal part of medieval life and traditions.

Before leaving on her journey after a considerable delay, Joan exchanged her traditional peasant dress for men's clothing, being supplied "with a tunic, long hose, and leather boots" as well as a horse (Brooks, 34). Joan's hair was also cut above her ears like a man's. After portending the French defeat near Orléans, the governor had a priest attempt to exorcise her, but the priest conceded that Joan was not under any demonic influence.

To Chinon to See Charles VII

After a long and restless wait, the governor finally permitted Joan to leave for Chinon. He provided her with a sword, another horse, and an escort of seven men. Joan and her entourage left in 1429 through dangerous enemy territory. She was 17 years old.

Although Charles attempted to hide from Joan at his castle in Chinon, Joan found him out. She repeatedly did and said things to cause others to marvel at her, most notably when she privately told Charles something that convinced him she was no ordinary maid. But Charles knew he had to verify that Joan was truly who she said she was: an instrument of God sent to bring about his crowning and save France from England.

Joan thus underwent three weeks of questioning. Women examined her and confirmed that she was indeed a virgin. Joan reportedly vowed to never marry, defying the custom of young women who were expected to take a husband and bear children. Her virginity not only confirmed her purity but proved that she was not a witch, as it was believed in those days that witches could not be virgins. During the questioning process, Joan was confident and cheeky. When a churchman stated that "if [God] wants to deliver [France], it is not necessary to send soldiers," Joan quipped back, "In the name of God, the soldiers will fight and God will deliver them" (Brooks, 45). When "asked if she believed in God, Joan indignantly snapped back, 'Better than you do'" (Brooks, 45). After this period of investigation, Charles sent Joan off on her dangerous quest to lead the French army into battle against the English. She was given armor, two battle standards, her own squires, pages, heralds, and chaplain, and several experienced knights.

In Battle

Joan of Arc went on to lead several campaigns for the French, most significantly the battles at Orléans and Patay. Scholars disagree as to whether Joan's role in the battles was as a figurehead or as an active strategist. Either way, she functioned as a symbol of national pride, resistance, hope, and can-do-itness.

Before Joan, now dubbed the Maid of Orléans, Charles and many of the people of France had largely given up hope. The English appeared too formidable. Joan encouraged the French soldiers, motivating them to fight, inspiring them to believe. She did not kill anyone, though she carried her sword (this alone was transgressive). Eager to save France, Joan braved the battlefield, directing the soldiers when to strike, urging them steadily onward toward the enemy. Esteemed captains conferred with Joan. Mighty knights acquiesced to her commands, such as when she ordered all the men to stop cursing and to make confession before battle. Essential to Joan's influence were her appearance, her conviction, and her intelligence.

POWER SUIT, WEAPONS, AND ABILITIES

The sight of young Joan astride a white horse in gleaming armor, wielding a sword or battle standard, emboldened the men she led in battle. The image contrasts sharply with that of the Joan who arrived in the city of Vaucouleurs, a humble maid in conventional dress, coding her as youthful and female, not at all mature and masculine. Joan's reason for wearing male clothing and cutting her hair is unclear. Many suppose that Joan dressed in this way so as to appear modest and to not tempt the men with whom she traveled. Unintentionally or otherwise, she donned the clothes that would best empower her, in a way that long hair and dresses (feminine identifiers) would not. In the same way, Lieutenant Jordan O'Neil discarded the markers of femininity (her long dress, soft body, menstrual cycle) in pursuit of achieving her goals as a warrior in the navy. After Joan's capture, her male clothing symbolized her resistance to conventionality, to the oppressive and corrupt government that insisted upon punishing her and ultimately martyring her.

Joan employed an assortment of weaponry. As the legend has it, her sword was found just where she said it would be, "buried near the altar in St. Catherine's Chapel at Fierbois. . . . In the chivalric tradition of King Arthur and his famous sword, Excalibur, the sword was miraculously found in the chapel" (Brooks, 48–49). Because of this, the people associated Joan's sword with divine (and possibly supernatural) power, which greatly heightened their awe of her. Another weapon that was indispensable to Joan was the voices that allegedly gave her counsel and thus led to the French victories at Orléans and Patay. Joan's faith in God astounded religious scholars. Her boldness in the presence of royalty, her ability to persuade men of power to do her bidding, and the courage to face off with her Goliath-like enemies, the English, at the age of only 17, were considered to be a measure of her faith.

Indeed, Joan's boldness and courage were out of the ordinary. She was anxious to lead the men into battle and became frustrated when they were delayed. She sent the English three letters, boldly requesting that they yield to the French. In the second letter to Lord Talbot, the commander, "she advised him to give up the siege and go back to England or she would force him to do so. She also demanded the return of the herald who had delivered Joan's first message" (Brooks, 60). In response, the English called her a "cowgirl" and threatened to burn her (Brooks, 60). When she was shot by

Girl Heroes

Girl heroes have played an important role in American popular culture since the early 20th century. Supergirl, Batgirl, Nancy Drew, Orphan Annie, Pippi Longstocking, the Powerpuff Girls, Hermione Granger, Buffy, and Carmen Cortez lead a host of girls who have appeared in comic books, television, and film. Caped teenaged crusaders, such as Supergirl and Batgirl, had powers like their adult male counterparts, and although they never over-shadowed Superman or Batman, they still enjoyed considerable popularity. Nancy Drew sparked a craze among young girls, inspired them to be smart, courageous, and adventurous. Red-haired Annie and pig-tailed Pippi Long-stocking were popular hoydens; Pippi Longstocking, in particular, was strong, tough, and feisty, constantly transgressing the quiet, demure, and sweet-girl archetype. The Powerpuff Girls' claim to fame was based on the ironic contrast of their sweet girlishness and their rambunctious super powers. Hermione Granger, one of Harry Potter's best friends, is depicted as super studious, smart, disciplined, and skilled with the wand and magic potions. Buffy was 15 when she started slaying vampires and saving the world on the television show that debuted in 1997, and Carmen Cortez is a tough and smart sleuth in the sister and brother dynamic duo in the *Spy Kids* film series (2001, 2002, 2003).

an arrow in the chest and taken away by her men, she pulled the arrow out herself. In Paris in the early part of September 1429, she rode up before the enemy and "threatened they would be put to death if they did not" surren-der (Brooks, 94). Shot in the thigh with an arrow, Joan had to be forced off the battleground again. The battle in Paris was a loss, because Charles ordered Joan and the soldiers to withdraw.

Thus in short order, Joan ascended to fame and acclaim, becoming a legend in her own time. The French attributed her accurate predictions of what would happen to her supernatural abilities. When she allegedly prayed for a dead baby who came back to life, they believed she was a messenger of God. In this way, she was akin to modern fictional heroes like Buffy the Vampire Slayer and The Powerpuff Girls, who were also sent to save humanity from oppressive forces in times of desperate need. It is a mighty archetype, glimpsed also in tales of American Western heroes who arrive in troubled towns to save the day.

After liberating a town from the English, Joan's successes were celebrated as miracles; women and men reached out to touch her. Joan also had an uncanny influence over the army, leading several thousand men who report-edly never questioned her orders.

TRIAL AND MARTYRDOM

After Joan was captured by the Burgundians on May 30, 1430, her spiritual strength was sorely tested. She tried, unsuccessfully, to escape the clutches of her enemies on more than one occasion. Charles would not ransom her, so in November of that year she was sold to the English for ten thousand francs.

Joan was a prized prisoner. Indeed, the English had wanted her in their grasp since she had first appeared in all her glory to fight them, for not only was she a nuisance to them, she frightened their men. Many of the English considered her a witch. To counter this effect, they determined to sully her impeccable image, which they did by trying her for heresy. Under the circumstances, there could be only one outcome.

The trial began early in 1431 and lasted three months, during which time Joan was aggressively questioned by some 70 clergymen. She was not permitted an advocate, but she did speak boldly as she was accused of sinning against God by dressing like a man, wielding weapons, and using magic and sorcery. The ecclesiastical court attempted to prove that the voices she heard were demonic in nature. At one point, Joan "looked directly at Bishop Cauchon [who facilitated the trial] and said, 'You say you are my judge. Consider well what you do, for in truth I am sent by God and you put yourself in great peril" (Brooks, 124–125). At night, Joan was shackled and watched over by male guards and prevented from taking part in religious rituals. Remnants of the transcripts from the trials remain, bearing witness to the fact that, incredibly, Joan remained alert throughout the long questioning process.

On May 24, 1431, Joan agreed to sign a confessional document to escape death. By signing, Joan "promised never to bear arms again, that she would cast off her male clothes, admit her sins and renounce her voices, and submit completely to Church authority" (Brooks, 142). It is unclear what happened next, but some argue that Joan was tricked into changing into men's clothes, thus breaking her pledge. Predictably (a heretic could not be killed unless she was a repeat offender), Joan was "pronounced a relapsed heretic and burned in Rouen's square by English soldiers" on May 30, 1431 ("Timeline"). Denied confession or communion, she reportedly cried as she was put on the executioner's cart.

Joan was bound to a stake. Above her was a sign: "Joan the Maid, liar, pernicious, seducer of the people, diviner, superstitious, blasphemer of God, presumptuous, misbelieving in the faith of Jesus Christ, idolater, cruel, dissolute invoker of devils, apostate, schismatic and heretic." Before her death, Joan prayed, kissed a cross that she requested to be brought to her and then repeatedly called out the name "Jesus" before a large audience of townspeople and nobles. She was 19 years old.

In 1450, Charles VII ordered an investigation of Joan's trial. A number of people who had known Joan in her childhood and young adulthood provided evidence and witness of her good reputation. In 1456, "the Church overturned Joan's conviction . . . [and] Joan is declared a martyr who was wrongly executed by corrupt partisan clergy" ("Timeline"). In 1920, Pope Benedict XV canonized her Saint Joan of Arc.

JOAN OF ARC, THE FILMS AND TELEVISION MINISERIES

In the absence of factual evidence, and given the obviously mystical elements of her tale, film and television producers and directors characterized the historic Joan in ways that were largely imaginative, each generation projecting its own distinctive interpretation upon the heroic tale. For example, all that is known about Joan's physical appearance is that she was a "strong peasant of square build. Her hair was black, her eyes dark brown, and her complexion swarthy" (Brooks, 18). But the "true" facts never are what is important when constructing a heroic character; truth is found in the depth of the character and in the universality of the message her story conveys.

In the 1928 silent film, director Carl Theodor Dreyer cast French actress Maria Falconetti in the role. She looks older than a mere 19 as she confronts her judges. Her hair—shocking for the early 20th century, let alone the 15th—is shaved close to her head. Although her hair and eyes are dark, her complexion is pale. This Joan is solemn-faced and (thanks to the exigencies of silent film) wordlessly intense and dramatic.

In the 1948 film starring Swedish-born Ingrid Bergman (of Swedish and German descent), Joan appears with golden hair and blue eyes. This Joan is sweet and wholesome, but when the situation demands it, forceful and noble in ways that reflect the might of the Hollywood studios of the time. In the 1999 film version, director Luc Besson cast Milla Jovovich in the role. Jovovich had become an icon of female heroism in the 1990s—boyishly thin, an unconventional Hollywood beauty, but as striking as a model in a fashion magazine. Jovovich's Joan is girlish, impetuous, aggressive, and neurotic. In the television miniseries of the same decade, Leelee Sobieski renders a wholesome, ordinariness to Joan. She speaks softly, exudes femininity, and her vulnerability comes through even when she is in armor leading French soldiers. Of the four actresses, she was the youngest to portray Joan and the closest to Joan's real age.

Rather than depict Joan as a one-dimensional hero, one who is brave, impenetrable, and masculine through and through, these producers and directors refashioned her in ways that dramatized her perceived weaknesses, her victimization, femininity, or fanaticism. In the 1928 silent film, which covers Joan's trial and martyrdom, Dreyer makes use of multiple close-ups, focusing on Joan's expressions. She alternates between a faraway look, sadness, serenity, and fear. In her chamber, she is overcome with emotion, but is serene when she sees a shadow in the shape of a cross on the floor. In other scenes, she is shown being harassed by men but is then rescued by an empathetic priest. In another scene, she passes out when she is taken to a torture room. However, when Joan is questioned, her answers, which appear in captions, are bold and forthright.

When Joan is transported to the place of her martyrdom, the onlookers show compassion. A woman gives her nourishment to drink. Men, women, and children cry for her, and someone calls out, "you have murdered a saint." After Joan is martyred, the people riot. This film clearly intends to inspire audiences to feel compassion for Joan the victim. It is her victimization, rather than her courage or zeal, that is underscored by the emotional close-ups, the men who harass her, the priest who rescues her, and the townspeople who protest her unjust death. Rather than depict the heroic scenes of Joan in battle array, audiences see only the victim and martyr.

The 1948 film, *Joan of Arc*, largely depicts Joan's rise to leadership as a struggle to control her femininity. At the beginning of the film, Joan is depicted as an ordinary member of the family, a young woman who is expected to help prepare meals and do as she is told. Underscoring her femininity and traditionalism, she wears a peasant dress and a long braid. In a weak moment when she is alone, she cries and doubts her ability to do as God wills her (i.e., facilitate the crowning of Charles VII and lead the French to victory over the English). When she appears before the governor, she is timid at first, then becomes more forceful. Outside, the people laugh at her. A man mocks her peasant dress. She is encumbered by weakness and self-doubt and the constrictions of society that belittles her attempt to exert control and power.

As with so many action heroes, Joan's physical transfiguration heralds her increasing power. After Joan cuts her hair, puts on men's clothes, and wins the support of Charles VII, she speaks as an equal to military commanders and launches French soldiers boldly into war. When she speaks, her voice booms and exudes the sort of confidence associated with masculinity. After one battle, she becomes overwhelmed with emotion and cries over the carnage. Men come to her aid and try to comfort her. They are accustomed to death in times of war and are thus unfazed. "I thought victory would be beautiful," she tells them. "But it is," one of them says. It was believed that the real Joan of Arc also cried at least once when watching soldiers die during battle. This scene dramatizes a feminine response to war. A subsequent scene, during which Joan waits impatiently to be dismissed by Charles VII so she can get back to battle, demonstrates how Joan has overcome her previous feminine response.

In this film, Joan appears much more forthright and bold during her trial than she appeared in the silent film. In the same strong speaking voice she learned to wield during battle, Joan answers her judge's questions. At one point, she raises her voice, telling her judges that "you are my mortal enemies!" In another scene, she points at the bishop and tells him "take care not to judge me wrongly, for in truth, I am sent by God and you place yourself in great danger." Only when she is alone with those who have compassion for her does she speak softly or allow herself to cry. But in the presence of her judges, she maintains her boldness and courage. She has effectively learned how to present herself as a hero. When she faces her impending death, she says, "my victory is my martyrdom." When she is shown in a culminating scene bound to a stake, she appears not as a power-less victim, but as an empowered martyr. Indeed, a priest echoes this senti-ment, stating that "[her corrupt judges] made her a symbol," emphasizing that the plans to destroy her will be her and France's victory.

The Messenger presents yet another approach to the story of Joan of Arc. In this film, Joan's voices are sinister, and dissonant music plays in the back-ground when she hears them. Her visions are ghastly too: a deadpan boy and grown man alternately shown sitting in a chair in the middle of the for-est. There are no light and angelic voices or melodic harp sounds to appease audiences. Thirteen-year-old Joan (played by Jane Valentine as a child) watches from her hiding place with fright as her sister is stabbed and raped by one of the fiendish soldiers plundering her small village. Joan blames her-self for the murder of her sister. She is angry and hysterical when she demands of a priest in a subsequent scene why she could not have died instead.

Jovovich plays the older Joan as compulsive and demanding. Although she appears waving her sword in the air while on her horse and defending herself against English soldiers, she is not shown killing anyone. Indeed, she stops a French soldier from killing an English prisoner of war for his teeth, clearly horrified by the act. This Joan is, nevertheless, an exuberant warrior, appearing in several scenes, screaming, contorting her face, and urging the men on. She is relentless, waking the men prematurely from their rest so they can go on to battle, working her men past the point of fatigue.

After Joan is captured and imprisoned, Luc Besson, the director, introdu-ces a character listed as "The Conscience," played by Dustin Hoffman, who comes to Joan and questions her. Although Joan is bold during the trial, she crumbles before her conscience, raving neurotically to herself about her innocence but ultimately confessing to her conscience that her mission was not divinely inspired, that her exploits were motivated by vengeance against the English for the death of her sister.

IMPACT

The number of films and television miniseries that depict the real and imag-ined story of Joan of Arc reveals the extent of her power as an enduring symbol of courage and faith, not only to France, but to the world. More than five hundred years have passed since the death of Joan, and yet her life and death continue to be found meaningful.

Joan did not fret against others for conforming to gender roles. She simply stayed true to her personal calling. She also challenged the dominant religious institutions of the day by exerting unwavering confidence in her personal spiritual journey and intimate revelations as she believed she received them. She trusted in her own counsel and spoke brazenly before her enemies and the powers that be.

Joan of Arc was one of the first transgressive female action heroes, who, in real life as well as in the mythology that grew up around her story, shattered conventions of how young women should behave and what roles they must submit to.

See also G.I. Jane; Xena: Warrior Princess.

FURTHER RESOURCES

Benson, Edward. "Oh, What a Lovely War! Joan of Arc on Screen." In *The Medieval Hero on Screen*, ed. Martha W. Driver and Sid Ray. Jefferson, NC: McFarland and Company, 2004.

Brooks, Polly Schoyer. *Beyond the Myth: The Story of Joan of Arc*. Boston: Houghton Mifflin, 1990.

Cook, Bernard A. *Women and War: A Historical Encyclopedia from Antiquity to the Present*. Santa Barbara, CA: ABC-CLIO, 2006.

Fraser, Antonia. *The Warrior Queens*. New York: Vintage, 1990.

Jones, David E. *Women Warriors: A History*. Dulles, VA: Brassey's, 2000.

Maid of Heaven. "Timeline of the Life of Saint Joan of Arc." http://www.maidof heaven.com/joanofarc_timeline_history.asp.

Silvey, Anita. *I'll Pass for Your Comrade: Women Soldiers in the Civil War*. New York: Clarion Books, 2008.

"Women as Warriors in History: 3500 BC to the 20th Century." http://www.lothene. demon.co.uk/others/women.html.

Captain Kathryn Janeway, the lead in the television series, *Star Trek: Voyager*, strikes a power pose. (© Paramount /Courtesy: Everett Collection.)

Kathryn Janeway

Kathryn Janeway was the stalwart captain of the *USS Voyager*, and as such was the only female starship commander to be the main focus of any of the six *Star Trek* television series. Gene Roddenberry created the first three television series: *Star Trek* (The Original Series) (1966–1969), *Star Trek: The Animated Series* (1973–1974), and *Star Trek: The Next Generation* (1987–1994). After Roddenberry's death in 1991, his work inspired *Star Trek: Deep Space Nine* (1993–1999), *Star Trek: Voyager* (1995–2001), and *Star Trek: Enterprise* (2001–2005). Prodigious as this list is, it is only the beginning; the *Star Trek* franchise has been one of the most successful of its kind, yielding 11 feature films and counting, numerous books, and several video games. Without question, the key elements of the formula that has made *Star Trek* successful for over 40 years are the beloved ships and their charismatic captains.

The archetypal Star Trek captain, James T. Kirk (William Shatner), helmed the starship Enterprise in the original and animated series. Kirk's name and masculine exuberance were synonymous with Star Trek for the first 20 years of the franchise. The distinguished Jean-Luc Picard (Patrick Stewart), who captained the Enterprise D in *The Next Generation*, set the pattern by neither copying nor competing with the iconic Kirk; rather he was positioned as older and more cerebral. The next *Star Trek* featured the first African American captain, Benjamin Sisko (Avery Brooks), who commanded Deep Space Nine space station with a calm, inquisitive, and often mystical persona. Then came Kathryn Janeway (Kate Mulgrew), who led the crew of the starship *Voyager*. Returning to a more **stereotypical** hero, *Enterprise*, set at the earliest point yet of the *Star Trek* history, put the manly Jonathan Archer (Scott Bakula) in the captain's chair.

The decision to have a female captain at the helm in a *Star Trek* television series was a landmark moment. The traditions of the show, as well as the times, dictated that although the captain might not have to be male, she had to be a strong-willed leader, physically tough, and above all brave and fearless in the face of danger. With her steely expression and self-assured pose, Janeway appeared ready to meet the criteria. She looked dashing and strong in the unisex Star Fleet uniform, which (unlike the miniskirts of The Original Series, which echoed the styles and attitudes of the 1960s) was characteristically angular, concealing her feminine figure. Her voice was distinctly low; she issued commands in a clipped and authoritative fashion. Her original hairstyle, known as the "bun of steel," **coded** Janeway as a character who was just as competent and tough as her male compeers.

In fact, Janeway, in appearance and behavior, came across as a **second-wave feminist's** ideal power woman—one who was neither diffident nor riddled with conventional markers of femininity that supposedly equated her with weakness, and who was the equal of any man. At the time, Janeway was considered to be the culmination of 25 years of *Star Trek*'s commitment to equality and humanism—the fulfillment of a promise long deferred, the last and best of a long line of female characters who would go where "no man had gone before." And yet, even within the seven-year run of the show, this was proved to be false, as Janeway's character was revealed to be not the pinnacle of the female action hero, but just one more fascinating stop along the way.

ORIGINS

The Original Series

Roddenberry was a product of his times, and his times were the 1960s, a period of intense social change that witnessed a groundswell of idealistic forward thinking—the perfect time for a television series about the future. It was only natural for Roddenberry to add controversial characters and humanistic themes to what he perceived as a Western series in outer space clothing, his "*Wagon Train* to the stars." Thus he cast Nichelle Nichols, one of the first African American women to appear in an American television series, as Lieutenant Uhura, creating the first of the long line of *Star Trek*'s iconic female characters. Given Uhura's sexy costume and "desk job" status, this casting might be considered insignificant or even tokenism today, but at the time it was revolutionary. Hiring a woman of color as a regular cast member was a highly progressive choice, not least because the character was not depicted, as was the norm in film and television at the time, in a negative or narrowly defined fashion.

Roddenberry challenged conventional media constructions as well as social norms by putting an African American woman on the bridge. As an officer, Uhura was highly visible and played a more prominent role in dramatic situations than many of the male officers. Most importantly, her fellow officers treated her seriously, as a peer. Uhura, the only full-time female character on the series, was a memorable figure, part of the team that went on to make the first six *Star Trek* movies. But Uhura was not Rodenberry's only strong woman character, nor was she technically the first.

In the pilot for *Star Trek*, filmed in 1964, Roddenberry cast Majel Barret as Kirk's first officer—an extraordinarily bold move indeed. But Rodenberry lost that challenge to the status quo, for although NBC picked up the series, the executives demanded that the female first officer be removed. Barret was instead cast as a part-time character, Nurse Chapel, the type of position to which women were historically relegated. But the battle had been waged, and Uhura was on the front lines.

After the euphoria of seeing an African American woman as a bridge officer wore off, critics and second-wave feminists began to complain that a mere presence was not enough. Sherrie A. Inness points out that Uhura "spent most of her time stuck on the bridge of the USS *Enterprise* like an interstellar receptionist." And like most of the women—notably the alien women—who appeared in the series, Uhura's body and femininity were dramatized by a short and fitted dress that showed off her voluptuous form, glamorous eye makeup, elaborate hairstyles, soft lighting and alluring close-ups (Inness, 114). Even so, Uhura's job as communications officer was unlike any job African American women filled in real life (most often as domestics) or in other television and film. She had power, skill, and presence in addition to beauty. She saw little action compared to her brawny costars, but the road to equality had to start somewhere, and on *Star Trek*, it started with Uhura.

Its split personality when it came to conventional femininity notwithstanding, The Original Series was well known for challenging other oppressive social constructs. Let the record show that Roddenberry's original (discarded) idea had been for both women and men to wear the short-skirted uniform on-board ship. The series featured a diverse cast and fearlessly tackled radical themes. In addition to Uhura, who hailed from the so-called United States of Africa, the series featured helmsman Sulu (George Takei), of Japanese and Filipino ethnicity, and a Russian navigator Chekov (Walter Koenig). Leonard Nimoy (Spock), a man of Jewish descent, was credited with adapting a Jewish hand symbol as the iconic Vulcan salute that accompanied his solemn "Live long and prosper."

Nimoy rose to superstardom playing the famous part-Vulcan, part-human science officer. Spock's heritage and the inner conflict it inspired frequently played a prominent role in the series, leading to the exploration of multicultural themes and interracial relationships. The episode "Let That Be Your Last Battlefield" openly condemns racial prejudice. Captain Kirk and Lieutenant Uhura share the first interracial kiss on American television in the episode "Plato's Stepchildren." Given America's long and turbulent history in race relations and the fact that the **civil rights** and **black power movements** were in full swing, this was no minor occurrence.

The six *Star Trek* movies featuring the original cast and subsequent *Star Trek* series continued to reflect progressive changes in American society. In the first *Star Trek* movie, Nurse Chapel became Doctor Chapel. Women and people of color were seen on the bridge in ever-increasing numbers. But though the spinoffs overshadowed their progenitor in terms of production quality and longevity, they never matched the breadth of vision or the social impact of The Original Series.

The Next Generation

In *The Next Generation*, the senior medical officer was Beverly Crusher (Gates McFadden), and her favorite nurse was male. In the pilot, one male crewmember actually wore the short skirt that Roddenberry had so long ago envisioned—so did the ship's counselor, Deanna Troi (Marina Sirtis),

Women Firsts

1901	Annie Edson Taylor is the first person to go over Niagara Falls in a barrel.
1926	Gertrude Ederle is the first woman to swim across the English Channel.
1932	Amelia Earhart is the first woman to fly solo across the Atlantic.
1960	Oveta Culp Hobby is the first woman to serve as Secretary of Health, Education, and Welfare and director of the Women's Army Auxiliary Corps (WAAC).
1967	Althea Gibson is the first African American tennis player to win a singles title at Wimbledon.
1969	Shirley Chisholm is the first African American woman to serve in the U.S. House of Representatives.
1970	Diane Crump is the first female jockey to ride in the Kentucky Derby.
1981	Sandra Day O'Connor is the first female Supreme Court justice in the United States.
1983	Dr. Sally K. Ride is the first American woman in space.
1984	Geraldine Ferraro is the first woman to run for vice president on a major party ticket (Democratic).
1985	Wilma Mankiller is the first woman chief of the Cherokee Nation of Oklahoma.
1989	Ileana Ros-Lehtinen of Florida is the first Hispanic woman to serve in the U.S. House of Representatives.
1992	Carol Moseley-Braun is the first African American woman to serve in the U.S. Senate.
	Mae Jemison is the first African American female astronaut.
1993	Janet Reno is the first woman U.S. attorney general.
1997	Madeleine Albright is the first woman to serve as the U.S. Secretary of State.
1998	Lt. Kendra Williams is the first female combat pilot to bomb an enemy target (Operation Desert Fox in Iraq).
1999	Lt. Col. Eileen Collins is the first woman to command a space shuttle mission.
2000	Hillary Clinton is the first First Lady to serve in the U.S. Senate.
2005	Condoleezza Rice is the first African American woman to serve as U.S. Secretary of State.
2006	Effa Manley is the first woman elected to the Baseball Hall of Fame.

(continued)

2007	Nancy Pelosi is the first woman to serve as Speaker of the House of Representatives.
	Drew Gilpin Faust is the first female president of Harvard University.
2008	Hillary Clinton is the first woman to win a presidential primary.
	Sarah Palin is the first woman to run for vice president on the Republican ticket.

regularly, though she got a wardrobe change early in the first season to a one-piece outfit (it took a few more years for her to turn up in the standard unisex Star Fleet uniform). But these were reactive rather than proactive modifications, for by the late 1980s, when *The Next Generation* debuted, women (at least those influenced by second-wave feminism) had distanced themselves from clothing that fed into derogatory images of women as sex objects, catering to the **male gaze**.

In a more radical move, Lieutenant Tasha Yar (Denise Crosby) was cast as chief of security. This was a breakout role for a woman, even in *Star Trek*, where women had not yet been shown in fighting roles. Tasha Yar wore a boyish hairstyle—a stark contrast to the long and glamorous styles that had been a trademark of female characters in The Original Series—and was a master of hand-to-hand combat. Her toughness was briefly "softened by showing her more feminine side" when she was kidnapped (relegating her to the stereotypical damsel in distress) and by a short romance with Data (Brent Spiner; Inness, 114). Historically, the tough male hero eschewed romance, which was associated with the femininity and softness, and was believed to have an emasculating effect on male heroes.

Where her character might have gone it is impossible to know, for Crosby, dissatisfied by the size of her part in an ensemble cast, left the show before the end of the first season. But Tasha Yar represents a giant step forward along the road of equality, and is the direct precursor of the dynamic female action heroes that would rise to prominence in later series.

Deep Space Nine

Deep Space Nine upheld the progressive and **transgressive** tradition of *Star Trek* by featuring an African American commander (later captain) of a vast multicultural space station. Sisko was not known to back down from a fight, but he was also portrayed as a deep thinker and an affectionate single father to his teenaged son. The space station he commanded teemed with assorted human and alien life forms, allowing the exploration of countless multicultural issues and the strong promotion of tolerance in all social situations.

Deep Space Nine's resident tough girl was Major Kira (Nana Visitor), a woman raised in harsh circumstances under the Cardassian occupation who went on to become a resistance leader and eventually a high-ranking officer in the Bajoran army. She had a boyish hairstyle, was dressed for action, and was as good a fighter as Tasha Yar. But unlike Tasha, and reflecting the nascent girl-power movement during which she grew as a character, she engaged in several intense romances and reveled in dressing up when the occasion required.

Moreover, Kira had something that no other regular character on Star Trek had had before—not Tasha Yar, not Beverly Crusher, and not Uhura. She was day in and day out a command officer. There was only one step left to take.

Kate Mulgrew

Born on April 29, 1955 in Dubuque, Iowa, Mulgrew began studying acting in her early teens. She attended Northwestern University, University of Minnesota, and Guthrie Theatre. At 17, she attended the Stella Adler Conservatory of Acting and received an Associate of Arts degree in 1976. She made a critical start in professional acting when she landed a role in the soap opera *Ryan's Hope* in 1975. Since then, she has appeared in several films, such as *A Stranger Is Watching* (1982) and *Throw Momma from the Train* (1987), and television programs, such as *Cheers* (1986), *Murder She Wrote* (1987, 1992, 1994), *Murphy Brown* (1992), and *Law and Order: Special Victims Unit* (2006).

In recent years, she has performed in the theater, in *Tea at Five* (2003, 2004, 2005), *Our Leading Lady* (2007), *Iphigenia 2.0* (2007), and *Equus* (2008–2009). She has received much recognition for her acting abilities, winning the Golden Satellite Award in 1998 for Best Performance by an Actress in a Television Series for her role in *Star Trek: Voyager*, an Audience Award for Favorite Solo Performance in *Tea at Five*, and the Obie Award (2008) for Outstanding Performance in *Iphigenia 2.0*. Mulgrew has been married twice, currently to Tim Hagan. She has two sons and a daughter.

POWER SUIT, WEAPONS, AND ABILITIES

Kathryn Janeway's power suit was her gold uniform, with its four gold pips worn on the right side of her collar, indicating her rank and authority. Aboard a Federation starship, no rank eclipsed that of the captain, and though there had been brief glimpses of female captains on *Star Trek* before, until *Voyager*, only male captains had featured as the central figure of a series.

Janeway appears in her uniform in most episodes and in promotional photos. In these photos, Janeway invariably strikes a commanding pose, with impeccably straight posture and a confident facial expression, her arms akimbo or crossed over her chest. These poses and expressions, as well as the uniform, code Janeway as a powerful leader, one who can be safely charged with undertaking dangerous missions in the far reaches of the galaxy, protecting her ship and its crew, and engaging in battle when necessary. Though there are many scenes, particularly later in the series, where we see Janeway in more casual clothing (and with longer, looser hair), these glimpses only serve to show just how much tougher than the traditional woman she is when she puts the uniform back on.

All Starfleet captains are trained not only for leadership but for combat. Previous captains—Kirk, Picard, Sisko—flaunted impressive fighting skills, from hand-to-hand combat, to phaser battles, to tactical ship-to-ship warfare. Captain Kirk, who always relished a good fight, regularly appeared in combat mode. He fought with punches, wrestling-like moves, his phaser, and with the powerful weaponry with which his ship was equipped. As cerebral as Captain Picard was, with his refined English accent, penchant for reading the classics, and fondness for Earl Grey tea (not to mention the fact that he was the oldest of the *Star Trek* captains), he was known for his physical fitness and bravery. Captain Sisko, although more soft spoken and spiritual than the others, was a giant of a man who was all but invincible in a physical fight.

Unlike the male captains that preceded her, Janeway was depicted far less often in the role of a combatant; however, when she does appear in a scene that requires fighting or weapons skills, she rises to the occasion without hesitation or fear of failure. In the episode "The Chute," Janeway wields a phaser rifle when she leads an away team to rescue two male officers who are wrongly imprisoned on the planet Akritiri. In "Macrocosm," Janeway relies on assorted weapons and her intellect to single-handedly fight an alien macrovirus that has stricken her crew. To save the day, Janeway (calling upon her scientific background) builds an antigen bomb. In "The Killing Game, Part II," Janeway is forced to kill one of the Hirogen, an alien species, during a holographic simulation. In "Dark Frontier," the crew, led by Janeway, battles the formidable Borg, a cybernetic species first introduced in the *Next Generation* series.

But throughout the seven years of *Voyager*, Janeway's primary ability was her power to lead, which she did with a balance of knowledge, experience, fairness, and strength of will.

VILLAINS

Voyager, like all the other *Star Trek* series, featured an unusual and imaginative cast of characters, both good and bad. Among the reoccurring villains in the series were alien species such as the Kazon, the Vidiians, Q, and the

Sally Ride: First American Woman in Space

Among the challenges still facing American society is the underrepresenta-
tion of women who excel in math and sciences, and in related fields still
dominated by men. Sally Ride is one woman who broke many barriers in her
achievements as a physicist and astronaut.

Sally Ride was born on May 26, 1951, in Encino, California. Ride was a stellar
student and tennis player. At Westlake School for Girls (now Harvard-Westlake
School), Ride was influenced by Dr. Elizabeth Mommaerts, a physiology teacher.
Upon graduation in 1968, Ride attended two prestigious institutions, Swarthmore
College and Stanford University. She graduated from Stanford with a BS in English
and physics. She received a PhD in physics in 1978. In 1983, at the age of 31, she
became the first woman and youngest astronaut to enter space aboard the space
shuttle *Challenger.*

Borg. The Kazon caused trouble for the crew of the *Voyager* for the first
two seasons. Their main goal was to steal alien technology, but they also
posed a personal and professional challenge to Janeway because of their
"misogynistic bent" (Ruditis, 125). The Vidiians were a diseased alien species who hunted down life forms to steal their organs for survival.

Q (John De Lancie) was a popular character who had harassed Star Fleet
captains since *The Next Generation.* An outcast from an omnipotent alien
species, Q was a mischievous character whose insatiable curiosity about
human beings led him to develop a unique relationship with Janeway, one
that was "primarily based upon her womanhood. He was constantly com-
menting on her gender, questioning her ability to be a leader, and irritating
her by calling her "Madame Captain" and "Kathy" (Inness, 117).

Alien villains were not the only source of conflict for Janeway. Indeed,
the ship's crew itself encompassed an inherent conflict. The Maquis, a group
of renegade Star Fleet officers of various species who had opposed the Federation's treaty with the Cardassians, were added to *Voyager*'s original crew
from the first. Mistrust, differing philosophies, and a patched chain of command led to extensive turmoil in the first three years of the series.

In addition to alien and internal conflicts, Janeway also faced a steady
stream of deadly astronomical anomalies, ship breakdowns, malfunctioning
holograms, and time distortions—all in a day's work for a *Star Trek* captain.

VOYAGER, THE SERIES

Audiences watched with mixed emotions—some with bated breath, others
with curiosity, and many with skepticism—as "Caretaker," the pilot episode

of *Voyager* made its debut. Would it still be *Star Trek* with a female captain? The opening graphics and orchestral music were in keeping with the vastly improved special effects and movie-quality production values that had replaced the clunky graphics of *The Original Series*. The stylish lines of the USS *Voyager*, the gracefulness of the ship as it swooshed across the starry vastness of space, the assorted galactic images—all signified the enormous importance of the moment and reassured viewers that the show would receive equal treatment with the previous *Star Trek* series.

In the first episode, the USS *Voyager* is cast into an unexplored area of space known as the Delta Quadrant, some 70,000 light years away from home (the Alpha Quadrant). Audiences are introduced to Janeway and her crew: science officer Tuvok (Tim Russ), the first Vulcan of color, like Spock in demeanor, only without the inner conflict; Tom Paris (Robert Duncan McNeill), a cocky pilot whose release from a Federation Penal Center Janeway has engineered; Harry Kim (Garrett Wang), a boyish officer of Asian American lineage; and the doctor (Robert Picardo), the ship's medical holographic medical man.

Not long after arriving in the Delta Quadrant, Janeway runs into the Maquis: Chakotay (Robert Beltran), one-time Star Fleet officer of Native American ancestry, and his crew, including B'Elanna Torres (Roxann Dawson), a half-human, half-Klingon ex-Star Fleet engineer with a turbulent personality denoting her Klingon ancestry. When Chakotay's ship is destroyed, it is decided that his crew must merge with Janeway's. Janeway maintains her leadership role, while Chakotay becomes second in command. Chakotay never does challenge Janeway's position, but rather acquiesces to a very nontraditional role, making him an appealing character to feminist critics who call him "a dream guy for a feminist heroine" ("Janeway/Chakotay," *Get Critical Star Trek Columns*).

This most ethnically diverse *Star Trek* cast yet was augmented by the addition of Neelix (Ethan Phillips), a Leprechaun-like alien, and Kes (Jennifer Lien), a child-like member of an alien species with telepathic powers and a nine-year life span.

Much of the first year of the series was spent establishing, sometimes in heavy-handed ways, Janeway's authority and capabilities to a presumably doubting viewership. In addition to the bun of steel, the deep voice, and an expression frequently devoid of the soft, warm, and smiling expressions largely denoted as feminine, she frequently appeared in posed shots in various power positions. As Ruditis explains, "camera angles can often be broken down by their very basic purposes. Scenes filmed from a high angle—with the camera pointing down at the actors—imply weakness and vulnerability, as conveyed by the fact that the audience is effectively looking down on the characters. With a camera placed at a low angle, the reverse is true" (Ruditis, 59). In this way, the camera shot establishes Janeway from the start as "a captain of strength, poise, and power" (Ruditis, 59).

Unlike the flirtatious Kirk, as well as the more choosey but still romanti- cally inclined Picard and Sisko, Janeway refrained from pursuing romance. This was a choice, not a personality trait or an attitude specific to her gen- der (though because it is a more transgressive choice for a woman, it attracted more criticism). It is a long-established tradition that military offi- cers should not fraternize with lower-ranking shipmates because it threatens the chain of command. Janeway decided early on that despite the fact that the *Voyager* crew were the humans in the quadrant, it would undermine her role as captain to be involved with a fellow officer. Other opportunities were virtually nonexistent.

It is clear that it is a sacrifice, meant to show Janeway's strength of char- acter, and that in other circumstances she would not choose to be alone. In "Caretaker," Janeway says farewell to her fiancé, not realizing that they would be separated for years. Over the first two years of the series, there is an obvious attraction between Janeway and Chakotay. This accelerates in the late second-season episode "Resolutions," when the characters are quar- antined alone together on a planet for four months and come to believe that they will be together there for life. The extent of their relationship is left to the imagination of the viewer, and interpretations therefore vary. But it is at least possible to conclude that, no longer bound by their responsibilities to the crew of *Voyager*, they entered into a physical relationship. Their even- tual rescue was undeniably bittersweet if not agonizing, as they put aside their relationship once again, this time for good.

But there are other ways in which Janeway was characterized in feminine ways. For example, she appeared in some scenes, particularly with other female characters like Kes, who idolized Janeway, as a nurturer. Inness asserts that the stereotypically feminine role "is a way to mitigate [her] very evident toughness" (Inness, 116). Inness points out other examples that demonstrate how Janeway's power is undermined. In the second season, Mulgrew's "bun of steel" is replaced "with a softer more feminine coiffure in some episodes"; in the holodeck, "which can create any kind of scenario that a visitor imagines, she typically adopts romantic, feminine roles, a reminder to the audience that Janeway is still a woman, despite her tough demeanor" (Inness, 116–117).

Star Trek fandom was often loudly critical of Janeway. Some refused to accept her as a captain. Others accepted her but disliked her personality, or her voice, or her hair. Many loved her but wanted romance for their favorite character, arguing that other captains were permitted to pursue love. One critic asserted that it was not "a victory for feminism to suggest that women—or men—are better off living and dying alone just to demonstrate their independence and self-possession" ("Janeway/Chakotay," *Get Critical Star Trek Columns*).

Another critic asked, with a clearly **third-wave feminist** voice, "why can't Janeway fight space battles and fly through nebulas, and grow vegetables and

Hillary Rodham Clinton: Making Waves in Politics

In television, producers can create characters that are rarely seen in the real world. *Voyager* debuted the first female captain in a *Star Trek* series. In 2005, American audiences saw the first female president in television history, President Mackenzie Allen, played by Geena Davis, in *Commander in Chief*. In 2008, Hillary Rodham Clinton made history when she ran a fierce campaign for the presidential nomination of the Democratic Party. She ran neck and neck with Barack Obama, who eventually won the nomination and was elected the first African American president in 2008.

Born on October 26, 1947, Hillary, a high achiever, was academically sharp as well as active in extracurricular activities. In the 1960s, she attended Wellesley College, a prestigious women's institution, where she discovered social activism, opposing the Vietnam War and supporting greater diversity on campus. She earned her BA in political science and went on to receive a law degree from Yale Law School in 1973. In 1975, she married William Jefferson Clinton, who was elected president of the United States in 1993. By this time, Hillary had a successful career in her own right as a practicing attorney as well as a reputation as an avid feminist. After eight years as the First Lady, Hillary was elected as the U.S. Senator from New York in 2000 and 2006. Though she lost the 2008 presidential primary, after he was elected, Obama offered her the office of Secretary of State, which she accepted.

play with kids and find lasting love? Why are wonderful careers and domestic happiness always presented to women as an either-or, even in the 24th Century?" (Green, "Having It All"). The same critic contended that "a lot of women don't identify with Janeway—because she's too self-reliant and sure of herself, because she doesn't "give in easily to fear" (Green, Michelle, "Having It All"). In contrast, others declared that "Janeway's not military enough, because she touches people and cries in front of subordinates and asks for second opinions" ("Janeway/Chakotay," *Get Critical Star Trek Columns*).

Such criticisms (and parallel complaints that the male characters were too soft—that it was a show for feminists only) illustrate the many pitfalls of trying too hard to break new ground. By contrast, Avery Brooks's casting as Sisko on *Deep Space Nine* took place with nary a murmur of complaint. This may reflect the different approaches taken toward the respective shows, or perhaps the belief of some that it is easier for mainstream audiences to see a man of color in a position of authority than a woman.

If the latter, much of Janeway's lasting importance may lie in the fact that, like Uhura, she was simply there—this time in the captain's chair rather than just on the bridge, dressed for power rather than for **eye candy**, taking part in away missions and armed to the teeth rather than stuck in that swivel chair in the background. Perhaps that in trying so hard to get her there—to establish her worth, toughness, and authority—the producers of the show (who strengthened Sisko's character arc with a special relationship to Bajoran prophecy) didn't pay enough attention to Janeway's personal journey. If so, this was an oversight that *Star Trek: Voyager* rectified with a vengeance in the last four years of its run.

By the end of the 1990s, the Star Ship *Voyager*, slowly chugging its way back home from the Delta quadrant, was, while not viewed as a major hit, still a mainstay of the popular *Star Trek* franchise. Meanwhile, back on planet Earth on the cusp of the 21st century, third-wave feminism was in full swing. When Kes, the soft-spoken third female costar of the show, left the series, a new character had to be introduced; and on a show dedicated to promoting women's rights, it was unthinkable to replace one female with anything other than another. But there were no unwritten laws against changing the nature of the character. Enter Seven-of-Nine (Jeri Ryan).

Seven exploded onto the show like a supernova. Suddenly, here was an action character with a gripping backstory: human child taken by the Borg, fitted with their dehumanizing implants, turned into a mindless killing machine—until the day Janeway found her and in the best Star Fleet traditions, determined to save her—to remove as many implants as possible, to give her back her free will, and to help her re-find her humanity.

Tall, blond, sexy, powerful, emotionless, confused, hard, cold, and beautiful, Seven-of-Nine had an effect on every episode, on every other character. They alternately guided her, feared her, fell in love with her, mistrusted her, were defeated by her in any and all contests of strength, and befriended her—all experiences that, for her part, she had never had before. Audiences, men and women alike, identified with her journey and clambered for more. Following in the steps of Spock, Data, and Odo, *Star Trek* had created its latest "other" character, someone driven by internal conflict and a desire to be (or not to be) human. Only this time it was a female action hero in an outfit that looked suspiciously like Emma Peel's old catsuit. The writers of *Voyager* had finally found their niche.

Even as Seven took her place as a third-wave feminist icon, B'Elanna suddenly found her own story in an unlikely romance with Tom Paris that spanned the last three seasons of the series. Fiery where Seven was cold, passionate where Seven was cerebral, B'Elanna, daughter of a warrior race, was nonetheless a full-fledged action hero. A character, like Spock, with a built-in racial conflict, B'Elanna embarks upon her own hero's journey for enlightenment. She combats her temper, her fears, and her own heritage frequently by facing wholly female challenges: experiences of love, marriage, pregnancy, and childbirth.

Nothing illustrates the intermingling of second- and third-wave feminism like the interactions of Janeway (representing the former) and Seven and B'Elanna (representing the latter) in the latter years of *Voyager*. Indeed, it was as a mentor, and without the forced hints at aborted romance and the need to prove at every turn how tough she was, that Janeway finally came into her own. In the end, she was a complete character, loving Seven fiercely as a daughter, caring for her crew because they needed her and depended upon her, fighting heroically to protect them all, even if it meant her death.

How rare it was on television to see a female leader in her forties like Janeway in a position of unquestioned power mentoring two younger action heroes about duty and social responsibility in addition to family and emotional happiness. A woman in her forties (Mulgrew was a few short months away from turning forty when *Voyager* debuted on January 16, 1995) in a leadership role has long been a contentious issue in American society. Although age, associated with experience, prestige, wisdom, and other positive terms is socially acceptable and even preferable for men in positions of leadership, it frequently signifies something altogether different for women. The television and film industry has long supported and indeed perpetuated these stereotypes; older women are inevitably cast as passive mothers or grandmothers.

In the end, *Voyager* and Janeway succeeded in proving that audiences would accept a female captain, though whether or not it was a good show remains up for debate. What is not in question is that, almost as an afterthought, they created the toughest, most powerful, and most dynamic trio of women ever to costar on the same television series. Janeway, Seven, and B'Elanna blew the roof off whatever was left of the notion that women should be relegated to a limited number of conventional roles. *Star Trek* once again proved that the sky's the limit.

IMPACT

Voyager garnered a large fan base, although, as with *Deep Space Nine*, it could not best the popularity of *The Next Generation*. Greg Fuller, who tracked the Nielsen Ratings for all the *Star Trek* series, blamed the modest viewing figures on the limitations of UPN, the network on which *Voyager* appeared, and the increased number of other science fiction shows that had recently emerged (Fuller, "*Star Trek* Ratings History). One such competitor was *Xena: Warrior Princess*, which achieved massive popularity with a broadly drawn female action hero, proving, if nothing else, that it wasn't the notion of tough women that kept *Voyager*'s ratings down. And no one can deny that, as Michelle Erica Green contends, "Janeway is a great role model for girls who want to be leaders and scientists, and for older women who get endless warnings about females only being valuable while they're young, nubile, and unthreatening" (Green, "Having It All").

Mere months after Janeway successfully led *Voyager* home and the show ended, *Star Trek: Enterprise* debuted. As if the franchise, knowing it had fulfilled its duty to cast minorities and women in transgressive roles, felt justified in lightening up for a moment, *Enterprise* was very much a boys' show, with a Kirk-like captain and lots of rollicking fisticuffs. Of the two female characters, only one (T'Pal) fits the bill of an action hero, and she was inspired more by the popular Seven-of-Nine (complete with form-clinging bodysuit and great strength—she was a Vulcan) than Janeway.

But there was no backpedaling on the feminist issues that matter. For even in this most manly of *Star Trek* shows, the characters' interactions with women revealed an unquestioned equality. Though *Enterprise* was set two centuries before The Original Series, there were no anachronistic attitudes, no Uhuras, for whom "being there" was enough. And if there were no female Federation starship captains, it is because there were no other Federation starships.

For over 40 years—almost all the length of time that female action heroes have appeared on television—the women of *Star Trek* have been breaking through barriers. Indeed, one can mark the way stations along the road of women's struggle for equality by their changing roles. Today, the world applauds Uhura's appearance on the bridge in 1966, though to second-wave feminists of the day, it was not enough. In the 1980s and 1990s, heroes like Tasha Yar and Captain Janeway seemed to fill the bill, but to third-wave feminists, who wanted it all, their advances were not enough. Blockbuster characters like Seven-of-Nine, B'Elanna, and T'Pal satisfy today's expectations, but what about tomorrow's? One can only wonder, in the best tradition of *Star Trek*, what the future will hold.

See also Emma Peel; G.I. Jane.

FURTHER RESOURCES

Benardi, Daniel Leonard. *Star Trek and History: Race-ing toward a White Future.* New Brunswick, NJ: Rutgers University Press, 1998.

Fuller, Greg. "*Star Trek* Ratings History." http://www.treknation.com/articles/ratings_history.shtml.

Geraghty, Lincoln. *Living with Star Trek: American Culture and the Star Trek Universe.* New York: I. B. Tauris, 2007.

Green, Michelle Erica. "Get Out Your Phasers, Ladies." http://www.littlereview.com/getcritical/trek/feminist.htm.

Green, Michelle Erica. "Having It All in the 24th Century." http://www.littlereview.com/getcritical/trek/havitall.htm.

Inness, Sherrie A. *Tough Girls: Women Warriors and Wonder Women in Popular Culture.* Philadelphia: University of Pennsylvania Press, 1999.

"Janeway/Chakotay (Yes, That Way)." http://www.littlereview.com/getcritical/trek/jccomnt.htm.

Mainon, Dominique, and James Ursini. *The Modern Amazons: Warrior Women On-Screen.* Pompton Plains, NJ: Limelight Editions, 2006.

Roberts, Robin A. "Science, Race, and Gender in *Star Trek: Voyager.*" In *Fantasy Girls: Gender in the New Universe of Science Fiction and Fantasy Television*, ed. Elyce Rae Helford. Lanham, MD: Rowman and Littlefield, 2000.

Roberts, Robin A. *Sexual Generations:* Star Trek: The Next Generation *and Gender.* Champaign: University of Illinois Press, 1999.

Ruditis, Paul. *Star Trek Voyager Companion.* New York: Paramount Pictures, 2003.

Sobstyl, Edrie. "We Who Are Borg, Are We Borg?" In *Athena's Daughters: Television's New Women Warriors*, ed. Frances Early and Kathleen Kennedy. Syracuse, NY: Syracuse University Press, 2003.

StarTrek.com. http://www.startrek.com/startrek/view/series/VOY/index.

Star Trek Voyager Rants. "The Face of a Woman." http://www.chicagowriters.com/startrek/janeway.html.

Totally Kate: The Official Web Site of Kate Mulgrew. http://www.totallykate.com.

Adrian Smith, co-creator of the *Tomb Raider* video game franchise, holds a model of Lara Croft. (AP Photo/Alastair Grant.)

Lara Croft

Lara Croft is the protagonist of the *Tomb Raider* video game series. Croft, archeologist and acrobat extraordinaire, is an English aristocrat customarily outfitted in a sleeveless shirt, short shorts, a small backpack, and a holster with straps that gird her hips and upper thighs and cradle her firearms of choice, two semiautomatic pistols. Shortly after her debut in 1996, her popularity skyrocketed. Croft, the subject of over 20 video games, multiple comic books, and novels, has appeared, in digital form, on magazine covers such as *Time* and *Newsweek* and in advertisements for various products. Real-life look-a-like models have been used for promotional and public appearances, and in 2000 and 2003, actress Angelina Jolie portrayed her in two films. Preparations for a third film are reportedly underway as of this writing. A decade after Croft's creation, Guinness World Records declared her the most popular female video game hero of all time.

Reasons for Croft's success abound. Her appealing, if not excessive, physical characteristics, exotic background and lifestyle, and nonstop action factor aside, Astrid Deuber-Mankowsky, a professor of media studies in Germany, explains in her seminal book concerning all things Croft (entitled *Lara Croft: Cyber Heroine*), that Croft was received with so much excitement because of the innovative technology and graphics used in the making of the series. She adds that the employment of a female lead in a medium (video games) that had been dominated by male protagonists for a mostly male audience was considered cutting edge.

As with sports (until very recent history), girls were not expected to want to play video games, especially not those that ventured into the violent and rough terrain of action-adventure games. Nor were they expected to enjoy the perceived masculine concepts of competition and individualism. However, Lara Croft triggered a phenomenon. In record numbers, young girls came out to play with as much enthusiasm as the boys, though what they reaped from the experience went beyond the ordinary game-playing encounter. Croft inspired some girls to want to be archeologists and imparted a sense of empowerment and invincibility. Croft, one of a steadily growing number of female action heroes during the period, was considered a product of, and to a certain degree an impetus for, the nascent girl-power movement.

ORIGINS

Before there was a Lara Croft, there was Rick Dangerous, developed in 1989 by Core Design, a video game developer based in the United Kingdom. Although inspired by the famous adventurer and archeologist Indiana Jones, Rick Dangerous appeared in 2-D video games as a rotund character, not at all like his rugged, swarthy, and fit predecessor. But this did not stop him from traipsing effortlessly through perilous and strange locations, pistol and dynamite in hand.

Women and Extreme Sports

Extreme sports, also known as action sports and adventure sports, have taken the world by storm in recent years. The term itself surfaced in the late 1980s and refers to physical activities that entail speed or heights that surpass ordinary standards and involve a high amount of adrenalin-producing risk. Some sports that can be classified as extreme are skydiving and wingsuit flying, surfing, rock climbing, snowboarding, mountain biking, and bungee jumping. Mountain Dew television advertisement campaigns, sportswear marketing in magazines and television, extreme sports television shows, and television programming such as Fuel TV have helped popularize extreme sports in mainstream culture.

The many tough girls in action television and film through the years reflect women's progressively changing lifestyles. Shows like *Charlie's Angels*, *Wonder Woman*, and *The Bionic Woman* in the 1970s showed women skateboarding, race car driving, running marathons, and riding motorcycles. Since the 1990s, women such as Lara Croft and the new Charlie's Angels have been depicted in films with more athletic prowess than their predecessors; these are women who surf, dive, and fly in wingsuits. The horror film *The Descent* follows a group of active women who go on a physically demanding cave expedition. Males still dominate the increasing number of extreme sports television shows, but Jolene Van Vugt is one of a few women who are breaking the mold. Van Vugt is the only woman on the popular stunt show *Nitro Circus*. She has received numerous awards in motocross and dirt bike events.

In real life, women are increasingly participating in extreme sports for competition and recreation. Sarah Burke, a freelance skier, has won three gold medals at the X Games, a sports event owned by ESPN that features extreme sports. In regions such as the Pacific Northwest, where outdoor activities are plentiful because of the abundant supply of rivers, lakes, forests, and mountains, women regularly appear hiking, climbing mountains, whitewater rafting, snowboarding, and participating in marathons and triathlons just for the fun of it.

Toby Gard, a video game character designer who was working for Core Design at the time, came up with the idea to create a woman protagonist, a counterpart to Rick Dangerous, who would be given her own game. He was allocated a substantial budget to do so, demonstrating that Core Design was serious about the project, though at the time a female lead was considered an uncertain venture. In the video game world, most games were based on male heroes, with females cast as victims or prizes, such as fairy tale princesses who needed to be rescued. If a game followed the comic book format of a traditional band of superheroes, there might be one woman in the midst of male heroes. *Street Fighter II*, released in 1991 by Capcom, had Chun-Li, a Chinese agent. She wore an odango hairstyle (two buns on either side of her head), brown pantyhose, spiked bracelets, and combat boots, and could decimate her adversaries with several different powerful kicks as well as discharge fireballs from her hands. But Chun-Li was not just an option for girls. Boys too picked the female protagonist when playing the game, because she was just as effective as the male characters.

Gard realized that given a chance, and if the playing field were level, many male game players had no problem opting for a female character. In his quest to create a character that would challenge the pin-up girl archetype—the stereotypical brainless sex symbol—he eventually invented Lara. One of his early prototypes was a South American woman named Laura Cruz, but the English aristocrat Lara Croft won the final vote. The name Croft was culled from an English phone directory, and Lara was chosen because it seemed American and, consequently, was believed to be more marketable to an American audience. Lara Croft thus debuted in 1996 in *Tomb Raider.*

Lara Croft has an elaborate backstory, one that has undergone modifications as needed over time. The backstory also changes with each incarnation, allowing the creators to freely explore various scenarios. One narrative explained that Lara Croft was born on February 14, 1968 in Wimbledon, Surrey, to an affluent father, Lord Henshingly Croft. Little information was given about Croft's mother. At 21, Croft was the only one to survive a plane crash in the Himalayas (this storyline was developed in 2006 by new developers Crystal Dynamics, who developed the last three major video games in the series). In another storyline, Croft was only nine years old when she survived a plane crash with her mother, Amelia Croft, in Nepal. Following the crash, her mother disappeared and Croft, alone, traveled for 10 days to Kathmandu, where she contacted her father, named in this version Richard, an archeologist. He died mysteriously when Croft was 19 according to another storyline.

Croft was provided with a comprehensive and elite education, primarily in private schools in England and Switzerland. She received athletic training and mastered multiple languages. She is reportedly a good cook and has a degree in needlework. According to one version of Croft's backstory, her parents were disappointed that Croft decided to travel the world alone and engage in risky behavior, such as visiting dangerous environments. Against their wishes, she chooses the life of an adventurer rather than marry, produce children, and become a homemaker, activities that have long been traditionally expected of women in real life. In the video games, she does not have a love interest. Neither is she supported by her parents; she writes travel books to fund her adventures. In adulthood, Croft lives alone in the sprawling Croft Manor with her butler Winston, also known as Jeeves.

Croft's makers gave her an intriguing personality and identity. She's confidant, independent, and thrill-seeking. She is also benevolent, making time in her high-action life to "work with underprivileged children and the mentally disabled," though later versions of the *Tomb Raider* games reveal a more combative, hard, and violent personality (Herbst, 24).

About the Video Games

Tomb Raider was launched with the help of revolutionary 3-D technology and other advancements. The look of the game was like none ever seen before. Included were narrative scenes that played out like a film and numerous flashbacks to drive the narrative or establish the backstory. The graphics and sound effects were realistic. Lara Croft's lithe movements, from the feminine swinging of her hips and, later, the whipping action of her trademark long ponytail, to the fluidity of her climbing, walking, running, and rowing motions, dazzled game players. Nothing was overlooked, including the way her chest heaved even when she stood motionless.

There are currently nine major Lara Croft games: *Tomb Raider, Tomb Raider II, Tomb Raider III, Tomb Raider: The Last Revelation, Tomb Raider Chronicles, Tomb Raider: The Angel of Darkness, Tomb Raider: Legend, Tomb Raider: Anniversary,* and *Tomb Raider: Underworld.* Several of these games, such as the first three and last, include expansion packs that offer additional chapters. In these games, Croft traverses exotic and dangerous locales in Asia, Europe, and Africa, encountering human villains, dangerous animals, and mysterious creatures. Thanks to Lara Croft, game players get to solve puzzles, navigate through scabrous environments, and contend with a variety of adversaries.

POWER SUIT, WEAPONS, AND ABILITIES

Though her look has undergone changes over the years, Croft's appearance always exudes toughness and sexiness. Indeed, at one point, Gard had Croft's breast size reduced, worried that she was becoming too sexy. Her outfits may change from game to game, but the colors remain muted and characteristic of an outdoorswoman—browns, blacks, and greens. Sometimes she wears shorts that show her bare midriff; sometimes for special sequences, say, for colder environments, she wears body suits. Some scholars claim she exudes "femininity" and that her clothes are functional, "enabl[ing her] to leap easily into action" (O'Day, 213–214).

With whatever she wears, Croft's body is exposed—the exaggerated bust, extraordinarily small waist, and round hips (her dimensions are recorded as 34D 24 35). She is both athletic and sensual. She stands five feet, nine inches tall and weighs 130 pounds, which, according to her body mass index, is on the low end of normal weight. Yet her figure is not as extreme as that of the Barbie doll, who, if she were real, would stand five feet nine inches tall, measure 39-18-33, and weigh 110 pounds.

Women of *Resident Evil*

Resident Evil is a popular video game series that was released several months before the first *Tomb Raider* game debuted. There are currently some 11 installments in the series. Advertised as a survival horror video game, the *Resident Evil* games revolve around a town named Raccoon City, wherein the Umbrella Corporation has conducted terrible experiments on humans and animals, turning them into vicious, cannibalistic creatures. Each game features playable characters, members of a Special Forces unit called "S.T.A.R.S." and minor characters who appear throughout the various games. Game players may choose to play a male or female protagonist. Among the female playable characters are tough uniformed women like Jill Valentine, an expert fighter, who employs a flamethrower. However, where Valentine shows fear, Chris Redfield, another team member, is fearless. Another character, Rebecca Chambers, wields gun power, but her alternate costumes expose her midriff and voluptuous shape. Claire Redfield, a college student who is an expert in assorted weaponry, dons a body-clinging outfit with shorts or jeans. Ada Wong is a spy with a dramatic fashion hairstyle and a sleeveless red dress.

The game's popularity spawned several film adaptations starring action hero Milla Jovovich as the protagonist. Jovovich is joined by a cast of male and female survivors. Like her male compeers, Jovovich's character works mostly alone and is the most capable fighter of them all. The films include *Resident Evil* (2002), *Resident Evil: Apocalypse* (2004), and *Resident Evil: Extinction* (2007).

Although Croft's primary weapons are her dual semiautomatic pistols, which she carries in her holster, she has at her disposal an array of weaponry and equipment to assist her in her journeys. Included in her arsenal is an M16 rifle, a grappling hook, a shotgun, a submachine gun, Uzzis, grenade launchers, a harpoon gun, and an assassination crossbow. She also utilizes various high-powered vehicles, such as a snow scooter, motorboat, and jeep.

Throughout the games, Croft encounters individuals—strangers, colleagues, and friends. Some, like French colleague Jean-Yves in *Tomb Raider* 4, help her by divulging important information (she later saves him). Some provide immediate assistance, as Ahmed does in the same game when he carries a torch to illuminate Croft's path inside a tomb. Some literally save her life, as in *Tomb Raider* 6, wherein a Bedouin tribe member called The Shaman heals Croft following her harrowing experiences in Egypt.

VILLAINS

Croft comes into contact with numerous villains in each major video game. A number of these enemies include humans endowed with occult powers or transformed into monsters. Other villains include a cannibal, zombie, mafia leader, cult members, hired assassins, a former mentor, and various traitorous colleagues. There are also female antagonists, such as Jacqueline Natla, CEO of Natla technologies and former ruler of Atlantis in the first game, and Sophia Leigh, owner of a cosmetics corporation, in the third game.

But villains are only one of many obstacles Croft must overcome. The *Tomb Raider* games are made more difficult because of the puzzles that must be solved, as well as the hazardous environs players must navigate. In most games, players risk an early demise due to a fatal fall off a cliff, drowning in quicksand, or any number of devious deathtraps.

TOMB RAIDER FILM SERIES

The adaptation of cartoon characters, comic book heroes, and most recently video game protagonists to film is not new and is not always a success. But when it was revealed that Lara Croft was going to be the subject of a movie, American fans were thrilled. Simon West, an English director whose filmography includes the action-packed film *Con Air* (1997), featuring Nicolas Cage in the male lead, directed the first film, *Lara Croft: Tomb Raider* (2001). Jan de Bont, who directed Speed (1994), *Twister (1996)*, and *Speed 2: Cruise Control* (1997), and produced *Equilibrium* (2002) and *Minority Report* (2002), directed *Lara Croft Tomb Raider: The Cradle of Life (2003)*.

Angelina Jolie, one of the most popular young stars of her era, was cast as Lara Croft in both films. Jolie has acted in a long list of films, in which she is frequently a protagonist, or at least a strong minor character. In real life, Jolie has been portrayed by the media—gossip columns included—as a uninhibited personality and a glamorous beauty. Born on June 4, 1975, to actor John Voight and former actress Marcheline Bertrand, Jolie rides motorcycles, flies planes, gets tattoos, adopts children from other countries, and serves as a goodwill ambassador. Following two divorces, she is currently in a relationship with actor Brad Pitt. They have three biological children and three adopted children.

Jolie is no stranger to **transgressive** roles. In *Hackers* (1995), she played an adolescent female computer geek. In *Foxfire* (1996), she played one of several girls who take matters into their own hands when they assault a villainous teacher. She played an officer who is aided by a quadriplegic detective to solve serial killer crimes in *The Bone Collector* (1999), a villain in *Sky Captain and the World of Tomorrow* (2004), and an assassin in both *Mr. and Mrs. Smith* (2005) and *Wanted* (2008). She provided the voice for Tigress, a fighting female tiger, in *Kung Fu Panda* (2008).

The Croft that is depicted in the films is similar to the one players loved in the video games. In both mediums, Croft "echoes many iconic figures from the action-adventure tradition: she is a bit James Bond (neo-imperialist agent), Indiana Jones (archaeologist adventurer), Batman (has an estate and an eccentric butler) and Tarzan (swings from ropes and dives off waterfalls), and a bit Modesty Blaise, Barbarella and Tank Girl" (O'day, 215).

In *Lara Croft: Tomb Raider (2001)*, Croft outthinks and outfights various antagonists (including giant supernatural stone creatures), successfully retrieving parts of an artifact called the Triangle of Light that the Illuminati, a secret society, want to use to control time. In *Lara Croft Tomb Raider: The Cradle of Life (2003)*, Croft teams up with a man, identified in the film as a former lover/love interest, to keep Pandora's Box, which contains within it a devastating plague, out of the hands of a death dealer who wants to sell it to the highest bidder.

In both films, traditional male and female roles are turned upside down. Croft, taking on the role of tough action hero, is constantly in motion, fighting, racing against time, dodging blows, and leaping into the vortex of danger. In the opening scene of the first movie, she walks cautiously through a simulated training sequence, with her hands poised over her guns like a hero out of a Western, before engaging in a fight with a machine that her personal assistant, Bryce, has created to help her train. When she engages in hand-to-hand combat with the main villain in the first movie, she gives as much as she gets in a brawl that leaves both bloody—but Croft is the one left standing. This fight is notable because, traditionally, if women fought, the brawl was usually with another woman, not a man.

When Croft does get hurt, she has no patience with it. In this film she appears hypermasculine. Even John Rambo and Jason Bourne stop long enough to tend to their injuries. Croft refuses to let a wound slow her down.

In Croft's films, she dominates, while men are reduced to subordinate or supporting (minor) roles. She has a male butler and personal assistant who clean up after her and serve her needs. Croft is never seen being self-indulgent or just relaxing; she is always doing, whereas the villain, Manfred Powell (Iain Glen), appears in one scene getting a massage, and in another lounging in a chair while others do his bidding.

Actors well known for their work in popular action movies appear in both films, but they function as sidekicks. Compared to Croft, these men frequently underperform. For example, Daniel Craig, who plays Alex West, Croft's colleague in the first film, has played in a number of action hero roles, including James Bond in the highly successful film *Casino Royale* (2006). Croft has to rescue him when he gets shot by Manfred Powell (Iain Glenn). In *Lara Croft Tomb Raider: The Cradle of Life* (2003), Gerard Butler, who plays the gallant lead in *300* (2007), is cast as Croft's former love interest, Terry Sheridan. Although Sheridan is a tough guy, a former MI6 agent, he (not Croft) is depicted as needy, asking Croft "where do I fit in?" when talking about their failed romantic relationship. Croft is coy,

Mary Flanagan: Changing the Video Game Industry

Mary Flanagan is the director of TiltFactor Laboratory, a company that specializes in socially and environmentally conscious video games. Feminists contend that video game protagonists such as Lara Croft are too sexy and send the wrong message to both male and female game players. Flanagan's answer is to create games that are constructive and educational. Her company is one of the few alternatives to the male-dominated industry in countries (primarily America and Japan) that produce video games.

"The Adventures of Josie True" is a game created specifically for girls that was released in 1997. This game casts a young Asian girl named Josie True as the protagonist. True goes on an adventure with an African American character named Ms. Trombone, and they meet several female historic figures along the way. Games such as these not only promote diversity, something that is commonly missing in video games and other media, but represent women and young girls in empowering, nonsexual, and nonviolent ways.

unresponsive, and emotionally detached—not interested. When a helicopter carrying the villains takes off, he gives up the chase, while Croft bounds from atop a building and grapples the landing skids of the helicopter to attach a tracking device. Later, though Croft softens somewhat toward Sheridan, she stabs and kills him when he unscrupulously tries to steal Pandora's Box. Djimon Hounsou, who portrayed Juba in *Gladiator* (2000), plays Kosa, one of Croft's many international friends. In the second film, though he towers over Croft, is well muscled, and looks every bit the formidable warrior, Kosa flinches when besieged by monsters in an African forest, and Croft stands fast, unnerved.

But Croft is no conventional hero. "Unlike her predecessors," Susan Hopkins writes, "the contemporary action hero is not always a 'good' girl—instead she can be selfish as well as selfless, competitive as well as co-operative, fierce as well as kind" (Hopkins, 209). Croft demonstrates all those traits and more in the films. She flaunts her prowess and high-tech gadgets, so much so that the men in her life, Gerard and Djiou, frequently point out to Croft her insatiable need to show off and always do things the hard (and most dramatic) way. For example, she slides headfirst, with legs entwined to a rope, arms aimed and firing at villains above and below, instead of taking the nearby stairs. She also parachutes down to a fast-moving jeep on the African plains. Croft has a coy explanation for her behavior, demurring to her friends, "I don't want to disappoint you." When training (which is nonstop), Croft appears driven, constantly pushing herself to be better.

Belying the "good girl image," Croft is immodest. After taking a shower, she discards her towel in front of her butler. She is resistant to the idea of wearing nice dresses like a respectable lady. The exception is the very end of *Tomb Raider II*, when, wearing a dress, she fights the machine that was constructed for her nonstop training program. In one scene, she's dressed in a leather motorcycle outfit and impolitely rests her legs on the back of a chair at an upscale auction. Croft exudes sex appeal, and this is underscored by the stares she gets from men when she is in public.

But Croft remains detached, ignoring the way men look at her, just as she is removed from social rules that might govern her behavior in other ways. Although she is athletic and beautiful, Croft is also smart, embodying traits that are valued among a new generation of girls seeking to be ambitious, smart, and sexy. Her various modes of adventuring include wingsuit flying, which reflects a small but growing number of women who participate in extreme sports. Childlike, Croft pouts and tells her father (who is dead), whom she encounters in the first film with the help of a powerful artifact, how "unfair" it is that he was taken from her so soon. Unlike male heroes in recent films like *The Incredible Hulk* (2008) and *Babylon A.D* (2008), who appear diligently cooking animal protein meals over a stove, Croft is depicted as impatient, using a microwave, and ineptly letting the food explode. Unlike those same heroes, she is not always so serious and grim-faced. Croft approaches her many fights and adventures with exuberant abandon, sometimes with delight, like the time she laughs as she narrowly escapes from a collapsing temple while being pulled by a dog sled.

Although international audiences responded with great fervor to the *Tomb Raider* films, American audiences were less receptive, though they rated Angelina Jolie as one of the best Croft incarnations ever.

IMPACT

The release of the *Tomb Raider* series sparked a frenzy on several fronts, with debates raging among academics and pop culturalists and excitement brimming over in the gaming world and in mainstream society. Generally, critics were confounded by Croft, though they all acknowledged that she represented a progressive and problematic new protagonist.

Many contend that Croft, for better or worse, is a transgressive character. Traditionally, female characters in video games were rarely the center of the action. As stated before, Croft epitomizes action as she tumbles, explores, sprints, and somersaults through various chapters in treacherous environments that were not, traditionally, permissible for women to venture into. She is also the star of her own show within the video game world.

Another indisputable fact is that she is admired by female and male game players alike. The *Tomb Raider* series is neither considered a "boys" game or a "girls" game. This appeals to some feminist critics who argue against the practice of relegating any form of play into rigid gender lines. Traditionally, boy activities included playing with toy cars and guns, climbing trees, and playing in the dirt, while girls were limited to playing house, or playing with Barbie and baby dolls. Croft, like so many other female heroes of the latter half of the century, challenges this paradigm.

Explanations as to why Croft appeals to boys vary. For one thing, Croft is as tough as any male video game lead, and for another, the graphics in her game bested most of the other games released in that period. One scholar asserts that boys like female video game protagonists because such a character "enables them to experience a greater range of emotional complexity"; it does not hurt that Croft is sexually appealing and provides a way in which males may dominate or control a female via the controls of a video game console (Kennedy, "Lara Croft").

Croft is alluring to modern young girls for different reasons. She is attractive, smart, powerful, wealthy, and not dependent on a man for love or to be her "knight in shining armor." She also represents an alternative to the traditional role of wife, mother, or homemaker, that is, the "weaker sex" or the image of the young girl who has trouble in the math and sciences and is considered too weak to participate in sports. Deuber-Mankowsky writes that "women, especially girls, enjoy following the tough adventurer. In her, as many will admit, they feel represented as a woman—a woman who is independent, eager to live life to its fullest, one who is liberated and feels superior to men," and explains how the "touch of immorality in a beautiful female body also accommodates women's fantasies of power" (Deuber-Mankowsky, 6, 7, 45). To the surprise of some critics, girls even like Croft's sex appeal. The overall acceptance of Croft appears to reflect the influence of what Claudia Herbst, a professor at Pratt Institute, refers to as "a new brand of **feminism**, recognized under the headings **"cyberfeminism,"** "cyber-girlzzz," and "girrrlpower," where the girliness, aggression, action, and a sexy appearance that was once disparaged as stereotypical and offensive, is idealized (Herbst, 28).

A number of critics insist that Croft's character is not at all empowering. Herbst asserts that Croft "is born out of a male fantasy" as well as the militaristic roots of the video game industry, and as such represents an "oversexualized" and violent woman (Herbst, 28). Whereas Croft may exemplify traditional masculine attributes in that she is tough and ultra athletic, Deuber-Mankowsky points out that her "femininity is reduced, in a very traditional manner, to her oversize female attributes" (Deuber-Mankowsky, 47). Herbst asserts that Croft's appearance, as well as her body movements, "borders on the pornographic" (Herbst, 28). Underscoring Croft's basic sex-object role was the so-called Nude Raider Patch that was made available to game players on the Internet.

The portrayal of Croft's body is troublesome in another way: the potential negative influence on young girls in terms of the issue of body image.

Herbst argues that Croft's seemingly flawless body is reminiscent of less liberated bygone days, pointing out that "the Victorian era [when society] favored tiny waists, achieved by the tight lacing of corsets. At the expense of vital organs, women's waists were squeezed to a minimum" (Herbst, 29). Another scholar writes how critics "fear that we will have a generation of young girls who grow up even more dissatisfied with their own bodies and who are willing to make more and more drastic interventions in order to recraft their bodies in line with these impossible images" (Kennedy, "Lara Croft").

Some find the interplay of Croft's hypersexuality and aggression disturbing. Herbst refers to Croft as a **dominatrix** archetype and gives her trademark stance as a case in point. Croft "is often staged so she is looking down on us. Her stance is usually rigid, her legs apart, her arms resolutely planted on her hips or, alternatively, pointing her guns at us. One eyebrow is typically raised, and her expression is angry, though her mean grin suggests she is enjoying her superiority" (Herbst, 30). Other critics argue that Croft is too aggressive, too violent. In an attempt to temper Croft's combativeness, developers, obviously aware of the criticism, depict a sorrowful Croft in response to seeing dead scientists in *Tomb Raider: Legend* and after making her first kill in *Tomb Raider Anniversary.*

While the arguments continue to play out, the *Tomb Raider* series continues to gain in popularity, which translates to an increased demand for new products and further interest in Croft. It also leads to the development of more tough female protagonists in other video games, and in other media. Sue-Ellen Case opens Deuber-Mankowsky's book with a massive list: "twenty-one video games operating on six different systems (including a forthcoming mobile phone game), a line of Lara Croft action figures . . . forty comic books, and a series of novels based on the video games" (Deuber-Mankowsky, vii). The popularity of Lara Croft has been co-opted by the adult world, where grown women publish pictures of themselves in Croft costume on the Internet.

Real-life models further promote Croft, the first appearing at a European Computer Trade Show in 1996. Since then, other models have made appearances as Croft around the world. Controversy follows some, like Nathalie Cook, who underwent cosmetic surgery to enhance her breasts to better emulate Croft, and Nell McAndrew, who was fired after she posed nude for *Playboy* magazine. The majority of models are, however, embraced by Croft fans, and Angelina Jolie, who played Croft in two films, is forever identified with the video game hero. The Croft character is reflective of the burgeoning trend toward reckless, sexy, and ambitious female heroes. Some critics worry that Croft's image is too sexy and too violent. Others are equally perplexed by Croft's message, but admit to being, like her fans, inextricably, drawn to Croft's power.

See also Buffy the Vampire Slayer; Jen Yu.

FURTHER RESOURCES

Deuber-Mankowsky, Astrid. *Lara Croft: Cyber Heroine*. Minneapolis: University of Minnesota Press, 2005.

Herbst, Claudia. "Lara's Lethal and Loaded Mission: Transposing Reproduction and Destruction." In *Action Chicks: New Images of Tough Women in Popular Culture*, ed. Sherrie A. Inness. New York: Palgrave Macmillan, 2004.

Hogan, Jay. "Movie Characters That Challenge Gender Roles." http://www.helium.com/items/203433-movie-characters-that-challenge-gender-roles.

Kennedy, Helen W. "Lara Croft: Feminist Icon or Cyberbimbo?" http://gamestudies.org/0202/kennedy.

O'Day, Marc. "Beauty in Motion: Gender, Spectacle and Action Babe Cinema." In *Action and Adventure Cinema*, ed. Yvonne Tasker. New York: Routledge, 2004.

"Official Tomb Raider Site." http://www.tombraider.com/server.php?change=Landing Page.

Spicuzza, Mary. "Bad Heroines." http://www.metroactive.com/papers/metro/03.15.01/cover/womanfilm-0111.html.

Maggie Fitzgerald in the film *Million Dollar Baby*. (© Warner Brothers/Courtesy: Everett Collection.)

Maggie Fitzgerald

Maggie Fitzgerald is the title character in the Oscar-award-winning film *Million Dollar Baby* (2004). Fitzgerald, a female boxer, is played by Hilary Swank, who trained a mere three months for the role. In that brief time, she gained 19 pounds of muscle, rapidly acquiring the techniques, skills, and swagger needed to emulate a real boxer and produce credible-looking fighting scenes in the film (Swank performed in all the fighting scenes without the use of a double).

Though Maggie Fitzgerald is mild mannered and endearing and emerged from humble beginnings, she packs a powerful punch in the ring. Her meteoric rise from novice to contender, and her battle with the notorious Blue Bear (played by real-life boxing and kick-boxing professional Lucinda Rijker) in a title fight, are the result of her extraordinary hard work, relentless ambition, and true-heartedness. She also receives indispensable guidance and support from Frankie Dunn (Clint Eastwood), owner of the L.A. gym where Fitzgerald trains, whom she convinces (he's hesitant because she's a "girl") to be her trainer and manager. Eddie Scrap-Iron Dupree (Morgan Freeman), a former boxer who works at Frankie's gym as a janitor, also plays a role in Fitzgerald's development.

During the climactic fight, Fitzgerald is caught off guard and punched by Blue Bear. The force of the punch causes Fitzgerald to fall and hit her head on a stool in her corner, resulting in a spinal cord injury that leaves her permanently paralyzed from the neck down. Fitzgerald, who does not want to live her remaining years confined by her paralysis, is assisted by Frankie to her death.

This moving film and its actors accrued much praise and many awards. At the 77th Academy Awards in 2004, *Million Dollar Baby* took front and center. Eastwood received a Directing Oscar and was nominated Best Actor. Swank received Best Actress, and Freeman won Best Supporting Actor. The film received the Best Picture award.

ORIGINS

Women in Sports and Boxing

The wide acclaim of *Million Dollar Baby* is particularly remarkable considering how recent a phenomenon women's boxing is. Historically, women and boxing have been almost universally considered incompatible. Down the centuries, men have garnered status and power through demonstrations of brute strength and physical prowess; reputations, decisions, disputes, territory, and even women have been fought over and won or lost based on the ritual of the fight.

Whereas a man is expected to demonstrate or appropriate physical power, women are often perceived in terms of gentleness, civility, and softness. For boys, the term *girl* conjures derogatory images, illustrated by the phrase

Amelia Earhart

Amelia Earhart (1897–1937), the famous aviator, was an unconventional woman for her time. Earhart enjoyed an active childhood, running, hunting, climbing trees, engaging in activities largely considered forms of play for boys. As a young adult, she dropped out of college after a year, and in 1920, during the era of the liberated "new woman," she took her first plane ride, a gift from her father. After working assorted jobs to save money for flying lessons, she chose Anita Snook as her first instructor. To make herself look more the part for her new career, Earhart cut her hair short. Though Earhart was not the first woman to fly a plane, she catapulted to fame by flying competitively and undertaking solo trips. American popular culture adored her. She appeared with famous leaders in numerous promotional photos. She married in her mid-thirties, an age that was then considered "late in life." Earhart also did the unexpected and kept her last name and insisted upon an equal partnership with her husband. In 1937, Earhart, Fred Noonan, and their plane went missing during a world flight. None were ever found. Earhart continues to be an iconic figure in American history.

"you fight like a girl," which refers to an individual's weak and ineffectual fighting ability. Even girls or young women may use the term *girl* in a negative way to one another. Girls who fight are deemed "bad girls," whereas "good girls" are not supposed to fight. Nor were they supposed to have muscles or get dirty. At various times throughout history, doctors have actively discouraged women from exercising and competing in sports.

When, at the start of the 20th century, the Olympic games were revived, only certain sports were deemed socially acceptable for women, including croquet, archery, golf, tennis, and swimming. Combat sports were taboo. Though the modern Olympics have always been popular, female athletes in the first half of the 20th century faced idle curiosity and at times severe criticism. Society did not completely accept the athletic woman. Sports were deemed a masculine activity, one that involved competitiveness and aggression; women were largely expected to be nurturing, domestic, and gentle. Though much progress was made in the second half the century, women's wrestling was only allowed at the 2004 Summer Olympics, and boxing is still banned at the Olympic Games.

Changing perceptions of women's sports have helped to alleviate, and in some cases reverse, the stigma attached to women athletes. In 1972, Title IX, an Educational Amendment, gave women and young girls equal access to sports, at least on paper if not immediately in practice. In the 1980s, women who excelled in gymnastics, figure skating, and track received intense media attention. With time, women who broke records and gender barriers made headlines. The advancements of women in sports paralleled the progress women were making in penetrating male-dominated fields and breaking out of traditional roles as well as ways of dressing and behaving. In the 21st century, women athletes are depicted as strong, beautiful, and tough. They not only participate in sports, but in radical extreme sports.

Though amateur and professional boxing has been a staple in men's sports since ancient times, and in film since the 1930s, women's boxing has been a harder sell. There are records of public boxing matches between women, including in the 1700s when women boxed in London. But it was not until the 1990s that certain female boxers, like Leila Ali, daughter of famed boxing champ Muhammad Ali, and managers like Don King helped to inch the sport toward the mainstream. It is no coincidence that during this period, unconventionally tough women were appearing more and more frequently in the traditionally male-dominated action film genre.

The earliest attempts to address women's boxing in film include the documentary *Shadow Boxer* (1999), featuring Lucia Rijker, and the film *Girlfight* (2000). In *Girlfight*, Diana (Michelle Rodriguez), an adolescent female boxer, learns to box and ends up in the ring in a fight against her male love interest. These two films reflect the slow emergence of this marginalized sport into the national consciousness, setting the stage for the release of *Million Dollar Baby* in 2004. Not surprisingly, mainstream critics and audiences were astounded.

Million Dollar Baby

Million Dollar Baby has it roots in F. X. Toole's *Rope Burns: Stories from the Corner* (2001), a book of short stories about boxing. The film, released following a peak year for women in professional boxing, and bolstered by the continuing popularity of female athletes, which had been growing since the late 20th century, is based on Toole's short story *Rope Burns*. Presumably, the character Maggie Fitzgerald is fictitious. But some allege that she is based on real-life boxer Juli Crockett or, possibly, Stephanie Dallam, whose career ended when she sustained a disabling injury following her first fight.

Paul Haggis, the Canadian-born screenwriter, producer, and film director who wrote the screenplay for the film (Toole died in 2002), went on to write many tales of male heroism. Since his success in *Million Dollar Baby*, he has written the screenplays for such movies as *Crash* (2005), *Flags of Our Fathers* (2006), *Quantum of Solace* (2008), and *Terminator Salvation* (2009).

Clint Eastwood

Another major player in the making of *Million Dollar Baby* was Clint Eastwood, who directed, produced, and composed the plaintive music for the film, in addition to playing the male protagonist. Eastwood is a legendary actor whose career has spanned over five decades. He has accumulated, among other honors, five Academy Awards, and played some of the toughest guys in film history. He is noted for his appearances in various genres—Western, cop, war, prison, and vigilante films.

Eastwood was born in California in 1930 to hardworking blue collar workers. In 1950, during the Korean War, he was drafted into the army. His acting career began in the mid-1950s, but did not take off until he played the role of Rowdy Yates in the Western television series *Rawhide*. Tall and lanky, Eastwood went on to play a string of laconic heroes. He made famous his squinty glare, raspy voice, and quotes like "Make my day." In the 1960s, he starred in a series of Sergio Leone's spaghetti Westerns, such as *The Good, the Bad, and the Ugly* (1966). From the 1970s onward, he portrayed such characters as a rock climber, truck driver, convict, and no-nonsense police officer in the *Dirty Harry* film series. Eastwood began directing in 1971, and slowly broadened his horizons to include mainstream films such as *Bridges of Madison County*. Recently, Eastwood directed, produced and starred in *Gran Torino* (2008), where he portrays a tough neighborhood vigilante facing off with a local gang.

Eastwood comments that Hilary Swank was chosen to play the role of Maggie Fitzgerald because he "knew just by the way she moved that she had good athletic ability" and "had no doubts about her acting at all" (Seller, "Literature to Film Lecture").

Hilary Swank

Swank, who was just 30 when the film was released, was born in Nebraska in Midwestern America and raised, for a time, in a trailer park in Bellingham, Washington. As a child, she excelled in swimming and gymnastics. After her parents divorced, she and her mother lived in a car while Swank pursued her dream of becoming an actress (and escaping her life of poverty). Her breakthrough roles were in the television series *Evening Shade* and *Growing Pains*. In 1994, she starred in *The Next Karate Kid*. Five years later, she received a Best Performance by an Actress Academy Award for her portrayal of an adolescent boy who wants to be a girl in *Boy's Don't Cry* (1999). She has since starred in several films, such as *The Reaping* (2007), *Freedom Writers* (2006), *P.S. I Love You* (2007), and plans to portray real-life heroine Amelia Earhart in a forthcoming film.

Swank's preparation for Maggie Fitzgerald was physically demanding. Boxing trainer Hector Roca and weight lifter Grant Roberts were enlisted to train Swank, a task that because of the film schedule, could take no longer than three months. Swank sparred with real female boxers, including Lucia Rijker. Recalling her exacting training experience, Swank stated, "I had never boxed before, and I don't think I really understood it—you don't

Laila Ali

Laila Ali has greatly helped popularize the sport of female boxing, owing in large part to her father's notoriety as well as her successful boxing record and her appearances in the media. Laila was born in 1977 to former boxing champion Muhammad Ali and Veronica Porsche Ali. After graduating from Santa Monica College with a business degree, Ali owned a Balloon and Halloween mask shop. Her first fight took place against April Fowler in 1999. Ali has won all of her 25 fights, 21 by knockout. Her first husband managed her career until they divorced in 2005. In 2007, she married Curtis Conway, a former National Football League player. They had their first child in 2008.

Ali remains a fixture in mainstream media, appearing on magazine covers and television shows. She has appeared on *Dancing with the Stars*, *American Gladiators*, and a reality show supporting weight loss for overweight teens in *The N's Student Body*. In recent television commercials, Ali promotes healthy physical activity for children.

fully respect what someone does until you step into their shoes even for a moment. Getting into the gym and training with Hector, I remember feeling so out of place the first day. But he was so patient and diligent, and pushed me so hard—he really pushed me to the limit, where you think you can't go any further, and then all of a sudden you break through that, and then the next thing and the next thing and the next thing. I tried to remember the sense memory of what it felt like when I learned how to punch correctly, so I could bring that feeling to my performance when Maggie reaches that point" ("Million Dollar Baby").

POWER SUIT, WEAPONS, AND ABILITIES

Maggie Fitzgerald exemplifies hero status and power. Her power is coded in her appearance, effectiveness in the ring, and can-do attitude. In the ring, Fitzgerald wears the customary sports bras, boxing trunks, and gloves. While training at the gym, she undergoes a visual transformation as her skills progress, from grubby, oversized T-shirts and sweats that hide her body to new, higher-quality gear that reveals more of her developing muscles. Although her body is on display at this point, it is the same for male boxers in other films. Such display functions as a way to signify the boxer's power, strength, and ability.

Fitzgerald's tough appearance is demonstrated in other ways. She is never dolled up with makeup in the film and wears jeans when she is not at work or in the gym. Although her hair is long (short hair is frequently coded as masculine), her hairstyle is plain rather than billowy and glossy. In the ring, she, like several other female boxers, opts to wear her hair in assorted braided hairstyles. At the restaurant where she works during the day, Fitzgerald wears a server's dress uniform, but her muscled calves reveal her strength and athleticism. Furthermore, the camera does not objectify Fitzgerald in traditional Hollywood fashion, such as through soft lighting, sensual music, lingering close-up shots on her body, and admiring male glances.

Another way Fitzgerald is depicted as tough is through the progression of her skills. At the start of the film, Fitzgerald has little, if any, technique or skill—though she has ample earnestness, heart, and commitment. After several training sessions with Dunn, Fitzgerald appears in scenes sparring, jumping rope, and punching bags with greater speed, ease, and improved technique.

Fitzgerald, as well as the other women fighters, demonstrates a great deal of power in the ring, and has the characteristic bruises to show for it. Like men, women fighters bear their teeth, grunt, punch powerfully, and become riddled with scars, lacerations, black eyes, bruises, and other injuries. These women have come a long way from the age-old fear women had of breaking their nails—a hackneyed device that even crops up in films like *Indiana Jones and the Temple of Doom* (1984). In that film, high-maintenance nightclub singer "Willie" Scott (Kate Capshaw) reluctantly goes along on many of the escapades of archeologist Indiana Jones (Harrison Ford). Unlike Scott, who cries out every time she chips a nail, the women boxers of *Million Dollar Baby* are not afraid of the consequences of appearing in public bruised and battered. When Fitzgerald goes to the hospital following a fight, she tells Dunn that she is not worried about her injuries or in pain.

The way in which Fitzgerald and other women are depicted in *Million Dollar Baby* was considered "a radical portrayal of a strong woman in the boxing genre of Hollywood cinema as well as a general challenge to the mainstream media's representation of female athletes" (Boyle et al., 103). The norm has long been that women are portrayed as sex objects, as "'sexy' sideshow entertainment" or as sexy athletes "limited to 'foxy boxing'—the boxing version of a mud wrestling match—as well as images of Hollywood 'darlings,' half-naked but for a pair of strategically placed and oversized boxing gloves" (Boyle et al., 103). In traditional boxing films, women were depicted as wives and love interests.

Fitzgerald's power not only stems from her muscles, her ability to knock out her opponents, and to tolerate pain, but in her tenacity. If she had not stubbornly refused to take no for an answer, she would have missed the opportunity to train with Gunn and rise through the ranks in boxing. Dunn had insisted that he could not train Fitzgerald because she was "a girl" and "too old." Despite age, gender, and her impoverished background, Fitzgerald pressed steadily forward, working through the pain and challenges, working in an environment traditionally hostile to women, training long and hard, while she lived frugally in a dilapidated and sparse apartment and subsisted on leftovers she brought home from the restaurant where she worked.

Fitzgerald's power is also illustrated by her independence. Women are often represented in film and television in female relationships and in community settings. Fitzgerald's solitary life is exemplified in the fact that she is the only woman working out in the gym, and she is never found chatting with one of the guys. Outside the gym, Fitzgerald does not associate with friends or participate in social events. She does not have a love interest, thus she challenges not only social conventions (in one scene, her mother depicts Fitzgerald, who is in her thirties, as a misfit because she has not settled down, gotten married, and had children).

VILLAINS

The villains in the film are largely depicted as Fitzgerald's female opponents, as well as her immediate family. Fitzgerald's family is depicted as manipulative and cruel, greedily taking all the material gifts Fitzgerald offers without providing any emotional support or even attending her matches. Fitzgerald's opponents are flagitious brutes, especially Blue Bear.

The Blue Bear, Fitzgerald's ultimate opponent in the film, is depicted with the same vividness as any male villain in a male boxing film, though with some gender-specific touches. In the tradition of good versus evil, Blue Bear epitomizes malevolence. She is a former prostitute, with a reputation for hitting hard and for executing illegal moves and getting away with them. Her masculine qualities are stressed—she sneers and is physically intimidating, and she is ethnic. People of color have been chronically represented as bad guys, villains, and ne'er-do-wells in film. African American women in particular, as argued by feminist critics Bell Hooks and C. Williams, "are often perceived as hypersexual, animalistic, and overtly masculine" (Boyle et al., 111).

MILLION DOLLAR BABY, THE FILM

Million Dollar Baby has been celebrated as an important film for women because it shows that women can be tough and because it gives exposure, with the same zeal as for men's boxing, to a sport that has yet to be fully accepted in the sports world or to the general public. There is no doubt, according to many critics, that Maggie Fitzgerald is a tough boxer, a hero of the ring, and that her life is transcendent, and that, even in the end, despite the controversial issue of euthanasia, she exercises control of her body. However, some challenge Fitzgerald's depiction and the appropriateness of

Benefits of Sports Participation for Boys and Girls

- Strong bodies can fight illnesses.
- Become graceful; sports teach balance, grace, and poise, which carry over to other areas of life.
- Fight fat; one of the biggest reasons for fat is lack of exercise. Sports and exercise keep you trim and firm.
- Control anger and anxiety; exercise in nature's best tranquilizer; it actually helps keep you calm!
- Eat and sleep better; proper nutrition and rest improve every area of life.
- Learn to take criticism; this is a lesson we all need to learn in order to improve performance.
- Overcome shyness; learn to be assertive, make decisions.
- Attain goals.
- Learn how to deal with success as well as failure—self-esteem doesn't depend on continually winning.
- Discover career and job opportunities that you didn't know existed. Become an athletic director, athletic trainer, a manager of a professional sports team, a sports medicine physician, a sports information director, or sports marketer!
- Meet new friends; avoid boredom.
- Be able to talk to your friends about sports—a popular topic of discussion and interest.

Source: "Mythbusting: What Every Female Athlete Should Know," http://www.womenssportsfoundation.org/Content/Articles/Issues/Title-IX/M/Mythbusting-What-Every-Female-Athlete-Should-Know.aspx (accessed August 2009).

her shocking death, contending that Fitzgerald, though a valiant character, is still subordinate to Dunn, her trainer and manager, and does not attain complete independence and power.

In *Million Dollar Baby*, power is clearly coded. Power is appropriated by those who are male, youthful, have position, attain their goals, and live by the code of boxing. The film blatantly demonstrates that boxing is a masculine sport. The opening scene establishes masculinity by showing two men engaged in a fight in the ring. At the gym, Fitzgerald is the only woman. When Fitzgerald importunes Dunn about training her, Dunn tells her that he does not train girls, that fighting girls are a "freak show" (out of the norm and abominable). He repeatedly refers to Fitzgerald as a "girl" (inferring she is not a man, that she is weak), and assumes she will cry (because she is a girl).

Fitzgerald's age is also a point of contention. In a tense moment, Dunn tells Fitzgerald that at 31 she is too old to fight. "Fighters are generally twenty-one," he tells her, and "it takes four years to train." In the gym, Dunn and Dupree are the oldest men in the room. Dunn works in his office; Dupree cleans and watches as the men spar and train. Everyone else is youthful, strong, sweating, and mobile.

Although Fitzgerald is considered "too old," a female, and without status and economic power, she strives toward her goals. According to the boxing genre, Fitzgerald, the underdog, still has every opportunity of appropriating the codes of boxing and attaining her dream of becoming a champion. The boxing codes are identified in the voiceovers, intoned by Dupree, or visual signs appearing in scenes. For example, at the beginning of the film, Dupree narrates that "boxing is about respect, getting it for yourself and taking it away from the other guy," and explains that a good fighter must have skill *and* passion. In Dunn's office, a sign reads "tough ain't enough."

After Dunn agrees to take her on, Fitzgerald proves that she is passionate and tough enough, and that she can learn new skills; indeed, her physical evolution is the crux of the story. However, the critical turning point occurs in her last fight, when Fitzgerald lets down her guard, failing to protect herself (a point Dunn painstakingly tries to drill into her before the accident) from the sneak punch that disables her and causes her to lose the championship (her dream) and ultimately her life. Fitzgerald's death positions her as a tragic hero for many, but for some critics, it throws doubt on her central role in the film. Boyle, Millington, and Vertinsky contend that Fitzgerald's death is evidence that she is not the focal point of the story, that her demise "eliminate[s] her threat to the masculine hegemony over boxing" and "enables the narrative to re-center Frankie [Dunn]" (Boyle et al., 113).

In life, Fitzgerald is a powerful figure but still inferior to Dunn, her manager and trainer. As a manager, Dunn automatically appropriates more power and control than any of his boxers, though he is never abusive to the degree of managers in the "[real] boxing world, where manager-athlete relations are [frequently] characterized by unequal and often exploitative power relations and boxers are known to use slavery and prostitution metaphors to describe managers, trainers, and promoters" (Boyle et al., 107). Notwithstanding the harmonious relationship that develops between Dunn and Fitzgerald, Fitzgerald reinforces her inferior position by calling him "boss," a term black slaves used to refer to their slave masters.

Fitzgerald's inferiority is also reinforced by her role as surrogate daughter to Dunn. Frankie, for an undisclosed reason, laments his broken relationship with his biological daughter. Fitzgerald in turn laments over her father who had died a long time ago. Reinforcing this father-daughter relationship, Fitzgerald actually tells Frankie that he reminds her of her "daddy," and Frankie, conversely, looks after Fitzgerald, who is represented as a dewy-eyed and unsophisticated Midwesterner come to the dangerous city, daring to penetrate the perilous sport of boxing. Dunn giver her a brilliant green boxing robe with the words "mo chuisel," a Gaelic term roughly meaning "pulse of my heart." This relationship—albeit an endearing one—is considered by some critics "to counteract [Fitzgerald's] depiction as an independent and headstrong woman" (Boyle et al., 107).

Fitzgerald's power is further undermined when she is contrasted with the two other male characters. Although Dunn and Dupree are past their fighting prime with lackluster careers, both men achieve their goals. Dupree, a former fighter turned janitor, who is dependent on the generosity of Dunn, and whose boxing career was terminated prematurely following a brutal fight, laments that he has not had the opportunity to redeem himself. He is so poor that he must live in a small space at the dark and ramshackle gym and cannot afford to buy a new pair of socks. In the end, Dupree gets another chance to fight when he rescues a gaunt gym member who is being pummeled by a stronger, more experienced boxer who had been teasing him throughout the film. At the end of the film, when Dunn deserts the gym and his friend (Dupree) following the death of Fitzgerald, Dupree is left to manage the gym and thus appropriates the power Dunn once had.

Thanks to Fitzgerald, Dunn gets the chance to bring a fighter to a title fight, which he had failed to do prior to working with her. Moreover, Dunn disappears, thus attaining mythic hero status, exemplified by the classic Western hero who leaves town once his job is finished. As previously mentioned, Boyle, Millington, and Vertinsky argue that the film was always about Dunn—about his personal struggles over the dissolution of his relationship with his daughter and his religious beliefs, his failure to follow through with fighters, and his transformation from chauvinist to someone who fully embraces the idea of women in boxing and, as a result, experiences one of the most meaningful relationships in his life. Indeed, he proves himself wrong: women can fight, and he can manage a successful boxing career.

IMPACT

The reactions to *Million Dollar Baby* were, in a sense, mixed. National and international audiences thronged to theaters six months after the film was first released. The Academy Awards recognized the director, major actors, and the film. But professional women's boxing experienced no surge in female fighters. There is evidence that more women were encouraged to box for exercise and to relieve stress, but then many women like to try out the new forms of fitness programs in vogue at the gym. Most women still were uneasy with the potential dangerous consequences of the sport, including bruises and broken bones. Among the more clamant objections to the film were those that came from men and women with disabilities. They viewed

Fitzgerald's death as limiting the endless possibilities for individuals with serious disabilities, particularly "for newly disabled athletes" who continue "to live a high quality life and . . . to compete" (Boyle et al., 111). The criticism notwithstanding, Fitzgerald, controversial and **transgressive**, helped to define the new wave of tough female heroes in the 21st century.

See also Chyna; Lara Croft.

FURTHER RESOURCES

Ascot Elite Entertainment Group. "Million Dollar Baby." http://www.ascot-elite.ch/libraries.files/Production%20Notes_Ascot%20Elite_engl.pdf.

Boyle, Ellexis, Brad Millington, and Patricia Vertinsky. "Representing the Female Pugilist: Narratives of Race, Gender, and Disability in *Million Dollar Baby.*" *Sociology of Sport Journal* 23 (2006): 99–116.

Hollywood, Leslie, and Shari L. Dworkin. *Built to Win: The Female Athlete as Cultural Icon.* Minneapolis: University of Minnesota Press, 2003.

Lawler, Jennifer. *Punch! Why Women Participate in Violent Sports.* Terre Haute, IN: Wish Publishing, 2002.

Lyman, Rick. "Far from Hollywood, a Boxer Whose Dreams Died in the Ring." *New York Times*, March 9, 2005.

Márquez, Maria Teresa, and C. Ondine Chavoya. *Women Boxers: The New Warriors.* Houston: Arte Público Press, 2006.

Oates, Joyce Carol. *On Boxing.* New York: HarperCollins, 2006.

Seller, Jay. "Literature to Film: Lecture on *Million Dollar Baby.*" http://hhsdrama.com/documents/LectureMillionDollarBaby.pdf.

Toole, F. X. *Rope Burns: Stories from the Corner.* New York: HarperCollins, 2001.

Weir, Tom. "Women's Boxing Far from Swank: *Million Dollar Baby* Success Hasn't Meant More Women in the Ring." *USA Today*, February 24, 2005.

Women Boxing Archive Network. "Lucia Rijker." http://www.wban.org/biog/lrijker.htm.

Bubbles, Buttercup, and Blossom attack the villainous Him in the animated television series *The Powerpuff Girls*. (© Cartoon Network/Courtesy: Everett Collection.)

The Powerpuff Girls

The Powerpuff Girls were the city of Townsville's resident superheroes, three adorable crime-fighting kindergartners in the animated television series that ran for six seasons (1998–2005). The series was a marketer's dream, spawning a feature film in 2001 and a stream of paraphernalia, clothing, toys, and other commodities. The girls were dubbed feminist icons and swiftly accrued an eclectic fan base of "1.9 million viewers, a number split evenly between boys and girls, and 24.5% of its viewers are adults" (Hains, 12).

The Powerpuff Girls comprised Blossom (voiced by Cathy Cavadini), Bubbles (voiced by Tara Strong), and Buttercup (voiced by Elizabeth Daily). The show was created by Craig McCracken, who also directed much of the series as well as the movie. Blossom, the unofficial leader, wore a pink dress with a thick black belt, like the black belt of a martial artist expert. She had long red hair and wore a big red bow. Bubbles, who was the most girlish and sweet of the three, had blonde pigtails and wore a powder-blue costume, and Buttercup, the aggressive hoyden of the group, wore a light-green dress and sported short black hair. Each of the girls had a large round face and enormous round eyes. The roundness of their features is a classic marker for femininity, innocence, kindness, and openness, the antithesis of the narrow-faced, square-jawed, and squinty glare of the traditional masculine hero. The girls also had disproportionately small bodies. Their appearance was deceptively nonthreatening, but if challenged or when facing off with a villain, the tops of their eyes narrowed and their mouths turned upward, signaling that the girls meant serious business.

The show used boundless humor and whimsical action to teach The Powerpuff Girls, and their viewers, life lessons. It was rife with feminist issues and messages, blending and bending traditional perceptions of feminine girlishness and toughness (as does their very name: power + puff). The recurring adult characters were a scientist, Professor Utonium, who looked the part of the straight-laced 1950s *Leave it to Beaver* archetype, an elderly dim-witted mayor; the mayor's voluptuous secretary, Miss Bellum; and the girls' kindergarten teacher, Miss Keene. The show featured a host of villains, was fast paced and always ended happily with The Powerpuff Girls triumphant.

ORIGINS

Craig McCracken, the man who created The Powerpuff Girls, launched his juggernaut on the new wave of **feminism**. In an interview, he explained that "there's this new feminism that's coming up, that's embracing things that are typically girlish and not saying, 'Oh, in order to be a feminist you have to denounce all of that pink stuff . . . you can have all those things, and be sexy and be feminine and be typically girlish, and still be a feminist'" (Hains, 14). Regarding his television series, he said "I just thought it was cool to see these cute little girls being really tough and really hardcore" (Hains, 14).

Tough Teens in Sports Flicks

The mainstreaming of teen girls in sports in the real world has inspired an increase in popular films on the same subject. In 2000, *Girlfight* and *Bring It On* were released in theaters. Both attained critical acclaim. *Girlfight* dealt with the nontraditional subject of an adolescent girl, Diana Guzman (Michelle Rodriguez), who boxed, and *Bring It On* followed high school senior Torrance Shipman (Kirsten Dunst), team captain of a competitive cheerleading squad. In 2002, the film *Blue Crush* was about a young woman who is a competitive surfer, having started in her youth; also, the British film *Bend It Like Beckham* became an enormous success, featuring Jesminder "Jess" Bhamra (Parminder Nagra) who dazzled as a star football (American soccer) player. Because her parents prohibited her from playing sports, she played in secret. In *Stick It* (2006), a film that capitalized on the previous success of films featuring sporty teens, Haley Graham (Missy Peregrym) was a gymnast with talent. She was also defiant, a trait which, in the end, was rewarded.

McCracken was on point. Indeed, a new movement had emerged in the 1990s, referred to as **third-wave feminism** or, simply, **girl power**. The movement advocated both femininity and power (intellectual, emotional, and physical), concepts that traditionally are at odds with each other.

Among the many players who helped shape this new brand of feminism were Riot Grrrls, an underground movement that wedded rebelliousness and femininity in their behavior, communication, and appearance. **Sexist** language became a playground, wherein women referred to themselves and one another in derogatory terms. Riot Grrrls dressed in "baby-doll dresses with lace Peter Pan collars worn with black boots, shaved heads, and cat's-eye glasses" (Hains, 2). The Spice Girls, a contemporaneous British band, disseminated girl power ideas to the mainstream in their songs, advice, and attitudes. **Second-wave feminists,** who coexist with the younger generation of third-wave proponents, were startled by the changes.

Second-wave feminism evolved during the 1960s. Activists marched, wrote books, songs, and scholarly articles, and appeared in interviews to challenge the status quo. Feminists advocated for equality of the sexes, the elimination of sexual harassment and **discrimination** in the workplace and other areas of life, rights for working mothers, and reproductive rights. In sum, they challenged the notion that women were inferior and subordinate to male dominance. Women wanted to be taken seriously, not treated like sex objects, protected, rescued, or controlled. The struggle for equality showed itself in the new ways women projected themselves. The film *Working Girl* (1988) is a case in point. To fit into the corporate struggle at work, working-class woman Tess McGill (Melanie Griffith) lowered the pitch of her voice, ditched her accent, cut her long, flowing, teased 1980s hair, and minimized her jewelry. In an extreme example, Lieutenant Jordan O'Neil shaved her hair off completely and built muscles in *G.I. Jane* (1997) in an effort to show that she could endure physical duress and equal the achievements of men. She wanted no special treatment or consideration because of her gender.

Progress in real life came slowly. But by the new millennium, the novelty of women achieving their goals had dwindled considerably, because so many women were excelling in life, at work, and in the media. Women presidents of companies, women leaders in various fields, and girls who excelled in math and science were received with less incredulity than in previous decades. This is not to say that life was a utopia for women in the new millennium; there's still plenty of room for improvement. Still, a watershed had been reached. Against this backdrop, young women challenged the second-wave notion that femininity, sexiness, and girlishness were "bad." To be looked at was a symbol of power, they argued, and was not innately offensive. Thus, primping and preening was as important as going to the gym, thinking for yourself, and getting good grades in subjects that traditionally challenged women. The popular television series *Buffy the Vampire Slayer* was one of the early symbols of the third-wave feminist movement. So was *The Powerpuff Girls*.

In the 1990s, television programming (in lockstep with radio, video games, and film) became increasingly **transgressive**. Shock talk shows, like *The Jerry Springer Show*, featured guests who bared their breasts, fought, and cursed. Although the shows were censored, audiences at the recording got an eyeful, and there was little left for the imagination for audiences at home. Lara Croft, the protagonist of one of the most popular video games of all times, was a voluptuous adventurer whose exploits stretched the limits of mainstream gaming. Cartoon networks, such as Nickelodeon, a formerly straight-arrow cable network, began showing cartoons with characters that were irreverent and deviant—and children loved them. The cartoon program *The Ren and Stempy Show* survived for several years on the odd humor of a chihuahua nicknamed Ren and a slow-witted cat known as Stimpy. For adults, female action heroes became increasingly regular. Films that featured strong, active women include: *La Femme Nikita* (1990), *The Silence of the Lambs* (1991), *Thelma and Louise* (1991), *Batman Returns* (1992), *Buffy the Vampire Slayer* (1992), *Bad Girls* (1994), *The Quick and the Dead* (1995), *Sailormoon* (1995), *Voyager* (1995), *Long Kiss Goodnight* (1996), *Batman and Robin* (1997), and *G.I. Jane* (1997). On television, shows like *Buffy the Vampire Slayer* (1997–2003), *Xena: Warrior Princess* (1995–2001), *Dark Angel* (2000–2002), *Charmed* (1998–2006), *Terminator: The Sarah Connor Chronicles* (2008–2009), and *Bionic Woman* (2007). These films presented reminders of the third-wave feminism version of the female action hero.

Craig McCracken

McCracken came of age during the 1980s, the decade of change between second- and third-wave feminism. Born on March 31, 1971, in Charleroi, Pennsylvania, McCracken studied at the California Institute of the Arts. He got his start with the Cartoon Network, where he introduced his three super-girls under a very different name: *Whoopass Stew*. After changing the show's title to *The Powerpuff Girls*, he re-launched his show to much acclaim. He is married to Lauren Faust, who also made contributions to the series.

Origins of The Powerpuff Girls

The Powerpuff Girls have an interesting origin story. The narrative was retold during the opening sequence of each episode; it was also retold in an expanded version in the movie. The television episodes merely showed how the girls were created; the movie told why.

According to *The Powerpuff Girls Movie*, the city of Townsville was rampant with villains and crime. Frustrated by this situation, a scientist, Professor Utonium, poured an assortment of ingredients into a pot to create the perfect girls, who would be able to relieve Townsville of its many problems. The ingredients were based on an old Mother Goose nursery rhyme that explains the differences between girls and boys. Girls, as the rhyme goes, were made of sugar, spice, and everything nice. While the voice-over narrated this story in a robust, vintage 1950s voice, the professor propelled flowers, stars, ice cream cones, hearts, rainbows, white rabbits, lollipops, and other sparkly contents into a pot. His assistant, a high-energy chimpanzee named Jojo, accidentally caused an extra ingredient, Chemical X, to spill into the pot. Chemical X, in grim, black packaging, was ominous looking, but when the girls appeared, they were smiling and blinking sweetly. The professor soon discovered that Chemical X had given them super abilities.

The role of Professor Utonium is problematic to some, progressive to others. In their advocacy for women in television and film who project strength, independence, and power, some scholars look critically at women who must depend not on their own wits or the advice of a female mentor but on men. In *Buffy the Vampire Slayer*, Buffy relies on a male Watcher. In *The Silence of the Lambs*, Hannibal Lecter is depicted as a mentor to the FBI hopeful, Clarice Starling. In *The Bionic Woman*, a male surgeon gives Jaime Sommers bionics and she receives directives from a man, and in *Charlie's Angels*, the three female detectives are subordinate to Charlie, the man in charge. According to Spring-Serenity O'Neal, Professor Utonium represents a single father who plays both the traditionally female nurturing role and the masculine role. Other scholars point out that this is an unfair criticism, since it is so easy to find a male influence somewhere in everyone's life.

Spice Girls

Although third-wave feminism has its roots in the underground punk movement of the Riot Grrrls in the 1990s, a number of mainstream celebrities figured prominently in the emergence of girl power. The Spice Girls was an all-
women English musical group that was enormously popular in the 1990s.
Like the Powerpuff Girls, each Spice Girl reflected a unique identity, which
was expressed by her behavior, fashion, and nickname. Geri Halliwell, formerly Sexy Spice, was known as Ginger. Melanie Chisholm was dubbed
Sporty Spice. Victoria Addams was known as Posh Spice, Melanie Brown was
nicknamed Scary Spice, and Baby was the moniker of Emma Bunton. The
Spice Girls were known the world over for their pop hits, as well as their animated videos, in one of which they do karate kicks. The group's music was
massively popular with women, especially young girls. The Spice Girls were
keenly aware of their status as role models. They thus advocated feminist
concepts and self-esteem, and became among the biggest promoters of the
term *girl power*. The Spice Girls also projected sex appeal, which was a contentious issue for adults whose young girls aspired to imitate the women.
The success of the Spice Girls culminated in several hit records; a film, *Spice-
world: The Movie* (1997); a television series, *One Hour of Girl Power*; television
specials; and a reunion tour in 2007–2008.

In the movie, after Professor Utonium's little girls appear, his parental duties
begin. The girls blink brightly at him, and he realizes they need names. Blossom
is given her name because of her "directness and opening right up to" the professor. Bubbles gets her name because she appears bubbly and friendly; while she
giggles, she covers her mouth. Buttercup receives her name "because it also begins
with a B." In response, Buttercup crosses her arms and frowns, freely showing
her displeasure, not feigning a sweet smile as a compliant little girl would do.

Anxious to be a good parent, he asks their kindergarten teacher, Miss
Keene, on their first day at Pokey Oaks Elementary, if they will "be okay."
Miss Keene, one of two recurring adult female townspeople that interact with
The Powerpuff Girls, is traditionally nurturing and kind. The girls, however,
do not understand the rules of social behavior, nor do they have a grasp of
their powers. Havoc ensues. After learning how to play a game of tag, they
use their super speeds to run. They shoot laser beams from their eyes,
destroying the school property, the fence, and breaking cement. The camera
pans above the school to show that it is hidden behind a plume of smoke.

POWER SUIT, WEAPONS, AND ABILITIES

The Powerpuff Girls wear the same costumes day in and day out, attire that
reflects both their power and their femininity. The costumes are simple and

undecorated, projecting both toughness and girlishness. The pastel colors, which are light, soft, and fun, correspond with the ring of color that surrounds the pupils of each girl.

The three different hair colors and styles denote the girls' sense of fun and individuality. They represent three universal hairstyles worn by little girls: long hair, pigtails, and short hair. Of the three, the most transgressive style is the short hair. Buttercup, who sports the short hairstyle, is also the toughest of the three. She is also the most eager to fight and to be shown frowning. The most traditional of the bunch, Bubbles, is a blonde with pigtails. Blonde hair is traditionally used to signify innocence, gullibility, femininity, and the beauty ideal. Blondes are also **stereotypically** cast as vacuous, and Bubbles displays this tendency. Blossom, with her long, red hair, is a more neutral character, although she is also bossy and self-righteous. Red hair is traditionally associated with having a temper.

Blossom, Buttercup, and Bubbles have superpowers. In some episodes, they try to work out conflicts without using their powers or getting violent, but mostly they meet each crisis with physical gusto. Like The Bionic Woman, the girls can run at super speeds. Their super strength gives them the ability to knock out, hurl, and generally incapacitate villains. The Powerpuff Girls also have access to "laser eye beams and ice breath" (Hains, 12).

VILLAINS

Most of the villains—a motley crew of quirky but stereotypical hoodlums with deliciously funny names—are male in *The Powerpuff Girls* series. Mojo Jojo is a chimpanzee whose brains show. Roach Coach is a grubby middle-aged man—a robot, actually—that is controlled by a cockroach. Al Lusion is a former magician who comes back to life as a zombie named Abracadaver. Major Man is a superhero who competes with the girls. Other monsters, creatures, and aliens that make appearances are the Broccoli aliens, The Giant Ant, a leech man, and nanobots.

Among the women villains are the Princess, Ima Goodlady, and Mask Scara. The Princess is a coddled young girl who turns against The Powerpuff Girls because they will not let her join their group (she has no powers). Ima Goodlady tries to get close to Professor Utonium, but it turns out she is not who she appears to be, but rather a villain named Sedusa. Mask Scara sullies the town by vandalizing billboards.

Sometimes, The Powerpuff Girls have to deal with more ordinary troubles, such as when the townspeople are inflicted with gas after eating the professor's chili in "Reeking Havoc."

THE POWERPUFF GIRLS, THE SERIES

With only his imagination limiting the activities of his villains and their goofy plots, McCracken comes up with numerous ways in which to endanger the people of Townsville and to demonstrate The Powerpuff Girls' skills and valor. He also creates havoc by poking fun at stereotypical female behaviors.

"Insect Inside" starts off with Bubbles screaming as she runs from an insect. Traditionally, women are depicted as being afraid of things that are scary or creepy, with the heroic male rescuing her from her fears. Buttercup, however, is the hero in this scene. She pursues the insect that is chasing after the frightened Bubbles. As part of her efforts, Buttercup punches the wall and uses laser beam eye action. Blossom jumps in, saying authoritatively, "Stop it girls. It's just a cockroach." Buttercup interjects, "Shut up . . . it's gross." After the professor ambles in, he gives the girls a lesson on why it's not good to kill insects and the importance of cockroaches. "It's not nice to harm an insect just because it's yucky on the outside," he intones, "it's the insect inside that's important. Who wants to touch it?" The girls scream in reply; Bubbles hides behind the professor's legs. The professor puts the cockroach outside.

In a subsequent scene, the same cockroach crawls to a nearby hotel, where Roach Coach (the robot being controlled by a cockroach inside his head) is waiting to get a report on The Powerpuff Girls. The cockroach tells him that the girls will not harm the cockroaches because of the professor's lecture. Emboldened by the news, Roach Coach executes his plan to destroy humans. But The Powerpuff Girls find an innovative means of dealing with him: imprisoning his army of cockroaches in a giant jar. When Roach Coach frees his minions, they form a giant cockroach using him as the core. Buttercup wants to squish the cockroaches, but Blossom reminds her of the professor's warning not to harm insects. Finally, Blossom is persuaded, and when they punch the giant cockroach, Roach Coach plummets to the ground and breaks into pieces. The little roach that was controlling him calls Bubbles a "stupid biped." Bubbles responds with a tough "Who you calling a biped?" But the joke is at her expense, underscoring her vacuity. In the end, the villain goes to jail.

In at least two episodes, male villains fruitlessly target The Powerpuff Girls' weaknesses in an effort to break up their tight sisterhood. In "Octi Evil," the villain, Him, who is depicted as a devil, taunts Bubbles, the weakest of the girls, through her stuffed animal Octi. Octi spouts lies to Bubbles, who becomes innocently befuddled and eventually starts a conflict with her sisters. However, the girls come together in a time of crisis, when Him morphs Octi into a giant monster. In "Buttercrush," the unlikely girl hero succumbs to a crush on a "bad boy," a villain named Ace who heads a recurring group called the Gangrene Gang. Buttercup comes to her senses after the gang manipulates her to get to her sisters. Episodes such as these firmly establish the strength of their bond and the importance of solidarity among the girls, especially when a villain (or male) is involved.

In "Rowdy Rough Boys," Mojo Jojo creates male counterparts to The Powerpuff Girls. McCracken uses this challenge to show that the girls cannot be defined in conventional terms and can overcome villains through unconventional means. The Mother Goose rhyme says that boys are made

Femforce

In 1985, the first all-women comic book hero team debuted. Among the many women to appear in A.C. Comics' *Femforce* were Miss Victory, who had super strength and could fly; Nightveil, who could also fly, plus she had magical powers; Tara, who could communicate with animals; Stardust, who could throw energy bolts; and Firebeam, who manipulated fire. These women were not only as powerful and capable as any male hero, they were frequently depicted as voluptuous, scantily clad women. On the cover of the comic books, they were drawn in suggestive poses, underscoring the historical challenge of how women have been represented in the media.

of snips and snails and puppy dog tails, and these are the ingredients Mojo Jojo uses to concoct his boy villains. The boys, however, are confounded when the girls do not cry like they want them to. After various attempts, "the girls eventually outsmart the boys and win by doing the one thing that the boys can't stand—being nice" (O'Neal, 10). "Being nice" is a traditional feminine trait. McCracken thus depicts niceness as a power.

In "Powerpuff Bluff," the villains learn just how far emulating girlie behaviors, including niceness and politeness, can get them. Early in the episode, three bandits attempt to rob a bank, a jewelry store, and the mayor's house. Each time, The Powerpuff Girls foil the attempt. The lead bandit conceives a plan to disguise himself and his cohorts as The Powerpuff Girls. Conveniently, three costumes, complete with face masks, hang in the corner of their jail cell.

The bandits start off again in the usual manner, dressed comically in their disguises. The image they project is disjointed. The men's arms are large, muscular, and hairy; stubble and crooked, discolored teeth show through their masks. The implied message is that girls can be sweet and powerful and pull it off, but burly men who feign sweetness are not believable. When the men start to rob the bank, they bellow in masculine voices. The lead bandit corrects them and shows them how to appropriately portray their new identities. In a particularly comedic moment, he skips across the bank to the nearest teller and asks very sweetly, in a high-pitched voice, assuming assorted girlish poses, if he could have all the money in the bank. The scene parodies how female forms of communication, verbal and nonverbal, can appear passive and indirect and yet effectively manipulate others. The tellers, including the mayor, who opens the safe, are easily tricked. As the bandits depart, the tellers and the mayor smile and wave. By behaving in traditional feminine fashion (mimicking The Powerpuff Girls, who are popular with all good Townsville denizens), the bandits go on to rob the jewelry story. Later, they go to the mayor's home and exploit his kindness. The mayor gives them cookies and intones, "what precious angels."

Miss Bellum, the mayor's assistant, is the only one who realizes that the bandits are imposters. Miss Bellum is a walking contradiction. Her face never appears to audiences, but her body, curvaceous and typical of the bombshell archetype, is always exposed. Her objectified sensuality belies her intelligence and common sense. In contrast, the mayor is dull and is dependent upon Miss Bellum. In some episodes he is depicted as having a romantic interest in her, though he is married.

Miss Bellum, with some difficulty, convinces the mayor that something is awry, but he gets confused and calls the police, who enter the girls' kindergarten class just when Blossom is explaining how the change she is collecting will be used to help the homeless, abused animals, and to "find good homes or adopt a child from a Third World country." The girls are promptly put behind bars. Buttercup and Bubbles initiate a breakout; Blossom is hesitant because she does not want to break any laws. The girls bring closure to the episode by beating up the imposters.

Perhaps the most unusual power of The Powerpuff girls is that they are stereotypically obedient and nice, classic **ingénue** archetypes. They are good-natured, generous, thoughtful, and obedient, and they reap the benefits of displaying these character traits. When they break rules, they apologize. They are constantly learning from Professor Utonium, who gently lectures them on polite behavior and other ethical precepts. In other words, the girls not only succeed by being aggressive and powerful, but because they behave in traditionally acceptable ways, by being friendly, smiling, and saying please and thank you. This stands in stark contrast with second-wave feminists' celebration of the female leads in *Thelma and Louise* (1991), who challenged the conventional good-girl construct and morphed into bad girls who rebel against **patriarchy**, attack rude and sexist men, and refuse to submit to the domineering men in their lives who won't commit until it is too late. Even third-wave feminist action hero Lara Croft flirted and was reckless.

There are several lessons learned in "Powerpuff Bluff." McCracken shows that people can be fooled by appearances, and that a glamorous assistant (Miss Bellum) can be intellectually sharp. McCracken also demonstrates that breaking the rules (as he does with his creation of super-powerful and feminine kindergartners) is sometimes necessary, that little girls can beat grown men, and that toughness, at the end of the day, is an asset.

IMPACT

Although *The Powerpuff Girls* was intended for young girls, the series had a broad appeal. According to one study, there were a number of reasons for the show's success. Male and female adults "enjoy [*The Powerpuff Girls*] for the clever pop culture references and felt the series targeted them, not children. . . . Simultaneously, girls enjoy viewing the cartoon's girls with enviable super powers defeating evil . . .; boys delight in imitating the male villains. . .; and both boys and girls enjoy watching child characters rescue grown-ups" (Hains, 13). Donna Potts contended that The Powerpuff Girls functioned as role models for young girls and lauded the series for showing that power is not undermined by girlishness and femininity.

Rebecca C. Hains, however, addressed some of the problems with the new girl heroes of television like The Powerpuff Girls. For all their promotion of female empowerment, many female action heroes of the 21st century inadvertently reinforce impossible objectives concerning body image, beauty, and ideal femininity. Hains further asserts that "the range of representations is still limited" to a certain demographic: "white" and "middle or upper middle class" (Hains, 19). These oversights, a sizeable loophole in the third-wave feminist dynamic, pose problems for young girls who do not fit those categories and leave them still searching for a relevant role model.

See also Charlie's Angels; Thelma and Louise.

FURTHER RESOURCES

Hains, Rebecca C. "Power(puff) Feminism: The Powerpuff Girls as a Site of Strength and Collective Action in the Third Wave." In *Women in Popular Culture: Representation and Meaning*, ed. Marian Meyers. Cresskill, NJ: Hampton Press, 2008.

Hains, Rebecca C. "The Problematics of Reclaiming the Girlish: The Powerpuff Girls and Girl Power." *Femspec* 5 (2005): 1–39.

Hopkins, Susan. *Girl Heroes: The New Force in Popular Culture.* Annandale, Australia: Pluto Press, 2002.

Hubel, Teresa. "In Pursuit of Feminist Postfeminism and the Blessings of Buttercup." *English Studies in Canada* 31 (2005): 17–21.

Mainon, Dominique, and James Ursini. *The Modern Amazons: Warrior Women On-Screen.* Pompton Plains, NJ: Limelight Editions, 2006.

O'Neal, Spring-Serenity. "Perfect Little Feminists: Resistance, Femininity, and Violence in the Powerpuff Girls." Proceedings of the Annual Meeting of the Association for Education in Journalism and Mass Communication, 2003. ERIC Document Reproduction Service ED481266.

Potts, Donna L. "Channeling Girl Power: Positive Female Media Images in the Power-puff Girls." *Studies in Media and Information Literacy Education* 1 (2001).

Princess Leia poses confidently with a blaster. (*Star Wars: Episode IV—A New Hope* TM & © 1977 and 1997 Lucasfilm Ltd. All rights reserved. Used under authorization. Unauthorized duplication is a violation of applicable law. Courtesy of Lucasfilm Ltd.)

Princess Leia

Princess Leia is famously known for being the twin sister (separated at birth and secreted away to a distant planet) of Luke Skywalker, powerful Jedi and one of the elite defenders-of-the-peace featured in George Lucas's fictional *Star Wars* universe. Although the first three films of the series (which ultimately comprised six films, released in 1977, 1980, 1983, 1999, 2002, and 2005) centered on Skywalker (played by Mark Hamill), Princess Leia (played by Carrie Fisher) was of only slightly less importance. Moreover, she quickly emerged as a heroic figure, displaying strength, bravery, and vitality equal to her two male protagonists.

Transcending her title, she turned on its head the depiction of the delicate, ineffectual princesses and fair maidens found in traditional fairy tales. For example, in *Star Wars Episode VI: Return of the Jedi* (1983), Princess Leia, disguised as a bounty hunter, goes alone into the treacherous underworld of crime lord Jabba the Hutt. Outnumbered and outarmed, she rescues her compatriot Han Solo, a smuggler and mercenary with a heart of gold, who has been frozen in carbonite. As Solo wakes from his glacial sleep, Leia kisses him. The moment harks back to the seminal fairy-tale kiss with which Prince Phillip revives Sleeping Beauty, thus removing the curse cast upon her by the jealous witch. In *Return of the Jedi*, it is the princess who awakens the sleeping man. When Leia's escape plan from Jabba's lair is foiled, Jabba makes her his slave. Forced to wear a metal bikini and fettered to Jabba, she briefly reverts to the more passive, ornamental female stereotype. But Leia metes out her own revenge when she later strangles Jabba to death with the very chain that binds her to him, firmly establishing that this is a female character who can have it all.

In addition to the six films, there is also the Expanded Universe. The Expanded Universe expands on the films and includes the comic books, literature, television series, and video games. In the Expanded Universe, the tale of Princess Leia unfolds with even more daring and drama—equal to if

Ahsoka Tano

Ahsoka Tano is the fiery and reckless adolescent Padawan, a Jedi apprentice, to Anakin Skywalker in the film *Star Wars: The Clone Wars* (2008) and its subsequent television series. Ahsoka is a Togruta who was raised in the Jedi temple. Her character is considered innovative and progressive because as an adolescent girl (and nonhuman) she shares much of the limelight with Anakin. She also challenges the traditional representation of submissive and ingénue girl characters. Constantly in the thick of action, Ahsoka teams up with Anakin on several dangerous missions. In the film, she brandishes her lightsaber and helps to rescue a baby from Jabba the Hutt. In the television series, she fights off an enemy ship, rescues R2D2, and protects a Republic Ship. Ahsoka proves that you don't have to be a boy or a human to be a hero.

not more expansive (at least career-wise) and unorthodox than her brother's formidable life story.

From childhood to adulthood, Princess Leia challenges societal and gender expectations. In her quest to combat the injustices and evils of the Empire, she rises to prominence as a politician, diplomat, rebel, and eventually a Jedi Knight of the New Jedi Order, with all the abilities of her famous brother. Moreover, Leia's ascent to power is characteristic of women in the Star Wars Universe. Female characters like Ahsoka Tano, featured in *Star Wars: The Clone Wars*, an animated television series that debuted in 2008, all have equal access to power. Tano, a 14-year-old Togrutan, is a Padawan, or Jedi apprentice, to Anakin Skywalker. She is not only a major character in the story, but a commanding fighter with the sort of feisty temperament that demands attention.

Indeed, Lucas's female characters are not only tough combatants, they are individuals with dynamic inner lives who control their own destinies. In the Expanded Universe, after many years of delayed nuptials and misadventures, Princess Leia and the swashbuckling Han Solo finally marry. They produce three children and go on to take part in numerous adventures, galactic battles, and of course, fairy-tale rescues.

ORIGINS

George Lucas and His Films

Although Lucas was born (1944) in the small town of Modesto, California, thanks to newspapers, television, and radio, few in that period in history were unaware of the tumultuous events going on in the nation. The years in which Lucas grew up were remarkable for the marches, sit-ins, and picketing of the **civil rights movement,** and the racial attacks against black and

Tough Princesses, Queens, and Rulers in History

Many historical women throughout the world have defied traditional representations of royal women as delicate and passive. Khutulun, the daughter of King Kaidu and niece of the notorious Mongol Empire leader, Khublai Khan, was a well-known warrior. Like other Mongol women, she fought in battles and is said to have challenged men to a fight for her hand in marriage. She remained unmarried her entire life. Although some scholars contend that Princess Urdujah is only a legend, she was known as a powerful ancient Philippine ruler who also fought in battles. Septimia Bat Zabbai, an ancient Arabian queen, fought forcefully, wrote history, and spoke several languages. Queen Jinga Mbandi, a West African ruler, formed a militia of men and women to fight Portuguese slave traders and rescued captive Africans who were being sold in the slave trade. During her illustrious reign (1558–1603), Queen Elizabeth of England endured foreign conflict, murder plots, and the colossal responsibility of managing one of the world powers of the time.

white protestors who refused to retaliate or defend themselves. After years of protest, beginning in the 1950s and culminating in the 1960s, President Lyndon B. Johnson signed the monumental Civil Rights Act of 1964, which eradicated **discriminatory** laws and practices. The Civil Rights Act of 1964 did not only benefit African Americans; it changed the lives of other marginalized groups, like women.

The civil rights gains, including the subsequent Voting Rights Act of 1965, did not put a stop to the protests. In the mid-1960s, militant African American groups emerged who resisted dominant white society. Counterculture groups were formed, protesting America's involvement in the Vietnam War, materialism, and mainstream culture. Native Americans, other ethnic groups, and women struggled for equality. Women in particular protested against a society they contended was controlled by men, who, in turn, controlled women's images and suppressed their rights.

Lucas's first film, released when he was in his late thirties, was a science fiction movie called *THX 1138* (1971). The film follows the life of a man named THX 1138 (Robert Duvall) in the distant future, when humanity lives in an antiseptic underground world and all aspects of existence are controlled by the powers that be. THX 1138 desires freedom and eventually makes a break for it. He must escape alone, however, without LUH 3417 (Maggie McOmie), his female roommate, who is captured. The movie ends with THX 1138 rising from an opening above the underground city, silhouetted against a vibrant red sky. Birds soar above him, and the background music is a section of Johann Sebastian Bach's *St. Matthew Passion*, an expansive piece with soloists, choir, and orchestra commemorating Jesus Christ's crucifixion and the events leading up to it. One of the major themes in this film is rebellion. Rebellion is a theme that Lucas explores throughout the *Star Wars* films. Rebellion also plays a large role in the struggle for racial and gender equality, and the construction of tough female action heroes in film and television who defy traditional passive and subordinate roles. Though this maiden effort was not a success, Lucas's subsequent films would grant him a notoriety that lasts to this day.

When *THX 1138* was released in 1971, the spirit of protest and rebellion in America was still strong, particularly among **second-wave feminists**. In his second film, *American Graffiti* (1973), Lucas continued to explore the theme of rebellion, focusing this time on his love of race car driving. This time, he hit the right note. Critics and audiences relished the film about young American males in the nostalgic 1950s indulging in the illegal activities of race car driving.

Because of the success of *American Graffiti*, Lucas received financial support from Alan Ladd of Fox Studios to produce his next project—a space opera that became the first of the *Star Wars* films. Ironically, the film that was to be a mega success was produced on a modest budget. While preparing for production, Lucas conceived an elaborate backstory for the film, which he dreamed of presenting in three trilogies for a total of nine films. Rather than start at the beginning, the original *Star Wars* (1997) was actually the fourth in the series. This trend was followed by a number of directors in the late 20th century in film series such as *Batman*, *Terminator*, and *Underworld*. It would be over two decades before *Star Wars Episode I: The Phantom Menace* (1999), *Star Wars Episode II: Attack of the Clones* (2002), and *Star Wars Episode III: Revenge of the Sith* (2005) were produced. The last three films envisioned by Lucas have not yet been made, and he has no plans to do so.

Thus Lucas began the tale when his main characters, twins Luke Skywalker and Leia Organa, were already budding adults. Skywalker, the male protagonist who is transformed (over the course of episodes IV, V, and VI) from immature and undisciplined wannabe to brave Jedi, was not a new concept for moviegoers. But Princess Leia, the female protagonist who could "take care of herself" and who knew how to wear the mantle of authority, was one of a rare breed.

One of a very few precursors to Leia was the African American vigilante, played by Pam Grier, in *Coffy* (1973). Grier is considered the first female to play an action hero in a feature film in America. Black women, with Grier at their head, of the so-called **blaxploitation** era, would continue to lead the way for two more years. Princess Leia's appearance in 1977 opened the door to the mainstream moviegoer. Then, in 1979, Sigourney Weaver's portrayal of Ellen Ripley of the *Alien* film series broke the door down (and half the wall along with it), triggering a crescendo that lasted into the 1990s and beyond. Currently, powerful female leads in action films, cable TV, and television appear with regularity.

But while Grier's character and Ripley were identified with professions where one might expect a certain toughness, Leia was presented as a *princess*, a term that since time immemorial has conjured up characteristics like "sweet-tempered," "feminine," "delicate," "obedient," "isolated," and "sheltered." A princess, according to literary archetypes, is the prize to be won by the hero. We picture a princess spending her days dressed in beautiful but impractical flowing dresses and robes, wearing expensive accessories that make movement difficult, waiting in her chamber by her canopy bed for her prince to come. She might have a sweet voice, few skills beyond the arts, and either a loving or dominating parent. The purpose of the princess, in fact, was to provide a reward for the hero, who is faced with many conflicts and engages in high action on the road to the attainment of his prize. A common device in fairy tales and myths is for the antagonist to capture the princess so that the hero (prince or knight in shining armor) can save her.

Lucas's princess has a low, authoritative voice; she is rebellious and fearless, and she is more than capable of appropriating the action. Moreover, these characteristics are not played for humor or presented as a novelty. Leia's importance to the action of the film is maintained throughout the first three movies that Lucas directs. Princess Leia's highly visible role in the original *Star Wars*, and indeed in the universe that Lucas created, projected something new to moviegoers: a world wherein it was not the norm that women's roles should be limited to marriage or supporting roles—a world where no one assumed that women were inferior to men.

Lucas continued to direct films following the success of *Star Wars Episode IV: A New Hope* (1977), notably the enormously popular *Indiana Jones* films (1981, 1984, 1989, 2008). Jones, the sardonic, deeply tanned and adventurous archeologist, was played by Harrison Ford, who Lucas had cast as Han Solo in the first three *Star Wars* film. Lucas directed other films like *Willow* (1988) and *Beverly Hills Cop III* (1994), featuring Eddie Murphy, an African American lead.

Lucas is considered one of the most influential and financially successful directors in America. His first wife was Marcia Griffin, whom he divorced in 1983.

Carrie Fisher

Born on October 21, 1956, in Burbank, California, to superstars Eddie Fisher and Debbie Reynolds, who divorced when she was a toddler, Fisher's career path was inevitable. She was 12 years old when she began singing professionally, and as a teenager, she performed on Broadway with her mother. After attending the Central School of Speech and Drama in England, she made her movie debut in the comedy *Shampoo* (1975). After starring as Princess Leia in 1977, she returned for the next two installments, *Star Wars Episode V: The Empire Strikes Back* (1980) and *Star Wars*

Queen Elizabeth

"I, too, can command the wind sir! I have a hurricane in me that will strip Spain bare when you dare to try me!"

Source: Queen Elizabeth's (Cate Blanchett) forceful reply to a Spanish minister's (Vidal Sancho) not-so-subtle threat in the film *Elizabeth: The Golden Age* (2007).

Episode VI: Return of the Jedi (1983). She did not appear in the subsequent three films, as they were concerned with events of the past.

In the 1980s and beyond, Fisher continued to appear in movies, though her ensuing action hero roles were limited mostly to cameos wherein she reprised Princess Leia. She has also written plays, novels, and screenplays, edited movies, and performed in a one-woman play. She has been candid about her struggles with drugs and bipolar disorder. She was once married to legendary folksinger Paul Simon of Simon and Garfunkel fame; Fischer has no children.

POWER SUIT, WEAPONS, AND ABILITIES

Princess Leia's trademark looks are her brunette hair, with two large buns affixed on each side of the head, and a draped white dress that covers from her neck to her feet. It is an overtly conservative style—a modest, almost Victorian style. The color white signifies purity and—like many films before and after—goodness. Black (like the term "dark side of the Force") is traditionally associated with evil. Many have challenged this construct over the years, including singer Janet Jackson, who in the late 1980s, preferred to wear mostly black, insisting that black, like the skin color of African Americans, had too long been denigrated. African American leaders like W.E.B. Du Bois and Marcus Garvey in the early 20th century made similar arguments as part of the ongoing struggle for racial equality.

Conforming to her appearance, Princess Leia does not exude sex appeal, nor does she ever appear in a compromising position with a man; her kisses are strictly on the lips. When she appears in skimpy clothing, it is because she is forced to appear so, not by choice. This serious, driven, focused woman stands in sharp contrast to the sexy image of the blonde, ditzy centerfold archetype—the image most second-wave feminists, who desired to be taken seriously in real life and not seen as sex objects, protested against.

The white robes were not Princess Leia's only outfit. She changed costumes several times across the three movies of the original trilogy. In one scene, she wore a vest, long-sleeve shirt, and pants; in others, she wore a costume as a disguise. At the end of *Episode IV*, when Princess Leia honors Skywalker and Solo, she wears an elaborate braided hair style and shows cleavage. In *The*

Empire Strikes Back, after she has broken her chains and strangled Jabba to death, she changes from her metal bikini back into her trademark outfit.

Whatever Princess Leia wears, her clothes never get in the way of her toting a blaster and using it. Most fans of *Star Wars* are familiar with the iconic weapon that Lucas introduces to audiences: the lightsaber. Children of the late 1970s grew up imitating the electric whoosh sound and slicing an imaginary (or toy) lightsaber in the air with dramatic flourish. The lightsaber is a futuristic version of that most ancient of chivalric weapons, the sword—but it has tremendous power, indicated by the fact that it is illuminated in neon red or blue.

Although Luke Skywalker was the only one of the twins to carry a lightsaber in the film series, it was understood that Princess Leia would get her chance, for she was destined to be a mighty Jedi like her brother (only Jedi are permitted to wield lightsabers). Instead, Princess Leia expertly wielded a blaster, a futuristic gun that shoots out a stream of deadly electromagnetic energy. She was, however, equipped with other supernatural powers, like her brother. She could sense the "Force," the invisible power that was classified as either good (light side of the Force) or evil (dark side of the Force) in the fictional universe (some classify the Force as a metaphysical religion or belief system). Luke Skywalker, Princess Leia, and friends followed the light side of the Force, whereas Darth Vader and his ilk followed the dark side.

Princess Leia was also competent in military strategy, piloting, and politics. What most viewers do not know, because Lucas did not reveal her complete backstory in the films, is that as a youth, Princess Leia received a privileged education and was trained in combat and political theory. She was a woman who could do it all (and more, including telekinesis and telepathy, according to the Expanded Universe). The Expanded Universe also explains how her adoptive parents did not stand in her way when she chose her life's path, one that was at odds with her peers, especially owing to her high status, who were expected to marry. This illustrates the real-life historical social expectations of women and underscores Princess Leia's rebelliousness.

When Princess Leia was in action, she was treated as an equal member of the team. That team included, at various times, Skywalker, Solo, Lando Calrissian (Billy Dee Williams), two droids (C-3PO [Anthony Daniels] and R2-D2 [Kenny Baker]), and a hirsute Wookie named Chewbacca, commonly referred to as Chewy (Peter Mayhew). Many of the men she met were attracted to Princess Leia's beauty and vied for her attention.

VILLAINS

In the *Star Wars* Expanded Universe, the villains include (in order of villainy): Darth Sidious, a cloaked figure who masquerades as Senator Palpatine; Darth Vader; and the army of Imperial Stormtroopers, human clones enveloped in white armor.

Vader, who personified evil to a generation of movie goers, wore all-black armor, including a frightening inhuman mask over his face. His raspy, technologically assisted breathing gave his deep and ominous voice a mechanical quality. Exacerbating this sinister image was the theme music that plays whenever he appears.

As senator-turned-emperor of the Galactic Empire, Palpatine, who is really Darth Sidious, functions as the most powerful political leader in the galaxy. Princess Leia, a leader in the rebel movement, as well as her Jedi brother and friends, is fighting to save the Galactic Empire (also referred to as the Republic) from his brutal rule. Deepening the plot is the fact that Darth Vader wants to turn his children, Skywalker and Princess Leia, to the dark side.

STAR WARS EPISODES IV, V, VI, THE FILM SERIES

In the opening scene of Lucas's *Star Wars Episode IV: A New Hope*, Princess Leia displays her toughness in a thrilling chase scene. Vader, aboard a large Imperial Cruiser, pursues Princess Leia's smaller rebel ship. But Princess Leia is no typical princess in distress. She maintains control of the ship and her emotions throughout the ordeal, even when Vader boards her ship (in this round, the Empire captures the rebels). Princess Leia talks tough to Vader, while guards restrain her. Vader plans to force her, by any means necessary, to disclose the whereabouts of the rebel's secret base. They will have trouble, for Princess Leia has a strong will. She also has hope, for before her capture, the fast-thinking Leia dispatched a message for help. Receiving the message seemingly by accident, Skywalker, displaying all his youthful energy, naturally bounds off to rescue her with the help of Obi-Wan "Ben" Kenobi (Alec Guinness), Solo, Chewy, and the droids.

This scene sets the tone for the rest of the movie as well as the way in which audiences perceive Princess Leia. Although she does get captured and needs to be rescued, she gets through the process with poise and brains. She is the first *Star Wars* character to be introduced to audiences, underlining her prime importance.

A similar situation occurred over two decades later when, in *The Matrix* (1999), Trinity (Carrie-Ann Moss) features in an initial pulse-racing scene with innovative martial arts effects. She fights several agents at one time. They pursue her. She runs. But she is so tough that when she falls down a flight of stairs, she immediately bolts upright while still on the floor, with her gun aimed. Her face is cool, emotionless as she undertones, "Get up, Trinity!" Barely in time, she gets to a phone booth where she "calls" for help and is immediately transported to a different reality. Although Trinity is rescued by others, she has, on her own, eluded her near-invincible pursuers.

Even if Princess Leia must be rescued from time to time, and even though she is heckled by Solo, who mockingly calls her "Your Highness" and other names, her persona as a hero is not seriously threatened (after all, she rescues Solo more than once too). Her rescues are only superficially the conventional role of a film damsel in distress who cannot help herself out of an impasse, and must scream and cry for help. But even when captured by her

Princess Projectra: A Comic Book Hero

Princess Projectra is a DC comic book hero of royal birth who debuted in *Adventure Comics #346* in 1966. Female comic book heroes have always been outnumbered by men. They are also historically represented with exaggeration and voluptuousness, but overall they project power and can-do-itness with as much vitality as their male counterparts. Projectra hails from the planet Orando. She appears with different looks over the years. Early on she has a short white bouffant hair style and wears a red heart-shaped bustier one-piece with a matching cape. In later appearances, she wears various bob hair styles and then long flowing tresses. In a stint as Sensor Girl, Projectra wears a red-and-white full-bodied uniform, with a cape and face mask, and has long blonde hair.

From the start, Projectra exhibits impressive powers. She first demonstrates her powers to the group of super heroes called the Legionnaires by transporting them underwater and to outer space. Projectra is not only gifted with the power to project illusions, but she can fight as well and is featured on numerous occasions rescuing others from harm and danger. Although Projectra is lesser known than other female comic book heroes like Wonder Woman and Storm, she was a force to be reckoned with and a formidable hero in the annals of comic book history.

enemies, Princess Leia does not scream or become hysterical; her facial expressions are cool and collected. When necessary, she helps the process of rescue along, as when she grabs Solo's blaster and shoots an opening in a wall when Skywalker and Solo get lost during the escape from Vader's Imperial Cruiser. Even Solo admires Leia's toughness and intermittently makes comments that allude to this fact. For example, after Leia grabs his blaster to make an escape, he replies, "I'm either going to kill her, or I'm beginning to like her." These and later double-edged statements reveal that Lucas wants audiences to know that not all men are intimidated by unconventional, assertive women. Although the opening in the wall Leia creates leads to a futuristic garbage bin and subsequent difficulties, suggesting that women's assertiveness can be problematic, the point remains that the group would not have escaped if someone had not acted.

In *Star Wars Episode V: The Empire Strikes Back* (1980), Princess Leia continues to play a pivotal role. She helps repair a ship and eventually helms a ship herself, a position all but universally held by men. At the end of the movie, using the Force, Leia senses that Luke is in trouble and spearheads his rescue. Displaying the ease with which she can fulfill any role as needed, Leia then takes on a more conventional role when she nurses Skywalker after his rescue.

One of Princess Leia's most heroic moments occurs when she enters Jabba the Hutt's domain and rescues Solo at the beginning of *Star Wars Episode VI: Return of the Jedi* (1983). In the previous film, Leia and Solo revealed their romantic feelings for each other. Although Leia's escape plan fizzles, she eventually takes revenge on Jabba when she kills him during a Skywalker-engineered rescue. It is typical of the *Star Wars* films, which depend largely on involved rescue scenes to provide drama, that those being rescued join in as quickly as possible, so that all members of the team can shine. Gender roles are not an issue.

In *Return of the Jedi*, we get our last on-screen view of the twins, now fully mature. Skywalker emerges as a traditional hero, having successfully completed his Jedi training and demonstrated extraordinary heroism. Princess Leia's journey, it is implied, is just beginning. She engages in combat, but she is also dressed (by cherubic bear-like creatures called Ewoks who live on the planet Endor) in traditional medieval princess garb, complete with long, flowing, neatly combed hair. Yet Princess Leia, as the movie reveals, is her brother's twin and has equal access to his power. This statement is striking, and accurately reflects the times in which it was made. When this movie was released in 1983, the struggle had yet come to complete fruition, much like Leia's unrealized Jedi power. But die-hard *Star Wars* fans knew that her day of reckoning would come.

STAR WARS EXPANDED UNIVERSE

The Expanded Universe, comprising video games, novels, and comic books, delineates the complete and spectacular life of Princess Leia. From this wealth of information we learn of a girl who is raised by her noble adoptive parents, Bail Prestor Organa, a politician, fighter and spy, and Queen Breha of Alderaan. We learn that she takes on many roles—as political leader, Senator, rebel leader, diplomat, and Jedi Knight. She eventually marries Solo and has children. Throughout her life, she is rescued, stages rescues, fights in myriad battles, and enjoys an equal and loving partnership with her husband.

The Expanded Universe also reveals Leia's complex personality in a way the films do not. Leia demonstrates an aversion to the slave system that operates in the galaxy. She was horrified when, in her late teens, she witnessed the ill-treatment of a Caamasi, a peaceful humanoid species, who was not permitted to enter a restaurant (a parallel to the experiences of African Americans during **segregation**).

Racism is only one of many themes explored in Lucas's films. His droids (or androids) and alien species are often depicted as symbols of marginalization. Like black slaves, droids were sold and treated abusively and dismissively. In *Episode IV*, Skywalker haggles over the price as he buys the two droids that would play a pivotal role in his life. At home, he treats them with casual condescension. Eventually, he develops respect for them. It is Solo, the more experienced space traveler, who befriends a Wookie and speaks his language, demonstrating his tolerance of other species.

IMPACT

Star Wars Episodes IV, V, and *VI* created a cultural—and marketing—phenomenon. Action figures, books, lunch boxes, clothing, and other paraphernalia reflected the public's obsession with all things *Star Wars*. In 1964, Hasbro came out with the first action figure, a military soldier named G.I. Joe. But the G.I. Joe nurse figure released in 1968 was a failure. It was a sign of the times that the Princes Leia action figure was a best seller.

The influence of *Star Wars* extended beyond consumer culture. Among the directors inspired by the series were Ridley Scott and James Cameron. Scott is responsible for the development of Ellen Ripley, protagonist of the *Alien* films, while Cameron created another landmark female action hero, Sarah Connor, protagonist of the *Terminator* films.

Two decades after its first appearance, the unquenchable interest in *Star Wars* brought fans of all ages to theaters to see *Episodes I, II,* and *III*. Sadly, the reviews from audiences and critics were mixed, and the films were not the watershed event that many expected. But the portrayal of Queen Padmé Amidala, the twins' biological mother, a strong, capable, and tough young woman, continues the Lucas tradition of telling heroic tales wherein the women are not just the prize, but adventurers in their own right.

See also Ellen Ripley; G.I. Jane; Jen Yu; Sarah Connor; Xena: Warrior Princess.

FURTHER RESOURCES

Decker, Kevin S., and Jason T. Eberl, eds. *Star Wars and Philosophy: More Powerful Than You Can Possibly Imagine*. Peru, IL: Open Court, 2005.

Hopkins, Susan. *Girl Heroes: The New Force in Popular Culture*. Annandale, Australia: Pluto Press, 2002.

Kline, Sally. *George Lucas: Interviews*. Jackson: University Press of Mississippi, 1999.

Morgan, Bell. "Princess Leia: Hero or Damsel in Distress?" http://www.movietrain.net/princess-leia-hero-or-damsel-in-distress.

The Official Web Site of Carrie Fisher. http://carriefisher.com.

Pollock, Dale. *Skywalking: The Life and Films of George Lucas*. Cambridge, MA: De Capo Press, 1999.

Rinzler, J. W. *The Making of* Star Wars: *The Definitive Story behind the Original Film*. London: Ebury Press, 2007.

Sansweet, Stephen J., Pablo Hidalgo, Bob Vitas, and Daniel Wallace. *The Complete Star Wars Encyclopedia*. New York: Del Ray, 2008.

Sarah Connor prepares to do battle in the film *Terminator 2*.
(© TriStar Pictures/Courtesy: Everett Collection.)

Sarah Connor

When first seen in *The Terminator* (1984) Sarah Connor, played by Linda Hamilton, is a cheery waitress whose biggest problem is what to do on a Friday night when her date cancels. By the end of the film, she is a commando fighter who accomplishes what her lover from the future and half the L.A. police force have died trying to do: destroy the indestructible Terminator. She is also the mother of John Connor, who, in 30 years' time, is destined to be the resistance leader in the ultimate battle against the machines. In *Terminator 2* (1991), Sarah Connor takes her role as a tough, hard-as-nails mother to a level not ordinarily depicted in the 1980s. This seminal character, along with the handful of other no-nonsense action women who went before her, paved the way for the onslaught of female action heroes in the 1990s and beyond.

The lasting success of any action film series (and the *Terminator* franchise is still going strong) greatly depends on its pivotal first movie, along with its characters and action-driven plots. New special effects are demanded by viewers for every film. But hair-raising narrative, Arnold Schwarzenegger's viselike hold on young male fans, and innovative action scenes notwithstanding, Sarah Connor was the lynchpin of director James Cameron's winning formula.

Connor is first portrayed as a traditional, nonthreatening waitress, a sweet and curvy young woman who bungles her way through food orders and must endure the wandering hands of the occasional obnoxious customer. Events (and Connor) change precipitously when a man from the future, Kyle Reese (Michael Biehn), arrives for the sole purpose of protecting Connor from the seemingly unstoppable cyborg villain, the Terminator (Arnold Schwarzenegger). Reese tells her that someday she will have a son who will grow up to save humanity from certain extinction at the hands of villainous cyborgs. On the run, the two fall in love and share a single night together before he dies—and before it is revealed that Reese will be the father of that son. By movie's end, violence, death, loss, and a terrible sense of impending doom have transformed Connor from hysterical woman to tough (and pregnant) female action hero. It is a sad, ominous ending—and yet her transformation has just begun.

Terminator 2: Judgment Day (1991), also known as *T2*, is widely touted as the best, or at least the most popular, of the *Terminator* films. Promos before the movie's release titillated fans with images of Schwarzenegger in cyborg persona with cool black shades, intoning, "I'll be back." However, it was Linda Hamilton who caused the biggest stir, when she showed up chiseled, militant, and dour, wearing camo gear and even cooler shades. The transformation was remarkable. From soft-bodied, feminine beauty to hard-bodied, athletic, warrior woman, Sarah Connor had morphed into the kind of woman who would sooner lead the battle than be the prize to be fought over. In this film, Connor's son John—the prophesied "great military leader" of the future—is 10 years old. But Connor, it turns out, is a failure as a mother, berating him for endangering himself and rejecting his expressions

Mother Warriors

Mother Warriors (2008), a book by model and actress Jenny McCarthy, features inspirational stories of mothers, including herself, who have battled their children's autism and won. She advocates alternative methods for treating the disorder. McCarthy defines a mother warrior as follows:

> A Mother Warrior is a mother who hears there is no hope for her child and, instead of retreating and mourning, breaks down walls, weaves her way through obstacles, follows her intuition even when people tell her she is crazy. She is a mother who believes in hope. A mother who believes in miracles and is able to carry on with strength and determination, even when her partner doubts her and offers no support. A mother who never gives up, even when she keeps hitting dead ends. These are the women who will continue to open the door so future generations of children don't have to suffer. These are the mothers with hearts of gold and shields made of the strongest armor.

Source: Jenny McCarthy, *Mother Warrior* (New York: Dutton, 2008), p. 216.

of love. She is half way to becoming a Terminator herself, and cannot give her son what he needs.

Despite this shocking betrayal of womanly sensibilities, female audiences fell over themselves to see this movie. The figures show it. *The Terminator* made $4,020,663 opening weekend and $78,371,200 worldwide. *T2* made $31,765,506 opening weekend and $519,843,345 worldwide. Women who traditionally had no interest in action or science fiction films loved it. Many joined gyms to sculpt their bodies like Hamilton, who in preparation for her role (and after having just given birth to her first child), worked out in a gym three hours a day with professional trainer Andy Cortes, followed a strict diet, and trained with Uzi Gal, an Israeli commando.

In the wake of *T2*, Hamilton became the poster woman (no longer poster girl) for female empowerment. Her ability to act, as well as her iconic single-mother role, reflect the changes taking place in the lives of modern American women, as well as how those lives were depicted in film and television.

Twenty-five years after she picked up her first pipe bomb, Connor's popularity and influence inspired a television series entitled *Terminator: The Sarah Connor Chronicles*. This remake involved a female Terminator sent from the future to protect John Connor and a brunette Sarah Connor, played by English actress Lena Headey.

ORIGINS

The 1980s, the decade in which the first *Terminator* movie was released, saw a torrent of social changes for women. Women were no longer expected to marry, bear children, and stay at home; premarital sex did not have the same stigma as, say, a century ago. Although some women put off marriage and children or opted out of both, many women married and then divorced, resulting in a large number of single working mothers. Women were also breaking into new careers, such as management positions in the business world. More women worked in the 1980s than in previous decades. Driving these changes was the increasing influence of feminist ideas and attitudes, which continued to permeate everyday life and popular culture.

In an effort to make television and films more relevant or in demand, producers and directors challenged traditional depictions of women—as passive, secondary characters—in ways that were either imaginative or emulated reality. The depictions were not flawless; many characters were portrayed as glamorous eye candy for male viewers or retained stereotypically feminine characteristics. This practice of trying to please both ends of the feminist spectrum began as early as the late 1960s, when television introduced the first single working women, female detectives, spies, and cops. Producers were careful never to stray from the underlying conventions that dictated that women should be nicely dressed and primarily concerned with their family responsibilities. They tended to use their "feminine wiles" rather than violence to achieve their goals. For superheroes like Wonder Woman and The Bionic Woman, who appeared early in the next decade, their innate attractiveness increased alongside their powers, as if the one must balance out the other. In the early 1970s, Pamela Grier was cast as a premier female action hero in blaxploitation films. Grier's action hero portrayals were not well known in mainstream society, as blaxploitation films were largely targeted to African American audiences, but she was an archetypal tough lady who also depended on sex appeal to attract a male viewership. At the end of the decade, the march toward empowerment reached a watershed with the portrayals of three women the likes of which had never been seen before: Princess Leia in George Lucas's *Star Wars* series (1977, 1980, 1983), Ellen Ripley in Ridley Scott's the frightening *Alien* (1979), and finally Sarah Connor.

The advent of strong and self-motivated female characters inevitably brings up social and gender issues like inequality or **sexism** in the workplace and women's struggle for career advancement. The hit comedy film *9 to 5* (1980), starring Jane Fonda, Lily Tomlin, and Dolly Parton as three disgruntled workers who combat a male chauvinistic boss, was a hit, inspiring a TV series and a still-running musical. The way in which the women undermined their boss triggered shouts of approval from many women who lived in a world where gender **discrimination** was much more openly practiced than it is now. In *Working Girl* (1981), Katharine Parker (Sigourney Weaver) is a conniving and overbearing female boss. When Tess McGill (Michelle Griffith), a temporary worker, expresses shock when she discovers Parker will be her boss, Parker asks if she is intimidated by the idea of working under a woman, thus reflecting the novelty of her position. In the new millennium, the question seems odd, owing to the significant increase of female managers in many fields.

Sarah Connor is a product of the changing times and evolving images of women in film and television. She is the direct descendent of a slender line of female action heroes. James Cameron, who was largely responsible for the *Terminator* film storyline, as well as Ridley Scott, who created Ellen Ripley, were both profoundly influenced by *Star Wars* (1977), directed by George Lucas. All three characters—Leia, Ripley, and Connor—embodied fierce independence, heroism, and other nonconventional traits, though Ripley and Connor were both visually and physically more progressive than Leia. Television female action heroes like Charlie's Angels were fashionably dressed and immaculately coiffed beauties. Jaime Sommers, the hero of *The Bionic Woman*, was depicted as distinctly feminine and generally operated in female spheres like a beauty competition, a hair salon, or a classroom—even though she could outrun a car, bend steel, and hear sounds imperceptible to ordinary humans. But Princess Leia, Ellen Ripley, and Sarah Connor appeared stronger and more serious; beauty was a secondary consideration—or, in the case of Ripley and Connor, neither mentioned nor overtly displayed. They did not smile easily or depend upon emotion to get what they wanted. They navigated with authority through the male-dominated environments in which they found themselves. Both Ripley and Connor transformed visually and emotionally, appearing more masculine, tough, and hard as time went on.

James Cameron

Cameron, who directed the first two *Terminator* films, was born in Kapuskasing, Ontario, Canada on August 16, 1954. He attended California State University, where he gravitated toward physics and English. After driving trucks and writing (a childhood hobby), Cameron taught himself how to make films. He got his professional start working with special effects and art design. *Piranha II: The Spawning* (1981), a film he directed, received negative reviews. During the making of the film, however, Cameron had a nightmare upon which the Terminator was eventually based. The success of *The Terminator* (1984), a low-budget film, catapulted him to success. He wrote the screenplay for *Rambo: First Blood Part II* (1985) and *Aliens* (1986), which he also directed. Both movies received wide acclaim. In 1989, Cameron created another strong female role: a submarine designer who does not cower to danger in *The Abyss* (1989). However, in the end, after she nearly dies from being submerged under water too long, she must be rescued by the mostly male crew. Cameron also directed *True Lies* (1994), *Titanic* (1997), and other various science fiction films. He has been married five times, including to Linda Hamilton (1997–1999). They have one daughter.

Tough Fictional Moms

During the silent film era, women adventurers tended to be unmarried and childless, much like their male counterparts. Eventually, fictional moms emerged, challenging the status quo. The *Fantastic Four* comic books, which debuted in the 1960s, featured a husband (Mr. Fantastic/Reed Richards) and wife (Invisible Woman/Susan Richards), along with the Thing (Ben Grimm), and The Human Torch (Johnny Storm). The Richards produced two superhero children, Franklin and Valeria. In *Aliens* (1989), the second installment in the *Alien* film series, Ellen Ripley, the protagonist, learned that her daughter on earth had died, but she would ultimately play surrogate mother to Newt, the young girl and only surviving colonist on LV-426, while Corporal Hicks functioned as a budding love interest. In *The Long Kiss Goodnight* (1996), Samantha Caine started off as a stereotypical mother akin to June Cleaver of the famous *Leave It to Beaver* television sitcom of the 1950s and 1960s, until she discovered that she was actually a super-skilled CIA assassin named Charlene, aka Charly. Elastigirl, of the film *The Incredibles* (2004), was a sensible mother, a former superhero who had settled down to an average home life with a husband in a dead-end job in insurance, an adolescent daughter, a young son, and a toddler. The entire family was endowed with super powers and forced, as a result of a series of events, into a life of crime fighting that injected excitement into their otherwise ordinary lives. Other supermoms include Xena Warrior Princess, of the eponymous television series; Sarah Connor, who appeared in film and on television; and the doomed but fiercely rebellious and powerful Sonja, who was impregnated with the first-ever Vampire-Lycan child in the film *Underworld: Rise of the Lycans* (2009).

Linda Hamilton

Hamilton was born on September 26, 1956, in Salisbury, Maryland. She studied acting in Maryland and New York. She got her first break in a soap opera before landing a role in the horror film *Children of the Corn* (1984). Hamilton's career skyrocketed after playing Sarah Connor in 1984 and 1991. She is noted for her role as Catherine (Beauty), who falls in love with a beast who resembles a lion, in the popular *Beauty and the Beast* television series (1989–1990), a reimagining of the classic fairy tale. With a clear eye on Hamilton's iconic status, Catherine is portrayed not only as a beauty but as a shrewd assistant district attorney in New York. Following the series, Hamilton appeared in several more films and made-for-TV films. She most recently dubbed voice-overs for the much anticipated *Terminator Salvation* (2009).

Hamilton has been divorced twice and has a son from her first marriage and a daughter from her second marriage, to James Cameron.

POWER SUIT, WEAPONS, AND ABILITIES

When *T2* was released, scholars, critics, and fans were awestruck by the new and improved Sarah Connor. Visually, Connor exuded power. Her ultra-fit physique and rock-hard arms, shown off to great effect by tank tops, cargo pants, aviator glasses, and sullen expressions, signified a level of toughness previously seen only with Ripley in *Aliens*.

Connor's appearance was all the more striking in comparison with her initial depiction in *The Terminator*, where her appearance was quite ordinary and conservative. In that first movie, she wore jeans and a cute jacket, and in a scene at home, an oversized shirt or pajama one-piece featuring a picture from the cartoon series *The Jetsons*. Her early scenes were accompanied by piano music, denoting her softness and femininity. Essentially, Connor was initially coded as nonthreatening, although other messages suggested subtle parts of her personality that would emerge full bloom in the movie's sequel.

In *T2*, Connor's first appearance is unsettling. She is chain-smoking and drugged up with medicine. This image, compounded by her unkempt hair and hospital gown, demonstrates serious images of weakness and defeat. It is, obviously, the shift from this look to the commando look that was so powerful, which had such an impact on viewers.

After Connor has pulled herself together following her escape from the hospital, she backs up her commando look with explosive action. It is explained in the film that she spent the years since Reese's death hiding from the law (and potential cyborg attacks), while training her son to fulfill his destiny. However, John is not the only one who learned a lot from their wandering existence from paramilitary camp to camp. Connor is savvy and seasoned; she speaks fluent Spanish, and has tough, militant friends who live under the radar; she also has access to a vast supply of weapons, which she clearly knows how to use. Connor has become decisive, determined, and hardened—traits that are necessary for her son's success—and has transformed her body in preparation for her role as a warrior. This transformation is not only physical—her outer transformation reflects her inward transformation. She must stay alert and hard. Emotion, she believes, is a weakness that can only threaten her own and her son's survival.

VILLAINS

The terminators are rightly known as among the most famous villains in film history. They were all machine, encased in human flesh (or, later, a semblance of it). They were designed by the machines themselves, after they took over Earth in the future. Terminators have but one directive, to infiltrate human encampments and terminate human life. The machines are nearly invincible. They have extraordinary strength and are able to withstand an assortment of attacks—fire, gun shots, car crashes. They also have enhanced vision and strategizing abilities, and they can mimic voices. Later models that emerge in *T2* and *Terminator 3: The Rise of the Machines* (2003) can shape shift, turning parts of their bodies into stabbing weapons if necessary.

Although terminators can be made to emulate any person of any gender, they are not human. Arnold Schwarzenegger played three different terminators, all simply known as "Terminator." In the second movie, the Terminator is reprogrammed by the adult John Connor in the future and sent back to Earth's past to help and protect Connor's younger self. In that film, the "bad" terminator, known as the T-1000, takes on the appearance of the first man he meets on Earth, a mild-faced policeman (played by Robert Patrick). In the third film, the villain is a svelte blonde woman in red leather, high-heel shoes, with the looks of a model (played by Kristanna Loken). Her appearance is a façade, for she is a terminator, known as the T-X or the Terminatrix (a play on the word **dominatrix**), who creates havoc for Connor, his love interest, and the Terminator himself.

THE TERMINATOR, THE FILM

During the majority of the scenes in *The Terminator*, Cameron has audiences believing that they are watching a classic tale about a knight in shining armor from the future who arrives in the past in a literal flash of light (accompanied by a violent jolt of sound) to rescue a powerless damsel in distress. Only Reese knows that the woman he has come to protect will develop into a legendary warrior—that everyone in the future he comes from will be in awe of her, for she is the one who will train her son to become the elite savior of the world. But Reese arrives in the past before she has evolved into the woman she is destined to become. She is, at that time of her life, youthful, fresh-faced, and girly. In scenes with her roommate, she giggles and is playful. Her body is soft and feminine, but not overly sexual, especially compared to her roommate, who wears short dresses, silk robes, and has sex with her boyfriend (She is depicted as sensual and as a "bad girl"; women like her are often targeted in horror films; indeed, she and her boyfriend are the first to be murdered by the Terminator.) The two young women beautify themselves in the mirror to prepare for a night out. Sarah has feathered shoulder-length hair and carries a pink bag. She works as a waitress, wearing a feminine pink uniform and apron.

Although Connor is depicted in a feminine and nonthreatening way, she is still, in many ways, an archetype of a young woman of the 1980s—a modern young woman who is not entirely a vision of sugar, spice, and everything nice. For one thing, she has a pet lizard, which her roommate is repulsed by, in a stereotypical response. For another, when audiences first see Connor, she is riding a motorcycle. Although she works in a stereotypical female

Madonna

Madonna is one of the most influential artists in American popular culture. Born Madonna Louise Ciccone on August 16, 1958, in Bay City, Michigan, Madonna's career has spanned nearly three decades to date. In school, she made good grades and was a cheerleader. Dancing was Madonna's initial passion; after moving to New York in 1977, she joined two musical groups before going solo in 1982 with her first album, *Madonna*. Madonna would go on to become a pop culture sensation.

In the 1980s, Madonna set the trends in fashion and helped spark the popularity of a new kind of girly sex appeal. While second-wave feminists pushed mannish suits and birth control, and desired to be taken seriously in work and social life, Madonna popularized a style of urban dress fused with lace accents and off-the-shoulder tops and crooned songs about romantic love and the right for a young girl to go through with her unplanned pregnancy.

Madonna owed her rapidly expanding appeal to the concurrent ascension of MTV (Music Television, which debuted in the 1980s), her controversial style (featuring explicit sexual and religious images in multiple projects, music videos, concerts, and other enterprises), sheer hard work, and marketing genius, including her ability to repeatedly reinvent herself. In the 1990s and into the new millennium, Madonna's celebrity status remained intact, and she has been as fashionable as ever. Since the 1990s, her hard body appearance has garnered envy as well as scrutiny, as women's bodies continue to be heavily criticized in American society. Married twice, Madonna has two biological children and two adopted children from Malawi.

profession, she has a job, a home that she shares with a female roommate, unconventional transportation for a woman, and a social life. Connor's financial and emotional independence, demonstrated when she goes out by herself after her date cancels, casts her as a progressive woman. Cameron rewards her independence, for the Terminator fails to find her when he goes on the rampage, killing all the other Sarah Connors he finds in the Los Angeles phone book who are at home, including a stay-at-home mother. He also kills her roommate and her boyfriend who stayed in to have sex. Connor eludes danger because she is not at the home, a symbol of domestic tranquility. Instead, Connor is active, working during the day and going out that evening.

In response to the discovery that other Sarah Connors in Los Angeles are being killed, Connor responds as any smart, single woman would: she goes straight to the nearest pay phone to call for help. Unfortunately, the phone does not work. When she walks outside, it is dark; Connor is guarded. Cities and darkness (nighttime) are usually coded as dangerous settings.

Historically, single women have been discouraged from walking in the city (or any location, for that matter) alone, especially at night, when they will be more vulnerable to predatory males. Criminals, vampires, and prostitutes (also known as "women of the night") are also associated with nighttime activity. If it were any other night, Connor would carry herself as a woman who would not be frightened by being alone. However, a killer is on the loose, and so Connor is *frosty*, a term meaning alert that Michael Biehn's tough Corporal Dwayne Hicks character uses in *Aliens* (1986). As a result of Connor's heightened awareness, she senses that she is being followed. Reese, who she does not yet know is on her side, has been shadowing her, watching over her from a close distance.

When Connor realizes she is being followed, she walks into the nearest public place, a dance club. Ordinarily, this would be an ideal safe place. There are lots of people around. It is too crowded for someone to consider inflicting harm on anyone, lest some stranger get involved and call the police. Connor calls the cops from a public phone inside the club but gets a busy signal. She then calls her roommate, who does not answer because she is in bed with her boyfriend and has on headphones and is listening to music with the volume turned up full blast. Connor leaves a message, asking her friend and boyfriend to help her and disclosing her whereabouts. The Terminator, hearing this message after he has murdered the roommate and her boyfriend, sets off in pursuit.

Connor calls the cops again. When someone finally picks up, she is assertive, commanding that the person not hang up on her. The cop she speaks to takes her seriously and even commends her for smartly hiding herself in a crowded club. Ordinarily, Connor, having done everything right, would be safe. Unlike many characters in horror films who make mistakes, causing audiences to groan, Connor is smart and resourceful. But Connor's adversary is not ordinary, and all is not well. The Terminator enters the club, spots Connor, whose picture he has seen at her apartment, and starts shooting. Reese is forced to come into the open; he shoots back, to no avail, then grabs Connor and drags her away.

Following this frightening encounter, Connor's character undergoes a period of transition, where she is depicted as a hysterical damsel in distress—a stark contrast to the cool, level-headed, emotionless Reese. In a car Reese has stolen, he explains that he has come from the future to protect her and the not-yet-born John Connor. Connor is catatonic with fear. She can not respond when he asks her if she has been hurt. Shortly thereafter, Connor becomes hysterical again, screaming at him to "let me go" and struggling with him. They are soon found by the police, who "liberate" Connor and arrest Reese. Inevitably, the Terminator tracks her down. He starts killing policeman after policeman, who are helpless in the face of his power. This time, Connor responds when she hears Reese call for her. She acknowledges that he is her "knight." They escape and go on the run.

Hiding out in a culvert, Connor moves closer to Reese because she is cold; indeed she is visibly shaking. Reese is indifferent to the temperature, suggesting that he is accustomed to harsh environments. After all, he has spent all his life either in hiding or at war with the machines. When she discovers that he has an injury, Connor's response is immediate. As she prepares to bandage it, she admits that she wants to "puke." Reese is once again indifferent and acts as if his injury is insignificant. Connor wants to talk to diffuse her anxious feelings, but Reese struggles to find something to say. Like most male heroes, he is laconic.

Gradually, Connor absorbs Reese's strange tale, but she has a hard time believing that she is destined to be a hero. She lacks confidence in herself. "Do I look like the mother of the future?" she asks him, "Am I tough? Organized? I can't balance my checkbook. . . . I don't want this." Reese tells her that she "must be stronger than you can imagine you can be." In other words, she must have faith. Then, he compliments the way she bandaged him. "It's my first," Connor says, suggesting that she has more ability than she gives herself credit for. Later, in a hotel, where they are temporarily hiding, they make love.

As the film nears its climax, Connor begins to exhibit more and more toughness, taking up the fight as Reese is forced to give it up. When Reese gets injured and appears immobilized, Connor lowers her voice and sternly commands him in military fashion to get up. After battling the Terminator in a factory with a pipe and igniting an explosive that has no lasting effect on the villain, Reese dies. Connor, in true heroic fashion, pulls a fragment of metal from out of her thigh, embedded there by the explosion, and embraces Reese one last time. After a gripping chase, the injured Sarah destroys the Terminator by crushing it under a hydraulic press. It is a dramatic turn of events: the knight has died and the damsel in distress has saved herself—and the son that lies within her womb.

T2, THE FILM

Cameron establishes Connor's new physique in the first scene in which she appears. Her back is to the camera, and she is doing pull-ups in a hospital for the criminally insane. She has landed in the facility after attempting to bomb a building and then foolishly divulging the story about Skynet (the corporation that will design the machines that will turn against humans) and the terminators. Neither the police nor her doctors believe her story, so she is labeled insane, and her son is put in a foster home. Pull-ups are considered particularly difficult for women, but Connor does them with ease. When doctors enter her room, she asks about an injury her doctor sustained by her hands. Thus we learn that since we last saw her at the end of *The Terminator,* Connor has become a violent and out-of-control woman. She appears on the edge, with unkempt hair and an attitude that seems to justify her incarceration. Although she initiates an extraordinary escape, she would

Real Beauty

In 2004, the popular Dove soap launched its Campaign for Real Beauty. The campaign advertised real women as models, representing many different body sizes, in billboards and magazine advertisements. The real models were frequently depicted wearing only bras and underwear. Many of the women reflected the true body types and sizes of most women in the American population. The size 12 and up models challenged longstanding beauty ideals projected in film, television, fashion magazines, and other media, that is, women who are excessively thin and preternaturally flawless. The Dove ads attempted to redefine America's concept of beauty. As many experts contend, women who carry extra weight can still be healthy and beautiful. Oftentimes, in the pursuit of thin bodies, women do more harm than good. Celebrities like 1970s singer Karen Carpenter, who died due to complications with eating disorders, have exposed the problems associated with unhealthy body concepts.

Similar campaigns are increasingly promoted in popular culture. For example, organizations and corporations sponsor campaigns for healthy self-esteem for young girls. Celebrities like Tyra Banks, a former model who hosts *America's Next Top Model* and *The Tyra Banks Show*, regularly advocates for real beauty. On her eponymous show, she has appeared without makeup, and in 2009 she discarded hair extensions in an effort to publicly support her convictions.

not have gained her freedom if not for the arrival of her ten-year-old son and the Terminator (who is on her side in this film).

Other women represented in the film are inept compared to Connor, who is the only woman to appropriate power. John completely ignores his foster mother, who goes to her husband, asking him to handle John in her place. The wife of the engineer who will be responsible for Skynet is shown pleading with her husband to pay attention to his family, but he, absorbed with his work, pays no attention to her. Later, when Connor tries to kill him to prevent him from producing any more technology that would benefit Skynet, his wife is powerless and terrified; she does not try to protect her husband or fight Connor. Fortunately, the Terminator and John arrive in time to stop Connor from killing them.

Although Connor is tough and heroic, throughout much of the film she falls far short of perfection. Scholar Yvonne D. Sims asserts that she is "flawed . . . with moments of vulnerability, irrational thinking, and paranoia" (Sims, 162). In an early scene (cut from the film as it was originally released), she dreams that she is being visited by Reese. She has a vulnerable moment, holding Reese tightly, reverting to the scared and powerless woman in the first movie. Although Connor complains that men are destructive, she, in fact, has become violent, destructive, and male-like to protect her son. In the act that parallels those of the terminators whom she hates so much, Connor relentlessly pursues the engineer to kill him, though he is not malevolent, only a family man merely doing his job. Connor has become so tough that she has almost erased her femininity. Scholar Harry Chotiner points out that, in relation to John, she, in fact, responds in masculine ways, whereas the Terminator is portrayed as the nurturer and protector.

Ultimately, the Terminator and Connor together destroy the T-1000, with Connor bringing him to the brink of destruction and the Terminator giving him the final push. Afterward, the Terminator tells Sarah and John that he must also be terminated, because the technology he carries within him is a liability. John, full of emotion and love, can't bear to see him go. It is Sarah, in tears, who has the strength to pull the lever and lower the Terminator down into the vat of molten metal.

IMPACT

In the next two *Terminator* movies (2003, 2009), Sarah Connor does not appear. Audiences are told in the third movie that Connor died after a battle with leukemia. But, in 2008, Sarah Connor's continued popularity spurred a spin-off, *Terminator: The Sarah Connor Chronicle*. This series capitalized on the trend of hot, new television shows with young, attractive female action heroes. The Terminator is depicted as a teenager named Cameron, played by Summer Glau. In this rendition, Sarah Connor, played by Lena Headey, is given a second chance at life by cheating death through time travel. The series was intended to fill in the details of the adventures of Sarah and John after *T2*, but production ended after two seasons despite a strong fan base and high ratings.

That Sarah Connor returned after nearly 10 years of absence—25 years after her first appearance—and competed successfully against fresh, new, contemporary TV shows demonstrates that Connor remains one of the most enduring figures in action film. Indeed, her journey parallels the journey that women have taken over the past hundred years. In essence, by becoming tough and deadly and putting on those sharp sunglasses, for a while Connor became the Terminator, a transformation that can be seen as summarizing the changing identity of women, with all its pros and cons, as they sought equality with men. It is thus a significant and transforming moment when Connor, about to kill an innocent man, stops before going all the way. She realizes, thanks to the intervention of her son, who for the first time shows the leadership qualities that she has imbued him with, that she does not have to give up on love and kindness and compassion to fight and win her battles.

This acknowledgement that it is a mistake to turn your back on your feminine side in the pursuit of supposedly male power marks a watershed for the female action hero. The idea that women have to choose between family and career is forever dead. From this will emerge the period of **girl power,** exemplified by Buffy and Xena and Lara Croft and other female action heroes who are beautiful and have emotions and can also kick ass with the best of the men. Thanks to Sarah Connor, the paradigm shifts, and as a result, female action heroes as well as the women who watch them or read about them can finally imagine what it would be like if women could have it all.

See also Ellen Ripley.

FURTHER RESOURCES

Brown, Jeffrey A. "Gender and the Action Heroine: Hardbodies and the *Point of No Return.*" *Cinema Journal.* 35 (1996): 52.

Chotiner, Harry. "'I Know Now Why You Cry': *Terminator 2*, Moral Philosophy, and Feminism." In *Terminator and Philosophy: I'll Be Back, Therefore I Am,* ed. Richard Brown and Kevin S. Decker, Hoboken, NJ: John Wiley and Sons, 2009.

Dougherty, Margot. "A New Body of Work: Bench Pressing with Linda Hamilton— Sarah Connor Gets Tough for *Terminator 2.*" http://www.ew.com/ew/article/ 0,,314767,00.html.

Inness, Sherrie A., ed. *Action Chicks: New Images of Tough Women in Popular Culture.* New York: Palgrave Macmillan, 2004.

Inness, Sherrie A. *Tough Girls: Women Warriors and Wonder Women in Popular Culture.* Philadelphia: University of Pennsylvania Press, 1999.

Mainon, Dominique, and James Ursini. *The Modern Amazons: Warrior Women On-Screen.* Pompton Plains, NJ: Limelight Editions, 2006.

Sims, Yvonne D. *Women of Blaxploitation: How the Black Action Film Heroine Changed American Popular Culture.* Jefferson, NC: McFarland and Company, 2006.

Tasker, Yvonne. *Spectacular Bodies: Gender, Genre, and the Action Cinema.* New York: Routledge, 1993.

Selene takes serious aim with a bow and arrow in the film *Underworld: Evolution*. (© Screen Gems/Courtesy: Everett Collection.)

Selene

Selene is a vampire warrior, one of the most popular female monster anti-heroes in film history, in two films (2003, 2006) in the *Underworld* series. When she is on the prowl, her eyes are electric blue; otherwise, they are dark brown. Either way, Selene has subtle fangs. Played by Kate Beckinsale, an English actress, Selene is a pretty vampire with pale but healthy-looking skin, dark hair cut in an adolescent-looking, shoulder-length bob, and a svelte body. She wears an all-black leather body suit with a black leather corset over her torso. Even when she is not feeding, blood smears her face in an exotic way. When on duty (her job is to eliminate lycans, otherwise known as werewolves), she is tough and unafraid. She spurns the advances of Kraven (Shane Brolly), the head vampire. She loves what she does and prefers her life over the lavish and decadent lifestyle of the vampires at the mansion. The oldest and most powerful vampires (all men) slumber in coffins below the floor of a special room inside the mansion, and must be awakened by certain trained individuals using specific rituals. But Selene is a woman of action, always on the move.

Women in vampire films were commonly featured as either damsels in distress, victims, Dracula's brides, or objects of romantic obsession. When bitten and turned into vampires, the vampire's victims were cast as beautiful but dangerous and slavishly attentive to him. When the vampire was around, they were clinging to him, deferring to him like timid children seeking protection.

The classic vampire storyline involved a vampire hunter, either a professorial figure or a loner bent on vengeance, who was engaged in relentless pursuit of the vampire. The vampire hunter was normally male, someone who appeared suddenly in town on a mysterious mission. The story was often set in a European town in the past. The plot usually involved deaths, a dramatic struggle, and a conclusion wherein the hero either beheaded the vampire, plunged a stake into his heart, or exposed him to sunshine, thus killing the undead fiend.

Not so with the *Underworld* films. The action takes place in modern times, and the vampires have accordingly evolved. They take their nourishment from bags of manufactured blood and use technologically advanced weapons with bullets made out of silver. They wage a centuries-old battle against the lycans, werewolves that were once enslaved to the vampires but who liberated themselves via the leadership of a Lycan named Lucian (Michael Sheen). The story goes that the progenitor, a Hungarian warlord named Alexander Corvinus (Derek Jacobi), survived a plague and became a true immortal. He had two sons: Markus (Tony Curran), who was bitten by a bat, and William (Brian Steele), who was bitten by a werewolf.

Selene's portrayal is, within the context of the vampire horror genre, revolutionary. Although she works within the heavily regulated system of the vampire world, a world that is dominated by a class of predominately male warriors, she is independent-minded and mentally and physically strong.

Trinity

Trinity (Carrie-Ann Moss) was one of the major characters in the *Matrix* film series (1999, 2003, 2003). What is so extraordinary about Trinity is that she was not only portrayed as computer savvy, she was the one who started the wildly popular series off in a spectacular fight scene. Historically, the first scene in a film introduces the first victim, frequently a woman or a person of color. Trinity was being chased at the beginning of the first film in the series, but she was not the typical victim. She fought back fast and hard, appearing as a blur of meteoric fighting moves. When she tumbled down a flight of stairs, she aimed her gun with lightning speed, got up, and fled to safety.

As the love interest, Trinity did not always play second fiddle. She looked smart and cool in black leather. She strutted around and participated in various action scenes, including several rescues. She was a member of the special group force that helped train Neo (Keanu Reeves). When Neo appeared to be dead, Trinity's kiss brought him back to life—a dramatic reversal of the traditional fairy tale, wherein the prince saves the sleeping beauty. Trinity was killed in *The Matrix Revolutions* (2003), but reappeared in comic book and video game adaptations.

She is the antithesis of the groveling, weak, and overly indulgent vampires who stay at the mansion, lounging on chairs, loitering, and gossiping.

While on the hunt for lycans in the first film, she comes across a human that the lycans are following. The human's name is Michael Corvin (Scott Speedman), a descendant of Alexander Corvinus, who, because of his bloodline, is a candidate for Lucian's scheme. Lucian, who continues to lead the lycans, wants to change Corvin into a hybrid, both vampire and lycan, thinking that his creation will end the ancient feud. Corvin eventually does become a hybrid creature. But for a time, he is what Daniel Garrett calls "a dude in distress" (Garrett, "If One Person is Strong"). Over the course of the two films, Selene and Corvin fall in love and unite in a relationship that is portrayed in mostly equal terms.

Selene is a woman who has it all, in **third-wave feminist** terms: she is pretty, powerful, confident, and in love.

ORIGINS

Though several writers contributed to the films, Danny McBride is credited as the main writer for both *Underworld* (2003) and *Underworld: Evolution* (2006). Born on December 29, 1976, he is younger than most who have found major success in the film industry. He was born well after the period when America was undergoing dramatic changes brought on in large part by the **civil rights movement**, the hippy movement, and the **second-wave feminist** movement. He came of age in a time when America was transitioning to a world of increasing racial and gender inclusion and environmental consciousness.

McBride enjoyed an adventurous youth. His father, who was in the navy, shuttled the family to locations such as Hawaii, Guam, Florida, and the Philippines. McBride took full advantage of a free, adventurous lifestyle. When he became an adult, he played in bands, formed a low-budget film company (The Scuba Dudes Action Team), appeared in films, and eventually collaborated with Len Wiseman, who directed the first two *Underworld* films.

Len Wiseman

Wiseman was born on March 4, 1973, in Fremont, California. He was strongly influenced by comic books. Comic books, generally considered a nostalgic part of a boy's life in America, have played a huge role is establishing the mythic hero complex. Comic books featured heroes who were usually male, muscular, and noble. But they also created a number of important archetypal female action heroes, such as Wonder Woman. Still, the female action heroes in comic books appeared mostly to male audiences.

Wiseman attended De Anza College in Cupertino, California, where he produced two short films. His professional career started as a property assistant in big-name films such as *Stargate* (1994), Independence *Day* (1996), and *Men in Black* (1997). The opening scene in his first movie, *Underworld*, shows Selene squatting on a window seat, overlooking the city, surly and authoritative, resembling a female *Batman*. Wiseman married the star of his films, Kate Beckinsale, in 2004.

Kate Beckinsale

Kathryn Bailey Beckinsale was born on July 26, 1973, in Finsbury Park, London. After leaving New College, located in Oxford, early to start a film career, Beckinsale played several conventional roles. She met and dated Michael Sheen, and they had a daughter, Lily Mo, who was born in 1999. Beckinsale and Sheen broke up during the filming of *Underworld*; shortly thereafter, she started dating Wiseman, whom she eventually married.

Beckinsale played a variety of roles immediately following the *Underworld* films. She then returned to playing action heroes, such as in *Van Helsing* (2004), where she played the tough Anna Valerious alongside Gabriel Van Helsing (Hugh Jackman), famous vampire hunter, and in *Vacancy* (2007), where she was cast as an ordinary woman-turned **final girl** hero who single-handedly takes on killers and rescues her husband.

POWER SUIT, WEAPONS, AND ABILITIES

Since Emma Peel first lounged onto the screen in *The Avengers*, the black leather suit or cat suit has been a popular costume choice for female action heroes. Trinity, in *The Matrix* (1999), was sexy, athletic, smart, and fierce in hers. Selene is equally formidable in her leather outfit. In a review of the first film, Skye commends Selene's attire, stating that "there is no gratuitous cleavage" (Skye, "*Underworld*"). But though Selene's body is fully covered, her thin, feminine shape is exposed. However, the eye of the camera does not draw the audience's attention to this fact with objectifying close-ups.

Selene also wears a leather piece that looks and fits like a corset. Traditionally, corsets have signified restraint, containment, and bondage for women. In the first film, it is evident that Selene is bound to something. The vampires run a tight ship. There are orders to follow, procedures to maintain, and males who dominate. Viktor (Bill Nighy), one of the leader vampires, has forbidden those without clearance from reading and knowing their history. Over the course of the two films, Selene comes to realize that she has been used and manipulated by Viktor, her adopted vampire father, and that the entire **patriarchy** is in on it. She stands up to Viktor and kills him, then breaks away from the coven. Rebelling further, she aligns herself with Michael Corvin and falls in love with him. Even though she upgrades her abilities as she struggles against her enemies, she continues to wear the corset. By the end of the film, Markus and William, the original brothers, are destroyed. Selene has achieved a new beginning, but faces an uncertain future.

Selene depends on her fighting skills as well as weapons. Her skills, honed over the centuries as a lycan hunter, are sharp. She tends, however, to favor her weaponry (an assortment of guns and automatic machine pistols, knives, and throwing stars) over hand-to-hand combat. The guns are faster and more efficient, particularly because some of her opponents are stronger than she is.

Selene, nonetheless, has superhuman strengths and abilities. She can leap to and from great heights, landing gracefully and ready for action. In *Underworld*, she grabs Corvin (before they become friends) by the neck and holds him aggressively above her against a wall. Both vampires and lycans heal quickly if injured by a cut or shot—unless, for example, vampires are shot with bullets infused with ultraviolet technology. The appearance of Selene's physical prowess is enhanced by the help of new film technologies. For example, when she hurls stars at a lycan, the throwing stars propel through the air in slow motion, an effect popularized by the *Matrix* films, wherein bullets fly and Neo (Keanu Reeves), "the chosen one," dodges them in stylish slow motion. This effect was parodied in *Shrek* (2001), a computer-animated film, in a scene where the lovely Princess Fiona, in full regalia, surprises her male attackers with martial arts moves. Selene's physical powers are

Aeon Flux

Aeon Flux, a secret agent in an avant-garde science fiction world, was originally the protagonist of an MTV animated series. The series tackled mature themes and images and was noted for its sexual and violent content. The film, *Aeon Flux*, released in 2005, cast Charlize Theron as the main character. A cool-headed assassin, she's svelte and athletic, swaddled in form-fitting futuristic costumes. She's also a clone, as is everyone else living in a special habitat on Earth that is enclosed by an impenetrable wall. In the process of discovering her identity, Aeon Flux learns that some cloned humans have evolved enough to procreate. The film's antagonist attempts to prevent the humans from reproducing, keeping them enclosed within the gate of the city's walls. Aeon Flux single-handedly saves humanity by destroying the wall and the machine that produces clones.

increased when Alexander Corvinus tells her to take his blood (as he lies dying). In this way, Selene becomes more strong and powerful.

Selene has other traits that illustrate her power. She is free thinking and hard working (like Starling in *The Silence of the Lambs* and its sequel). She is constantly at work, mulling over her own history and the best way to achieve her goals, devoting her life to her mission rather than playing a passive role. And she is fearless.

VILLAINS

Traditionally, vampires and werewolves are portrayed as villains in films. They are the classic monsters who terrorize humanity. In the *Underworld* series, vampires and lycans have little to do with humans; they are too busy at war with each other. There are three main factions: the lycans, the vampires, and the group of humans led by Alexander Corvinus.

The lycans, who dwell in Spartan and grimy underground areas in the city, are an oppressed minority, having been enslaved and systematically hunted and killed by the vampires. Lucian struggles to teach the lycans to behave in a more brotherly fashion (women do not figure in his band) toward one another and to be less brutal and uncouth. Unlike the vampires, lycans can roam in human form during the day. But they turn into werewolves when the moon is full. They can also turn at will.

The vampires of *Underworld* dress well, have parties, and reside in a lush mansion. Since the beginning, they have lived affluent lives. They represent the upper class, civilization, and culture. Among them, there are warriors whose function is to eliminate lycans. Vampires generally feel repulsion and animosity toward the lycans, emotions that are equated by scholars to racial hatred.

The group led by Alexander Corvinus is depicted as an elite squad of human males who are under his command. They clean up after conflicts between lycans and vampires so as to keep their existence a secret from humanity.

Selene's main adversaries emerge as the vampire patriarchy, those who desire to perpetuate the feud between the two species of monsters. This patriarchy is represented by the oldest, most powerful vampires and by the original werewolf, William.

UNDERWORLD, THE FILM

The new millennium brought forth enormous changes for women—and for the female action heroes who represented their aspirations. The world is drastically different from the one that existed a hundred years ago. In the 1900s, women were expected to conform to certain roles and behaviors. They had not yet achieved the right to vote, but were expected to give birth, raise children, and not challenge a world dominated by men. The feminine ideal was a woman who spoke softly and politely. In the feature films that emerged in the early years of the century, women were **typecast** as love interests, mothers, sisters, and damsels in distress.

By 2000, women had finally made their mark as leaders in business, politics, and other traditionally male-dominated fields. Young girls and women competed in sports and had a vast array of conventional and unconventional extracurricular activities from which to join. Few doors remained closed.

The female action hero in the new millennium crops up in an ever-widening array of roles. She might be a detective, cop, adventurer, vigilante, superhero, or FBI agent. She might appear in a leading role, as a sidekick, or as a minor character, displaying characteristics that might include physical strength, power, vulnerability, aggression, sex appeal, or a desire for thrills and peril. In ever-increasing numbers, women who were unconventionally strong starred or had supporting roles on film. Among the most notable actresses and the films they starred in were Angelina Jolie in the *Lara Croft* series; Milla Jovovich in *The Messenger: The Story of Joan of Arc*, the *Resident Evil* series, and *Ultraviolet*; Halle Berry in *Catwoman*; and Charlize Theron in *Aeon Flux*.

Selene gave the audiences of the new millennium exactly what they wanted. She was cool, tough, serious and sexy. Unlike earlier female action heroes, like Sarah Connor in *Terminator 2* (1991), Selene did not have muscle definition. Her body shape was similar to that of Buffy the Vampire Slayer, from the popular television series that debuted in 1997. These and other action heroes had the lean, feminine shapes—subtly sporty but not overstated—that the girl-power audiences desired. Though she has a feminine body, Selene disrupted other notions of femininity when she introduced herself as a Death Dealer, a vampire warrior who preys on the despised lycans.

Selene is with another (male) Death Dealer in the opening shot of the first movie. She is perched on a ledge, unconcerned by the fact that she is many feet above the ground. It is Selene who gives the final okay to pounce upon the lycans below. Her male colleague is killed during the subsequent fight, but Selene stays alive as she twirls her gun, long leather jacket flapping behind her, and takes control of the situation. She runs into the underground tunnels and begins taking down werewolves. She is greatly outnumbered, but her only fear is that soon, without lycans, her profession may "be obsolete." "Pity," she says, cockily, "because I lived for it." At least one lycan manages to escape, though not unscathed.

Back at the mansion, Kraven tries to undermine her power. He tells her she takes her duties too seriously. He doesn't acknowledge her skill (she brings back a new weapon used by the lycans) or believe her when she tells him she is concerned that there may be more lycans then they originally thought. He fails to allow her to lead a team to investigate. Kraven is only concerned about the need for her to dress appropriately and elegantly for an ensuing party.

Selene ignores his superficial concerns, and conducts her research on the computer, wondering out loud why lycans would be tracking a human. A female vampire, Erika (Sophia Miles), reacts approvingly to Michael Corvin's picture on the computer screen. Selene is not interested. She is only thinking about work and has no traditional regard for love interests or parties. And she has no respect for Kraven, whose leadership abilities she doubts. He is, as she says, "a bureaucrat, not a warrior." Viktor, the vampire who turned Selene into a vampire and adopted her, put Kraven—not Selene—in charge while he slumbered.

Selene, challenging the role of compliant female, rebels against Kraven and conducts an investigation on Corvin on her own. Corvin, an innocent victim, does not realize he is caught in the middle of an ancient battle. Nor does he know that he is going to be used as a pawn. Thus Corvin is given a subordinate role, one that was reserved for women in traditional films.

When Selene confronts the clueless Corvin (he does not know why the lycans are interested in him), Lucian and other lycans show up. Selene fights admirably but Lucian still manages to bite Corvin. Selene comes to the rescue, leading Corvin to a car. The scene echoes the scene in *Terminator* (1984), in which Reese rescues Sarah Connor from the cyborg, taking the power position at the wheel, while Connor becomes hysterical—except that in *Underworld*, Selene takes the wheel, while Corvin sits passively in the passenger seat. Though he is relatively calm compared to Connor, in other scenes he screams and is clearly powerless.

In another echo of *Terminator*, Corvin notices that Selene has been shot (this is in line with his medical profession but also demonstrates a nurturing

Venus and Serena Williams: Tennis Superstars

Venus and Serena Williams are two of the most widely known tennis stars in the world. Although they are not the first African American women to play professional tennis, their skill, reputation, and records make them among the most legendary in a sport that is dominated by whites. Born in 1980 (Venus) and 1981 (Serena) and raised by supportive parents in the gang-ridden neighborhood of Compton in Los Angeles, California, the Williams sisters began to play tennis at an early age. Both Venus and Serena debuted as adolescents and went on to attain spectacular fame into their late twenties. They are known as athletic players who grunt and scream and play with extraordinary power and fearlessness. Both women have won numerous major championships, launched highly successful endorsement deals and fashion lines, and have helped to popularize women in sports with mainstream audiences.

side), saying, "you've lost a lot of blood." She says, coolly, "shut up. Hold on. I'll be fine." One of the characteristics of an action hero is the ability to sustain injury and endure pain stoically. Since Selene is a vampire, she is unconcerned because she knows her injuries will heal quickly. When their car plunges into water, it is Corvin who does the rescuing, challenging Selene's position as the hero of the two. His rescue has an impact on Selene, and she beings to see the lowly human with different eyes.

Selene is punished for her rebellion and for involving herself with a human and bringing him to the mansion. While Kraven argues with Selene, Erika is alone with Corvin, who is resting on Selene's bed. When Erika sees Corvin's lycan, she panics, flying to the ceiling in a flash, hissing at him like a feral animal, both repulsed and in fear of him. He wakes, jumps from Selene's window, and escapes. Erika's reaction is telling, demonstrating the depth of the vampires' dread and hatred of lycans.

Selene's rebellion is not over, but when she goes to Viktor, her "father figure," for help, she assumes a subservient role. Starting the process of waking Viktor (before his time), she resembles a child who goes to a parent to tattle tale behind her sibling's back. Selene tells Viktor "I desperately need your guidance," and that she fears Kraven is involved in some covert alliance with the enemy (the lycans). She explains that Kraven will not stop pestering her with his advances, and that Lucien, whom Viktor thought was dead, is alive and well.

She finds Corvin, who has come to the mansion (he has nowhere else to turn), and takes him to a safe place. Selene explains how Viktor saved her from the lycans who murdered her family, and how she accepted his offer to turn her into a vampire to take revenge on the lycans (in truth, it was Viktor who killed her family, but she does not know this yet). When Selene is about to leave, Corvin tells her he does not want to be left alone. He is frightened and has become dependent on Selene. They share their first kiss, but Selene then leaves him.

Selene's hopes are dashed when, in a subsequent scene, she returns to the mansion to speak to Viktor, who is now awake but weakened from his slumber. Viktor chides her for waking him up (breaking vampire rules), and warns her that the "[vampire] counsel will decide [her] fate" for her transgression. Selene is confined to her room. The themes of rules and confinement have special import for feminists, who condemned the patriarchal society for forcing women to comply with social and gender rules that confined them to roles such as mothers and wives—or literally to their homes. Feminists desired liberation, equality, and freedom to exert power just as men historically did. Moreover, they wanted to exert control over their lives, their bodies, and their career choices. Ironically, Erika is the one who releases Selene from her confinement, although her motive is not founded in noble sisterhood. Erika wants Selene out of the way, so she can become Kraven's queen.

From there on out, Selene is essentially banished from her home. She and Corvin join forces to battle their enemies. Before Lucien dies, he persuades Selene to bite Corvin. Her bite is the final ingredient to complete his transformation.

Although Selene takes the lead in this film, it is Corvin who is positioned as the new superpower. As a result of her bite, he is extraordinarily strong. In the climactic fight with Viktor, Corvin matches Viktor's strength blow by blow. But it is Selene who executes the final strike when she leaps above Viktor, slicing his face in half with a sword. The movie ends with the encroaching vampires backing off, sensing, rightfully, that Selene and Corvin won't be easily taken.

UNDERWORLD: EVOLUTION, THE FILM

The first film ends with Selene in victory, but needless to say, she is presented with more challenges in the film's sequel. Selene and Corvin have a perilous confrontation with Markus. Afterward, Corvin shifts into protector role as the sun rears above the horizon and burns Selene's hands. Corvin covers Selene in blankets, fortifies an abandoned building with black paint, and protects her from the sun. This underscores her weakness and his invincibility (the sun does not bother Corvin). When Markus follows Selene and Corvin to Alexander's home, Corvin takes him on. Selene tries to assist Corvin; Alexander tells her to "wait. You're no match for him." Selene ignores his warning, causing Markus to fly away, but Corvin is badly hurt and appears dead.

For the first time ever, Selene's impenetrable expression crumbles and she sobs over Corvin's body. Her tears code her as feminine, and her behavior is intensely human and feminine. Without Corvin, Selene is faced with her own physical limitations and agrees to take Alexander's blood. In this scene, Selene illustrates how her independence and power are limited. Her advancement is dependent on a patriarch. The transfer of power works, and even Markus comments on her improved strength during a subsequent fight. The problem with his compliment is that it reinforces the idea that a woman's power must be validated by a man. But not all is lost.

In the final battle, Selene and Corvin (who lives!) do their own fighting. Selene takes on Markus and Corvin battles William, but the fights end in different ways. Selene pushes Markus into the whirling blades of a helicopter; Corvin, using only his physical strength, rips off William's head. This illustrates that Selene still cannot overtake a powerful villain by hand-to-hand combat alone.

When the sun comes up, Selene is exposed and has nowhere to run. But she survives. Alexander's blood has enabled her to withstand the sun's rays, making her a true immortal.

IMPACT

The two films did extremely well at the box office. *Underworld* grossed $95,708,457, while its sequel, *Underworld: Evolution*, grossed $111,340,801. Selene was an instant favorite among men and women, although mainstream critics were less easy to please. The success of the two films spawned a sequel, but, to the disappointment of her many fans, Selene did not play a major role. *Underworld: Rise of the Lycans* (2009) told the story of the origins of the lycans and how they came to serve the vampires, and what led to their emancipation. According to this movie, the essence of the conflict lay in the taboo relationship between Lucian, a werewolf with some standing with the vampires (but also sympathetic to the abused werewolf slaves), and Viktor's daughter, Sonja (Rhona Mitra). Sonja got pregnant, but the relationship and the child were considered "abominable" to vampires, and thus Sonja was executed in front of Lucian.

The theme of forbidden love was also prominent in the first two films. It was clear that Corvin's lycan identity represented a race that was despised, mistreated, and brutally tracked down and killed. Selene was depicted as a member of the dominant, upper-class race of vampires. When the two fell in love, they challenged one of the most sacred rules of vampires. Like Shakespeare's *Romeo and Juliet*, *Othello*, the 1967 film *Guess Who's Coming to Dinner*, and others, Len Wiseman's *Underworld* not only challenged gender roles but society's perceptions of biracial love. As for Selene and Corvin, their love survived; they set off together to deal with the aftermath of the vampire-lycan drama, finally living as equals.

See also Buffy the Vampire Slayer; Emma Peel; Xena: Warrior Princess.

FURTHER RESOURCES

Creed, Barbara. *The Monstrous-Feminine: Film, Feminism, Psychoanalysis.* New York: Routledge, 1993.

Garrett, Daniel. "If One Person Is Strong, Must the Other Be Weak?" http://www.horschamp.qc.ca/new_offscreen/person_strong.html.

Grace. "Underworld: Evolution." http://www.heroinecontent.net/archives/2006/08/underworld_evolution.html.

Hopkins, Susan. *Girl Heroes: The New Force in Popular Culture.* Annandale, Australia: Pluto Press, 2002.

Öhlund, Eva. "Female Monsters." http://www.eng.umu.se/monster/eva/documents/female_monsters.htm.

Phillips, Kate. "Post-Feminism in Action: A Critical Analysis of the Motion Picture *Underworld.*" http://www.associatedcontent.com/article/233970/postfeminism_in_action_a_critical_analysis.html?cat=38.

Skye. "Underworld." http://www.heroinecontent.net/archives/2006/09/underworld.html.

Storm unleashes her powers in the film *X-Men*. (TM and Copyright © 20th Century Fox Film Corp. All rights reserved. Courtesy: Everett Collection.)

Storm

Storm is a powerful mutant, best known for her association with the X-Men, a team of superheroes created by Marvel Comics in 1963. Storm, the first female African American hero to appear in comic books, made her debut in 1975 in *Giant-Size X-Men #1*. According to the Marvel Universe (the fictional universe peopled by Marvel Comics characters), Storm, who has free-flowing white hair, blue eyes, and medium-brown skin, stands at 5 feet, 11 inches and weighs 127 pounds. Though many of her male peers and nemeses flaunted colossal bodies, Storm, artistically depicted as having an athletic and voluptuous form, was nonetheless a formidable foe. Endowed with phenomenal combat skills and the amazing ability to control the weather, she was among the most powerful of the X-Men. Storm was significant in other ways. She served as the leader of the X-Men and other groups and figured prominently in assorted comic book storylines and in other media in which the X-Men appeared, including an animated television series, films, and video games. In 1996, she received her own four-issue comic book series, titled *Storm*.

Like any super action hero, Storm led a tumultuous and dramatic life. Her parents died when she was just five years old. Homeless, she turned to pick pocketing until, as a preteen, she returned to her mother's homeland, Kenya, where she was worshipped as a goddess because of her powers. She remained there, protecting the community, until Professor Charles Xavier, the founder and leader of the X-Men, recruited her to his team. She quickly established herself as a leader of the X-Men and a teacher at Xavier's School for Gifted Youngsters. Over the years, Storm temporarily changed her looks (sporting a Mohawk), lost her powers, gained them back again, battled many foes, and was proposed to several times. She eventually married King T'Challa, also known as the Black Panther, another African American comic book hero, becoming Queen of a fictional African nation called Wakanda.

Both Marvel Comics and its rival, DC Comics, have created many comic book characters that have defied time and mercurial societal trends. Storm is a prime example of this success. The two defining aspects of her persona are her racial identity and her social status as a mutant. In the *X-Men* comic book series, mutants were loathed, though they had powers that surpassed those of ordinary humans. The source of the X-Men's power, which frequently translated into unusual physical appearance and superhuman abilities, was a human mutation.

Present-day academics consider that mutants in real life symbolize marginalized groups who, historically, have been misunderstood, feared, despised, and denigrated by mainstream society. In 1963, when *X-Men* debuted, the United States was reeling from the sight of the harrowing protests against **segregation** and **racism** taking place as the **civil rights movement** came to a head. The X-Men represented African Americans, who were likewise subjected to racism, **discrimination**, and segregation. In the 1960s, protests against such treatment and disparities climaxed with the emergence of two diverging movements among African Americans: the nonviolent civil rights movement and the

Tough Girls with Magical Powers

Witch is a term historically given to individuals, male or female, who practice magic. The witch is one of the earliest power roles attributed to women. However, the term is laden with negative connotations. Images of gnarled and cadaverous women who lurk in swamps and forests gathering ingredients for malevolent potions fill the cannon of ancient lore and serve as a foundation for a number of horror films and comic books. There were, however, exceptions.

Many women endowed with magical powers challenge stereotypical depictions. Glinda, the good witch in the iconic film *The Wizard of Oz* (1939), was depicted as beautiful, angelic, and powerful. Samantha (Elizabeth Montgomery) was a lively and attractive housewife (and, later, a mother to a daughter who also has powers) in the television series *Bewitched*, which ran from 1964 to 1972. At first glance, Samantha was submissive and traditional, but, ultimately, she was the one with the power, while her husband was frequently depicted as gangly, inept, and excitable. The television series *Charmed*, which ran from 1998 to 2006, coincided with the burgeoning mainstreaming of Wicca on college campuses and in cities. *Charmed* featured four Halliwell sisters who grappled with everyday life, family, marriage, love and breakups, fashion, and, most importantly, the perilous battles against demons and other evil entities. In the *Harry Potter* film series (adapted from the bestselling books), boys and girls attend schools to learn magic spells and potions. Hermione Granger is one of the two best friends of the titular protagonist. She is frequently depicted as the academically superior of the two; she is quick with the wand, extraordinarily studious, and never one to shirk from danger. Although Gandalf is a formidable wizard in *The Lord of the Rings* movies (adapted from the popular books), the Lady Galadriel, an Elf with magical powers, is equally powerful and stunningly beautiful. She plays an instrumental role in helping the Hobbit, Frodo Baggins, succeed in his journey to destroy the nefarious One Ring.

militant black-power movement. Shadowing these true-life social movements were two of the mutant groups of the Marvel Universe: the X-Men, organized by Xavier, and the militant mutant faction known as the Brotherhood of Evil Mutants, helmed by Magneto. It is thus not hard to understand why the *X-Men* comic books were among Marvel's most popular in the 1960s.

Popular comic books have often made a smooth transition to other media such as animated cartoons, television series, films, and narrative video games. In the early 21st century, there has been an explosion of modern-day films revolving around the heroic adventures of comic book superheroes. The list includes Superman, Batman, Spider-Man, the Hulk, Fantastic Four, Iron Man, and the X-Men. Women superheroes, however, remain disproportionately under-represented in comic books as well as their film adaptations. Women of color, like Storm, are even more rare.

ORIGINS

Stan Lee played a major role in the creation of the X-Men, developing characters with unusual characteristics, backstories, and abilities. For example, Professor Charles Xavier, a man with a brilliant mind and a telepath, was a paraplegic confined to a wheelchair. Like Dr. Martin Luther King Jr., who was the face of the contemporaneous civil rights movement, Xavier served as the "champion" of his people, the mutants (Sanderson, 9), also turning his sprawling mansion in New York City into a school for mutants.

The first members of the X-Men team were Cyclops, Marvel Girl, Angel, Beast, and Iceman. In the ensuing years, the X-Men found many allies and welcomed new members to help them battle their enemies. They faced a variety of equally strange and unusual villains, many of them led by the arch nemesis of the X-Men, Magneto.

The *X-Men* comic book series was cancelled in 1970, but returned in 1975 with a fresh stock of new and unusual characters, many of them with an international flavor that reflected the end of the Vietnam War and America's renewed interest in international relations. Storm, representing Kenya, made her first appearance; as did Colossus, representing the Soviet Union; Nightcrawler, representing West Germany; Wolverine, representing Canada; and the Native American mutant, Thunderbird. Two legendary Marvel Comics writers and one artist were instrumental in creating this new line of characters.

Len Wein, Dave Cockrum, and Chris Claremont

Comic book writers Len Wein and Chris Claremont and artist Dave Cockrum are credited for creating Storm.

Len Wein, who was born on June 12, 1948, in New York City, began writing comics in his mid-twenties. He wrote storylines for some of the most popular comics at both DC Comics and Marvel Comics, the two companies that remain to this day the supreme comic book publishers in America. Wein had a hand in writing stories for such DC superheroes as Daredevil, Supergirl, Zatanna, The Flash, and Superman. When he switched over to Marvel Comics, Wein wrote storylines for the likes of Spider-Man, the Hulk, Thor, and the Fantastic Four. In 1975, Wein collaborated with artist Dave Cockrum to bring Storm to life. Cockrum, born on November 11, 1943, in Pendleton, Oregon, produced drawings for *X-Men* from 1975 to 1977.

Wein only wrote for *X-Men* for an issue and a half before being replaced by Chris Claremont. Claremont, born in London, England, on November 30,

Seattle Storm and the WNBA

Women are frequently symbolically associated with the gentle aspects of nature; however, a storm is a natural event that signifies power and might. One of the most famous storms is the comic book hero who can manifest any weather pattern she desires. Another storm is the all-women's basketball team based in Seattle, Washington, which plays in the first professional women's basketball league in the United States. The Women's National Basketball Association (WNBA) was established in 1996, but not without considerable controversy, as many critics doubted that a women's basketball league could be as successful as a men's league.

The realities of life in the WNBA contrast sharply with those of the men's National Basketball Association (NBA). The NBA was founded in 1946, making it some 50 years older than the WNBA. It features 30 teams, whereas the WNBA features a mere 13 teams. Overall, the NBA receives far greater resources for marketing and player endorsements. Male teams and star players loom larger in the minds of most individuals than do women players.

The Seattle Storm, however, is in a unique position. In 2008, Seattle's men's basketball team, the Sonics, relocated to Oklahoma City, and the Storm (which had been attached to the Sonics), was sold to a group of women. As a result, the Storm was allowed to stay in Seattle. The continued success of the team has made the Storm one of the best professional teams in the city, helping to break down barriers to audience acceptance and interest in women in historically male-dominated athletic professions.

1950, stayed with the series until 1991. He is considered to be responsible for Storm's origin story as well as for her high profile in the comic books.

Marvel Comics

Marvel Comics, a major comic book publisher established in 1939, was the home of the X-Men, as well as Spider-Man, the Fantastic Four, the Hulk, Iron Man, and Captain America. Popular heroes in the early years included the Human Torch and Captain America.

The popularity of comic book superheroes surged in the 1960s with the emergence of characters such as the Hulk, Spider-Man, Thor, Iron Man, and the X-Men. Marvel was well aware that from the first, comic books were wildly successful amongst young, male readers, and they catered to that audience. Historically, males dominated not only the colorful pages of the comic books and their readers, but the production staff as well. Women and persons of color were always a minority, although they have made some progress in recent years.

Racial and Gender Representation in Comic Books, Television, and Film

The history of the representation of race and gender in any media form—comic books, television, and film—invariably reflects the inferior status of women and people of color. With the emergence of film as a popular medium in the 1920s, comic books in the 1930s, and television in the 1950s, long-standing traditions of male heroism and masculinity, previously confined to oral storytelling, books, and theater, were made available to virtually everyone, and were thus strengthened and perpetuated.

Throughout the media, women were generally relegated to subordinate, weak positions—largely consigned to roles as screaming and powerless damsels in distress. Minorities, particularly African Americans, were reduced to negative images such as cannibals, thugs, or infantile buffoons with features that parodied their physical differences. To be sure, there were exceptions. Film portrayed a few female heroes in the **serials** of the 1920s; however, these heroes, such as Helen of *The Hazards of Helen*, were still encumbered with numerous traditional limitations. They faced danger with reckless abandon, but they wore long inhibiting skirts and were constantly being bound and gagged. Compared to the male adventurers and heroes of the day, they were less forceful and wielded far less power.

The smattering of pioneering female and minority characters that appeared in early comic books was unspectacular. Inspired by adventurers like Amelia Earhart, the 1930s saw the introduction of several aviatrixes—Betty Lou Barnes, Peggy Mills, and Jenny Dare—but "they were all stereotypical beauties and consequently did not offer a significant threat to the male domination of comics" (Inness, 143). In the same decade, Lother, "the African 'Prince of the Seven Nations' gave up his chance to be king of the jungle in order to play manservant to Mandrake the Magician" (Walker, "Black Holes"). In addition to this dubious life choice, Lother's characterization was problematic because he did not challenge societal roles, reinforcing African Americans' real-life social, economic, and political disempowerment. Wonder Woman, a female pioneer in comic books, and supervillainess Catwoman appeared in DC comic book series in the 1940s. In the mid-1950s, Sheena, queen of the jungle, made her mark in television, though her characterization (hampered by her primary purpose of providing **eye candy** to male viewers) did not compare with the likes of Wonder Woman, who fought and did incredible things, like lift trains. The African American comic book heroes of the 1960s and 1970s, including Black Panther, Black Lightning, and Black Goliath, still constituted "sidekicks and supporting characters" (Walker, "Black Hole").

Storm was the first major African American female superhero in comic books or elsewhere. Her advent was during the heyday of **blaxploitation** films, which featured, among others, Pam Grier, an African American actress who is considered a pioneer in female action hero films. The same

Martha Washington

Martha Washington is one of the newer comic book heroes, a tough-fighting African American woman who debuted in the series *Give Me Liberty* in 1990. Visually, Washington challenges the typical comic book hero. She wears a short natural (unstraightened hair) and has true-to-life features. In other words, she is represented to look like an African American woman, not a European woman. Frequently, African American features are toned down on fictionalized characters, reinforcing societal conceptions of the Eurocentric beauty ideal.

Washington is subversive in other ways. According to scholar Sherrie A. Inness, Washington is "one of the toughest and most realistic women to hit comic books." She is level-headed and emotionally in control. The series she appears in frequently deal with socially and racially conscious themes. Rather than rely on superpowers, strength, and abilities, she is endowed with intelligence and superior fighting skills. Unlike many female comic book heroes, her body is not objectified through tight-fitting and scant clothing and exaggerated feminine features. Instead, Washington is slim and athletic and dons a military uniform. As a soldier of the future, Washington frequently functions as a group leader and is a major champion of society and the environment, battling destructive and dangerous foes.

Source: Sherrie A. Inness, *Tough Girls: Women Warriors and Wonder Women in Popular Culture* (Philadelphia: University of Pennsylvania Press, 1999), p. 153.

decade saw a significant influx of female action heroes, such as The Bionic Woman and Charlie's Angels.

During the 1980s, the concept of rugged masculinity and dominant male heroism, while still the standard, at least moved over enough to make room for alternatives. The number of women and, to a lesser degree, women of color, mushroomed considerably. This radical shift in how women and persons of color were being depicted marked real-life societal changes, wherein people of color were becoming further integrated into mainstream society, and women were enjoying greater freedoms than ever before by increasingly appropriating behaviors, attitudes, and lifestyle choices that were once denied them.

Although women and minorities continued to take on more powerful and positive roles into the 21st century, women continue to be depicted as sex objects, and both women and minorities still lag behind male heroes in terms of numbers. This is particularly true in comic books. Some critics, like Sherrie A. Inness, argue that comic book publishers have failed to use their influence to create more positive female action heroes (potential role models for young girls). They continue to rely heavily on age-old male heroes and to reinforce stereotypical images of female characters as sex objects.

POWER SUIT, WEAPONS, AND ABILITIES

Storm's appearance and abilities have differed across the various comic books, the animated television series, and the films. When she first started out with the X-Men team in the comic books, she wore a black headband, a long cape, a black barely there costume, and thigh-high black boots. In the 1980s, Storm donned a radical look, including a Mohawk and black leather. In other incarnations, she wore different outfits, all of which put her shapely body on display. Storm's least-revealing outfit was the silver-colored full-body power costume she wore in the popular animated cartoon that appeared in the 1990s. In this adaptation, Storm was especially commanding, as illustrated by her regal, low-pitched, and sonorous voice and her trademark big and unruly hair.

Halle Berry brought a softer-faced, more subdued (smooth and glamorous white hair, youthful disposition, petite dimensions) superhero to the *X-men* films (1994, 2003, 2006). Although Storm showed off her powers and abilities—including her leadership role—Wolverine (Hugh Jackman) dominated the movies with his powerful build, exciting claws, and barely tamed aggression. He was also depicted as tougher during hand-to-hand combat, though the comic books established otherwise.

According to the comic book storyline, Storm was a powerful combatant, who had proven her fighting abilities in several key situations. However, she was most known for her mutant abilities. These allowed her to "simulate the creation of any form of precipitation such as rain or fog, generate winds in varying degrees of intensity up to and including hurricane force, raise or lower the humidity and temperature in her immediate vicinity, induce lightning and other electrical atmospheric phenomena, and disperse natural storms so as to create clear change" ("Storm," *Marvel Universe*). Storm could also manipulate the winds to enable her to appear as if she were flying. When Storm's blue eyes turned white, watch out, she was jumpstarting her powers. Storm was also considered "extraordinarily skilled at picking both locks and pockets"—skills that were honed during her years as a thief.

VILLAINS

Villains galore wreaked major havoc on the X-Men and on the vast population of normal humans who did not have the mutant gene. Like various factions in the *Underworld* films, the villains of the X-Men refused to listen to ease the tense relations between mutants and humans.

The main enemy of the X-Men was Magneto, who formed groups such as the Brotherhood of Evil Mutants to exact revenge on his enemies, to conquer the world, and to prevent "the same persecution happening to mutants" that he had experienced (Sanderson, 35). A fine example of the intriguing backstories created for *X-Men* characters, Magneto was a former victim of a concentration camp in Auschwitz, Poland. His family was killed there by the Nazis, as were one million or more other Jews during the 1930s and 1940s. Following the end of the war and his subsequent freedom, a "mob prevented him from rescuing" his wife and daughter, who died in a fire (Sanderson, 34).

Magneto had amazing powers, including his brilliant mind and the ability to control electromagnetic energy. His original fellow villains included Toad, who was able to leap great distances, a powerful illusionist called Mastermind, the Scarlet Witch, and Quicksilver. In the *X-Men* films, Mystique, a metamorph, was cast as a member of Magneto's team, although according to the comic books, she started her own divergent organization, the Freedom Force. Members of the Freedom Force included "Destiny, a blind mutant who could foretell the future; Avalanche, who generates small earthquakes; Pyro, who mentally controls flame; and the X-Men's perennial foe, the Blob" (Sanderson, 39). The *X-Men* comic books featured an array of such groups, including the Imperial Guard and the Morlocks, as well as individuals, both mutant and alien, who worked tirelessly against the X-Men.

THE COMIC BOOK SERIES

In the original comic books, Storm was depicted as a tough and powerful woman, having ascended from a difficult and traumatic childhood to become the leader of the X-Men and marry an equally powerful character, Black Panther. The details of her story were fraught with adventure, captures, challenges, and triumph.

Born Ororo Monroe in New York, Storm's parents were N'Dare, an African princess, and David Monroe, an ordinary man who worked as a photojournalist. Ororo's loving parents were taken from her when they were killed in an airplane crash near their home in Cairo, Egypt. She was only five years old.

Orphaned, Ororo was taken under the wing of a man named Achmed el-Gibar, leader of a gang of thieves. He taught Ororo how to steal. She was a fast learner. She met Charles Xavier for the first time when she tried to pick his pocket. He prevented the robbery, but Ororo managed to escape. Some years later, she traveled to Kenya. On the way there, she killed a man in self-defense when he tried to rape her. Overcome with guilt, Ororo vowed never to kill again.

She eventually met a young T'Challa, otherwise known as Black Panther, a prince of the fictitious African country Wakanda. In a major role reversal, it was the female, not the male, hero who did the rescuing, when Ororo saved T'Challa from men who were trying to abduct him. Ororo and T'Challa spent time together before Ororo finally reached her mother's homeland.

In Kenya, Ororo was guided by a wise woman named Ainet. Ainet "taught [Ororo] to be responsible with her powers" ("Storm," *Marvel Universe*). Historically, men loom large as the teachers and guides for women. For example, Maggie Fitzgerald, the female boxer in *Million Dollar Baby* (2004) and Chun Li, as depicted in the film *Street Fighter: The Legend of Chun-Li* (2009), are managed and directed by men who help to develop the woman's power. Chun Li, in particular, is taught by her male teacher, Gen, to be responsible with her power and how to release her anger. This role reinforces the dominance of men and the inferiority of women.

That said, there are plenty of examples of **transgressive** mentoring relationships. The comic book character Wonder Woman, for example, honed her skills on an island inhabited by all women, and Gabrielle, who was once a meek and traditional farm girl, was taught the way of the warrior by the powerful Xena in the television series *Xena: Warrior Princess*.

While in Africa, Ororo became a goddess whose job it was to protect and watch over the tribe with which she dwelt. As a protector, Ororo was positioned in a role normally filled by a man. In American society, power has been historically relegated to men. But in mythology as well as other world belief systems, women were often depicted as powerful gods and thus worshipped and invoked by ordinary humans who desired special favors and protection. Women were also shamans and venerated elders.

However, all of Ororo's potential was not tapped until she joined the X-Men. After becoming a member, Ororo received the code name Storm and, after several years, replaced Cyclops as leader of the team. In a subsequent confrontation with the Brood, a heinous alien race, Storm became infected with an alien egg that, if allowed to gestate, would "transform her into one of the aliens" ("Storm," *Marvel Universe*).

The Brood made their debut in *Uncanny X-Men* #155 in 1982. They were terrifying insect-like extraterrestrials with oblong heads and ferocious teeth. Like the aliens who appeared in the famous *Alien* film series (1979, 1986, 1991, 1997) featuring actress Sigourney Weaver as hero Ellen Ripley, the Brood required hosts for reproduction. Storm attempted to commit suicide when she found out that she had been impregnated, a valiant gesture that was actually carried out by Ellen Ripley in *Alien 3* (1992). Storm destroyed the embryo, but was saved from death by the Acanti, a whale-like alien species.

Despite this rescue, Storm was no typical damsel in distress; nor was she a powerless victim. In a subsequent story, she rescued one of the male mutants, Angel. Callisto, a female leader of the Morlocks, abducted Angel to mate with him. Storm fought her in a duel and won. Callisto was ousted and Storm replaced her as the new leader of the Morlocks. Shortly after this episode, Storm underwent a dramatic change.

Influenced by Yuko, a female ninja, who "was the most care free spirit that Ororo had ever met," Storm shaved her flowing locks and adopted a

Mohawk ("Storm," *Marvel Universe*). However, her compeers disliked her new appearance—after all, it was a masculine look and thus unfitting for the usually conservative and predictable leader they had come to know. The negative reception underscored how Storm, though unconventionally powerful, still had to conform to traditional expectations. In the real world, women have long been expected to maintain feminine hair styles, and iconoclastic looks stir up adverse reactions. Storm soon reappeared with her long hair restored.

In another story, Storm accidentally lost her powers. During the time when she was without her mutant abilities, Storm continued to play a pivotal role in the storylines. Forge, a mutant character who invented the weapon that took her powers away, cared for Storm as she recovered from the accident. They fell in love, but Storm withdrew from Forge when she found out that he had created the weapon. Storm took the loss of her powers hard. As in later *X-Men* films, Storm was depicted as a mutant who was not ashamed of her powers.

Going back to Africa, Storm joined a team called the New Mutants, only to return to beat Cyclops in a "duel for leadership" of the X-Men ("Storm," *Marvel Universe*). She accomplished this feat without having the use of her mutant powers. Her powers were eventually restored by Forge, who then proposed to her. But the pair was still doomed, for Forge interpreted her hesitation as a rejection and pulled back.

Storm had no time to mourn her loss. A villain named the Nanny apprehended her and turned her into a child, though not before Storm unfortunately destroyed the machine that changed her. After she was changed back to her rightful age, she led one of the two X-Men teams that were formed at that time. Imprisoned by a villain named Khan who wanted to make Storm his queen, Storm single-handedly escaped and launched the X-Treme Sanctions Executive, a mutant group formed to assist the United Nations. After several more adventures, Storm returned again to Africa, where she eventually wed T'Challa. The wedding was billed as a monumental occasion, wherein two very powerful heroes forged a mighty partnership.

Prominent African American romance writer Eric Jerome Dickey was charged with retelling the tale of how Storm and Black Panther met and married (as well as Storm's youthful life as a pickpocket). However, his version, entitled *Storm* and published in 2008, cast T'Challa—not Storm—in the more heroic terms. Indeed, Storm was regarded as a simple thief and her royal bloodline omitted, while T'Challa was depicted as a mighty warrior who was descended from legendary ancestors. It was T'Challa who rescued Storm (reversing the original storyline) at their first meeting.

Moreover, T'Challa was depicted as a young man on his walkabout, or rite of passage—a ritual that ushers an individual from one state to another. In T'Challa's instance, his walkabout would usher him into manhood. Following an often-touted male interpretation of the universe, Ororo's rite of passage into womanhood was referenced by the loss of her virginity, which occurred shortly after meeting T'Challa.

In subsequent *Black Panther* comic books, Storm joined her new husband on various adventures. But it was in her own comic books, *Storm* Volume 1 (1996), *Ororo: Before the Storm* (2005), and *Storm* Volume 2 (2006), wherein Storm emerged as a central character, whose life was not solely defined by her membership in an organization or to her husband.

IMPACT

As Storm approaches four decades since her debut, her impact on popular culture remains relatively limited. Though she broke new ground for women and people of color—groups largely under-represented in media—and, thanks to the films, is reasonably well known to the general public outside comic book fandom, she has not elicited the enthusiastic responses that other female action heroes or classic male heroes have received.

Female action heroes like Wonder Woman, Foxy Brown, Princess Leia, Ellen Ripley, Sarah Connor, Buffy the Vampire Slayer, Lara Croft, and Xena loomed large in the minds of both audiences and critics. These characters spawned lucrative paraphernalia, cult followings, and extensive fan followings. Storm's comparatively limited success may be due to the fact that the more popular female action heroes tend to stand alone, or at the least stand front and center.

Storm's titular comic books are few in number. In most comic book series, Storm must share the limelight, competing with other, equally powerful mutants. In the *X-Men* films, Storm's role is marginal, with only intermittent demonstrations of her spectacular powers. Storm's dubious status—her immense power and toughness notwithstanding—illustrates the ongoing struggle for female action heroes to prevail in the male-dominated comic book industry.

See also Catwoman; Ellen Ripley; Foxy Brown; Wonder Woman.

FURTHER RESOURCES

Dickey, Eric Jerome. *Storm*. New York: Marvel, 2008.

Foster, William H. *Looking for a Face Like Mine*. Waterbury, CT: Fine Tooth Press, 2005.

Housel, Rebecca. "X-Women and X-istence." In *X-Men and Philosophy*, ed. Rebecca Housel and J. Jeremy Wisnewski. Hoboken, NJ: John Wiley and Sons, 2009.

Hudlin, Reginald. *Black Panther: Back to Africa*. New York: Marvel, 2008.

Hudlin, Reginald. *Black Panther: Civil War*. New York: Marvel, 2007.

Hudlin, Reginald. *Black Panther: Four the Hard Way*. New York: Marvel, 2007.

Ilea, Ramona. "The Mutant Cure or Social Change: Debating Disability." In *X-Men and Philosophy*, ed. Rebecca Housel and J. Jeremy Wisnewski. Hoboken, NJ: John Wiley and Sons, 2009.

Inness, Sherrie A. *Tough Girls: Women Warriors and Wonder Women in Popular Culture*. Philadelphia: University of Pennsylvania Press, 1999.

Marvel Universe. "Storm." http://marvel.com/universe/Storm.

Pierce, Jeremy. "Mutants and the Metaphysics of Race." In *X-Men and Philosophy*, ed. Rebecca Housel and J. Jeremy Wisnewski. Hoboken, NJ: John Wiley and Sons, 2009.

Robichaud, Christopher. "Professor X Wants You." In *X-Men and Philosophy*, ed. Rebecca Housel and J. Jeremy Wisnewski. Hoboken, NJ: John Wiley and Sons, 2009.

Sanderson, Peter. *Ultimate X-Men*. New York: Dorling Kindersley, 2000.

Stafford, Nikki. "Holy Butt-Kicking Babe, Batman!" In *Girls Who Bite Back: Witches, Mutants, Slayers, and Freaks*, ed. Emily Pohl-Weary. Toronto: Sumach Press, 2004.

Walker, David. "Black Hole: Why Aren't There More Black Superheroes?" http://paralleluniverse.msn.com/comic-con/black-superheroes/story/feature.

Thelma (right) and Louise sit on top of Louise's 1966 Thunderbird convertible in the film *Thelma & Louise*. (© MGM/Courtesy: Everett Collection.)

Thelma and Louise

Thelma and Louise are outlaws on the run in the eponymous film released in 1991. From the start to the finish of the film, Thelma (Geena Davis) and Louise (Susan Sarandon) undergo dramatic transformations. Initially, they are defined as stereotypical females. Thelma, with big hair and made-up face, is a submissive housewife. Her husband, Darryl (Christopher McDonald), is depicted as insensitive and chauvinistic. Louise, primly coiffed, with lipstick, eye shadow, and a perfect complexion, works as a waitress and is in a dead-end relationship with a boyfriend named Jimmy (Michael Madsen).

In this film, the women's personalities, occupations, as well as the town in which they live, underscore the confinement they feel. As a housewife, Thelma's world is limited by the boundaries of her home; her function is, essentially, to serve her husband's needs and to keep order in and maintain the cleanliness of the home. As a subordinate figure in the household, Thelma is expected to defer to her husband and seek his approval on issues, big and small. Louise, who has greater freedom than Thelma because she is single, is nevertheless caught in a dead-end relationship with a man who scorns the marriage Louise desires. Like Thelma, Louise is positioned as a caretaker—albeit a paid caretaker—perfunctorily performing her duties as a waitress, seeing to the needs of the diners, serving their beverages and food, and cleaning up after them.

Both women live half-heartedly—though this fact is not addressed until later in the film—in the confines of a small Arkansas town. Southern towns, particularly small ones, are generally depicted in films as provincial. In this fictionalized representation of a small Southern town, men and women rarely transgress gender roles. Men dominate the police force, make condescending remarks about women, and are depicted as **sexist** and crude; women are expected to be presentable, pretty, polite, and on the sidelines— a pointed example of this occurs when Louise, sitting in a car with her hair tousled and make-up worn off, is gawked at in surprise by older women who would never be caught dead in public in such a state of disarray.

The lives of Thelma and Louise are irrevocably altered when the women go on a road trip. The trip starts innocently enough, but takes a shocking turn when Louise murders a man who attempts to rape Thelma. Next, a vagabond steals Louise's life savings, prompting Thelma to rob a convenience store to replenish their funds. Both women willingly continue to break the law to evade capture, eventually blowing up a truck driven by a man who obscenely catcalls and gestures at them.

During the progression of the women's escapades, Thelma and Louise become increasingly tough, both emotionally and visually, shedding the codes of femininity that defined them at the start of the film, but never entirely losing their comedic politeness. At the end of the film, they are cornered by the police whose many vehicles chase Louise's 1966 Thunderbird convertible toward the edge of a gaping canyon. Shockingly, Thelma and Louise opt to drive off the cliff, the camera capturing the moment in a

> ### *Set It Off*
>
> *Set It Off* (1996) is a film that featured four African American women who robbed a bank, each one for personal reasons, most of which involved racism and poverty. The film starred prominent actresses Jada Pinkett as Lita "Stony" Newsome, Queen Latifah as Cleopatra "Cleo" Sims, Vivica A. Fox as Francesca "Frankie" Sutton, and Kimberly Elise as Tisean "T. T." Williams. Following a tumultuous pursuit, only Newsome survives, escaping to Mexico with the money they had stolen.
>
> The film is significant, among many reasons, because it exposes real issues related to the discrimination and inequities African Americans face in contemporary America. It gives voice to a unique perspective of a group that has been historically marginalized by society as well as the media.

freeze frame shot as the car soars into the air. Many audiences were befuddled, angry, and sad. Others were ecstatic, preferring to see the women die rather than face the failure of capture.

Once the dust settled, academics and critics were left with the daunting task of coming to terms with *Thelma and Louise*. Many thought the film was excessively critical of men, caricaturing them as bumbling buffoons, sexist troglodytes, immoral charlatans, and lewd ogres. Others thought the film bordered on camp, situating the women in unrealistic adventures. Others contended that Thelma and Louise were "feminist icons," women who took charge of their lives and boldly spoke and behaved in ways that caused many women, in real life, to applaud and root for them. Even so, their violent behavior was controversial, and their assumptive suicide was a point of contention for those who **read** their deaths as a cop-out or a symbolic punishment for **transgressive** behavior (Fournier, 61). Critical response aside, Thelma and Louise's leap off the cliff, however fatalistic, was intended by screenwriter Callie Khouri and director Ridley Scott to be triumphant.

ORIGINS

Bad Guys, Bad Girls

In *Thelma and Louise*, women are portrayed as the "bad guys." For women, bad behavior holds particular importance, as women have historically been denied equal access to power, independence, as well as the opportunity to be depicted as cool bad guys.

Since frontier times, American women have struggled to overcome the constraints of social customs and expectations that contained them within domestic spaces and labeled them as the weaker sex (emotionally, mentally, and physically). Women's appearance and behavior were controlled by a restrictive feminine ideal; their dreams, hopes, and aspirations were severely limited compared to men who could travel alone, go anywhere at any time, exert confidence and aggression, and pursue adventure and ambitious careers. Traveling, living alone, and venturing into male spaces—whether a male-dominated industry or environments coded as masculine, such as the frontier (the Wild West), saloons, the open road, and the battlefield—were taboo and considered too dangerous for women. Aggression, confidence, and ambition were largely perceived to be masculine traits and were not acceptable in women. Moreover, particularly in frontier times, bad behavior was more acceptable in males than females. These perceptions persist—albeit, to an increasingly lesser degree—into modern times.

In *Public Enemies* (2009), Johnny Depp played John Dillinger, a legendary Great Depression–era bank robber who epitomized the traditional, cool, and powerful outlaw. The media and public idolized Dillinger, an archetypal antihero. Nerveless, cocky, confident, and a rebel, he is extremely good at being bad, from breaking himself and his friends out of prison to stealing money from banks and firing weapons. According to Sturken, "the [male] outlaw was mythologized as someone who defied the system (the law, capitalism, and the work ethic) for the vicarious pleasure of the constrained and law-abiding citizen who followed his exploits" (Sturken, 24). Notably absent from the lively cast of bad guys and gangsters were female thugs. Women were depicted as glamorous love interests, prostitutes, and secretaries, illustrating that women were denied status in the underworld, as well as in normal society. Thelma and Louise defy these sorts of traditions, demonstrating that girls can be tough enough and bad enough.

Callie Khouri

Callie Khouri, the woman who wrote the Academy Award–winning screenplay for *Thelma and Louise*, never intended to be a writer. When she sat down to craft the story, she did so for personal reasons, from the perspective of a woman who had worked for years in a male-dominated industry, and who was frustrated with the way she saw women like herself treated. She was not alone. Women across the world have battled **discrimination** and **sexism** throughout history.

Although America was founded on the principles of freedom and independence, women, as well blacks (most of whom were enslaved in the South) and other ethnic groups, were denied many privileges, opportunities, and freedoms primarily enjoyed by white men. In America's early years, a woman might dream of becoming a doctor, an athlete, or an inventor, or of owning a home of her own, but laws and social beliefs kept women, especially wives, from realizing those aspirations. In the 18th century, far-sighted and progressive women joined the abolitionist movement to protest the institution of slavery. In the late 19th century, women organized to fight for

Cagney & Lacey

Thelma and Louise were famous outlaws in the 1990s; *Cagney & Lacey*, on the other side of the law, were famous detectives in an award-winning television show in the 1980s. The show was revolutionary because it featured two realistic women detectives. Christine Cagney (Sharon Gless) was single, focusing solely on her career, and Mary Beth Lacey (Tyne Daly) was married with children, balancing a stressful career and family. Prior to the television series, most women in police and detective shows were glamorous and thin (television series such as *Charlie's Angels* were a case in point). Cagney and Lacey, however, were generally not objectified by the camera with close-up shots of their bodies or through fashionable clothing and glossy makeup and hairstyles. The women also contended with serious issues such as abortion, domestic violence, tough urban crimes, and dramatic human emotions. *Cagney & Lacey* ended in 1988.

the right to vote, as well as to better conditions in the cities for the poor and underprivileged.

In 1920, when women obtained **suffrage**, the pace of progress increased. Gains were most visible in the passage of laws to protect women from discrimination, sexism, and sexual harassment and to advance equality in the changing face of America's workforce. As more women, single and married, moved into the workforce, expanding into careers traditionally dominated by males, they confronted new challenges such as balancing career and home life, dealing with sexist attitudes that kept them out of management positions, and alienation.

Carolyn Ann Khouri was born in 1957 in San Antonio, Texas, and raised in Texas and Kentucky. She was seven years old when the Civil Rights Act of 1964 was enacted, thereby establishing laws to end racial **segregation** and (under Title VII) discrimination in the workplace based on race, sex, or religion. **Second-wave feminism** was in its infancy. Khouri studied landscape architecture at the University of Purdue in Indiana before deciding she wanted to be an actress. She worked in a theater and took several jobs, such as waitressing. After moving to Los Angeles in 1982, she worked as a receptionist, a production co-coordinator, and a music video producer. As a producer, Khouri was troubled by the negative and highly sexual images of women that were popular in music videos. She also experienced struggles in romantic relationships and dissatisfaction with her career.

The story of Thelma and Louise, conceived and written in a mere six months, was both therapeutic and redemptive for Khouri. She explains how "she was fed up with producing music videos, in particular because of their predominantly sexist narratives: 'In order to get my karma straight about women, I had to write this script'" (Sturken, 16). Second-wave feminists would have applauded her, for they objected to the centuries-old tradition of depicting women as sex objects who were weak, inept, and timid. Feminists promoted sisterhood and female power, encouraging women to overcome and challenge the status quo and not let themselves be defined by their relationships to men.

Even after Khouri's screenplay was accepted and film production had begun, she never lost sight of her message: "the primary feeling she wanted in the film was of wanting to bust out. 'I wanted to bust out of my life. . . . I was the product of a lot of wasted years and bad relationships and ennui and frustration at not really knowing what I wanted to do'" (Sturken, 16).

The theme of "busting out" figures prominently in *Thelma and Louise*. Khouri also wanted to create female protagonists who reflected the lives of real, ordinary women. The result, an action/outlaw film told from the perspective of ordinary women, was, in the early 1990s, radical. Women, especially the type of women Khouri wrote about, who might normally be cast as love interests or other subordinate characters, or at best as the protagonists of a melodrama or chick flick, were simply not seen as capable of being female action heroes—or female action antiheroes.

But *Thelma and Louise* was not just an action or outlaw film; it blended other genres, such as the buddy movie, the road movie, the Western, and the comedy. Traditionally, the films in these categories featured male protagonists and were made with male audiences in mind. The male hero reinforced social perceptions of ideal manhood and, presumably, fed male fantasies of power, dominance, and over-the-top action. In these fictional worlds, men dominated, while anything associated with femininity was suppressed or coded as weak, inferior, expendable, and a snare.

By creating female heroes that real women could relate to, Khouri did the unthinkable: she transferred the point of view of an action-adventure road trip film from men to women. In effect, Thelma and Louise became a study of female fantasy. For example, when Thelma and Louise blow up the truck of the disrespectful and lewd truck driver, they do so for all women who have ever been disrespected by a man. When Thelma and Louis assert their power in other aggressive and sometimes violent ways, they do what real women might want to but cannot do.

To some, this made the film unfair to men and excessively violent. According to Khouri, the way in which the men were depicted was based on real experiences. In actuality, Khouri's characterization of the males in the screenplay was less harsh than what is ultimately seen in the film. Scott and the male actors made changes to the male characters, producing more broadly drawn examples of negative male archetypes. In response to critics who object to the film's violence, Khouri points to other action films, where male protagonists employ excessive violence, some of which is directed at women, which do not attract such criticism. In fact, male action hero films are among the biggest money-making genres. Scholars, like Marita Sturken,

Bonnie Parker

Bonnie Parker was the female member of the infamous Bonnie and Clyde criminal duo. The duo itself was part of a gang of robbers whose crime spree ran from the early to the mid-1930s. Born on October 1, 1910 in Rowena, Texas, Parker grew up in dire poverty, but she excelled in school and emerged as a gifted writer. She was married when she met Clyde Barrow, a man who was regularly in trouble with the law. Barrow and his gang had committed numerous robberies and murders. It is unclear what role Parker played in the violent acts that followed. In addition to being known as Barrow's girlfriend or *moll* (the term used to describe the romantic interests of gangsters and other criminals), Parker went along on the crime sprees, was jailed for a time, and lived a harrowing life on the run. Fueling her sensationalized public persona was a photo of Parker posing with a cigar in her mouth and wielding a gun. In 1934, she and Barrow were killed by officers as they tried to escape capture.

author of *Thelma and Louise* (2000), argue that, compared to typical action films, *Thelma and Louise* features far less violence.

The violence and punishments inflicted upon the men in the film are further examples of how Khouri reversed gender norms. Whereas women were expected to be nonviolent, polite, gentle, and to respond passively to sexism, it was more socially acceptable for a man to "act out" and respond aggressively to an offense.

Khouri went on to explore themes such as sisterhood and good-girls-gone-bad in subsequent films. She directed *Divine Secrets of the Ya-Ya Sisterhood* (2005) and *Mad Money* (2009).

Ridley Scott

The film *Thelma and Louise* garnered Ridley Scott both attention and acclaim; however, this film was not Scott's first encounter with female action heroism. Scott directed *Alien* (1979), in which the crew of a space freighter is attacked, violated, and slaughtered, one by one, leaving only Lieutenant Ellen Ripley, a character who appealed to feminists and mainstream audiences alike, to defeat the terrifying and powerful alien. Scott later directed another transgressive female action hero in *G.I. Jane* (1997), the story of Jordan O'Neil, who trains in an all-male elite branch of the military. Other action films he directed include *Blade Runner* (1982), *Gladiator* (2000), *Black Hawk Down* (2001), and *American Gangster* (2007).

Geena Davis and Susan Sarandon

Born Susan Abigail Tomalin on October 4, 1946, in New York City, one of nine children, Sarandon obtained a bachelor of arts degree in drama from the Catholic University of America. She has played an assortment of roles in films since 1970. She appeared as a vampire in *The Hunger* (1982), an imprisoned nurse in a prisoner-of-war camp in *Women of Valor* (1986), a sultry witch in *The Witches of Eastwick* (1987), as well as a heroic mother, a nurse, and a grandmother. She is well known for her commitment to activism. She married her college sweetheart, whom she subsequently divorced in 1979. A later relationship produced a daughter, and she has two sons with fellow actor Tim Robbins.

Davis was born Virginia Elizabeth Davis on January 21, 1956, in Wareham, Massachusetts. She graduated from Boston University, worked as a model, and appeared in her first film, *Tootsie*, in 1982. The film centered on a man named Michael Dorsey (Dustin Hoffman) who, after turning 40, is no longer able to get an acting part until he dresses up like a woman. Davis has appeared in several unconventional roles, including a traditional wife and mother turned professional catcher in *A League of Their Own* (1992), a film about an all-women's baseball team during World War II; a female pirate in *Cutthroat Island* (1995); an amnesic mother and school teacher who discovers she is an assassin in *The Long Kiss Goodnight* (1996); and the first female president in the television series *Commander in Chief* (2005–2006). In 1999, Davis competed in the trials for the Olympic Archery team. In 2007, she established the Geena Davis Institute on Gender and Media. She is currently married to her fourth husband. They have three children.

Both Geena Davis and Susan Sarandon received nominations for Best Actress for their roles as Thelma and Louise.

POWER SUITS, WEAPONS, AND ABILITIES

At the start of *Thelma and Louise*, the protagonists were coded as ordinary, traditional, and feminine; they had not yet appropriated full power or toughness. The women's neat and pretty hairstyles, orderly clothes, clean and fresh complexions, and subservient roles as waitress and housewife coded them as good women—women who did not break laws or social roles, and women who were not empowered.

By the film's end, Thelma and Louise were tough, bad women, having taken on attributes traditionally associated with masculinity and criminality. They went without makeup; their hair was disheveled; they wore jeans and sleeveless T-shirts; and committed crimes. They also wore hats that had belonged to men, Louise trading her jewelry for a hat worn by an elderly man, and Thelma stealing a hat belonging to the truck driver whose truck they detonated in retaliation for his crude and sexist remarks. These hats signaled their physical ascent to toughness; the manner in which Thelma obtained her hat in particular marked it as an emblem of her personal development and valor. Both Thelma and Louise wielded guns with ease and confidence.

Underscoring the transformation of these two women was the hardness of their facial expressions, their acclimation to—and growing pridefulness in—their newfound freedom and position as scofflaws and the ease with which they made decisions.

THELMA AND LOUISE, THE FILM

One of the reasons Thelma and Louise are such popular characters is that they claimed the power that men normally appropriated. They epitomized rebelliousness, not only because of the crimes they committed, but because they were women disrupting gender norms. Audience reactions were strong in large part because transgressive women, particularly female outlaws, were atypical in film. Changes in society, such as women's significant involvement in the Gulf War (1990–1991), made audiences more receptive to powerful women.

The road trip that starts the notorious exploits of Thelma and Louise begins happily. Both women are talkative, smiling, and ebullient, behaving in very feminine ways. The trip gives both women an opportunity to escape from their uneventful and restrictive lives and especially their traditional identities. Thelma in particular has not traveled much. She has never ventured far from her home and is too timid to ask her husband for permission to go on the trip to the cabin with Louise. This is Thelma's first rebellious act. While she is depicted as childlike, gullible, sheltered, and submissive, Louise is single and depicted as more assertive, transgressive, and worldly. Louise appears to have more world smarts and to be more independent than Thelma. She owns a gun and brings it along for protection, which shocks Thelma (who holds it skittishly). Nonetheless, Louise is still cast as a traditional woman—she wants to marry her boyfriend, she works as a waitress, and she lives in the same small and suffocating town.

The women visibly enjoyed themselves, reveling in the freedom of the road—a freedom that normally belonged to men. Enjoying the liberation of riding in Louise's convertible, they sing along to the radio, their hair whipping under a great expanse of sky. The open road and the vast sky underscore their sense of freedom. Out of town, Thelma's inhibitions disappear, and she pleads with Louise to stop at a country bar. At the bar, Louise is reserved, drinks sparingly, and disapproves of Thelma's overdrinking and dancing with an aggressive stranger. While Louise is in the women's restroom, the man attempts to rape Thelma in the parking lot. Louise arrives in the nick of time and fatally shoots the man. Louise decides they should not go to the cops, saying no one would believe their side of the story since Thelma has been seen drinking and dancing with the man. Louise's attitude is in no way a transparent and unlikely device for the purpose of moving along the plot. The long-held myth that rape was a woman's fault is perpetuated to this day, though it also continues to be challenged in the plethora of literature, education, campaigns, and other methods that are used in schools, colleges, universities, and television.

After Thelma commits murder (partly out of self-defense and partly as personal vindication), she and Louise become criminals on the run. Like Lieutenant Jordan O'Neil in *G.I. Jane* (1997), who underwent a dramatic transformation, shedding the accouterments of her femininity (her menstrual cycle, soft body structure, long hair, and earrings) to beat the system of a male-dominated, elite military training program, Thelma and Louise must discard stereotypical feminine traits to survive on the run. They put away hysteria, indecisiveness, and bubbly talkativeness. Thelma must also put away her pursuit of reckless fun, for a second mistake—a one-night stand with a hitchhiker—results in the loss of Louise's savings (which the hitch-hiker steals). Louise must also reject her boyfriend's proposal of marriage. As their transformation progresses, the mood of the film becomes heavier, the conversations in the Thunderbird more serious and sparse.

Scott enhanced the women's transgressiveness further by depicting the men in lesser or unconventional roles. When Thelma and the hitchhiker, J.D. (Brad Pitt), have sex, "the camera spends much more time focused on his [muscled] body than hers" (Sturken, 81). Thelma's husband is depicted as the abandoned spouse, a position traditionally relegated to wives, and is con-signed to the domestic space for subsequent scenes. With Thelma gone, the house is in disarray, pizza boxes littering the living room floor. Louise's boy-friend becomes the jilted love interest. The cops are depicted as ineffectual, as they remain mystified over the sudden and unusual crimes; they can't seem to catch up to the women outlaws, not even at the last, dramatic moment. Ironi-cally, the lead detective in the case shows empathy for the women. Normally, detectives are portrayed as hard and relentless soldiers of justice, while empa-thy (and kindness) are considered typical traits of femininity. Here, men are depicted as victims of crime too, not just the female protagonists.

For Thelma and Louise, the crimes they commit following the shooting at the bar demonstrate their desire to remain free. Desperation propels Thelma to rob a store at gunpoint after the hitchhiker steals the money they planned to use to get to Mexico to avoid capture and imprisonment. When a policeman stops them for speeding, they lock him in the trunk of his car; then they blow up the truck of a man who harasses them on the road. The latter action was considered a triumph for all women treated as sex objects. When the women hone their shooting skills in another scene, they are steely, tanned, and focused.

In the final, climactic scene, a hoard of FBI agents in cars chase Thelma and Louise, whom the law now characterizes as armed and dangerous women. Before deciding to drive over the cliff, the women kiss briefly on the mouth. Sturken contends this kiss was not lesbian in orientation but rather symbolized the women's friendship. When the women drive off the cliff, the camera captures the Thunderbird in a freeze frame before the screen fades to white and the film ends. Khouri is "adamant that the film does not end with suicide," explaining that "they flew away, out of this world and into the mass unconscious. Women who are completely free from all the shackles that restrain them have no place in this world," for they can neither go back to their metaphorical prison (their former lives) or be imprisoned for their crimes (Sturken, 73).

IMPACT

The film was a sensation with mainstream audiences, feminists, and academics alike, sparking numerous fan clubs. Thelma and Louise became instant pop culture icons; their names are still used to refer to any woman who rebels against society or challenges authority. The film paralleled a trend in mainstream television, escalated by talk show host Oprah Winfrey, wherein ordinary women in life and literature who transcended obstacles and challenges were spotlighted. Ultimately, the film challenged and influenced how society perceives gender roles. The very fact that Thelma and Louise were outlaws (antiheroes) helped to widen the horizons of and introduce fascinating nuances to the budding genre of female action heroes.

See also Catwoman; Chyna; Jen Yu.

FURTHER RESOURCES

Fournier, Gina. *Thelma and Louise and Women in Hollywood.* Jefferson, NC: McFarland and Company, 2007.

Neroni, Hilary. *The Violent Woman: Femininity, Narrative, and Violence in Contemporary American Cinema.* Albany: State University of New York Press, 2005.

Owen, Susan A., Sarah R. Stein, and Leah R. Vande Berg. *Bad Girls: Cultural Politics and Media Representations of Transgressive Women.* New York: Peter Lang, 2007.

Read, Jacinda. *The New Avengers: Feminism, Femininity, and the Rape-Revenge Cycle.* New York: Manchester University Press, 2000.

Sims, Yvonne D. *Women of Blaxploitation: How the Black Action Film Heroine Changed American Popular Culture.* Jefferson, NC: McFarland and Company, 2006.

Sturken, Marita. *Thelma and Louise.* London: British Film Institute, 2000.

Vares, Tiina. "Action Heroines and Female Viewers: What Women Have to Say." In *Reel Knockouts: Violent Women in the Movies*, ed. Martha McCaughey and Neal King. Austin: University of Texas Press, 2001.

Wonder Woman as she appeared in the 1970s television series. (AP Photo.)

Wonder Woman

Wonder Woman was America's first female comic book superhero. She debuted in 1941 in an issue of *All-Star Comics* during World War II. Her patriotic origins were signaled by her red corset (decorated with a gold emblem) and her blue-and-white star-spangled shorts, an ensemble that came across as a one-piece bathing suit divided by a gold belt. Her iconic accessories, among them the gold tiara, bracelets, and lasso, functioned as weapons. Her knee-high, red high-heeled boots completed her look. Boots are worn by many male and female superheroes, however, Wonder Woman's boots were feminized with the heels and by fact her legs and thighs were bare.

Wonder Woman's creator, William Moulton Marston, had female empowerment in mind when he constructed his female superhero, though his radical ideas came two decades before the feminist movement took off during the 1960s, finally penetrating mainstream America. Marston once said that he believed women would rule the world—despite the reality that men dominated society as well as comic books—but he was told that Americans would not respond favorably to autonomous female superheroes. Defying tradition, Marston infused his new character with feminist ideas. He constructed Wonder Woman using the popular method of fusing mythical characters and storylines and endowing the resulting hero with extraordinary powers.

Wonder Woman's origins were feministic too. Wonder Woman, whose name was actually Diana, came from an island called Paradise. Paradise Island was populated by women (referred to as Amazons) who had been liberated from bondage to a man (Hercules). The Amazons lived peaceably and were led by a commanding woman (Queen Hippolyte). Theirs was an advanced society. Entanglement with men was outlawed. Queen Hippolyte warned Wonder Woman to stay romantically uninvolved with handsome Captain Steve Trevor, whose plane crashed on Paradise Island during World War II, because such romantic entanglements would cause her to lose her powers. Wonder Woman was not the only one who had to contend with romantic difficulties. Superman had the same problem.

Wonder Woman was an astounding success. Her most celebrated years were in the 1940s, which was a high time for comic books (known as the Golden Age). With television in its infancy, comic book reading was one of the most influential and popular activities for young boys. For a quarter century, Wonder Woman continued to be a comic book mainstay, joining forces with an elite group of superheroes in the *Justice Society* and the *Justice League*. She did change with the times, however. In modern adaptations, Wonder Woman is a hard-faced, muscled woman, no longer the cherubic-looking, classically shaped female beauty of the 1940s.

Wonder Woman's status as a national icon was augmented when by the recognition of a prominent feminist, Gloria Steinem, and by the launching of several television series. In 1972, Steinem, one of the founders of the feminist publication *Ms. Magazine*, put Wonder Woman on the cover of the first issue. In 1973 and 1977, Wonder Woman appeared in the animated cartoons *Super Friends* and *The All-New Superfriends Hour*. In 1975, Linda Carter was cast as the celebrated hero in the television series *Wonder Woman*. Carter, a woman of mixed heritage, including Irish, Mexican, and Spanish ethnicities, had long, ebony hair, pale skin, and blue eyes, just like the character she played. The *Wonder Woman* series was on the air for three seasons and was considered a hit. The show continues to be a cult classic to this day, so much so that a direct-to-video animation movie was released in 2009.

ORIGINS

Wonder Woman was conceived from a composite of the world as Marston knew it and his soaring imagination. Marston strongly believed in female power and the equality of the sexes. Indeed, he asserted that women were more powerful than men. In 1937, he made an unusual forecast, stating that in "the next one hundred years will see the beginning of an American matriarchy—a nation of Amazons in the psychological rather than physical sense [who] would take over the rule of the country, politically and economically" (Daniels, 19). In defending his Wonder Woman creation, he wrote, "Wonder Woman is psychological propaganda for the new type of woman who should, I believe, rule the world," and was confident that Wonder Woman was in line with "a great movement now underway—the growth in the power of women" (Daniels, 22).

Marston crafted Wonder Woman to meet his personal requirements for an ideal, powerful woman. This woman was patriotic, feminine, and nonviolent. Marston wanted Wonder Woman to have "all the allure of an attractive woman but with the strength of a powerful man. He wrote in a letter that "I have given Wonder Woman this dominant force but have kept her loving, tender, maternal and feminine in every other way" (Daniels, 23). Allegedly, Marston's idea of beauty looked a lot like one particular woman, Olive Richard, who assisted him in his academic studies and also lived with him and his family. Like Wonder Woman, Richard had dark hair and blue eyes; she wore silver bracelets on both wrists.

Among the assortment of powerful accessories attached to Wonder Woman was the magic lasso, which enabled Wonder Woman to retrieve the truth from anyone by wrapping the lasso around their bodies. Marston, it turns out, had a life-long interest in lie detectors, and pioneered several studies.

Bondage was a prominent theme in Marston's Wonder Woman stories. Marston knew bondage scenes had heavy sexual connotations. He also knew that that was a powerful marketing tool that could be exploited in film and literature, like comic books. The same tool was used frequently in episodes featuring Emma Peel, a spy in the 1960s British show *The Avengers*. In one

Mother Teresa: A Real-Life Wonder Woman

Mother Teresa, a woman of action and faith, devoted her life to helping the sick and the poor in countries throughout the world. Born Agnese Gonxhe Bojaxhiu on August 26, 1910, in the Ottoman Empire, Mother Teresa left home to join a missionary when she was 18 years old. In 1929, she taught children in India. In her late thirties, she began working in the slums, reaching out to help those in desperate need. Often times, Mother Teresa was herself in need and subsisted on the help of others for food and shelter. In 1950, she started the Missionaries of Charity, first in India and then elsewhere. This organization continues to thrive today, providing resources and shelters for orphans, individuals with serious health issues and disabilities, and for those who have lost their homes due to natural disasters. Mother Teresa's generosity soon became known throughout the world, and she was honored by world leaders and dignitaries and toured the globe. She worked well into old age, despite mounting health problems. She died in 1997 at age 87.

film study, Marston concluded that "scenes in which the title character is bound and whipped . . . caused a strong, disguised captivation emotion in the minds of the audience" (Daniels, 17). Marston relied heavily on bondage scenes, wherein Wonder Woman was repeatedly bound and gagged. The bondage symbolized captivity, but Wonder Woman always broke free, illustrating that a powerful woman could not be kept suppressed.

Despite many naysayers and a society that did not welcome strong, powerful women (even in a fantasy world), Wonder Woman was immensely popular, acquiring numerous devoted readers, most of them young boys. Marston shrewdly picked comic books as his medium for change. Along with film and television, comics play a large role in the socialization of modern Americans, particularly young children. Marston was most interested in reaching boys, whom he felt "needed his message most" and thereby hoped to achieve his goals "by exposing millions of boys (who would become men by the 1960s) to the ideals of **feminism**" (Daniels, 33).

William Moulton Marston

Marston was born on May 9, 1893, in Saugus, Massachusetts. He received his PhD in psychology at Harvard University in 1921. During the early 20th century, when Marston was an impressionable young college man, American women were undergoing a dramatic change. Suffragists, who had had their start at the turn of the century, were celebrating the Nineteenth Amendment, which gave women the right to vote. During this period, the **New Woman**

emerged. She wore radical knee-length dresses and short hairstyles, was boyishly thin, and smoked cigarettes. In the theaters, female leads starred in
adventure film series and **serials**, such as *The Hazards of Helen* and *The Perils of Pauline*.

Marston had a prodigious career. He taught at universities and invented a
systolic blood-pressure test, a precursor to a lie detection device; he conducted numerous studies, wrote essays on popular psychology, and worked
as a consultant in the film industry. His most notable achievement was the
creation of Wonder Woman. Under the pseudonym Charles Moulton, Marston authored Wonder Woman comic book stories until his death in 1947.

Marston's views on female empowerment were atypical of the 1940s.
Though women were exerting increasing independence and assertiveness, such
as delaying marriage, staying single and enjoying social activities and dating,
the march to progress had slowed considerably since the Nineteenth Amendment had passed. Advances made during the World War II had ground to a
halt. Delaying marriage was a particularly meaningful choice, as many women
believed that marriage signaled the end of their freedom and independence.

Marston's unusual ideas carried over into his home life. He had four children, two with his wife, Elizabeth Holloway, and two with Olive Richard.
The two merged families lived, for the most part, in one home.

POWER SUIT, WEAPONS, AND ABILITIES

Wonder Woman's costume is legendary. In the comic books she is shown in
her classic suit, the red corset and blue shorts with white stars. Free from
the heavy, constricting clothes of the early 20th century, Wonder Woman
was able to run, leap, and engage in combat with no trouble.

The colors and the stars were an homage to the American flag, and rightfully
so, considering she was launched in the midst of World War II. Patriotism was
high among many Americans who longed for the opportunity to make contributions. They were given their chance as Tuskegee Airmen. African American
men were trained to be pilots in a **segregated** facility at Tuskegee Institute.
They performed spectacularly. Women also were also permitted to play a
role—albeit limited—during World War II, as nurses and secretaries in the military and as factory workers on the home front.

When the television series emerged in the 1970s, Wonder Woman received
several new additions to her wardrobe. She had a Wonder Wet Suit, a Wonder Biker costume, a Wonder Skateboard suit, and a cape. These outfits not
only made her more effective at her job but demonstrated that Wonder
Woman was an active, athletic woman. Wonder Woman excelled in activities that were normally attributed to masculinity.

Wonder Woman, decked in her power outfits, contrasted strongly with
her **alter ego**, Diana Prince. Many superheroes had an alter ego, someone

Betty Friedan

The following quote comes from the opening paragraph of Betty Friedan's iconic book, *The Feminine Mystique* (1963). The book aimed to speak for housewives and mothers in the 1960s, many of whom eventually became working mothers or delayed marriage and children for careers:

> The problem lay buried, unspoken, for many years in the minds of American women. It was a strange stirring, a sense of dissatisfaction, a yearning that women suffered in the middle of the twentieth century in the United States. Each suburban wife struggled with it alone. As she made the beds, shopped for groceries, matched slipcover material, ate peanut butter sandwiches with her children, chauffeured Cub Scouts and Brownies, lay beside her husband at night—she was afraid to ask even of herself the silent question—"Is this all?"

Source: Betty Friedan, *The Feminine Mystique* (New York: W. W. Norton, 1963), p. XX.

who was usually dramatically weaker than the superhero. The alter ego was merely a mask, a façade, behind which superheroes hid their true identities from the world. Superman's alter ego was Clark Kent, the bumbling journalist who worked at the *Daily Planet*. Both Clark Kent's and Wonder Woman's alter ego, Diana Prince, wore glasses to obscure their appearance, to signify weakness (both superheroes had perfect vision), as well as to project the stereotypical persona of the smart but socially awkward person (nowadays known as the geek). Prince began as a nurse and then was promoted to military intelligence. She was depicted as weak and inhibited, and frequently positioned as a damsel in distress. Trevor, who preferred the powerful figure that was Wonder Woman, was not attracted to her.

Diana Prince was shown transforming into Wonder Woman in several ways. In the early comic books, Prince ran into a different room and discarded her work clothes at meteoric speed. Beneath her unassuming outfit was her power suit. Later, Prince used her magic lasso to change outfits. In the television series, Prince, who normally wore her hair in a ponytail, spun around in place to became Wonder Woman, instantly revealing her true identity, hair billowing, with upbeat music underscoring her transformation.

Wonder Woman wielded numerous powerful weapons, all of which originated from Paradise Island and were either made of superior materials or had supernatural origins. The golden belt she wore helped her maintain her power while away from Paradise Island. The tiara could be used as a boomerang. The bracelets, which were worn by all Amazons, served as a symbol to remind all the women of their former bondage to Hercules. They also deflected bullets. With the golden lasso, Wonder Woman could extract the truth from someone and erase memories. Wonder Woman also had an invisible plane that she used to travel from one place to another. Other accoutrements included the Sandals of Hermes, which she used for dimensional travel; the Gauntlets of Atlas, which increased her powers; as well as ceremonial armor and clothes.

Wonder Woman was instilled with natural abilities, separate from her arsenal of power, such as altruism, empathy, daring, and intellect. She also had super strength, which was exhibited in nearly every comic book story, and could jump 150 feet in the air. She was also immortal. Considered one of the most powerful superheroes in comic books, she was virtually unconquerable—except that if an enemy bound her bracelets together, she became powerless. Also, as previously mentioned, marriage would cause her to lose her powers.

VILLAINS

Wonder Woman had numerous antagonists, many of whom were given recurring roles in the comic book series. Many of these antagonists were women (and in this Wonder Woman differs from many other female action heroes), some of whom controlled female slaves and were intent upon Wonder Woman's destruction. The Cheetah and Queen Clean were among her most notorious foes. The Cheetah was a character who evolved out of her intense jealousy over Wonder Woman. She relentlessly pursued Wonder Woman with the intent to destroy her. But Wonder Woman's early missions were not necessarily to defeat her enemies. When possible, Marston demonstrated how Wonder Woman encouraged villains to leave their wicked ways in nonviolent ways. In a storyline in Sensation Comics, the Cheetah started dancing wildly and asked for Wonder Woman's opinion. Wonder Woman gave her positive feedback and then encouraged her to pursue dancing as a way to get the attention she desired. Cheetah, who was touched, claimed that she would never "let the Cheetah personality control me again!" (Daniels, 59).

Other villains included Dr. Poison, a woman disguised as a man; Dr. Psycho, who hated women; and, in the comic books, sundry mythical creatures. The television series introduced assorted bad guys, such as Nazi agents, terrorists, and aliens.

WONDER WOMAN IN COMIC BOOKS

Comic book history is divided by ages. The Golden Age ran from the 1930s through the 1950s. The Silver Age includes the period between 1956 and 1971. The Bronze Age covered the 1970s and 1980s. And the Modern Age consists of the comic books published from the mid-1980s onward.

Wonder Woman emerged during the peak of comic book popularity and is thus one of the longest running superheroes in comic book history. Over the many decades, she has evolved and been transformed, sometimes intentionally, sometimes as an expediency. Many storylines conflicted with each other and with her original conception, but that is not uncommon in comic book lore, where characters repeatedly die and are resurrected or reinvented at the whim of various (and revolving) writers, artists, and the demands of the market.

The Golden Age

When the first Wonder Woman comics were released in 1941, Marston infused the storylines with patriotism and feminist issues. Many of the early episodes kept her at the heart of the action against wartime spies and villains. Her "wartime slogan was 'Keep 'em flying!' and in 1943 she was even shown leading marines into battle against Japanese troops" (Daniels, 34). The Japanese, one of the Axis powers during World War II, were the enemy.

During this period, Wonder Woman's origin story was published, explaining that she came from a powerful island peopled only by women, who were all very intelligent, athletic, and beautiful. When Trevor's plane crashed on the island, Queen Hippolyte established a contest to ascertain which woman would be best suited to assist Trevor back to America and help in the noble cause of the war. America was referred to as "the last citadel of democracy, and of equal rights for women" (Daniels, 25). Women would not receive significant equal rights until the passing of major legislation bills in the 1960s and beyond; Marston, by projecting his own idyllic version of America, was in fact predicting it.

Disguised to hide her identity (Diana was actually a princess, the queen's daughter), Diana entered the Amazon Olympics and won. In this revolutionary storyline, Marston demonstrated to America that a male captain required the help of a woman, and that only one woman was needed to grapple with America's harrowing issues. For a while, each issue of the comic book featured a biographical section of women of achievement, educating young boys (and the few girl comic book readers) about women who were doing extraordinary things in a society that largely limited them through laws, traditions, and practices.

In a society that traditionally depicted women as the weaker sex in film and television, Wonder Woman exercised toughness at every turn. Although reluctant to commit violence, she did not back down from a fight when all else failed. During a confrontation with Amazons from Atlantis, Wonder Woman wrestled down an opponent, during which she gave a free lesson, "tackle 'em low—didn't you ever play football, Big Girl?" While putting the woman's head between her own knees, she quipped, "roll 'em in a bundle—this is what we Amazons call the kitten hold," and while tethering her wrists behind the woman's back, she instructed, "on Paradise Island where we play many binding games, this is considered the safest method of tying a girl's arms!" (Daniels, 65). On the cover of one issue, Wonder Woman executes a strangle hold on the Vanishing Mummy. On the cover of a 1943 comic, Wonder Woman appears

The Amazons

The Amazons, an all-women warrior society, are most often associated with Greek mythology. Greek legend abounds with tales of powerful women who battled men and were led by women queens, believed to rule a land situated in Asia Minor. But the Greeks were not the only ones who told stories of legendary women warriors. Amazons, referred to by assorted names, were rumored to have lived in many other parts of the world. The Amurianos, for example, were a strong-bodied, all-women society that allegedly lived in Brazil. China and the Philippines also told tales of combative and fiercely independent women warrior societies. In today's world, the term *Amazon* commonly refers to any woman who is tall and athletic.

with bindings unraveling from her body (she has untethered herself from a train track just in time), arm and back muscles flexed, while single-handedly hoisting the front of a train off the tracks. On yet another cover, we see her lassoing an airplane and navigating it safely to the ground.

Wonder Woman's heroism aside, she was not a fan favorite to everyone. Some people were outraged by the abundance of episodes in which women, including Wonder Woman, were in bondage. The bound-and-gagged damsel in distress is a trademark of early films and television series that viewed the world in terms of what men liked to see and regularly objectified women. Marston filled each comic book with at least one bondage episode, and in at least one episode, Wonder Woman is spanked by another woman.

The sexual (if not **sexist**) images, as well as Wonder Woman's skimpy costume, disturbed many women. Josette Frank, who was one of a group of experts hired to ensure that Marston's comic books did not go too far in their subject matter and depictions, wrote a letter stating that the comic book "does lay you open to considerable criticism from any such group as ours, partly on the basis of the woman's costume (or lack of it), and partly on the basis of sadistic bits showing women chained, tortured, etc. I wish you would consider these criticisms very seriously because they have come to me now from several sources" (Daniels, 61). Marston, however, saw his comic books as far less harmful than other comic books that exhibited excessive violence. He did not change his approach, and Wonder Woman rapidly became one of the greats of the Golden Age. But her iconic status would be severely challenged in the next age.

The Silver Age

Two issues threatened Wonder Woman's existence in the Silver Age. The end of World War II made the theme of patriotism and related storylines irrelevant and unpopular. After Marston died in 1947, subsequent writers struggled to carry on Wonder Woman's legacy. In the 1950s, Wonder Woman was depicted as a watered-down version of her former self. Daniels argues that among the reasons Wonder Woman's power was undermined was because of "the new trend toward romantic tales," and Robert Kanigher's interest in appealing to female readers; as a result, Wonder Woman appeared on one of the early covers reflecting her newfangled modifications, "simpering and seemingly helpless" in the arms of Steve Trevor as he crosses a stream (Daniels, 93). Other modifications included depicting Wonder Woman in various traditional ways, such as "a model showing off the latest fashions, to a 'lonely hearts' newspaper columnist," and a "movie star" (Daniels, 98). During this period, Wonder Woman/Diana Prince demonstrated an intense infatuation with Trevor, and she fought a lot less often than she did in the 1940s.

In the 1960s, Wonder Woman underwent still more changes. For one, she was given a different origin story. In the original story, Queen Hippolyte formed Diana from clay and goddesses supplied her soul. In the new revision, Diana was born to human parents. Her super powers were gifted to her from the gods, and she appeared as two youthful precursors, as Wonder Tot and Wonder Girl, a preteen. Sometimes, all three incarnations appeared in a single issue. Wonder Girl was a hit with many young girls, who enjoyed reading about her adventures and the drama involving her several love interests or romantic pursuers, including a young Steve Trevor, Merboy, Bird-Boy, the Glop, and others. Wonder Woman also appeared in unusual circumstances, marrying a monster in a 1965 issue.

Making the jump to television was inevitable, though it took a couple of false starts to get there. In the mid-1960s, the portrayal of women in the media shifted, greatly influenced by the appearance of Emma Peel, the martial-arts-fighting secret agent in *The Avengers*, which debuted in America in 1965. Two comic book heroes, Batman and the Green Hornet, appeared on television in the 1960s. Bruce Lee, the kung-fu specialist who played Kato, the Green Hornet's sidekick, made his American debut after a successful career in Hong Kong. Peel and Kato helped to popularize martial arts in American film and television. Kanigher duly endorsed a pilot for a proposed series, "Who's Afraid of Diana Prince," but the show was not picked up and the pilot was never broadcast.

In an effort to cash in on the burgeoning martial arts trend, the comic book Wonder Woman was given a new identity: she appeared as an ordinary, young, single woman trained in martial arts. Mike Sekowsky, an artist, explained the reason for Wonder Woman's change: "I felt girls might want to read about a super female in the real world, something very current. So I created a new book, new characters, everything" (Daniels, 125). Diana was touted as an independent, fashionable, and glamorous woman who went to boutiques and beauty salons. Like Peel, she worked undercover. Her mentor was a man named I Ching.

Rosie the Riveter

Since Wonder Woman's debut, the popular comic book hero's moniker has become synonymous with the universal woman who has it all or can do it all. Another important female icon who emerged during World War II was Rosie the Riveter. Originally the subject of the hit 1942 song "Rosie the Riveter," Rosie came to symbolize the new working woman, who was called upon to work in factories when the male workers went to war as soldiers. One striking image of a powerfully built Rosie depicted her "on lunch break, her riveting gun on her lap as she uses a dog-eared copy of *Mein Kampf* as a foot stool" (Dungan, "Bentonville"). This picture, created by famed artist Norman Rockwell, appeared on the 1943 cover of *The Saturday Evening Post*. In countless other promotional posters, Rosie appeared in her trademark work uniform, overalls or pants, as did her real-life counterparts, who posed in pictures in factory settings. The images memorialized a monumental moment in history for women, who had previously been prohibited from male-dominated factory industry.

Another iconic image of this era was the woman of the "We Can Do It" poster. This poster featured a stoic-faced woman wearing a polka dot headscarf on her head and a blue work shirt, flexing her right arm muscle. J. Howard Miller created this poster for Westinghouse Electric Corporation to promote women's participation in wartime efforts. Images such as Wonder Woman, Rosie the Riveter, and the "We Can Do It" woman inspired and empowered women across the country. However, at the close of the war, women were expected to return home and settle back into traditional gender roles.

Source: Tracie Dungan, "Bentonville: Crystal Bridges Museum Obtains Rosie the Riveter," http://www.rosietheriveter.org/painting.htm (accessed September 2009).

Feminists protested Wonder Woman's materialistic persona and transformation into a traditional woman. They wanted their hero back. On the cover of the first issue of *Ms. Magazine*, Wonder Woman, in classic uniform, lunges forward, towering over a town that is ravaged by mayhem, tanks firing all around. Above her image are the words: Wonder Woman for president. In an essay written by Joanne Edgar that appears in that issue, Edgar laments that Wonder Woman "relinquished her superhuman Amazon powers along with her bracelets, her golden magic lasso, and her invisible plane. She became a human being" (Daniels, 131, 132).

Bronze Age

The decade of the 1970s was good to Wonder Woman. Not only did she return to vintage form in comic books (1973), she appeared in the television cartoon *Super Friends* and *The All-New Superfriends Hour*. Another attempt was made to get a live-action Wonder Woman onto the small screen in a made-for-television movie starring Cathy Lee Crosby (as a blonde) in *Wonder Woman* (1974). That goal was finally achieved with the television series of the same name, which ran from 1975 to 1979.

Modern Age

In the 1980s and beyond, Wonder Woman has continued to change. Before launching the "Crisis on Infinite Earths," which was an attempt to clean up loose and conflicting storylines by creating fresh new scenarios for superhero characters, Wonder Woman married Trevor. (The "Crisis on Infinite Earths" also introduced the concept of multiple dimensions, from which writers could create countless versions of stories for any superhero.)

In subsequent re-creations in the 1990s, Wonder Woman was depicted with more musculature and showed more fierceness. Fighting in comic books was illustrated with increasing violence and brutality. Paul Kupperberg, an editor, said that Wonder Woman "mirrored the evolution of women and attitudes towards them" and "that some of her appeal came from her role as 'a tough hero for the guys . . . and she's not bad to look at!" (Daniels, 184). Other female action heroes in the 1990s also underwent similar transformations, melding sex appeal with toughness. In an alternate dimension story, Wonder Woman and a middle-aged Superman are expecting their first child, whom they portend to be one of the most powerful heroes ever, considering that the child would fuse two of the most formidable superheroes.

IMPACT

Wonder Woman's emergence and success in the 1940s was unparalleled by any other woman in comic books during that time or since. Her continued success has defied the odds, though changes in the structure of the comic books helped to welcome young female readers. By and large, women as well as men were drawn to the 1970s television series. Since Wonder Woman's spectacular beginnings, she has become an icon for female empowerment, as well as a term for any woman who can multitask with finesse or show abilities that transcend traditional norms.

See also Catwoman; Storm.

FURTHER RESOURCES

Daniels, Les. *Wonder Woman: The Complete History*. San Francisco: Chronicle Books, 2000.
DC Comics. "Wonder Woman." http://www.dccomics.com/sites/wonderwoman.

Fleisher, Michael L. *The Original Encyclopedia of Comic Book Heroes: Volume Two, Featuring Wonder Woman*. New York: DC Comics, 1976.

Hopkins, Susan. *Girl Heroes: The New Force in Popular Culture*. Annandale, Australia: Pluto Press, 2002.

Inness, Sherrie A. *Tough Girls: Women Warriors and Wonder Women in Popular Culture*. Philadelphia: University of Pennsylvania Press, 1999.

Pingel, Mike. *The Q Guide to Wonder Woman: Stuff You Didn't Even Know You Wanted to Know . . . about Lynda Carter, the Iconic TV Show, and One Amazing Costume*. New York: Alyson Books, 2008.

Robinson, Lillian. *Wonder Women: Feminisms and Superheroes*. New York: Taylor and Francis, 2004.

Wilde, Lyn Webster. *On the Trail of the Women Warriors: The Amazons in Myth and History*. New York: Thomas Dunne, 2000.

Xena wields a chakram in an episode in the television series *Xena: Warrior Princess*. (AP Photo/Flat Earth Productions.)

Xena: Warrior Princess

Xena, played by Lucy Lawless, was the hero of *Xena: Warrior Princess*, the hit television series set in Ancient Greece that appeared between 1995 and 2001. "Nearly five feet eleven inches" tall and solidly built, Xena was an imposing figure (Weisbrot, 7). Her sidekick was a youthful peasant girl-turned-warrior named Gabrielle, played by Reneé O'Connor.

Gabrielle debuted in the pilot episode, "Sins of the Past," of *Xena: Warrior Princess*. Gabrielle is a fair-haired young woman, a former peasant girl. She was described as a "spirited runaway . . . who idolizes the Warrior Princess for her strength, courage, and independence" (Weisbrot, 163). The two first met when Xena rescued Gabrielle and other girls being attacked by male warriors. After much pleading, Xena permitted Gabrielle to join her.

Like Xena, Gabrielle was a rebellious figure because she rejected the conventional life of womanhood and opted for the hard, perilous, if thrilling life of a warrior, a role that is conventionally **coded as** masculine. Gabrielle's visual transformation began when she traded her peasant girl's dress for warrior garb, a top that bares her midriff (first, a brown surplice top and later, a green lace-up bodice), a medieval version of a sports bra, and a short skirt. In the beginning, Gabrielle spent most of her time aping Xena; gradually, she developed more independence and individuality, becoming a formidable fighter, though never as great as Xena.

Although Xena functioned largely as a mentor to Gabrielle (Xena taught her how to fight and to use weapons), the two forged a close friendship that some coded as a lesbian relationship. Writers, however, maintained a sense of ambiguity. Their relationship was rendered all the more complicated when Xena and Gabrielle appeared in a hot tub together in "A Day in the Life" and when Xena gave Gabrielle a "Sleeping Beauty kiss" to waken her from a sleep induced by witchcraft in "The Return of the Valkyrie" (Hayes, 127).

Xena made a deep impression on audiences as a **third-wave feminist** hero, a woman who projected both power and femininity. Even more important was that Xena was the star of her own show and was consistently depicted as a victor—the one people turned to in times of need. An action hero in every sense of the word, she thrilled viewers by wielding swords and other weapons and riding her horse, Argo (played by Tilly). Xena also somersaulted, executed martial arts kicks, grunted, and grimaced. Her trademark battle cry, "yi-yi-yi," became identified with a new kind of female power in television.

The progress of tough girls in feature films was slow but inevitable. Action women have appeared on film almost from the beginning; early on in the silent era female adventurers like Helen, of *The Hazards of Helen*, leaped into action without hesitation and engaged in daring stunts in the course of their adventures. By the 1960s, there was a smattering of films featuring female action characters, such as the lethal Bond girls in assorted *James Bond* films, the antiheroes Catwoman (Lee Meriwether) in *Batman: The Movie* (1966), and The Woman (Millie Perkins) in the cult classic *The Shooting* (1966). But these women saw little real fighting and were not as aggressive as the women of action who would appear in the following decades. Later films such as *Foxy Brown* (1974), *Alien* (1979), *Terminator* (1984), and *Red Sonja* (1985) revealed women's increasing assertiveness and power, mirroring similar developments in the lives of real women who were steadily gaining equality in American society.

The history of tough girls on television lags behind the film industry, and does not really get into gear until the 1960s. Most early female action heroes were spies, detectives, or cops. In the 1970s, *The Bionic Woman, Charlie's Angels*, and *Wonder Woman* helped to popularize action women who were both glamorous and tougher than in previous years. Still, these women were not the rough-and-tumble sort; for myriad reasons, they were frequently depicted as nonviolent. For one thing, network executives wanted to appeal to television audiences, whose tastes were considered conservative and traditional; for another, they wanted to maintain the femininity of the female characters. A number of female action heroes, including Wonder Woman (*Super Friends* and others), Princess Ariel (*Thundarr the Barbarian*), Cheetara (*Thundercats*), and She-Ra (*She-Ra: Princess of Power*), made their first appearance in animated television series during the 1970s and 1980s.

In the 1990s, the film industry again took the lead by ushering in a new era with a wave of tough girls. Films like *La Femme Nikita* (1990), *Thelma and Louise* (1991), *Batman Returns* (1992), *Buffy the Vampire Slayer* (1992), *Mortal Kombat* (1995), *The Quick and the Dead* (1995), and *Tank Girl* (1995) all featured tough action women. On television, history was made slightly later when, in1995, the first female Starfleet captain got her own series in *Star Trek: Voyager* and *Xena* debuted as the first major female warrior on television who was not a cartoon.

Xena's entrance was a milestone for tough action women. She helped pave the way for other forceful female action heroes on television, where audiences were still unaccustomed to seeing women at the forefront of the action with such an aggressive, in-your-face style. But the mainstream tide had turned. In 1996, the most popular video game protagonist was Lara Croft, a high-action character whose success spawned two films and a slew of paraphernalia. A muscled woman named Chyna took the pro wrestling world by storm when she debuted as a World Wrestling Entertainment character in 1997. By the dawn of the new millennium, television audiences had come to expect women to be tough, and Xena delivered.

ORIGINS

Xena had her beginning in three episodes of *Hercules: The Legendary Journeys* (1995–1999), a television series created by Christian Williams. Both series featured action, fights, as well as camp and humor.

Female Comic Book Heroes in Films

Red Sonja and Electra are among the few women of comic books who made it to the big screen as leads. Red Sonja debuted in *Conan the Barbarian #23* in 1973. Like many characters in comic books, her appearance changed over time. Typically, she had long red hair and was clad in a bikini, wielding her trademark sword. Like Conan, her male counterpart, she was a courageous and powerful warrior. As one origin story goes, Red Sonja lived an ordinary life with her parents until, when she was 17 years old, vicious men destroyed her home, killed her family, and raped her. A goddess then endowed Red Sonja with super skills but warned her that the only man she would be able to enter into an intimate relationship with was one who could subdue her in a fight.

The comic book series was adapted into an unspectacular film in 1985. *Red Sonja* was notable because a woman warrior (played by Brigitte Nielsen) was the titular character, but in fact, Conan (Arnold Schwarzenegger), who appeared in several of his own films, played a significant role in the film.

Electra first appeared in the 1981 issue of *Daredevil*, a comic book series that featured a male protagonist. Indeed, she was Daredevil's love interest— but her future was far from ordinary. She met the Daredevil, then Matt Murdock, while they both attended Columbia University in New York City. After her father was accidentally killed by the police, Electra left the university and went to China, where she was trained by ninja and became a powerful assassin, catapulting her into a wayward and violent life.

In 2003, Elektra (Jennifer Garner) appeared as a supporting character in the film *Daredevil*. In the 2005 film *Elektra*, which followed events of *Daredevil*, she was given the titular role. *Daredevil* made over $179 million, but *Elektra* grossed only $57 million.

The television Hercules was based loosely on the Greek demigod or hero of numerous myths and legends. The Hercules legends comprise his birth and childhood (he was the son of Zeus, a powerful god, and a mortal named Alcmene), the so-called 12 labors of Hercules (which Hercules undertook to earn forgiveness for murdering his children while under the influence of Hera, a goddess and wife of Zeus), and immortality. The Hercules legends include many fantastical and dangerous adventures. His bravery, strength, and power, as well as his sexual prowess, have long been a template for male heroism. Hercules epitomized the young male's quest for a perfect and sizable body—an impossible goal for many individuals whose body types were naturally lean or small—and the idea that only males with muscles could attain hero status. Women's roles in the legends of Hercules were largely reduced to goddesses and flawlessly beautiful love interests.

It is no surprise that the ancient hero Hercules has inspired a number of film, television, comic book, and video game adaptations. Italian film companies were the first to produce what were known as sword and sandal films, featuring a muscle-bound Hercules, during the 1950s and 1960s. Many of these films were released in America dubbed in English. Arnold Schwarzenegger, having made a name for himself with a successful bodybuilding career, made his acting debut in *Hercules in New York* (1970), directed by Arthur Allen Seidelman. In this film, Schwarzenegger was billed as Arnold Strong, an appropriate name considering his legendary physique. Lou Ferrigno, who also appeared as the Incredible Hulk in the 1970s television series, played the title role in *Hercules* (1983) and *The Adventures of Hercules* (1985). Both films were directed by Italian Director Luigi Cozzi. Since the 1970s, Hercules has appeared in assorted television series.

Kevin Sorbo first played the part of Hercules in a series of made-for-television movies released in 1994: *Hercules and the Amazon Women*, *Hercules and the Lost Kingdom*, *Hercules and the Circle of Fire*, *Hercules in the Underworld*, and *Hercules in the Maze of the Minotaur*. The movies were so well received by audiences that producers created the series the following year.

In many ways, Sorbo reinforced the longstanding concept of the role: he was swarthy with long, thick hair, extraordinarily powerful, and well muscled. But he was not characterized as all brute and brawn; he was a hero with considerable depth and congeniality, and the show, with its light, campy, and humorous turns, made for an interesting spin on the ancient hero. Unlike a Western hero (the archetype for distinctly American male heroes), this Hercules was not a conventional lone figure; he had a sidekick, a winsome, strapping blonde named Iolaus (Michael Hurst), and on some occasions, Salmoneus (Robert Trebor), a somewhat wily opportunist.

Executive producer Rob Tapert, who "chiefly gave *Hercules* its vision and vitality," played an instrumental role in coming up with the preliminary ideas for a woman warrior who would appear in several *Hercules* episodes (Weisbrot, 1). Longing to tap into his love of martial arts movies, he considered a role for actress Brigitte Lin, who starred in *The Bride with White Hair* (1993), a Hong Kong wuxia (martial arts) film, a love story that pits two fighting lovers against each other. In the end, Tapert did not pursue Lin, because she did not speak English, and he felt that, at 40 years old, "her chances of breaking into American cinema aren't good" (Weisbrot, 6) (This may be true, but Michelle Yeoh, whose career began in Hong Kong action films, continues to appear in action films into her late forties.) In pursuing his idea for "a beauty who comes between Hercules and his best friend, Iolaus," Xena was born, a woman who would embody "beauty," "sensuality," "power," "ferocity," and "implacable will" (Weisbrot, 6, 7). Lucy Lawless, an up-and-coming actress from New Zealand, was cast in the role. Before her appearance as Xena, Lawless played Lysia, an Amazon, in

Hercules and the Amazon Women, and Lyla, a love interest, in the series episode "As Darkness Falls." Lawless and Tapert would eventually marry.

Xena and Hercules

Xena's three-episode arc in *Hercules* included "The Warrior Princess," "The Gauntlet," and "Unchained Heart." The first episode depicts Xena's villainous background as a warlord. Her hair is dyed black "to give her a fierce look, a darker, more sinister look" (Weisbrot, 12). Intent on destroying Hercules, Xena seduces his friend, Iolaus. The episode starts off with a mock reversal of the traditional woman-in-peril scene:

> a tall young woman fetches water from a well. Just beyond her vision two unsavory figures ready their knives and whisper to each other . . . the woman's placid expression suddenly gives way to a frenzied yell, as she decks one man with her water bucket before he can strike, then knocks down his accomplice. Other armed men swarm around her, but she makes short work of each, grunting as she kicks, punches, and flips them in turn. Then, glaring in disgust at her dazed and prostrate assailants, she adds a tongue-lashing that reveals her to be the real conspirator. "Pathetic!" the Warrior Princess scolds them. "If you can't learn to fight better than that, then you're never going to defeat Hercules. And I want him *dead*!" (Weisbrot, 12, 13)

In "The Gauntlet," Xena begins her metamorphosis from bad to good. Witnessing a horrific attack on innocent villagers executed by a character named Darphus, Xena "recoils" and rescues a baby (Weisbrot, 14). Later, Darphus forces Xena to walk the gauntlet, but she survives and directs her energies toward killing Hercules, thinking she will vindicate herself before her soldiers. When Hercules and Xena have their climactic meeting, there is a dramatic fight between the two great warriors. When Hercules overcomes her, Xena faces her impending death bravely, telling Hercules to finish the job: "Prove you're the greatest warrior." Hercules, however, relents, telling Xena that "Killing is not the only way to prove you're a warrior." Later, Hercules and Xena fight side by side to save a village that Darphus and his army is plundering.

"Unchained Heart" reveals a repentant, enamored, and softer Xena. (In a plot arc that parallels that of Jaime Sommers in *The Six Million Dollar Man*, Xena was supposed to die in this episode, but this time the producers recognized before the fact that her immense appeal with audiences would spawn the spin-off, *Xena: Warrior Princess*, so they let her live.) In a conversation with Hercules, Xena divulges her immense guilt for her evil ways. "I have done terrible things. I've killed so many men I'll never wash the blood from my hands!" she tells him. "You've already started," he tells her. "There's the goodness in your heart." The two fall in love. But when Hercules asks Xena to stay with him, she declines, defying age-old traditions wherein women in

Sonia Sotomayor

Sonia Sotomayor is the first Hispanic and third female justice on the U.S. Supreme Court. She was born on June 25, 1954, in a predominately Puerto Rican section of the Bronx in New York City. Her mother, Celina, was born in Puerto Rico, served in the Women's Army Corp, and later became a nurse. Her father, Juan, died in his early forties. As a result, Sotomayor and her brother were raised for the remainder of their childhood by their mother, who encouraged them to dream big. Supported by her mother and inspired by fictional characters like Nancy Drew and Perry Mason, Sotomayor aspired to go to college and become an attorney.

Sotomayor graduated from Princeton University and Yale Law School despite being one of the few Latinos represented in the student body and faculty. She maintained excellent grades, pushed for the study of Puerto Rican history, and was actively involved in on-campus activities. In 1976, she married Kevin Edward Noonan. On August 8, 2009, Sotomayor was sworn in as a U.S. Supreme Court Justice.

love eschew their personal passions and dreams to settle down in marriage and childbearing. Xena chooses the solitary warrior's path. However, hers is to be a journey of redemption, dedicated to rescuing the powerless and defending the victims of tyranny, a journey that will be shared by a cast of assorted colorful characters, including her faithful sidekick, Gabrielle.

Robert Tapert

Tapert was born on May 14, 1955. While attending Michigan State University, he formed a friendship and working relationship with Sam Raimi, who directed *The Quick and the Dead* (1995), starring Sharon Stone, and the wildly popular *Spider-Man* movies (2002, 2004, 2007). Tapert and Raimi produced their first film together, *The Happy Valley Kid*, while in college. Tapert starred in the leading role, a student who goes on a killing spree dressed as a cowboy. He has produced a number of films, such as *The Grudge 2* (2006), *30 Days of Night* (2007), and *Drag Me to Hell* (2009). He served as writer, director, and producer for several episodes of *Xena: Warrior Princess*.

Lucy Lawless

Lucy Lawless was born Lucille Frances Ryan on March 29, 1968, one of seven children, in Mount Albert, New Zealand. Ryan attended Auckland University, intending to become an opera singer, but dropped out before graduating. She traveled to Europe, where she lived the life of an "adventurer": picking grapes in Germany and traveling through Switzerland and Greece (Weisbrot, 121). In Australia, she mined for gold "in the Outback, a hard, arid region, often bitter cold, removed from coastal cities like Perth by more than five hundred miles of dusty roads. Nearly all of the miners were men, and she matched them in surveying, digging, driving trucks, and handling heavy industrial equipment" (Weisbrot, 122). In 1987, Ryan became pregnant, and in 1988, she married her boyfriend, Garth Lawless.

Lawless's acting career bloomed soon after, starting with TV commercials and a comedy show. In 1991, she attended the William Davis Center for Actors Study. In the following year, she appeared in a television movie, *Rainbow Warrior*, and other projects. In 1995, her life and career took a major turn when she accepted the part of Xena and divorced her husband. In 1998, Lawless married Robert Tapert, the executive producer of *Xena: Warrior Princess*. They have two sons.

In addition to *Xena: Warrior Princess* and crossovers to the *Hercules* series, Lawless has appeared in such television series as *The X Files* (2001) and *Battlestar Galactica* (2005–2009), and in the films *Euro Trip* (2004), *Boogeyman* (2005), and *Bedtime Stories* (2008). She provided the voice for Wonder Woman in the animated movie *Justice League: The New Frontier* (2008). After appearing in the reality television show *Celebrity Duets*, in 2006, Lawless performed in concert in 2007 and 2008 and released two albums, *Come 2 Me* and *Come to Mama: Lucy Lawless in Concert: The Roxy Theater in Hollywood*.

POWER SUIT, WEAPONS, AND ABILITIES

Among the many iconic costumes that female action heroes have worn, Xena's sexy warrior garb—leather bustier with armor overlay and her warrior-style skirt, armbands and shoulder pieces, and knee-high boots—was a standout that created a craze in fandom. No different from the warrior clothes worn by Hercules and other mythical characters like Conan the Barbarian, Xena's outfit likewise revealed her athletic build. This outfit is markedly different from the most popular female action hero costume: the black leather catsuit introduced by Emma Peel in *The Avengers* and Catwoman on *Batman*, and the similarly form-clinging dark bodysuits worn by Lara Croft in the *Tomb Raider* video game series, Seven-of-Nine on *Star Trek: Voyager*, and Selene in the *Underworld* movies.

In addition to her warrior outfit, Xena frequently donned costumes to disguise her true identity as a way to foil her conniving enemies. A score of other female action heroes have done the same. Foxy Brown, in the titular 1975 film, dressed up as a prostitute. Going undercover was the main premise of the 1970s *Charlie's Angels* show as well as *The Bionic Woman*.

Many of Xena's disguises found her dressed in traditional women's clothing that coded her in traditional female roles. In "Warrior . . . Princess," Xena pretends to be a princess and dresses up in a gown, but she makes for an awkward conventional princess. In "Here She Comes . . . Miss Amphiboles," Xena dons a blonde wig when she enters a beauty contest. This episode gave the writers an opportunity to inject criticisms on modern-day beauty contests. For example, Gabrielle complains that the contest is "a feeble excuse for men to exploit and degrade women" (Hayes, 70).

Xena was well skilled in the use of an assortment of weapons. However, she favored the chakram (a circular object that has a boomerang effect), the sword, and her martial arts combat skills, which she learned in her childhood, and, later in life, from Lao Ma. In contrast to Hercules' brawny fighting skills, Tapert wanted to showcase flashy martial arts moves, kicks, flips, and tosses, which Xena (with help from special effects, camera tricks, and skilled stunt coordinators) performs with ease.

VILLAINS

Xena challenged and was challenged by numerous villains, many of them representing historic, ancient, or mythic figures, as well as foes who were created just for the show. Xena's enemies included warriors, gods, pirates, giants, monsters, and other fantastical creatures. Villains like Draco and Callisto (a woman) were equal parts fierce and good-looking. In "The Giant Killer," Xena helped the biblical David fight the giant Goliath, and in "Adventures in the Sin Trade, Parts I and II," Xena taught Amazon women how to fight to conquer a female shaman.

XENA: WARRIOR PRINCESS, THE TELEVISION SERIES

Xena's debut heralded a new, tougher, female television hero: one who was depicted with some femininity and a lot of sex appeal. The opening credits dramatize this approach. Celtic music starts off the opening sequence, rising to a crescendo of triumphant chords normally associated with the classic male hero (soft, romantic strains usually indicate the appearance of women—alluring damsels in distress and love interests—in films associated with mythic heroes).

In subsequent scenes, Xena appears in dynamic action. In one scene, she stands on a cliff overlooking an ocean from which the god Poseidon erupts. Xena faces him, shouts aggressively, and raises her sword in the air. She appears like a miniature doll in contrast to the hulking, looming figure of the sea god. This scene codes Xena as fearless. A quick succession of shots shows men raiding a village, close **fetishizing** shots of Xena adjusting her warrior costume, and images of Xena fighting and grimacing. In another shot, she faces the camera, smiling prettily, her teeth gleaming. As Xena fights, flips, kicks, throws her chakram, and practices moves with her sword, a voiceover describes how Xena is the answer to "a land in turmoil [that] cried out for a hero" and explains that Xena is "a mighty princess forged in the heat of battle . . . her courage will change the world."

Throughout six seasons, Xena was consistently portrayed as a fierce, formidable, intelligent warrior. After all, she was created to be "smarter, faster, stronger and tougher than even the gods, though she might have flaws, she could never appear weak" (Hayes, 136). Xena was also laconic and frequently pensive and severe, like a number of famous male heroes (Conan, as depicted by Arnold Schwarzenegger in the *Conan* film series is a case in point). But Xena's zest for fighting frequently exceeded that of male heroes, who often fought with restraint and only when necessary. In this she resembled Jen Yu, from *Crouching Tiger, Hidden Dragon* (2000) and Lara Croft, from the *Tomb Raider* films, whose reckless zeal for daredevil antics, danger, and combat largely defined them. This was a historically unconventional way to depict a woman.

Like many male heroes, Xena experienced romances that were destined not to last. Two of her relationships, one with a warrior named Borias, produced a son named Solan, and another relationship with Ares, the god of War, yielded a daughter named Eve. Xena gave up Solan, because she was at the time living the life of a pillager; she decided to raise Eve, but due to circumstances—she and Gabrielle were put to sleep for 25 years—she didn't get the opportunity to do so. Xena's love interests came and went; men betrayed her, or seduced her, but Xena continued to eschew the traditional marital life of homemaker and child rearer. Interestingly, Borias, before his death, was the one (not Xena) who desired to settle down and make a home with Xena.

For all her power and toughness, Xena's femininity was a prominent feature of her character. Visually, Xena's beauty, long hair, and feminine form coded her as female. Although she was athletic and powerful, she did not have the excessive musculature of her compeer, Hercules, or other male warriors she encountered. Thus she did not **transgress** the conventional body type as did say, the pro wrestler Chyna, with her massive frame, or even Sarah Connor, with her sculpted arms in *Terminator II* (1991). Although Xena's sex appeal was obvious, she was nevertheless often awkward when she had to feign a traditional female role.

Some aspects of Xena's character mitigated her warrior persona. For example, over time Xena's friendship with Gabrielle evolved into an equal partnership. When Xena was pregnant with Eve, Gabrielle frequently took the central role in the action while Xena remained on the periphery. In contrast to the conventional lone, all-self-sufficient hero, Xena eventually depended on Gabrielle for protection and for friendship. Reneé O'Connor explains how Xena's pregnancy, as well as her friendships, made her "more vulnerable" and how "the more people she invests in emotionally, the more vulnerable she is as a warrior" (Hayes, 141). Some critics argued that the friendships and the appearance of the baby could be coded as symbols of progress, as they disrupt the **patriarchic** pattern of the lone male hero who is depicted without friends, family, or any other social networks. Xena challenged her own transgressiveness when she periodically wrestled with the guilt of her past life and the uncertainty of whether or not to give up her violent, warrior lifestyle.

But Xena never did give up her warrior lifestyle. In fact, in the last episode, "A Friend in Need, Part II," she allows herself to be killed so that she can enter a spirit world where she will remain to fight the Lord of the Dark Land to avenge the 40,000 souls whose deaths she is responsible for. Importantly, Xena fights alone, for she is separated from her loyal friend Gabrielle. Thus, in the end, Xena appropriates the classic stance of the male hero, as a lone crusader of the innocent and powerless.

IMPACT

Xena's influence in popular culture was extraordinary. Her fan base included women and men, boys and girls. A number of lesbians embraced Xena as a role model. Overall, Xena's strength and power appealed to a broad demographic, demonstrating that America was ripe for a television hero who challenged the status quo of past female action heroes like The Bionic Woman, Charlie's Angels, and Wonder Woman, who projected more glam than toughness, more **eye-candy** allure than raw and breathtaking ability. Xena helped to usher in a wave of assertive women (and girls) onto television shows like *Buffy the Vampire Slayer, La Femme Nikita, Charmed,* and *Powerpuff Girls,* who not only talked tough but fought hard.

See also Buffy the Vampire Slayer; Chyna; Princess Leia.

FURTHER RESOURCES

Early, Frances, and Kathleen Kennedy, eds. *Athena's Daughters: Television's New Women Warriors.* Syracuse, NY: Syracuse University Press, 2003.

Hayes, K. Stoddard. *Xena, Warrior Princess: The Complete Illustrated Companion.* London: Titan Books, 2003.

Hopkins, Susan. *Girl Heroes: The New Force in Popular Culture.* Annandale, Australia: Pluto Press, 2002.

Inness, Sherrie. *Tough Girls: Women Warriors and Wonder Women in Popular Culture.* Philadelphia: University of Pennsylvania Press, 1999.

Nelson, Rhonda. "The Female Hero, Duality of Gender, and Postmodern Feminism in *Xena: Warrior Princess.*" http://whoosh.org/issue13/nelson.html.

Ross, Sharon. "Tough Enough: Female Friendship and Heroism in *Xena* and *Buffy*." In *Action Chicks: New Images of Tough Women in Popular Culture*, ed. Sherrie A. Inness. New York: Palgrave Macmillan, 2004.

Stafford, Nikki. *Lucy Lawless and Reneé O'Connor: Warrior Stars of Xena*. Toronto: ECW Press, 1998.

Weisbrot, Robert. *Xena, Warrior Princess: The Official Guide to the Xenaverse*. New York: Doubleday, 1998.

Glossary

Ageism—the tendency to regard older persons as debilitated, unworthy of attention, or unsuitable for employment.

Alter ego—another side of oneself. In comic book terms, this phrase refers to the persona or role superheroes may take on to disguise their true identity. Alter egos are normally presented as a polar opposite of the superhero. Alter egos may be depicted as weak and socially awkward.

Black power movement—a movement among African Americans who advocated black pride and social, economic, and political empowerment. This movement emerged on the heels of the civil rights movement of the 1960s.

Blaxploitation—a term that refers to the popular body of low-budget African American films made during the 1970s. The genre features African American leads, street vernacular, drugs, crime, and prostitution. Many felt the films exploited African Americans through the objectification and stereotyping of African Americans as pimps, prostitutes, and other negative characters. The term had negative connotations for many African American directors during that time, who strove to create films that depicted African Americans in positive and nonstereotypical ways.

Bombshell—a female archetype that describes a woman who is very attractive, sexually appealing, and voluptuous.

Civil rights movement—a period of social protest during which African Americans and their supporters fought to eliminate segregation and gain equal rights. The movement spanned the 1950s and the first half of the 1960s. It culminated in the passage of the Civil Rights Act of 1964, which ended segregation, and the Voting Rights Act of 1965, which provided voting rights protection to citizens. These laws supported civil rights for African Americans and other marginalized groups.

Coded as—refers to how an object or person represents or symbolizes something else.

Cyberfeminism—a term coined in 1991 to refer to the feminist community in cyberspace, the realm of electronic communication.

Discrimination—negative and/or exclusionary treatment based on class, race, gender, or any other category rather than individual merit; prejudice.

Dominatrix—a female archetype who dominates others, especially men; a female archetype who plays the dominant role in a sadomasochistic sexual relationship or encounter.

Eye candy—someone, usually a woman, who is visually attractive.

Feminism—the doctrine advocating social, political, and all other rights of women equal to those of men.

Femme fatale—a female archetype that refers to a seductive woman who leads men to difficult, dangerous, or disastrous situations; siren.

Fetish; fetishize—an object that is designed to create an erotic response; the act of treating an ordinary object as a fetish.

Final girl—a female archetype that refers to the last woman or girl alive to confront a villain.

First-wave feminism—a movement that spanned the 19th and early 20th centuries. The main goal of first-wave feminists was suffrage (the right to vote).

Gaze/male gaze—a term introduced by Laura Mulvey in her essay "Visual Pleasure and Narrative Cinema" and used frequently in feminist film theory and communications media studies to refer to the way in which films are projected to audiences from a dominant male perspective. For example, women in film who are subjected to close-ups of their bodies are said to be subjected to the male gaze. The gaze denotes power. Historically, men hold the power of the gaze, but women may also appropriate that power.

Girl power—a term that emerged concurrent with third-wave feminism to refer to women who take control over their own lives or situations; may also include women who have social, political, or economic influence. Although the term *girl* was once universally considered a derogatory term for women, third-wave feminists embraced it, as youthfulness is considered an important feature in third-wave feminism.

Glass ceiling—a symbolic wall that excludes others. This term commonly refers to the systematic exclusion of women's advancement in the workplace.

Ingénue—a female archetype to refer to a woman who is depicted as artless, innocent, and unworldly.

New Woman—a term that emerged in the late 19th century used to describe women who defied social expectations of how they should behave and dress. The New Woman eschewed the previous generation's corsets, long dresses, and polite behavior. She was assertive, smoked cigarettes, and wore short hairstyles, short dresses, and makeup.

Patriarchy—a social system in which men dominate.

Phallus—a representation or symbol of the penis as an embodiment of power.

Racism/racist—hatred or intolerance of another race; a person, idea, or behavior exhibiting racial hatred or intolerance is referred to as a racist.

Read—to interpret.

Second-wave feminism—a movement that emerged during the 1960s and 1970s among middle- to upper-class white women who actively challenged gender inequalities operating in America. Second-wave feminism coexists with the new third-wave feminist movement. Some of the major issues of second-wave feminism are to challenge social constructions of gender, male-dominated institutions and workplaces, and other patriarchal structures and thinking. Different racial groups, such as African American and Native American women, have developed separate forms of feminism to reflect their disparate histories and concerns.

Segregation—the policy or practice of separating people of different races, classes, or gender.

Film serial; serial queen—films that are produced in short installments. The female leads of early 20th century film serials or series were referred to as serial queens.

Sexism/sexist—attitudes or behavior based on traditional stereotypes of sexual roles; discrimination based on gender.

Stereotype—an overly simplified and standardized conception or image imposed on a group of a particular race, class, or gender.

Suffrage movement—the women-led campaign for the right to vote that emerged in the late 19th century. Women secured their right to vote with the passage of the Nineteenth Amendment in 1920.

Third-wave feminism—a movement that emerged in the 1990s in response to the so-called failures of second-wave feminism. Among the prominent features of this movement is the advocacy of femininity and personal empowerment.

To-be-looked-at-ness—a term introduced by Laura Mulvey in her essay "Visual Pleasure and Narrative Cinema." Used frequently in feminist film theory and communications media studies to refer to the objectification of women in film. This concept may apply to television, advertisements, and other media forms.

Transformative—to change in a significant and dramatic way.

Transgressive—to violate or trespass a law, command, or moral or social code.

Typecast—to cast (a performer) repeatedly in a kind of role closely patterned after that of the actor's previous successes; to stereotype.

Vamp—a female archetype that refers to a seductive woman who uses her sensuality to exploit men.

Women's liberation—a movement that aimed to combat sexual discrimination and to gain full legal, economic, vocational, educational, and social rights and opportunities for women, equal to those of men; also referred to as women's lib.

Selected Bibliography

BOOKS

Apeles, Teena. *Women Warriors: Adventures from History's Greatest Female Fighters*. Emeryville, CA: Seal Press, 2003.

Braudy, Leo, and Marshall Cohen. *Film Theory and Criticism: Introductory Readings*. New York: Oxford University Press, 1999.

Cassell, J., and H. Jenkins, eds. *From Barbie to Mortal Kombat: Gender and Computer Games*. Cambridge, MA: MIT Press, 1999.

Collins, Gail. *America's Women: 400 Years of Dolls, Drudges, Helpmates, and Heroines*. New York: HarperCollins, 2003.

Driver, Martha W., and Sid Ray, eds. *The Medieval Hero on Screen*. Jefferson, NC: McFarland and Company, 2004.

Early, Frances, and Kathleen Kennedy, eds. *Athena's Daughters: Television's New Women Warriors*. Syracuse, NY: Syracuse University Press, 2003.

Gourley, Catherine. *Ms. and the Material Girls: Perceptions of Women from the 1970s through the 1990s*. Minneapolis: Twenty-First Century Books, 2008.

Helford, Elyce Rae, ed. *Fantasy Girls: Gender in the New Universe of Science Fiction and Fantasy Television*. Lanham, MD: Rowman and Littlefield, 2000.

Heywood, Leslie, and Shari L. Dworkin. *Built to Win: The Female Athlete as Cultural Icon*. Minneapolis: University of Minnesota Press, 2003.

Hooks, Bell. *Feminism Is for Everybody: Passionate Politics*. Cambridge, MA: South End Press, 2000.

Hopkins, Susan. *Girl Heroes: The New Force in Popular Culture*. Annandale, Australia: Pluto Press, 2002.

Inness, Sherrie A., ed. *Action Chicks: New Images of Tough Women in Popular Culture*. New York: Palgrave Macmillan, 2004.

Inness, Sherrie A. *Tough Girls: Women Warriors and Wonder Women in Popular Culture*. Philadelphia: University of Pennsylvania Press, 1999.

Isaacs, Susan. *Brave Dames and Wimpettes: What Women Are Really Doing on Page and Screen*. New York: Ballantine Books, 1999.

Jones, David E. *Women Warriors: A History*. Dulles, VA: Brassey's, 1997.

Mainon, Dominique, and James Ursini. *The Modern Amazons: Warrior Women On-Screen.* Pompton Plains, NJ: Limelight Editions, 2006.

May, Martha. *Women's Roles in 20th-Century America.* Westport, CT: Greenwood Press, 2009.

McCaughey, Martha, and Neal King, eds. *Reel Knockouts: Violent Women in the Movies.* Austin: University of Texas Press, 2001.

Mitzejewski, Linda. *Hardboiled and High Heeled: The Woman Detective in Popular Culture.* New York: Routledge, 2004.

Neroni, Hilary. *The Violent Woman: Femininity, Narrative, and Violence in Contemporary American Cinema.* Albany: State University of New York Press, 2005.

Osgerby, Bill, and Anna Gough-Yates, eds. *Action TV: Tough Guys, Smooth Operators, and Foxy Chicks.* New York: Routledge, 2001.

Owen, Susan A., Sarah R. Stein, and Leah R. Vande Berg. *Bad Girls: Cultural Politics and Media Representations of Transgressive Women.* New York: Peter Lang, 2007.

Pohl-Weary, Emily, ed. *Witches, Mutants, Slayers, and Freaks: Girls Who Bite Back.* Toronto: Sumach Press, 2004.

Reed, Jacinda. *The New Avengers: Feminism, Femininity, and the Rape-Revenge Cycle.* New York: Manchester University Press, 2000.

Robinson, Lillian S. *Wonder Women.* New York: Routledge, 2004.

Sheridan-Rabideau, Mary P. *Girls, Feminism, and Grassroots Literacies: Activism in the Girlzone.* Albany: State University of New York Press, 2008.

Sweeney, Kathleen. *Maiden USA: Girl Icons Come of Age.* New York: Peter Lang, 2008.

Tasker, Yvonne, ed. *Action and Adventure Cinema.* New York: Routledge, 2004.

Tasker, Yvonne. *Spectacular Bodies: Gender, Genre, and the Action Cinema.* New York: Routledge, 1993.

Tasker, Yvonne. *Working Girls: Gender and Sexuality in Popular Cinema.* New York: Routledge, 1998.

WEB SITES

DC Comics. http://www.dccomics.com.

Grimes, Sarah M. "'You Shoot Like a Girl!' The Female Protagonist in Action-Adventure Video Games." http://digra.org:8080/Plone/dl/db/05150.01496.pdf.

The Internet Movie Database. http://www.imdb.com.

Library of Congress. "American Women." http://memory.loc.gov/ammem/awhhtml.

Marvel. http://www.marvel.com.

Moby Games. "Female Protagonists." http://www.mobygames.com/game-group/female-protagonists/offset,550/so,1d.

MovieMaker. http://www.moviemaker.com.

Women in World History Curriculum. http://www.womeninworldhistory.com.

World Super Hero Registry. http://www.worldsuperheroregistry.com/world_superhero_registry_gallery.htm.

Index

About the Author

GLADYS L. KNIGHT is a freelance writer/researcher who lives in the Pacific Northwest. Her articles and essays have appeared in *Northwest Transporter* magazine and several reference books published by Greenwood and ABC-CLIO. Her first book, *Icons of African American Protest: Trailblazing Activists of the Civil Rights Movement,* was published in 2008. She received a B.A. in communication at the University of Puget Sound in Tacoma, Washington.